ENDORSEMENTS FOR

"*Beyond Self-Help* is absolutely tremendous and genuinely important.
Dietrich Bonhoeffer's life is a reflection of what Jason Pankau talks about in
this book based on the Omega Course. Communicating the things of God
—becoming Christlike—is done person-to-person in Christian community.
In terms of what the church needs in America today, this hits the nail squarely
on the head."

ERIC METAXAS
New York Times Best-Selling Author of *Bonhoeffer: Pastor, Martyr, Prophet, Spy*

"This is one good book!!! Jason Pankau engages us with a most comprehensive
process of Christian discipleship. Being "trained in righteousness" is not
a "sometimes" thing, but rather an exercise that emerges from intentionality,
undergirded with a theology that touches the ground, all the while squeezing
every bit of goodness out of the lives God gave us. This book cuts through
the cultural clutter that so easily besets us and leaves us with the promise of
a more authentic faith. It is a step-by-step "naming" of the exercise of living
abundantly, claiming that profound resource of unconditional love of the
Father, while staying anchored by and held accountable to the biblical text.
For anyone searching for credibility, relevance, and impact in their Christian
witness, this roadmap for personal growth and spiritual maturity is a must read."

AMBASSADOR ROBERT SEIPLE
Chairman of the Board, Institute for Global Engagement
Former President of World Vision and
U.S. Ambassador-at-Large for International Religious Freedom

"Jason Pankau nailed it. His storytelling is both relevant and rive
I laughed and cried reading this book. More importantly, I'm act
going to DO some things differently after reading it"

BOB MUZIKOWSKI
Founder and President of Chicago Hope Academy

"To a society that is sick with the notion that we can really help ourselves from "good to great," Jason Pankau reminds us of God's roadmap from a drifting existence to experiencing all that God has in His heart for our lives to be: filled with a faith you can lean on, aligned with His holy will, purposeful in His Kingdom, and truly satisfying because we are uncovering through the study of Scripture the "us" that He made us to be. *Beyond Self-Help* meshes the wisdom of God's Word with the best research business and academia have to offer. Building on a decade of research and writing, Jason Pankau offers a systematic approach to the study of God's Word that leads the reader from the illusion of "self" righteousness to a life both defined and driven by our Father. This book helps the Christian understand what it means to live the phrase from Martin Luther's Morning Prayer "that all my doings in life may please You." It is an application of what Lutherans call the "Third Use of the Law," a guide essential for the sanctified living of Christians in our vocations, a pattern of God's definition of *real* life. *Beyond Self-Help* breaks Babel's notion that we can build ourselves up to God and shows the simple way the Bible teaches to build our lives on the Lord Jesus Christ."

REV. DR. CHARLES S. MUELLER, JR.,
Senior Pastor, Trinity Evangelical Lutheran Church, U.A.C., Roselle, IL.

"In this significant work, Jason helps us gain an in-depth, biblical perspective on what the 'abundant life' is really all about. 'Beyond Self-Help' provides for us a biblically-guided roadmap for how to identify, understand, and live out, the 'life' mission that God has defined for us. This is a great resource, filled with very useful and practical suggestions, for any Christ-follower who is serious about personally engaging in the transformative, disciple-making 'way-of-life' that Jesus calls us to."

KEITH TOLLEY
President, Vision New England

"If discipleship is a core duty as Christians then why is it lacking in so many churches? It is because we lack the confidence and resources to span the scope of areas to be covered. Jason Pankau is committed to the church and development of disciples of Jesus. 'Beyond Self-Help' collects some of the best disciplines, strategies and principles he has learned so men and women can live the abundant life God desires. It is applicable and comprehensive—add this tool to your toolbox."

DR. CARSON PUE
CEO Arrow Leadership
Author of *Mentoring Leaders: Wisdom for Developing Character, Calling and Competency*

"Today's Church is program addicted, which is a manifestation of our society's addiction to status and achievement, and neglect of real relationships. Real relational connection is the missing link in churches today. This book makes the case that this reconnection only comes as a result of being trained in righteousness. Only as we are relationally connected to God, one another and to our calling of servanthood will we become the Church that Jesus envisioned. We need a revolution in disciple-making if we are going to stem the tide of cultural drift away from God. Jason helps us see how essential mentoring is in God's plan to make disciples. This book is significant and ground breaking. It clearly shows us the Biblical pathway to real holistic discipleship and guides us into what we need to experience the abundant life. It's what the American church needs to reverse years of decline and grow once again."

MICHAEL LEE STALLARD
President, E Pluribus Partners
Co-author of the Bestselling book *Fired Up or Burned Out*

"As a theologian, NT Wright has recently written about WHY Christian character matters. As a pastor, teacher, mentor and coach, Jason Pankau writes about HOW we can help each other grow in Christian character. God made us for relationship (with Him and with each other), and Pankau has spent over a decade thinking and praying about, and teaching and doing, covenantal relationships. Listening to Jason share his wisdom and insights on discipleship, mentoring and relationships can be like trying to drink from a fire-hose, but now *Beyond Self-Help* puts that collected wisdom in a format that can be sipped, savored and put into practice. This book is for anyone who believes that Christian character matters and is tired of just hearing theories or trying to do it alone."

PAUL MICHALSKI
Management Committee Member, New Canaan Society, Inc.
Former Partner, Cravath, Swaine & Moore LLP

"Becoming a disciple of Christ is a lengthy process involving every area of our life. We can find books about individual facets of becoming a mature follower of Christ, but it is rare to find a discipleship process mapped out as clearly as in this book by Jason Pankau. Every person has a calling, but Jesus said that the road is narrow, and few people find the path toward the abundant life that can be realized in Christ. This book helps point the way."

MARK CURTIS
President and CEO Splash Car Wash Chain

"Jason Pankau has identified the Western church's key problem as having drifted away from Christ's intention to make us a community of people who powerfully receive and express the love of God. Jason's prescription for our malaise is to recognize that alone, we can't recover what we've lost, and to rediscover the practice of mentoring, which he contends will restore the church to its God-ordained functioning. He has presented a carefully conceived and finely tuned process of mentoring and enriched it with vivid illustrations and fresh language, making *Beyond Self-Help* a delight to read. He is optimistic that with a Christ-centered mentoring network in place for each of us, the church will be able to learn to love, make disciples, and lead each believer to the abundant life Christ promises, where each of us reaches his or her full potential. Any Christian who is tired of mediocrity and wants to pursue a more dynamic and fruitful "abundant life" would do well to read and follow the game plan Jason presents here."

REV. FRANK DRAKE
PRM International

"Becoming a disciple of Christ is a lengthy process involving every area of our life. We can find books about individual facets of becoming a mature follower of Christ, but it is rare to find a discipleship process mapped out as clearly as in this book by Jason Pankau. Every person has a calling, but Jesus said that the road is narrow, and few people find the path toward the abundant life that can be realized in Christ. This book helps point the way."

REV. DAVID HERNQUIST
Senior Pastor, Van Nest Assembly of God, Bronx, NY.

"Jason has written an encyclopedia of Biblical thought with regard to living wisely in God's direction. The questions asked invite you to a journey. The suggestions made form a focus for where your soul longs to be. The opportunities to live out Jesus' words...to live *more* abundantly...should you so choose, are found in this book."

WES ROBERTS
Leadership Mentor, Leadership Design Group

"Whether you've come to faith recently, believed in God your entire life, or are just seeking, you may wonder whether faith can be truly transformational. Can we really live the abundant life—that is, a life filled with love, peace, and joy? *Beyond Self-Help* responds with a powerful and practical "yes." Be bold and go beyond self-help!"

STEPHEN PALETTA
Founder and CEO of GiveBack

"Jason has written an encyclopedia of Biblical thought with regard to living wisely in God's direction. The questions asked invite you to a journey. The suggestions made form a focus for where your soul longs to be. The opportunities to live out Jesus' words...to live more abundantly...should you so choose, are found in this book."

REV. DR. MARTIN SANDERS
Author *The Power of Mentoring*, President Global Leadership
Professor, Alliance Theological Seminary, Nyack, NY

"Jason Pankau has written a systematic and compelling book about life change. He is a creative writer and thinker who challenges his readers to evaluate the depth of their own discipleship and impact on culture. Jason has translated many of his life successes on the athletic field, in the classroom and real ministry experience into Biblical principles that can transform any life. Dig in and seek after the abundant life in Christ."

REV. DR. MCKENZIE PIER
President, The New York City Leadership Center

"Jason has created an instruction manual for a full life! Filled with scripture's truths and wisdom, *Beyond Self-Help* lays out a logical road map for individual growth that is readable and actionable. Jason has inspired so many people with the desire to grow into their full potential as Christians. This book is the perfect way to begin the journey."

LYN S. KRATOVIL
Managing Partner, Bridge 1 Advisors

"Jason Pankau is **on target** with *Beyond Self-Help*! His approach to discipleship training (training in the Lord's mission) is remarkably consistent with the training conducted by the U.S. Army's Special Forces. America's elite fighting forces do not reach the pinnacle of their craft by accident. It is the result of sacrifice, discipline, dedication. Most of all, it requires a well designed and executed training program. The same holds true of developing our relationship with God. In this book, Jason coaches us in the art of Mission Analysis: determining God's mission requirements for us, followed by a plan for executing that mission. In Special Operations, Mission Focus is a key characteristic used to seize and retain the initiative in attaining strategic objectives. Coach Jason has truly cracked the code for gaining and maintaining mission focus through his Life Focus Process. This book is your mission essential asset for living a truly abundant life."

MAJOR ERIC ROITSCH U.S. ARMY (RET.)
Former Green Beret Commander

"It has been said that amateurs train until they get it right but professionals train until they cannot get it wrong. In his spiritual journey, Jason is not content just to get it right but is in constant training with God to press in to the richness of life in God. Nobody gets great without a coach. Jason has been well coached in His life's journey and he is able to coach you into that abundant place in God. In this book he pours himself out as a spiritual life coach to you.

Church leaders will love the spark this gives to their congregations. If you are looking to be challenged to greatness and trained for the Kingdom of God, then *Beyond Self-Help* is for you. I encourage you to use all the power tools he makes available in the book. Take the time to press into the questions. Pay attention to the coaching moments. Ponder over the stories of people like yourself who know there is more of God than what they have been experiencing. Get together with friends to share in the ways of God as you work through this book. In this way I can assure you that you will come into that abundant life God has for you where you experience and express the passion of His love in every part of your life."

JAMES LEACH
Co-founder, SageFire Ministries,
Author of *Field Guide to Your Dreams*

"Jason has captured the essence of life in his masterpiece, 'Beyond Self-Help.' Here Jason unlocks the principles of true biblical transformation. Christianity is more than just being saved from the penalty of sin. It is stewarding our lives for the glory of God, being conformed into His image. But how do we do that? How does God do this in our lives?

We tend to complicate the truths of God's word. Jason simply but thoroughly walks you through the path to spiritual greatness. Jason helps you understand God's mission for your life, challenges you to commit to the process of transformation, understand yourself and where you are in that process, then helps you chart the course you need to take to get the job done. The Christian life is all about the journey, growing to be more like our Savior and enjoying Him through the process. This is truly the way to really live.

We have been applying the principles Jason has skillfully unfolded from God's word in this book and have seen tremendous spiritual growth at Standing Stones Church. My own life has been transformed as I have been working through the concepts Jason teaches."

REV. BOB POWERS
Pastor Standing Stones Church, Vice President Hands on Africa

Beyond
self-help

The True Path to Harnessing
God's Wisdom, Realizing Life's Potential
and Living the Abundant Life

By Rev. Jason K. Pankau
with Lisa Leach and John B. Donovan

Beyond Self-Help
by Rev. Jason K. Pankau with Lisa Leach and John B. Donovan

Printed in the United States of America

ISBN 9781612155098

www.xulonpress.com

To my wife Jennifer,
whom God has used to grow me the most as my soul mate
and partner in life; asking you to be part of my inner circle
and letting God use our marriage to hone my character has been
the wisest thing I have ever done.

To my children Jarod, Jaden, Julianne and Josephine,
this book encapsulates the wisdom that God has
taught me to this point in my journey. It also describes
the true inheritance that I desire to pass on to you.

Acknowledgments

I owe an incalculable debt to the mentors, fellow church members, ministry team partners and those motivated by the Holy Spirit whom God has used to shape me and train me in righteousness.

I have included a list of the mentors that God has used to grow me as a disciple of Jesus over the past 22 years. This list is incomplete, and as with any list I have run the risk of leaving some names out, but here are those that have had the most impact on my journey.

Mentors – past and current intentional, peer and occasional mentors include: Tony Schwartz – South Barrington, IL; Jeff Hatton – Providence, RI; Rev. Frank Drake – Norfolk, VA; Bob Treichler – Providence, RI; Rev. Jack Diamond – Barrington, RI; Bob Kalander – Jamestown, RI; Jim Frost – Cumberland, RI; Dick Scoggins – Providence, RI; Rev. Dr. Ken Lyle – Northboro, MA.; Rev. Dr. Michael Lewis – Swansea, MA; Rev. Dr. Andrew Lee – Northboro, MA; Jeff and Mindy Caliguire – Newton; MA, Bruce Driesbach – Wolfoboro, NH; Neely Towe – Greenwich, CT; Rev. Dr. Martin Sanders – Nyack, NY; Paul and Christa Schoeber – Vancouver, B.C.; Bobb Biehl – Mount Dora, FL; Rev. Dr. Carson Pue – Vancouver, B.C.; Joe Zimmel – Greenwich, CT; Mark Curtis – Greenwich, CT; Parker Stacey – Greenwich, CT; Don Osgood – Stamford, CT; Steve Paletta – Greenwich, CT; Kris Revelle – Montgomery, NY; Jim Leach – New Canaan, CT; Rev. Dr. Charles Mueller Jr. – Roselle, IL; and hundreds of others whom I have lived in covenant community within small groups and on ministry teams. To the members of the churches that I have been privileged to serve as an ordained minister of the Gospel – Power Street Christian Fellowship, Beacon Community Church and Stanwich Congregational Church – God has used my time journeying with you to help me see His Kingdom vision.

A special thanks to John Donovan and Lisa Leach, my writing partners whom God has used to help make this book a reality. Also to Scott Greenlee for cover design and layout. You have worked tirelessly helping me to put this book together – well done, good and faithful servants.

Finally, to the Board Members of the Life Spring Network and all of the prayer and financial supporters who believe in the vision of reproductive disciple-making through mentoring networks and want to see the Church become the radical force for good in the world once again, this book is for you.

Give 'em Heaven.
Rev. Jason Pankau, President, Life Spring Network

TABLE OF CONTENTS

"Christianity without discipleship is always Christianity without Christ."

— *Dietrich Bonhoeffer*

FOREWORD

Have you ever had a moment that altered the whole course of your life? I've noticed they tend to arrive when we least expect it...

In my senior year, our high school football team was ranked third in the state and I was the MVP of our team. I played both offense and defense, and also served as the place kicker. Even though we had a couple of guys who were out with injuries going into the state playoffs, I expected that we would still go far. Instead, we lost in the first round to a team we had beaten 20-0 a few weeks earlier. I had worked very, very hard to help get our team prepared. The sudden loss stunned me. Now my high school football career was over, and I was left trying to figure out what happened. A few weeks after the end of the season, Mike Swider came to speak at a Fellowship of Christian Athletes meeting held at our high school. He was the strength and conditioning coach at Wheaton College; he also coached several Olympic athletes, including his sister who was a four-time Olympic speed skater. At that time, I had Olympic aspirations as a discus thrower and was eager to hear what Coach Swider had to say.

Swider looked like he could play Tarzan in a movie. He had shoulder length blond hair and the v-shape build of a sprinter. He looked more like a professional athlete than a coach. He stood in front of us and looked us over like we were a platoon of raw recruits.

"Men!" He bellowed. From that moment on, I was utterly glued to his every word.

"How many of you guys go to church?"

Nearly every hand went up.

"How many of you guys have read the Bible?"

The hands went down.

"That doesn't make any sense to me," he said. "You're going on the field and you haven't even read the playbook. How does that make sense to you?"

I nodded my head and thought to myself that it really didn't. Listening to Coach Swider speak that afternoon, it became clear to me that I needed to go deeper in my journey of faith. I needed to give it the same kind of commitment I gave to athletic endeavors.

A BIT OF MY JOURNEY

When I look back, it seems clear that God had been working on my heart for years. On some level I knew Him. I remember that both my maternal and paternal grandparents prayed for me. As a young boy, I sensed something special every summer when I spent two weeks at my grandma and grandpa's farm in Indiana. Every night at bedtime Grandpa would rub my back and pray out loud for me. It gave me a warm feeling. I felt loved and I looked forward to these times with my grandpa. Following high school, I attended Brown University in the Ivy League. By senior year, I was pre-season All-American and captain of the football team as well as a national qualifier and school record holder in the discus. After graduating with degrees in organizational behavior and business economics, I led Bible studies for athletes and coaches at Brown while I worked in the business world doing financial planning.

After three years working in the business world and leading various ministries as a volunteer, I heard my official call to ministry. I'd been fasting and praying, really seeking God for direction, especially with regard to my desire to dig into Scripture on a deeper level. One day I sat alone in a conference room during the lunch break. Everyone was gone, and as I wasn't eating, that gave me more time to spend seeking God. I looked up at the chandelier and heard God say, *"Get ready."* It was as if I heard an audible voice. Nothing like receiving your marching orders from the top! Out of obedience I embarked on a journey over the next seven years in which I attended seminary and helped to start two churches, one in Providence and one in the Boston area. It was during this time that my ministry to executives also began and I was invited to become a pastor at Stanwich Church in Greenwich, Connecticut, a suburb of New York City.

Greenwich is known as the wealthiest town in the wealthiest state, in the wealthiest nation in the history of the world. It is the home of many chief executive officers, investment bankers and hedge fund billionaires. Living amidst this extreme material prosperity and witnessing how it affects people opened my eyes to some important insights, which in turn led me to become an executive life coach to some very wealthy Americans.

In 2006 I was commissioned out of Stanwich Church to share what God is doing through this ministry of training, mentoring and equipping people to live their faith. Life Spring Network was created to take this ministry beyond the walls of Stanwich. God has used our team to train, mentor and equip communities of Christians to steward their lives from God's perspective and realize life's potential as reproductive disciple-makers.

TIME FOR A CHANGE

Like many people today, I am tempted to be an "achieve-aholic." Of course the New York City area is the achieve-aholic capital of the world. This lifestyle is marked by a continuous drive to accomplish more, not to mention receive recognition for it. Each day I see the damage it causes in people's lives. There have been times in this journey when my own achieve-aholism has spun out of control. One year, (my wife and I call it "the train wreck year") when I was simultaneously training for the Olympics, starting a church, attending seminary, meeting with athletes on campus, working as a financial planner by day and a watchman by night—all "for the cause of Christ,"—I hardly ever saw my wife Jen, the love of my life. Needless to say, my life's imbalance, well-meaning as it was, caused us great hurt. It took a crisis to bring this situation to a head and force me to rearrange my priorities.

With God's grace and guidance, I began to value relationships over super-achievement; since then our circle of family and close friends has grown in love. And by His grace that will continue, as we allow ourselves to be trained in His ways. It's great to be part of a flourishing ministry, but these days I'm mindful that it should not be at the expense of my wife and our four beautiful kids: Jarod, Jaden, Julia and Josie. No other way but God's way.

THEY CALL ME "COACH"

Coach. It certainly fits who I am. I love to encourage and mentor others to become the people God longs for them to be. I would like for you to think of me as your coach too. Interwoven throughout this book is my story; what I've learned along the journey. It is an honest account of my ups and downs, the times I tried to do it my way and the times I followed God's lead. My aim is that you can learn from my mistakes, from the ways God redeemed those mistakes and from the wisdom that I have been used by God to speak into people's lives.

Watch for this symbol Ω as you read along; these are your "coaching moments" where I ask you to take time to reflect, work out issues, or take action in your life.

COACHING AGAINST THE GRAIN

Following God's plan goes against the grain. God's ways can feel counterintuitive. Because of our imperfections and separation from God, we are blinded. Have you ever heard stories of people who are lost in the wilderness? They begin to believe the compass is wrong, and research shows that left to their own devices, they walk in circles and wear themselves out. That's how it is in daily life too; it's human nature. Yet, we are made in God's image and He's given us His life, His Word and His Holy Spirit as our compass. When we stay connected with Him and with each other, we experience the joy and peace that comes from living the abundant life.

WHY I WROTE THIS BOOK

Even in my college days, I was a good example of one of the church's most significant problems. I was a Christian but my life was all about me. I tried to self-help my way to greatness. (More on that in Chapter One.) Now I realize something about our culture: What was true for me on a personal level has also been true of the Church, at least in the West. We have collectively drifted away from the command of Christ to *"go make disciples" (Matthew 28:19)* and join with God in His Kingdom work here on earth. This book is an outgrowth of my concern over the collective ineffectiveness of the church and how I have experienced God reversing this trend in people's lives.

THE BAD NEWS

You've heard about the advancing secularization in society. Yet more disturbing is another trend, the secularization of the Church. It's not that the hymns, the prayers, the pews or other elements of church services have changed appreciably; it's rather that the rise of social pathology is no different *inside* the church than it is *outside* of it. In fact, the rising volume of atheist propaganda now cites this as evidence to bolster the idea that God doesn't exist!

What would you think, hearing that the social statistics on the Church (rates of divorce, pornography, etc.) are about the same as the world outside the Church? Would it not raise some questions in your mind? What would be your reason for seeking the Christian life in that case? I've noticed many in the Church who find no serious fault with their moral condition; they assume God has no expectations of them beyond their diligent but basically self-directed lives. Why would anyone be drawn to such mediocrity, given that the same life experience can seemingly be found outside the faith?

The ups and downs of people's faith in history reflect this basic fact about human nature: When there is outward prosperity, human beings rely on themselves; following God's ways is an afterthought. Not until there's a need or a crisis do people eventually cry out to God in their pain. America's current state of affairs shows clearly where we are on this continuum. Our faith has grown dull. Countries that used to receive missionaries from America are now sending theirs to us (we are the third largest missionary receiving country in the world) so far have we fallen into the dangerous trappings of the comfort zone. In fact, the present troubles we are facing as a country may actually be good news, if we respond to them by crying out to God for help.

"Then if my people who are called by my name will humble themselves and pray and seek my face and turn from their wicked ways, I will hear from heaven and will forgive their sins and heal their land."

(2 Chronicles 7:14)

WHICH ONE IS POORER?

If you compare life in America to many rural areas of the developing world, the contrast is staggering. Here indoor plumbing is the rule; there it is a rarity. Here electricity and modern appliances are the rule; there such things are beyond the reach of the common person. Here we take television and telephone communication for granted; there one person out of two has never made a telephone call and the vast majority have no access to television. We view ourselves as prosperous, but from God's point of view we are poor. The less fortunate of our world who know God have a love, a peace and a simplicity in their lives that far surpasses ours in the West.

Our outward wealth has led us directly toward inner impoverishment. Material prosperity has risen to historic highs as spiritual health (our desire to submit the will of God) has sunk to historic lows. The ready accessibility of media entertainment grows less and less effective in soothing the malaise in our innermost being. Statistics show that during the last half century, our broader society has been damaged. Consider that (according to research by David Myers in *American Paradox*) the divorce rate in the U.S. has doubled, the teen suicide rate has tripled, the recorded violent crime rate has quadrupled, the prison population has quintupled, the percent of babies born to unmarried parents has sextupled, co-habitation has increased sevenfold, and depression has soared to record levels.[1]

If you go to church, you may feel better informed by the teaching and uplifted by the music and the prayers. But if you do not engage in God's training in righteousness, then you will find yourself Monday morning just as empty as you were on Saturday night. It's possible that those attending church are in even graver danger, as they suppose themselves to be better off.

PROSPERITY UP, HAPPINESS DOWN

It should come as no surprise, then, that during a period when economic prosperity has soared, the National Opinion Research Center has recorded a decline in happiness among Americans. The question is why? And once we know why, what can we do about it?

NOTHING NEW OR IMPROVED

First, some myth-busting: According to Barna research, the most widely-known Bible verse among adult and teen believers is "God helps those who help themselves," which is *not* in the Bible, and contradicts its teaching. Our culture glorifies self. This way of life infuses every level of the Church, causing us to seek God and the abundant life in our own way. Like the companies who place a new label on an old product and call it "new and improved," Christians have simply transferred over their old habits and put them under God's Name. Even the way we do church in the West fosters an environment of self-help.

What is missing?
We *know* that multitudes are professed Christians, weekly assenting to the truths of the faith. Therefore, what in the world is going on? Why is there such a disconnect? How can we get back on mission with God? **THAT** is the subject I've set out to tackle in this book.

THE GOOD NEWS, REVISITED

Let's take a closer look at what the Bible *does* say. Jesus didn't promote self-help. Nor did He promote the kind of church growth models that have become popular. Jesus didn't say, "go make converts and bring them to church." Rather, He said, *"go and make disciples of all nations" (Matthew 28:18)*. Disciples. That means those who enter into ongoing discipline or learning. It is urgent that we identify and deal with this missing factor of discipleship in our churches. It is rare to find church members submitting to Christ as Lord of their *entire* lives and being trained in righteousness.

Another thing: Jesus didn't say, "Go witnessing." He said, *"You will be my witnesses" (Acts 1:8)*. Note the difference: One emphasizes doing it ourselves; the other indicates a relational truth about who we will *be*. Instead of believing a truncated Gospel, thinking only in terms of getting to Heaven or doing church, we are to enter a relationship with God as His disciple and *become* more like Jesus as eternal-life learners. The journey doesn't end when we come to Christ; it begins.

We face a stark choice: It can be summed up in the word "submit." Either we submit to the guidance and power of God in every aspect of our lives, or we will have to submit to the advance of secular values, both in society and within the church itself. The choice is as simple— and as basic—as the one posed in Deuteronomy 30:19: *"…I have set before you life and death, blessings and curses. Now choose life…."*

SELF-HELP OR SUBMISSION?

I've visited a lot of churches, coached a lot of churchgoers. Many churches spend the bulk of their resources putting on worship services to inspire, entertain and educate people, rather than focusing their efforts to actually train people in how to live their faith. As important as worship services are, without the requisite discipleship, people run off on their own to take what they have seen and heard and figure out how to integrate it into their lives—as if they *could*.

You might feel that submission is a form of "giving up"—something that should only be done when you are sure you can't handle something yourself and need to escape. But the Christ-centered life isn't about escape; it's about engagement and victory. Godly submission is the diametrical opposite of self-help. It is like the submission of David who, while facing Goliath, declared, "The battle is the Lord's." He knew that his own human skills would be inadequate but that the guidance and power of God would be invincible.

Hardly a week passes when those who keep up with the news are not given some evidence of the widespread weakness of Christianity in its efforts to engage the culture. The number of Americans who claim no religious affiliation has nearly doubled since 1990, rising from 8 to 15 percent. According to Barna research, only 10 percent of Christians profess to living with a Biblical worldview. This statistic is echoed by research done by a former mentor of mine, Bruce Driesback in the New England Research Project. He discovered that 90% of Christians say they don't know how to live their faith and wouldn't know how to make a disciple if they had the opportunity to do so. It is time we faced the facts the church is dying in every way that really matters to God.

It has become clear that the current approach to accomplishing the great commission isn't working. We can't just continue to offer more worship services and educational programs, as good as they are, and blindly hope that the drift we are experiencing will change. Nor do we need a fatalistic throwing-up-our-hands in desperation. Christians in the West face an important turning point. We will either continue along our current path of cultural drift and social corrosion or we will reverse the trend and be the head, not the tail. If we submit to God's ways and train, mentor and equip each Christian in how to live his or her faith and make disciples of others, we will become much more the salt and light God intended us to be. We'll have a transformative impact on the culture.

Sometimes it takes a crisis. Just as it took the "train wreck year" to get my attention, it may take some pain to help the Church make changes. When people you know are struggling with addictions, they don't usually change until they hit bottom; **our church culture is addicted to self-help, and crisis may be what we need.** We can pray for the "bottom" to come up so that we don't have to go so far down before seeking help from God. We must each renounce self-help or we are in danger of cutting ourselves off from God's blessing. The old phrase, "Christ is the answer," must take on a new urgency but not as mere assent to propositional truth. A truly Christ-centered life—serious discipleship—must be the goal of the Church and each of its members, no matter what the cost. That means submitting to the guidance and power of God.

DRIFTING OR TRAINING?

Followers of Christ don't "drift" toward abundant living. On the contrary, the drift that comes so naturally to us human beings is toward the negative. As an athlete, I know and appreciate that you can't take the field and play to your potential unless you have trained for that moment spiritually, emotionally, mentally, physically and relationally. Drifting is easy; training takes dedication and sacrifice.

We don't drift toward greatness any more than Michael Phelps drifted toward record-breaking Olympic victory in Beijing. Greatness requires training. This is not to assert that we can train our way to godliness in and through our own strength. Remember, apart from Him we can do nothing (John 15:5). This is training which is submitted to the guidance and power of God in our lives. It is allowing Him to form new habits and Christ-like character in us as we submit to His guidance in His strength. N.T. Wright described this as "developing our second nature" in his recent book, *After the Call: Why Christian Character Matters.*

For us to be filled with life and transform our culture, our training in righteousness must begin. I'm so convinced of this that I've spent years developing this material and sharing it with people all over North America in the forms of the Creating a Connection Culture Seminar, the Omega Course and the Omega Experience Seminars. The transformational impact that our ministry is having on many lives has encouraged me, and at the prompting of other Christian leaders I felt compelled to write this book so that yet more people can grow as real disciple-makers.

One of my main objectives in this book is to provide tools and suggestions that will help you submit to God and be reshaped and empowered in order that you might know the life that is truly life. The tools I offer are designed to help you identify areas in your life that you may have never examined in quite that way before. Together we'll examine terms like vision, priorities, values, identity roles, attitudes, perspectives, beliefs, and character. We will point out ways to unlock parts of your life that you might not have noticed before by seeing them from God's perspective.

If God is calling you to greatness, you must not allow the lure of becoming a "good moral person" to satisfy you. Striving to be good without the power of the Holy Spirit results in pride. Mark Twain was referring to this when he described some people as "good in the worst sense of the word." The bottom line here is, why settle for good when God is calling you to partake of His divine greatness? This book was created to help you seek and find God's plan for greatness in and through you.

LET THE TRAINING BEGIN!

In order to properly train, you need to first see where you are going and how life really works from God's perspective. Coach Swider challenged me to read the Bible in order to understand the playbook. That same Bible describes a very clear picture of life that is very different from the training that we receive from the world. In my own mentoring experience, (both giving and receiving) I have discovered and refined 18 truth statements that I call the 18 Natural Laws of Life Stewardship. They describe God's perspective on how life really works. Natural laws are fundamental patterns of nature and life. They describe things as they really are, as opposed to how we think they are or how we wish they were. A natural law is a law that cannot be repealed.

The existence of laws implies that we need some guidance. Just as the world we live in has natural laws such as the law of gravity, God created life to function according to spiritual laws too. When we live according to these truths, we thrive and experience the life God intends for us. When we don't, we gradually, almost imperceptibly, experience spiritual death.

Just for the record, this discussion of laws is simply about things that are demonstrably true. I'm not interested in promoting any form of religious legalism. That would only lead to an empty or false spirituality (at best) or worse, the kind of oppression that results in deep woundedness. I am concerned that we are not seeing life from God's perspective and are therefore missing out on abundant living. As one of my mentors told me long ago, "If you can't see it you can't do it." These laws are an attempt to help us see and align our lives with these vital truths of real discipleship.

As your coach, I will walk you through 18 Natural Laws of Life Stewardship and explain how you can use them to guide your training in abundant living. I will also introduce you to a pattern of thinking I have used to help people focus their lives and "get on with it" called the Life Focus Process©.

The Life Focus Process

The Life Focus Process begins by clarifying God's mission for our lives. Life experience and a biblical worldview teach us that when we choose to guide our own lives, we lead ourselves away from God's abundant life. We were never created to lead our own lives. Rather, we were created to be led by God and seek out His mission for our lives.

In keeping with other forms of training, the 18 Natural Laws of Life Stewardship are laid out in a sequence that moves logically from first principles toward those that are more advanced. Their progression also follows our journey through the Life Focus Process.

The early laws can be categorized under the label of clarifying God's life mission for us. This includes understanding God's vision, priorities, values and identity roles. The second set of laws details the anatomy of transformation, including our tendency to resist that process. This works with the Life Focus Process to guide us in making a true commitment to transformation. The third set of laws guides us in discovering an objective sense of ourselves. In this stage of the Life Focus Process we will discover who we really are from God's perspective, looking at both the nature and nurture components of our lives. The fourth set of laws helps us to wisely chart our growth towards Christ-likeness. In this stage of the Life Focus Process we learn how to set God-discerned goals for our lives and discover spiritual disciplines that can train us in righteousness in the various areas of our lives. The fifth set of laws guides us in staying on mission with God through the various seasons of life and adjust our lives according to the new revelation that He brings. Through this process you will find a roadmap of core essentials that align our lives under the Lordship of Christ and train us in the fullness of what He has in store for us.

TRAINING IS REIGNING

Training is work. You will encounter obstacles along the way. (You may have noticed that life is full of adversity, whether we're followers of God or not.) However, once you've committed yourself to the journey of transformation, every adversity can be used by God to move you more quickly along the road than you'd move without obstacles. How cool is that? That is the difference your turning to God will make. Think of your struggles as personalized weight training, and you may approach them with a whole different mindset. Hebrews 12 exhorts us to treat hardships as discipline. God will use every difficulty you face to grow your character and strengthen you as you turn to Him. The end result is the transformed person that God designed you to be. You may be the most surprised one of all, once you begin to see the kind of profound changes God works within you.

Are you, right now, where you have dreamed you would be? Have you settled for being a "good person?" Do you feel that the word "great" is a stretch in describing you? Are you ready to seek after more?

PACE YOURSELF

Is this a quick fix? No. It would be a mistake to think this is an overnight makeover; that's why I call discipleship a "journey." It would also be a mistake to think this book is a quick read. Don't rush through the material. Rather, as you find yourself challenged at various points, stop and reflect on what God may be telling you. You may not be accustomed to listening to the Holy Spirit's promptings, but that too is a habit you can cultivate. Just as Jacob wrestled with the angel of the Lord and said, *"I won't let go until you bless me,"* *(Genesis 32:26)* you may find that encountering these truths feels like a wrestling match at times. You are indeed doing some spiritual, mental and emotional weight lifting. As with most wise exercise plans, you should train to the point where you feel fatigued, then put the book down, rest, and pick it up again later. Press on, but pace yourself.

Another word to the wise: As with many other things in life, you will get even more out of this material if you engage in it with other people. This will not only give you moral support, but will also greatly enhance your growth process. Sometimes others can see things in us that we can't see. While I am offering to be your coach and will share with you through these pages, I wouldn't be doing my job if I didn't encourage you to find others who want to grow with you. Work with mentors and put yourself in a position of accountability so you can be that much more encouraged.

Is this book The Answer? No. It is, however, an introduction, a "primer for abundant living." **My intention is to give you the big building blocks. Your challenge is to grab hold of them, one at a time, and to work together with God and His covenant community to seek and find His abundant life.**

God is the Author and Finisher of your faith, so all I can do is cheer you on and share what I've learned. Before I made the choice to submit to God's authority in my life and engage with Him in His training process, I was trapped in a dungeon of self-help. The best I could hope for was worldly good, fame, money or prestige. But these prizes pale in comparison with what God has in store for us. A life of real meaning and powerful love that lasts forever is not some kind of fairy tale, it's tangible and accessible to us, starting now. Our Heavenly Father is offering it to us, daily. It's your birthright! **Are you ready to unpack this awesome gift that He put in you?**

As we begin this journey, let the words of a master disciple-maker (Coach) the Apostle Paul, encourage you:

⁷But whatever was to my profit I now consider loss for the sake of Christ. ⁸What is more, I consider everything a loss compared to the surpassing greatness of knowing Christ Jesus my Lord, for whose sake I have lost all things. I consider them rubbish, that I may gain Christ ⁹and be found in him, not having a righteousness of my own that comes from the law, but that which is through faith in Christ—the righteousness that comes from God and is by faith. ¹⁰I want to know Christ and the power of his resurrection and the fellowship of sharing in his sufferings, becoming like him in his death, ¹¹and so, somehow, to attain to the resurrection from the dead.

¹²Not that I have already obtained all this, or have already been made perfect, but I press on to take hold of that for which Christ Jesus took hold of me. ¹³Brothers, I do not consider myself yet to have taken hold of it. But one thing I do: Forgetting what is behind and straining toward what is ahead, ¹⁴I press on toward the goal to win the prize for which God has called me heavenward in Christ Jesus. ¹⁵All of us who are mature should take such a view of things. And if on some point you think differently, that too God will make clear to you. ¹⁶Only let us live up to what we have already attained. (Philippians 3:7-16)

How Hungry are You?

To learn more about the Omega Course, the Omega Experience and the ministry of the Life Spring Network visit our website at www.lifespringnetwork.org.

SECTION 1

Getting On Mission with God

CHAPTER 1

Does Your Life Belong to You?

LAW 1

The Law of Stewardship: *Life is a gift that we are responsible to steward with the decisions that we make until we die.*

Picture it with me again: There I was, running down the football field, king of the game. I was no slouch; I'd worked hard. The team had worked hard. We'd beaten the other team 20-0 a few weeks before; the state championship was in the bag!

But we lost in the first round…

You might see a trend in some of my stories: It seems that the times I was most disappointed and befuddled were times of deepest spiritual growth. What's with that trend? Could it be that those were the moments when I was more likely to listen? The super-confident MVP might not have asked for help. But the crushed high school senior with dashed hopes of a grand football career might be a tad more teachable. Just a tad.

"How many of you have read the Bible?" Coach Swider had challenged us a few weeks after that defeat. "You're going on the field and you haven't even read the playbook!" Maybe to some this would sound like a stretch. What would the Bible have to do with football? How could he assert that the Word of God was the playbook for an athlete?

2

Coach Swider knew a basic fact that we all need to know, whether we're athletes or not: *The earth is the Lord's and everything in it (Psalm 24:1).* That word "everything" includes you. You are the Lord's, whether you believe it or not. You do not own your life; it is a gift from God. Your life is infinitely precious to God, and He hasn't given it to you as something to squander. In fact, God has given you the responsibility to be His steward over your life. Yes, you have free will —another precious gift. But consider this: Each of us will stand before a holy God one day and give an accounting of how responsible we were with what He entrusted to us.

HOW DO WE "STEWARD" THIS LIFE?

Think of it: God has blessed you with the gift of life. He will guide and empower you to steward it wisely so that you will experience and express His love in the world. A steward is the manager of property that is owned by someone else. Some of you might use the word "trustee." In this case the owner (God) has placed confidence in us—and resources at our disposal—to make something good into something great. He has not simply left us here all alone to fend for ourselves or play in the football game without any playbook or training. But many of us live as though He does. We try to do it ourselves. But what kind of owner does that make God out to be? There's a better way! Coach Swider might have sounded tough, but it's true love that makes sure you're equipped before sending you out on the field.

It may seem radical to think of your life in these terms, that you are accountable to God for how you manage your heart, your soul, your mind, your strength, your life. It may seem like an imposition to suggest that God owns you, as though you don't have a free will. You may feel as though you don't have personal discretion over the most cherished aspects of your life. But in actuality, God's ownership of your life is not an imposition but a great relief. He hasn't taken away your free will, but neither has He asked you to perform solo. He wants to partner with you the whole way. And the buck stops with Him. St. Augustine wrote, "to serve him is perfect freedom."

3

That's not a head-in-the-clouds, mystical statement. St. Augustine was a man who knew what it took for the rubber to meet the road. He'd tried doing it his way, grown miserable and finally found relief in that awesome submission to God.

BIGGER THAN YOU THINK

Most people think of "stewardship" as having to do with a percentage of your income that you decide to donate to the church. Others have a slightly broader view, and include "time, talent and treasure" under that umbrella of stewardship. You might be picturing it right now: An upstanding, responsible citizen, neatly dressed, nice family, using his or her free time to volunteer for charities. Honest, dependable, generous… That's all well and good.

But the law of stewardship blows that picture wide open. It's a Copernican Revolution for your life: This law says IT'S ALL GIFT. Your whole life. This law says you're not the owner and you're not ultimately in charge. But this law also says that everything you do counts. Everything. If we don't get a hold of this basic truth, the wisdom of scripture will not make much sense. Concepts like we must die so that we might really live only make sense in light of the reality of life stewardship.

Consider the vine: *"I am the vine, you are the branches,"* Jesus says in John 15. We may know the verse well, but stop to observe the way fruit is produced. Do the branches strain and toil to push those grapes out? No, they just hang in there. Life flows through every stem— plenty is going on—but it's not supposed to be a stressful thing for the branches. Unless, of course, the branch is on its own. Try producing fruit when you're not on the vine; that is a quick recipe for death. We can be put out about the fact that we need to stick to the vine, or we can be in awe of the way God has designed us to flow with abundant life. To experience and express His love in everything is what it means to live the abundant life. Your choice: abide or die.

In short, you were designed to live a supernatural life. Nothing less than that will satisfy. Maybe—just maybe—that's the reason so many people are restless, ambitious, hungry for more. Is that you? You are right to hunger for more. But to look for this kind of life on earthly terms alone is like a branch trying to produce fruit all by itself. God has some divine sap for us that may seem hidden from view at first, but it's real and it's the stuff of a truly fruitful life. Not only that, but it's free for the asking; it's Standard Issue! South African devotional writer Andrew Murray quotes God as saying it this way: *"All that I have is yours. I have given it to you in Christ. All the Spirit's power and wisdom, all the riches of Christ, all the love of the Father—there is nothing that I have that is not yours. I am God who will love, keep, and bless you."* [2]

SO YOU'RE RICH: NOW WHAT?

So then, men ought to regard us as servants of Christ and as those entrusted with the secret things of God. Now it is required that those who have been given a trust must prove faithful. I care very little if I am judged by you or by any human court; indeed, I do not even judge myself. My conscience is clear, but that does not make me innocent. It is the Lord who judges me. Therefore judge nothing before the appointed time; wait till the Lord comes. He will bring to light what is hidden in darkness and will expose the motives of men's hearts. At that time each will receive His praise from God. (1 Corinthians 4:1-5)

Consider that phrase: *"The secret things of God."* It's not that God wants to keep His riches a secret. Rather, like life in the blood and sap in the vine, His secrets are well-protected but there for discovering. Yes, it does take a particular kind of hunger to discover them. In a way, that makes these riches all the more valuable. God has a built-in guarantee that they won't be opened to anyone who really doesn't want them. So if you do have this gnawing hunger, this sense of dissatisfaction that tells you there's something more, it may help to know that you have a gift in disguise. God doesn't give physical hunger without also giving something to satisfy it; the same is true for spiritual things.

A LEGEND IN MY OWN MIND

In my own mind, I had it all when I was a student at Brown University. Not only was I accomplishing all of the goals already mentioned, but my relationships were going well and my classes were too. My nickname on campus was the "total package." Was there anything wrong with this picture? Despite appearances, something was radically wrong. Deep inside, I was crying out for something more. I had begun my journey with God as a senior in high school, but it wasn't until my junior year in college that I made the biggest, scariest and most profound decision of my life. That decision was to truly engage God as the Lord of my life.

Here's the difference: Until that point I treated my relationship with God like the bulk of the Christians that I knew. I went to church, prayed and worked hard while I asked God to bless *my* life. Sound familiar? I knew where I wanted to go and I believed that God would give me the desires of *my* heart. (Notice the key word: MY.) Granted, I definitely experienced some change in my life due to the different disciplines that I engaged in, **but every now and then I would meet a Christian who had a noticeably different kind of love than the love I was striving to muster up in obedience. I noticed an ease and release to their lives that I didn't have yet. These people had a power in their lives that I had tasted on occasion but had not experienced moment by moment. I would read the Scriptures and learn about the power of the Holy Spirit but I had not yet let that power flow through me.**

At the end of my junior year in college I became convicted that all of my diligent study of the Scripture and desire to implement it into my life was not producing loving fruit. That is when I came to understand that I was simply trying to self-help my way to God and to a better life. What I didn't know at the time, but could *feel*, was that there was something more to life that I was missing. (Hint: It's called the abundant life.) Abundant life is rarely connected with the external trappings of success, and it is not something that we can obtain through our own guidance and strength.

I needed to adjust my relationship to God in order to experience that powerful release I saw in those people. I needed to go on a journey, one that I am still on. That journey has made me aware of real life from God's perspective, and I started to retrain in this new way. I have had to unlearn many things so that God could train me in His ways of desiring, feeling, thinking, behaving and relating. God wanted to revolutionize my life, not just die for my sins. When I engaged with Him in this way, I began to understand what it means to live the abundant life. While the desire for the abundant life is good, the way I was pursuing it kept it far out of reach. I was like the guy who bends down to pick up a ball, but his own foot kicks it farther away just as he steps up to it. And so on, down the road. The invitation of God to live the abundant life is not an invitation to self-help your way to godliness, but rather a life of submission and release of control.

THE DANGEROUS PRAYER

It was during this season of my life that I prayed a dangerous prayer. It went something like this: *"God, take away my pride and my desire to control life. Be the Lord and King of my life, and if there is anything in my life that resists your Kingdom from coming and your will from being done in my life please remove it. I give you permission to rewrite the story of my life. You are the potter; I am the clay. Mold me and make me. Have absolute sway. Guide and empower my life according to your will for me, Lord Jesus."*

That was my revolutionary shift, a sample moment of submission. (You will note in this prayer that God is God, and I am not.) Most of us don't like the idea of losing control. But God's control brings your life under a higher order than what you could muster. It's a paradox: As we submit to God's control, we gain greater control over our lives and become more effective in our life's purpose. Anything less is sleepwalking through life from God's perspective.

Which is better: Trying to scrounge up the love and power on your own, or letting God's love and power flow through you? God has destined you for greatness. But He doesn't call for greatness as a mere burst of extra effort or performance on your part. His main plan is to live His life of love in and through you.

KINGDOM THINKING

God is offering us His Heavenly Kingdom on Earth. Even better, He's made available His Kingdom *within* us! His aim is not for us to wait until we're in Heaven to live in His Kingdom but to use our lives to help usher it in, right here. I'm not talking about sitting around blissfully twiddling harps, either. Nor am I talking about trekking through the jungle to bring the Gospel to a remote tribe, though some of you may certainly be born to do that. I'm talking about the Kingdom of Heaven having everything to do with our everyday lives. We need to let go of our stereotypical views of Heaven and bust myths surrounding words like "mission." God's Kingdom is misunderstood and difficult to see when we are in control of our lives. But as we begin to let go of our old mindsets and controls, His Kingdom reality has more room to show up in our lives. We can begin to experience the lasting richness of life that God intends for us, a richness that is far beyond all we can ask or imagine.

If you're like most people, you may have assumed that we get to the Kingdom of Heaven after we die, and that it has no influence in our present lives. Yet one of the most important (and overlooked) teachings in the history of Christianity has been the Kingdom of Heaven as a present, not only a future, reality. Scripture makes it clear that Jesus came to earth to proclaim and usher in the Kingdom of Heaven *(Matthew 4:17).*

Not only that, but Jesus said, *"The Kingdom of Heaven is within you" (Luke 17:21).* Notice he did not say the Kingdom of Heaven *will be* within you but *is.* We may not have tapped into it all yet, but Jesus meant what He said. The Kingdom of Heaven, meaning the life that flows from God, is available to us, right now.

SPRING UP, O WELL!

If the Kingdom of Heaven is a present reality, then how do we access it?

Is it like a well that we already own, but just need a pump or a bucket to help us drink? You can begin with your own "dangerous prayer," too. Ask God to release His Kingdom reality within you. Or ask Him to show you something new that you need to understand. Use your words as a "pump" by simply saying to the well, "I submit Lord, command me and I will follow!" When we do this, God's life springs up within us and He builds His Kingdom. Our words are powerful. God created the world with His words, and then made us in His image, with the same kind of creative word power that He used. We have that pump or bucket and don't even realize it. We tend to think of the Kingdom of Heaven as an abstract concept, but God longs for us to dip into His well within us and "make it real." Submitting to Him is the way we tap into all the promises in Scripture that we think sound too good to be true. Our challenge is to let the Kingdom of Heaven be released into every part of our being so that God can use our everyday lives to build His Kingdom.

HOW WISE ARE YOU?

Teach us to number our days aright, that we may gain a heart of wisdom. (Psalm 90:12)

Maybe you are familiar with the phrases "carpe diem" (seize the day) and "life is short." But how familiar are you with the Scripture above and the truths contained in it? Here the psalmist is crying out to God for His guidance in life. Without God, no one is truly wise. **I define wisdom as knowledge applied to life that makes life work the way it was meant to work by God.** So how truly wise are you, using this definition of wisdom? God has given each one of us a gift of time before we die. How will you unpack this gift? God wants to act in your life, but you need to perceive that He is for you, active on your behalf, before you can be guided by Him. The way you see is crucial. Your perception of God and your perception of yourself will determine how you live. Once you see that He is God and you are not, you have a fighting chance at wisdom.

*The fear [respect, awe] of the Lord is the beginning of wisdom.
(Proverbs 1:7)*

DRIFT AND SELF-LEADERSHIP

I'll say this again and again: Without deliberate training, our natural
tendency is drift. To drift is human; to train is divine! Without a
conscious decision to invite God into our lives—not just as an observer
but in His role as Lord of our lives—the drift factor sets in. We must
get used to the fact that our relationship with God is to be one of
dependence and not independence. We resist dependence, thinking
it's unbalanced (as in co-dependence) or not "grown up." But it's
more grown up to depend on God, and it's safe, because He's the only
one who is truly healthy. Our dependence can grow with *every* event
in our lives and *every* act of obedience to Him. It may not suit our
egos that life works this way. On the other hand, that will no longer
be a concern to us when we experience the supernatural power of God.
In fact, God's love will begin to flow not just into us but also through
us, and we'll know the joy that comes from being a blessing to others
as God bears fruit through our lives. That is, *"fruit that will last"*
(John 15:16).

Not long ago, I listened as a young man told me about an opportunity
he had to move to a more senior position at two different companies.
The companies were similar and he was trying to make up his mind
which to choose. There were no ethical considerations with respect to
the industry the companies were in. On the surface, the two companies
looked the same. Equal choice, right? That's what this young man
thought. "God doesn't care about which company I go to," he said,
and picked the one he wanted.

Soon, however, he began clashing with one of the company's top
managers almost daily. Before accepting the position, he had met the
manager briefly; there was no way to tell from that meeting that the
man's personality and character could cause such difficulty. But it did.
I urged my friend to consider that God does care about the decisions
he makes. He cares about everything pertaining to his career. Also,

only God has the inside knowledge of all the people and other factors involved. He created them, remember? *Nothing is hidden from God's sight. Everything is uncovered and laid bare before the eyes of Him to whom we must give account (Hebrews 4:13).* As a committed Christian, this young man now realizes that in order to steward his life well he must not only think things through rationally, but also seek God's wisdom and guidance before making decisions. He has come to believe that God wants to speak to him and guide him in every area of life.

How can we avoid this drift into self-leadership? And what's the right balance? How much does God do and how much do we do? We might not know God's will in minute detail every hour of the day, but when we acquaint ourselves with His revealed will in Scripture, wise principles and listen for His promptings, we'll start to see His fingerprints on our lives more and more. The more we see Him at work in us, the deeper our peace. That is the *peace that passes understanding (Philippians 4:7).* That peace is but one fruit that develops when you are *abiding in God (John 15).*

HISTORY AS YOUR STORY...

Did you ever sit in a history class in school, wondering, "What does this have to do with *me?*" Then, if you were fortunate, you found out that one of your grandparents remembered something about the era you had to study, and suddenly you realized that history wasn't a bunch of random stuff that the teacher made up, but had to do with what actually happened. It still might have seemed ancient, but making a personal connection brings history to life for us. In the same way, we might hear the Scriptures differently if we see more clearly the connections in it for us, and remember that it all really happened. If you put your own name in all the slots that say "My people" or "Israel" or "Zion," you might perk up a bit in your awareness of the Scripture's application to your life. (Try it! I dare you!)

At the very center of history is the Atonement, or Jesus' restoration of our relationship to God as His children. Through His sacrifice, He made available to us the Father's rich resources, at His own expense.

It is critical to understand what we have lost in history so that we have a clear concept of what has been restored, what God wants to see manifested in our lives. It's like an inheritance already laid out in the will, but not yet drawn upon daily. I'm going to make a brief sweep through the last few thousand years in order to recap history's highlights and emphasize its relevance to your life. As you read, you might even picture yourself in there where it says "mankind."

GOD AND US, THROUGH HISTORY

In the beginning, mankind was created by God and existed in a perfect loving relationship with Him, filled with His presence, including His guidance and His power. But then came a succession of events:

The Fall and the Flood. When Satan entered the picture in the Garden of Eden and offered Adam and Eve an opposing will to follow, they chose to disobey God. Consequently, they lost connection with the guidance and power of God and fell from the perfect relationship status that they had enjoyed with Him. Out of His great love for us God began creating a pathway through which we could reconnect to Him. His first gift to humanity was to create physical death. Before the fall we were destined to live with God in perfection forever. Death is a gift to humanity because it limits our exposure to the influence of evil and gives us the possibility to reconnect with God's perfection in Heaven. Instead of simply destroying His creation, the gift of continued life that ends in a physical death gives us the opportunity to reconnect with God and be retrained as His followers. Upon death, those who die as God-seeking and God-fearing men and women are fully renewed as he removes our sinful desire, perfects our desire to do His will and gives us resurrected bodies to live in. It is true, one day we will all eject out of our earth suits.

So the descendants of Adam and Eve have found themselves in a bad state, separated from God and tempted by the Evil One to behave in destructive ways ever since. In short order, humanity devolved to the state that the desires of their hearts were "only evil all the time" (Genesis 6:5). This season in history proved that left up to our own guidance and power we choose evil and that life does not work unless we abide in God. It is in that corrupted life experience God found a righteous man and his family and decided to rebuild through them. So he brought the Flood.

God Fathers a Nation. After the Flood, God started over with Noah and his family and began to rebuild a people who would seek Him and experience and express His love. It is interesting to note that the lifespan of people after the flood decreased dramatically. As a general rule of thumb people today live one-tenth as long as before the flood. Another gift from God limiting our exposure to sin, but also creating an urgency for us to decide who we will follow as Lord of our lives. His plan was to use this nation to retrain humanity and restore the experience of life in His Kingdom. As they sought after God and followed His guidance for their lives, they re-entered His blessing, learning how to experience and express love again, God's way. During this season of history, people related to God primarily as Father, and their relationship with Him was very much like children learning how to love from a parent who is training them in righteousness (right living). They never broke out of the bad state into good, however; they only experienced better levels of bad with spurts of growth toward righteousness. Some people became God-fearing and God-following men and women, but on the whole the nation was still lost and in need of saving. It was during this season that God restored His guidance through the giving of the Law (Ten Commandments, etc.) and speaking through angels and prophets. Yet this, as we learn in the New Testament, served only to clearly illustrate that we can't follow God's guidance *without His power.*

The sacrificial system implemented during this season of Israel's history, was given to us as a graphic reminder that the wages of sin is death and in order for God to be just, something must die for our sins. Sacrificing animals never fully paid the price for our sins, however. In order for a real atonement to be accomplished for humanity's sin a perfect human sacrifice would be needed. Until that was accomplished in Jesus, humanity was simply paying it forward.

Arrival of Jesus the Son. Then God sent His only Son Jesus to be our Savior (pay the debt that we owe because of our sin) and our Lord (guide and empower us to live). For those of us who accept His payment for our sins, God no longer holds our sins against us, and our relationship with Him begins. In so doing, we move from bad to good. Unfortunately, most Christians' journeys of faith end right here. We are not properly instructed how to align ourselves under the Lordship of Christ. Such alignment leads to life lived through the guidance and power of God.

God Sends His Spirit. Christ's redemptive work for us on the cross is not the end of the story. God sent the Holy Spirit to empower us to experience and express the love of God in a supernatural way. This can happen when we are living in and through His strength. The Cross and Resurrection restored the Kingdom. Even though we cannot experience the Kingdom perfectly this side of the grave (because of the impact of our sinful nature, the Evil One's relentless attack and the fallen world system within which we live,) it has been restored in its perfection for us to draw upon. Through the power of the Holy Spirit, we can draw on much more of the Kingdom's abundant life than we realize. As we submit to God's Lordship and live in and through the power of the Holy Spirit, our lives move from good to great. Now that we live in the season of the Spirit, good isn't good enough. Greatness is being offered to all who will bend their knees in obedience to God the Father, receive Jesus as their Savior and Lord, and submit to the power of the Holy Spirit to guide and empower their lives.

Our Eternal Dwelling. For those who die connected to God—Father, Son and Holy Spirit—we will be restored to the perfect unhindered relationship that was experienced with God before the Fall. One significant difference from the previous perfect state in the Garden is that this time it is a permanent state of perfectly experiencing and expressing love. It is permanent because we chose to love and follow God during our life on earth. Upon death, God purifies and perfects our will to do the will of the Father, and since the Evil One has no influence on us beyond death, we perfectly experience and express love forever. I like to picture the story of God and mankind through history using the following diagram.

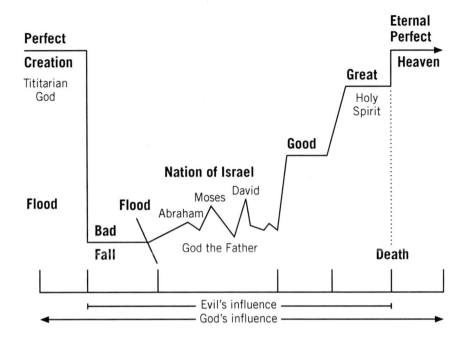

This is true history (His story). Now we must ask ourselves: How do we respond to what He has done? What will be our story? What kind of life experience do we want to choose for ourselves? How can we draw on the abundant life in the here-and-now Kingdom of Heaven within us?

ARE YOU READY TO DIE?

You might interpret this question two ways. Both are useful: Literally, are you done yet? Have you been all that you were born to be on this earth? Are you totally convinced you've fulfilled God's purpose for your life? Are you ready to move on to the next life? (If you're reading this, I am guessing the answer is "not yet.") And spiritually, are you ready to die to your agenda and whatever might be in your heart that is not of God? Are you at a point where you're willing to let go? You may notice that for a plant to flourish, it needs to be pruned, and anything that constitutes dead wood, withered old fruit, even extra foliage that is ungainly—needs to be cut off in order to give that plant a fresh boost. Just so, we need to die to self-leadership and seek God's plans for us if we are going to experience the abundant life. God wants to renew our heart, soul, mind, and strength and begin transforming the way we relate and what we do. That's how we become new creations. Priorities shift so completely that we enter into new passion, new power, new devotion, new understanding...

Therefore, if anyone is in Christ, He is a new creation; the old has gone, the new has come. (2 Corinthians 5:17)

By the way, dying to self-leadership and becoming a follower of God does not mean you will not be a leader in your sphere of influence. Godly leaders are needed. The world of business abounds with leadership courses, leadership books, leadership programs with their leadership CD's and DVD's. You see leaders everywhere scrambling to develop their capabilities so that their organizations can attain their competitive edge. Much of that material may be terrific and even applicable in a Christian setting. Just be mindful that leadership happens to coincide with our egotistical tendencies in a way that *"followership"* does not. When we are truly in Christ, submitted to the guidance and power of God, He will lead through us. And the best leaders are those who know first how to be excellent followers and let God lead through them.

God has good plans for us. Those plans may allow our shortcomings to come to the surface in ways that should help us become more dependent on Him. If we react by accepting deeper dependence, that's the kind of "dying" we're talking about. In return for what we're letting go, we receive guidance and power from God in a way that helps us meet the next challenge. Again, in our culture we associate growing up with becoming more independent. But in God's Kingdom, it is the more mature who are most dependent.

JESUS BUSHWHACKED THE TRAIL FOR US

*Therefore, since Christ suffered in His body, arm yourselves also
with the same attitude, because he who has suffered in His body
is done with sin. As a result, he does not live the rest of his earthly
life for evil human desires, but rather for the will of God. For
you have spent enough time in the past doing what pagans choose
to do – living in debauchery, lust, drunkenness, orgies, carousing
and detestable idolatry. They think it strange that you do not plunge
with them into the same flood of dissipation, and they heap abuse
on you. But they will have to give account to Him who is ready
to judge the living and the dead.(1 Peter 4:1-5)*

Jesus is not merely a good example. Nor is He wringing His hands
over the terrible condition of Creation. What Jesus came to do two
thousand-plus years ago is a cataclysmic action that exists outside of
time: The power of the cross reaches as far as your personal struggles
and is still potent to put the old sinful patterns to death. But we must
be willing, as this scripture states, to put following the will of God
above everything else, even our own physical well-being. We have all
experienced what life is like when we walk according to the patterns
of this world. We have all experienced the lifelessness of it all. When
we choose to follow God's ways, we will experience persecution from
those who are still enamored with chasing after evil, sinful desires.
They don't like the fact that we are experiencing and expressing the
love of God. We will also struggle with our old sin tendencies which
need to be healed and retrained in righteousness. During this retraining,
you might think of the cross as the most powerful weapon God could
ever place into your hands. It is the only weapon that can effectively
put to death sinful cycles.

NO MORE VICTIM MENTALITY

No doubt you know many people who feel helpless to change their
lives. They've fallen into a victim mentality and have not found a way
to break the vicious cycle. As helpful as many helping professions can

be, none can offer the complete transformation found in the cross. Only God deals cleanly with guilt, through our confession and His cleansing of unrighteousness. And only God cuts through false guilt and shame in a way that sets us free from a victim mindset. The enemy can duplicate many miracles, but only God can change a life for good, from the inside out.

Just as resurrection is only possible after death, new life patterns come into play only after we put the old ones to death on the cross. We do it first verbally, by "handing them over" to God with our mouths. With continued submission, you will begin to see change. Don't be surprised if, as you grow closer to God, you become more aware of sin. Don't dismay! That is a sign that you're growing in holiness. Often, the more healing we experience, the more sensitive we are to what grieves God's heart. As you abide in Him, you'll find that balance between hating sin yet also growing in forgiveness. As you are filled with His divine sap, you'll find yourself less daunted by the forces that try to slime you or pull you in the opposite direction. The more saturated you are with His Holy Spirit, the more easily those negative influences will roll right off of you, like water off a duck's back. God's ownership of your life includes a pretty awesome Protection Plan!

BORN TO OVERCOME

"In this world you will have trouble. But take heart, for I have overcome the world." (John 16:33)

You were made to be an overcomer. You were born for greatness. It is found in submitting to the One who invented greatness and created you to take joy in His life expressed through you. Being owned by the Creator of the Universe has its privileges.

CHAPTER 2

What Drives You?

LAW 2

The Law of Mission: *Every life (being and doing) is guided by a governing mission which is a combination of our vision, priorities, values and identity roles we have learned from our life experience and chosen as a path to an abundant life.*

If I were to ask you, "What is your mission in life?"…what would you say? The average person would draw a blank. That is not because the mission doesn't exist, but because most people have not consciously thought through that question. But consider this: We are living out a mission whether we are conscious of it or not.

DOWN TO THE CORE

A friend of mine tells me this story about her son: He had just graduated from boot camp, and for ninety days he had been instilled with the core values that underscore every aspect of Marine life: honor, courage, commitment. As this young man was traveling home for a ten-day leave with his family, he shared the sobering challenge he felt to somehow live up to those values. "I realize that wherever I go, people will say, 'That's what a Marine is like.' It's different; I can feel the pressure—to make sure I represent the Marines well."

His mother, secretly admiring his humility, suggested that *everyone* is "representing" something whether they realize it or not; he is simply ahead of the game by being conscious of it. "Think about it," she said. "How many of us go through life without thinking through our purpose or our values, never aware of why we're here or who we're representing in our lives?"

"Wow, you're right," he said. "I never thought of it that way."

Many of us tend to live in a human "default" mode. With this default setting, we pursue *our idea* of the abundant life, which includes most of the habits and tendencies we picked up in our younger years. We like to think of ourselves as discerning and able to make free choices, but the truth is, outside of the cross we're far more programmed than we think. Our habits and paradigms have molded the course of our lives. Furthermore, our culture bombards us with its influence through media.

THE QUEST TO ESCAPE BOREDOM

Actress Eva Gabor and playwright Noel Coward were dining in a New York restaurant when the subject of writer Barnaby Conrad came up. Conrad had taken part in a bullfight in Spain and was injured.

"Noel, dahling, have you heard the news about poor Barnaby? He vas terribly gored in Spain."

"He was **what?**"

"He vas **gored!**"

"Thank heavens!" Coward exclaimed with relief. "I thought you said he was **bored!**"

Entertainment is upheld as one of our culture's top priorities. The secular German philosopher Arthur Schopenhauer said that human beings vacillate between the two extremes of *distress* and *boredom*. His pessimistic view of life lacks God's input, but you may recognize how its truth is played out in the drift of human nature. The enemy of our soul understands this drift and promotes the fear of boredom in our lives. Have you noticed how we go to great lengths to avoid boredom? We do not tolerate peace and quiet well. We turn on the media at every spare moment. The ultimate condemnation of a movie or book is not to say that it is vulgar or evil or poorly structured— but to say that it is boring. In the tabloid headlines we see the little flings and swings of bored people that result in destruction of families and reputation.

To the mind thirsting for amusement, the activities of a Heavenly-minded person are considered to be dry and dull. *Holiness* is made to look boring. Heaven itself is depicted as the quintessential boredom. Who do you think thought up the picture of angels and saints sitting around all day on clouds, with bland-looking robes, halos and a harp or two? Not God! And while we're here on Earth, Christian life is thought to be constricting, with God as the Chief Killjoy. It has been human nature under enemy influence that has produced this version of Christianity.

HOLY ADVENTURE

Yet here are the facts: Countless testify to the *joy* and *adventure* of a holy life with God. Holiness is not the opposite of adventure; it's our *doorway* into it. My desire is to usher you into the amazing adventure God is offering us. A close relationship with the Creator of the universe empowered with His Holy Spirit cannot possibly be dull. Religion is boring, but God did not call us to be religious. We are called to be fully engaged in mission with God. Jesus came to lead and empower us to live a supernatural life. When we submit to Him, the adventure begins. We no longer fall prey to the old default settings or get knocked back and forth between distress and boredom like a tattered badminton birdie. Dismantling the old programming releases us to tap into our *true mission*.

LEARNING—AND UNLEARNING

In coaching people, I've realized that the first thing I need to do is understand what shapes their worldview, or what default mission is already operating in their lives. It takes a lot of listening. What are the main factors influencing a person's belief system? Upbringing and our experiences with authority are key. The most influential people in all of our lives are parents, teachers, authority figures and significant friends with whom we grew up. We may have wanted to be like these people, or we may have decided we *never* wanted to be like them. Either way, they were the ones who helped shape our lives and our outlooks. We made choices and decisions, conscious and sub-conscious, that were influenced by the events and people in our early lives. These choices helped install the buttons that get pushed in us. However, what was *done to us* doesn't have to determine how our lives will go; our *responses* to those circumstances will.

We are subject to God's principles. For example: *A man reaps what he sows (Galatians 6:7)*. This law of sowing and reaping is a powerful principle operating in our lives, whether we like it or not. Our thoughts, judgments, choices, actions and even dreams, feelings and memories are all seeds that get planted and sprout and grow into our belief system. Where we've reaped unhealthy habits or sin-tendencies, we may need to go through seasons of unlearning (putting old patterns to death through confession and healing of hurts.) That unlearning is best followed by refilling and retraining in righteousness (putting new patterns in place.) This transformation process is not limited to those who consider their lives to be a mess. It's the basic working out of salvation for any Christian; it's our life's journey.

What is there to unlearn? And how do we begin to even see these underlying forces in our lives? You might feel like you've just been put on assignment to rewire your house when you haven't studied as an electrician and don't know where to start. It helps to begin by looking "behind the wall." That's the equivalent of looking past our façade, the image we like to portray to the world, to find our underlying motivations. One clue might lie in the significant repeated patterns in your current life, and what memories you have that are associated with them.

AN INNER VOW

Take me, for example. You already know I've been the ultra-jock, sports fanatic, workaholic, bent on success at all costs. Where did that begin? I was raised in the Midwest, Catholic, with Lutheran grandparents. I first played football when I was nine years old; I was a heavy kid, and I only played center. The team I was on lost every game that year. I remember an awards ceremony in which I didn't receive anything. Something clicked in me at that moment; I said to myself, *"This will **never** happen again."* Notice the tenacious tenor of that promise: It's no less than an inner vow, and it promptly slid into place as a substitution for God's mission for my life. We all have these vows that we've made. You may recognize them more easily once you've heard stories like mine. I grew up in a culture that had a reward system built into it. And it's not that it was all bad; life of necessity has to include those kinds of rewards as we go along. It's part of life to receive praises for good behavior or trophies for excelling and achieving. My point is, we substitute those rewards for God's unconditional love and acceptance. And we substitute our own inner vows for God's greater plan for our lives. My sense of mission was to glorify myself, and it came about in reaction to that feeling of humiliation I had as a nine-year-old. As you will see, my "mission" looked so good that I easily assumed it was God's best for me. That is, until our little meeting...

A DIVINE AMBUSH

Right after final exams of my junior year at Brown, I had a week alone before traveling to the national track and field championships. Competing at the nationals was the realization of one of my dreams. Not only that, but my football coach had called me a few days before to give me more good news: I was voted co-captain of the team and pre-season All-American for the next year. Here was the realization of two more of my dreams. Let's just say that my overall mood was one of euphoria, and my momentum...off the charts.

I needed a place to stay before heading to the West Coast, and a friend kindly lent me his apartment. His place was nice, but it lacked one key component: a television. I found myself steeped in a quietness more profound than any I had ever experienced. This stillness ushered me into extended time in the Scriptures and in prayer.

During one of my morning prayer sessions, God showed up. He met me in the stillness. First, God showed me a vision of myself standing on a mountaintop, waving the flag of victory. It was as if God was celebrating me for doing things no one else in the world was doing. Then God shifted gears and made me feel the profound aloneness of the situation I had created for myself. It was palpable and real, and I felt the darkness of it. Then I was taken to a farm-like scene. I was standing at a crossroads; I needed to make a decision. In that setting, God entered into a dialogue with me as I prayed. As with any encounter with God, words fail to capture the deeper impact. But reduced to words, this dialogue would have been as follows:

ME "It seems I've been achieving my goals and realizing some of the dreams I have been striving towards."

GOD *"But that's just human good."*

ME "Well, I'm doing a lot of things at a really high level. My nickname is 'the total package.'"

GOD *"But you're not immersed in my greatness for you. You know very little of the God-guided, God-empowered life I want for you."*

ME "If this is about sin, well, I do feel convicted of my sin, and I confess my waywardness. But, all things considered, compared to most people, I'm pretty good, right?"

GOD *"You weren't created to be good. You were created to be great."*

ME "Well, surely I am on the right path! Rome wasn't built in a day! Why don't I just continue on this path I'm traveling? Obviously, it's a path of achievement."

GOD *"Do you remember those moments on your grandparents' farm in Indiana?"*

ME "Yes, I do. They were filled with peace, filled with You, filled with faith. There was an experience of abundance about those days. There was even something of grandeur about them, as though You were covering me with your truth and your protection."

GOD *"And how do those moments compare with what you're experiencing now?" (That was the moment of truth.)*

ME "Well in comparison, I have a sense of emptiness, of loneliness. Something is missing!"

GOD *"Look at where your pride has gotten you. Do you realize you're at a fork in the road? The choice is yours. You can keep going the way you're going in your own guidance and strength, and you can expect this to produce a life that's more of the same—achievements and relational experiences that will not satisfy your soul! If that's what you want, you can pursue it."*

ME "No, I want a life that is very different from that."

GOD *"If you take your road, you will continue to be in charge, and the accolades may continue. But I'm pointing out a road that may not have all the accolades, and on this road I am in charge. You need to surrender to my guidance and power in order to walk this road. Do you want to walk it?"*

By then I couldn't have been more eager to release myself to God. I wanted to be His true disciple. Instead of self-helping my way to God, I was being introduced to a better way. A real relationship with God as my Lord. A sense of *"Yes, God!"* rushed into me in a flood. The first step on my journey of true discipleship took place at that moment. Nothing has been the same since.

It was not a crisis or downfall that forced me to reflect on my life's direction. No, I was at the top of my game. But even there on the mountaintop, God knew how to get my attention. **He proved to me that course adjustments are not only for the down-and-out.**

I must admit that if God had told me then that I would be leading and teaching others how to seek and live the abundant life, I would have run. Fortunately, God only reveals what we need to know to take the next steps with Him—not what the rest of the road will look like.

If I were to sum up what some of those next steps meant for me, it would look like this: God invited me to take a first step and engage in real, vulnerable relationships where I would be sharing more of my inner self with others. I hadn't done much of this since I had been a child. My world trained this innocent vulnerability right out of me. God challenged me to invest more time getting to really know others rather than just working on building myself up. I needed to do this in little steps along the way. The biggest next step of them all was to pray that God would remove my pride and fill me with a true sense of self from His perspective, a work He continues to this day.

As you take steps like these and embark on relearning, God re-parents you. He, your Creator, reaches back into your life and touches those areas that are hurting. No parents, teachers or authority figures are perfect. But God is able to fill in the gaps you they left in you as you grew up. We'll take a deeper look at this in the next chapter, but for now suffice it to say that the abundant life requires and includes God's ongoing input and re-parenting. If He can touch that humiliated nine-year-old in me and plug in His Fatherly presence for my drivenness, He can reach your heart too.

A CLOSER LOOK AT OUR WIRING: THE FOUR ASPECTS OF MISSION

In order to help people begin to see what is really driving them, I ask them some questions. I ask them to check out the different types of wiring, so to speak, so they'll see better how it all comes together to "run" their lives.

I've discovered at least four components of our lives that work together to make up our sense of mission: Our vision, our priorities, our values, and our identity roles. I believe these four elements operate in our lives whether we call ourselves Christian or not. In the rest of this chapter I will discuss each of these components from the human perspective. In the next chapter we'll look at *God's* concept of these components. Sometimes it helps to take things apart and put them back together. We can then see better how each part functions.

OUR *HUMAN* VISION

Why did God create you and me and set the world in motion?
Our vision in life, sometimes called our *purpose*, is your take on *why we're here*. Is it that we were created to partake of His divine nature? Or is it "whoever has the most toys wins?" Our vision of God affects everything we do, even if we don't believe in God. It is key to what we think life is all about. Furthermore, our vision needs to keep growing throughout our lives. God is Eternal; who can fathom His plans once and for all? It is a lifelong process, understanding and expanding our vision.

Ω

Consider taking five to ten minutes right now to ponder this. Write it down if you like to use a journal: *Why am I here? How do I envision God? What is the meaning or purpose of my life?*

OUR *HUMAN* PRIORITIES

What do we consider to be of first importance? Do our lives reflect that? As we've said in Chapter One, we don't drift toward spiritual growth. Our natural sway is towards self-indulgence and self-promotion. Some of that is due to our tendency to focus on what is still uncertain. As an example, many women have found that the attention lavished on them by their husbands before the wedding has suddenly dissipated once the afterglow of the honeymoon is over. Once the commitment has been made, the husband has no lingering uncertainty about his marital status. Yet uncertainty about career advancement looms large in his mind, and his focus turns to that as a more pressing priority. He even views it as *part* of his devotion to his wife; it's considered the "right" thing to do.

The reason we focus on what is most uncertain is due to our desire to bring it under control and get a handle on our lives. However, anybody who has lived a while can tell you that this control is an illusion. The only thing that is certain is that we don't have a clue what will happen next. But that doesn't stop people from trying. As our lives fill with questions of material well-being and security, those concerns shove priorities of faith and family togetherness into lower slots on the mental list.

Ω

Why not ask yourself where you are on that priority spectrum now: *Where is my focus much of the time? What concerns me most? What are my priorities? Have they shifted over time? Have I neglected important relationships in my effort to control my life?*

OUR *HUMAN* VALUES

You might say that our priorities reflect our values; what we put first on the list reveals what we *value*. You may have found that a discussion of values can sound general and vaguely positive. For instance, many people would say they like to be generous in their attitude toward others, or that they believe it is important to be hardworking. These are certainly positive values. If we maintain such positive values in the abstract, but if they are not carried out in our priorities, we'll find that our culture soon shows very different values. In our culture we've seen a decline in certain values such as those of *respect* and *community-mindedness*.

One of my partners, John Donovan, recently completed a nationwide study of teachers on behalf of a national ministry. The most notable finding was the change in the everyday classroom experience among those who have been teaching since the 1970s. Without exception, the teachers said that the difficulty of managing a classroom today was vastly greater than in the earlier years of their career; consequently some of them couldn't wait to retire. They felt that children are not being raised to respect the authority figures in their lives and that this makes teaching them often a wasted effort.

This decline in community-mindedness and family values is accompanied by a rise in assertive individualism. According to the book *There's No Place Like Work*, society has changed its entire view of work from being a means of supporting family life to the primary avenue of self-fulfillment. Neglect of children has emerged as a salient consequence of this trend, with child abuse and delinquency being traceable to it as well. Our society will pay a high price for valuing career over family.

In the following section and at several other points in the book, I invite you to examine *seven values that lead to a genuinely abundant life*. First we will examine these values in the light of how we see them from the *human* perspective. This list—Guidance, Grace, Growth, Gifts, Glorification, Good Stewardship, Group (community)—takes its influence from a variety of sources, chief among them being Willow Creek Community Church's "Five G" membership class.

Ω

You might consider making this "Seven G's" list one of your regular spiritual workout sessions. As you read through the list, notice where you see yourself or identify with the behavior I've described. You can ask: *What are my values? Do I tend to lean toward the human concept of these values? What views or mindsets are fueling my life?*

THE SEVEN G'S: VALUES FOR LIFE (*HUMAN* CONCEPTS)

Guidance – Our *Human* Concept

Guidance goes to the core of our self-image and our natural desire to be in control of ourselves. We dread losing that control. Few things arouse more pity than the person who has lost control of his faculties to the point where his choices must be made by others. Our natural drift is to be guided by our own natural "global positioning systems." We do this in several ways:

- **We depend on our own understanding.** In other words, we just do our best to assess a situation and then act on the basis of that. This one is especially strong when we've been experiencing success. We don't handle success well; as soon as we succeed, our human tendency is to revert back to self-sufficiency.
- **We fly blind.** Certain life situations may force us to move forward without any confidence that we know what to do. In our sinful state we move ahead anyway without asking God or others for direction.
- **We consult books, other people, etc.** We acknowledge that we don't have all the answers, but we confine ourselves to human wisdom and cut ourselves off from God and His divine guidance for our lives.

Grace (unmerited favor, forgiveness, mercy) – Our *Human* Concept

If someone is lacking in graciousness toward us, our natural tendency can vary, but it is typical to respond in kind. To rise above it is something we find difficult, unnecessary, or even impossible.

A lack of grace also shapes our tendency to avoid reaching out to others in situations that involve hardship, believing they are none of our business. Of course, it may well be that we should avoid involving ourselves in the problems of others; it takes discernment to know where and when we might be called to help. But as anyone familiar with the helping professions can attest, the human response to need is often indifference on the one hand or a frenzied desire to solve every problem (and burn out) on the other.

Growth – Our *Human* Concept

Our human tendency is to avoid growth. We'd rather seek the easy life. Think of how this is reflected in television advertising. Tens of millions of dollars of research have proven beyond all doubt that advertising works because it taps into the deepest springs of human desire. An advertisement about debt relief doesn't show columns of figures or the furrowed brows of people in debt; it shows the carefree faces of people enjoying a hike in magnificent natural surroundings. We dream of an easier life, free of inconveniences and pain.

Yet we need to grow, and we tend to recognize this isn't possible without some sacrifice on our part. Perhaps with some reluctance, we try. But our striving, because it is usually done in our own strength under our own guidance, only lasts a short period of time before our old habits kick back in. Real growth only comes through a process of transformation by placing ourselves under the guidance and the power of God, being held accountable by God through others who are coaching us in our growth.

In our church communities, we expect growth to take place through two avenues: (1) education, including Bible study, sermons, Sunday school, and special programs; and (2) inspiration, characteristically from worship services, sermons and occasionally from testimony, public or private. But recent studies show that most Christians are simply not making growth changes in their personal lives. It takes more than just attending services, groups and classes in which we are being inspired and educated. We need to be coached and held accountable in order to grow.

Gifts – Our *Human* Concept

When we speak of someone as "gifted," it is usually a reference to natural abilities. Sometimes the gifts seem to be inherited, just like the color of hair or eyes. Recent literature on the subject has been downplaying the significance of natural gifts in favor of determination and skill.

When we attempt things in life, we're inclined to be "realistic" and avoid anything for which we feel poorly equipped. It seems that our job is to figure out what we are able to do and do it well. Unfortunately, this is only partly true. We are to discover our natural abilities in life and develop them to their full potential, but God also gives divine enablements to those who align themselves with Him and live in and through His strength. In other words, we may have gifts we don't yet know about, and God has designed us to do far more than we think we can. In this light, what is possible takes on a whole new meaning.

Glorification – Our *Human* Concept

Our celebrity-conscious society is saturated with images of glory. Anyone waiting at the supermarket checkout counter is besieged by headlines that glorify the exploits, if not the bodies, of people whom millions want to emulate.

Most of us are acquainted with people whose main goal in life seems to be the attainment of their own glory. In their presence, we become conscious of an invisible ledger sheet of credit and discredit, merit and demerit, praise and blame. Even times of celebration for these people are clouded by the spirit of unrelenting evaluation—all in the elusive quest of some personal glory, outshining everyone else in sight. The greatest problem for them is that even when they succeed, the satisfaction evaporates quickly. Is there not a touch of this syndrome in all of us? God wants to call us to a life beyond this, beyond self-aggrandizement, to real and abiding love for Him and for others. To bring glory to Him through our lives is truly one of the more challenging value adjustments.

Good Stewardship – Our *Human* Concept

On the natural plane, people say, "Well, it's my life," and assume that no one can dispute that; they own it and hopefully they enjoy it. Some people even assume they have the right to live carelessly or even to end it altogether. They live as owners and not stewards of their lives. Even when there's some understanding that our lives belong to God, we are still inclined to undertake the task of obeying God by managing our life as best we can with our own resources. We seek to gain control over as much of it as possible, thinking we're doing it for God. (If you run an Internet search using the phrase "take control," the result is more than 60 million items that enable you to take control of every conceivable aspect of your life.) One of the most quoted proverbs says, "God helps those who help themselves." *Poor Richard's Almanac* by Benjamin Franklin didn't use that proverb to promote the notion of pulling ourselves up by our own bootstraps. He wasn't advocating a lifestyle in which human behavior would have to happen *before* God's moves. Rather, he was encouraging his fellow humans to *respond* to God by adding action to their beliefs; by taking steps in line with God's standards. What began as a Christian exhortation ended up devolving into a justification for self-help!

Group (community) – Our *Human* Concept

In leadership literature, it is assumed that being in charge of a group should always be the goal. Often it is, but in many situations "followership" would be the more appropriate option. Dominating a group can be just as inappropriate as using it solely for personal advancement.

People who don't meet societal norms often find themselves feeling outcast and alone. Many people feel they don't belong and develop lifestyles that produce false intimacy. Their lives become organized around destructive behaviors.

Then there's the "us versus them" approach in relating to others. On one level, we naturally define ourselves as group members in part by our distinction from those who are outside the group. Yet God is calling us to a greater community, an interdependence and unity in diversity that far transcends our human understanding of community.

OUR *HUMAN* IDENTITY ROLES

Finally, there is the component of *identity roles*. We tend to adopt a separate way of behaving for each identity role, with the only unifying element being self-leadership. (There's the control again.) We develop a sense of what we want to achieve or receive—as consumers, family members, professional people, and so on—and we move into automatic pilot in those roles. If we haven't become intentional in the way we approach these roles, we will automatically succumb to the natural forces within us and the social forces around us to pursue the "vision" for each role that we are handed. We also have a tendency to divorce faith from life in general; we relegate it to a "religious identity." Ideally, our faith should permeate every identity role in our lives. Have you seen yourself doing this?

Ω

Some things to explore: *What roles do I want to play in life? What roles do I think others are expecting me to play?* **(Notice there might be a difference between those two, which could be a source of conflict.)** *What is the sense of identity that I have in the roles I am playing in the lives of other people?* **By the way, asking these questions is the beginning of your spiritual workout session.**

DISCOVERING YOUR REAL MISSION

You've heard plenty these days about "diversity," "open-mindedness" and "freedom of choice." In our culture we've come to think of commitment to someone or something as being "tied down" or "narrow-minded," which leads us to resist a singular focus. But true freedom actually *begins* with that kind of focus. In a study on children in a playground, it was found that without a fence, the children huddled together in the center of the play area and didn't play as actively. When they were given a fence clearly delineating the boundaries of the playground, the children ran all the way to the edges with great joy and abandon, playing with freedom. So it is in life: If we don't say "no" to certain things, we've essentially said "yes" to everything, which is no choice at all and is truly an anxious state to live in.

Something in us yearns for a singleness of focus in the direction that's right for *us*. If we are Christians, that means the one chosen for us by God, the One who has ordained good works *that we should walk in them (Ephesians 2:10).* The Scottish writer James M. Barrie, best remembered as the author of *Peter Pan*, wrote the following: "The life of every man is a diary in which he *means* to write one story, and writes another, and his humblest hour is when he compares the volume as it is with what he vowed to make it." I submit that it is an equally sad moment when a person sets off to accomplish one mission successfully—only to realize one day that it isn't what he was born to do. He climbed the ladder of success only to find that the ladder was leaning against the wrong wall.

Or as the cover of this book illustrates, we are all tempted to seek out a life of greatness through self-help, but in the end find that we were only pursuing a *reflection* of greatness and have not been making real progress. We are all being guided by an internal compass or a mission of some kind. Whose mission is it—yours or God's? That is what we will explore in the next chapter.

CHAPTER 3

What is "The Good Life?"

LAW 3

The Law of Abundant Life: *When your life (being and doing) reflects God's governing mission for your life, (vision, priorities, values and identity roles) you experience the abundant life.*

While in college, before Jen and I were married, I went down to Virginia Beach to meet her parents. Her father, Frank Drake, is a Presbyterian minister there. He is a deep man of prayer, and we had a prayer meeting during our visit. At some point in the meeting, I was prompted by the Holy Spirit to say the following prayer:

"Lord, please remove my pride."

I didn't think one short prayer would lead to such a big change, but it did. God's process of removing my pride transformed my senior year in college to quite an adventure.

As you may recall, I was the elected co-captain of the football team, and I was proud of that honor. Unfortunately, in the third game of the season I suffered a bad concussion and had to miss the next six games. This was especially upsetting because I had received interest from the Indianapolis Colts. They had invited me to their training camp during the previous summer so they could evaluate me. Working as a strength coach and an assistant linebacker coach during the summer,

I had also trained with their strength coach, Tom Zupancic. At the end of camp, he'd told me to go back to Brown and have a great season; the implication was that they were impressed with what they saw, and I'd receive very favorable consideration—possibly leading to a tryout—at the end of the year. This, of course, was exactly what I had intended to do.

But then came the injury. After the concussion, I was "damaged goods."

However! I was a two-sport athlete, and that still left the discus as a significant athletic opportunity for me. I began to focus intently on going to the Olympics as a discus thrower. The Olympic trials were looming, and that part of my life seemed to be going well, until just a month before the Olympic trials. I was injured again.

Did God not want me to move down the path of greater athletic achievement? Was this His way of dealing with my pride? On the one hand I had invited Him to remove my pride, but on the other I'd continued to go full steam ahead with my own plans. Was this His idea of an end-zone tackle from Heaven? I don't believe God was out to hurt or steal from me. His purposes are always to give us life and give it abundantly *(John 10:10)*. Even though I lost much during this season of suffering through injuries, what I gained was far more significant than what I lost. Through the experience of failure, I learned something of what real humility and dependence is all about. Through the experience of intense training, I learned to appreciate the significance of training as an essential precondition, not just of human achievement but as a path to attaining higher, more permanent goals. One Scripture that began to mean a lot to me back then is Psalm 1:1-6:

> *Blessed is the man who does not walk in the counsel of the wicked or stand in the way of sinners or sit in the seat of mockers. But his delight is in the law of the LORD, and on his law he meditates day and night. He is like a tree planted by streams of water, which yields its fruit in season and whose leaf does not wither. Whatever he does prospers. Not so the wicked! They are like chaff that the wind blows away. Therefore the wicked will not stand in the judgment, nor*

sinners in the assembly of the righteous. For the LORD watches over the way of the righteous, but the way of the wicked will perish.

A NEW DREAM

I was seeking God's will for my life, and yet He allowed these injuries to occur. It certainly didn't *look* like the good life He had planned for me. Was I frustrated? Of course! At those moments of frustration I had to make a decision. I could trust that God watches over me and believe that He allowed this to occur for reasons that would reveal themselves later, or I could become bitter and angry with God for not giving me what I wanted out of life. I chose to trust God. The void created by the death of my previously held dreams was filled…by dreams that have produced so much more that it is hard to put into words.

Yes, I had good plans. But to my amazement, God had even richer plans:

"For I know the plans I have for you," declares the Lord, "plans to prosper you and not to harm you, plans to give you hope and a future. Then you will call upon me and come and pray to me, and I will listen to you. You will seek me and find me when you seek me with all of your heart." (Jeremiah 29:11-13)

Do you believe that God has a good plan for your life? Look closely at this Scripture from Jeremiah and you will see the most common roadblocks to really believing this. First, why do you think God has to clarify the fact that His plans are to *prosper and not harm* us? Could it be that each of us has to wrestle with the pride of believing we know better than God how to guide our lives into prosperity? Or believing we know what true prosperity means? Second, many of us actually think God is a cosmic killjoy, out to punish us. We understand that taking orders from anyone else means discipline, challenge and hard work. This, of course, is true, but even on the human level it is not harmful. Training actually produces a life that we can live more abundantly. How much more effective and productive would God's discipline be, given that He is not fraught with human shortcomings?

Now look at the order of God's wording: *"Then you will call upon me..."* I like to say that any time you see the word "then" in Scripture, pay attention to it. There's a condition involved. People seem to want the pay-off without the work. In this Scripture, God is trying to show us that **when** we allow God to guide us to the very best life possible and we are willing to follow Him wherever he leads us, **then** we will receive the abundant life promised. In this verse, to truly **believe** (live by) means coming to God with all of our dreams and desires and asking Him to give us *His* dreams and desires for our lives.

What are your dreams and desires? What is your vision for your life? We are not naturally endowed with what Alfred North Whitehead called *"the habitual vision of greatness."* Our naturally occurring thoughts and desires tend to drift away from God. Our lower nature and even our souls are persistently seeking dominance over our spirits. Therefore our journey toward God's greatness must have intentionality. That intentionality won't happen without our spirits submitting to God's Holy Spirit. It won't happen without conscious decisions regarding vision and focus on our part.

Corporations have discovered that it's important to have statements of mission and values that capture what they're trying to accomplish. I've done consulting work to help companies create master plans and come up with their own mission, vision and value statements. If companies do it, how much more important is it for us to do it to begin to see the course God has in mind for our whole lives? *Without vision, the people perish...(Proverbs 29:18).* Without a vision for our lives, we're just hurtling forward on whatever roller coaster we may happen to be riding at the moment.

Ω

You might consider taking a few minutes right now to consider and even write out what comes to mind: *Lord, what would your governing mission statement for my life look like?*

GOD'S MISSION FOR US

We're going to look at the four aspects of mission once again, this time not from the human point of view but from God's perspective. So it's an instant replay: Vision, Priorities, Values and Identity Roles. Just as the "instant replay" footage on TV helps us see more clearly what is really happening in the game, so this repeat is a closer look through the scriptural lens and should reveal more accurately what God intends for our lives.

GOD'S VISION FOR US

He answered: "Love the Lord your God with all your heart and with all your soul and with all your strength and with all your mind;" and, "Love your neighbor as yourself." (Luke 10:27)

The reality of God's vision for our lives is so simple that it's easily missed, even if we've had a taste of it earlier in life. Here it is: **To experience and express love.** This is not a weak, self-indulgent or syrupy kind of love. This is a passionate, all-consuming and supernatural love that breathes life into us and finds powerful expression through everything we say or do.

What happens when we forget to focus on this one important mandate? Consider that old character in the familiar classic, *A Christmas Carol* by Charles Dickens. Though Ebenezer Scrooge had experienced love as a child, he allowed God's vision to be driven from his mind by the usual cares of commercial life. He was well known for creating misery for just about everyone around him, but as his nephew said, "He creates misery for himself most of all." In the story, Scrooge is startled by the appearance of his deceased business partner as a ghost, who denounces the selfish life of business he spent on earth, exclaiming, "*Humanity* was my business!" Later, after Scrooge's eyes are opened by the three spirits of Christmas, he repents. In one of literature's most captivating episodes, he becomes deliriously happy as he endeavors to express love toward everyone he had previously made miserable. With the barriers cleared, his joy is unbounded; he can see the world with God's vision.

CORPORATE VISION IS NOT EXEMPT FROM LOVE...

Just as there is a vision for stewardship of our lives as *individuals,* so there is also a *corporate* vision for stewardship. My area of expertise as a consultant and life coach in the business world is to help leaders see the bigger picture of life and create corporate connection cultures. True greatness is not a solo project! It requires harnessing the talents and skills of everyone involved through humility and *relationship excellence.* Too much of what is being taught to leaders only focuses on task excellence without helping them to understand the nature of *people.* It's good for professional people to recognize their own skills. It's also important that they recognize their need to have a positive impact on others. Even though I don't talk about God in corporate settings unless invited to do so, I do bring the perspective of God into those settings. I know that God wants each person to steward his personal life well. The same perspective and tools for being a good steward of your personal life are used for stewarding a corporate life. The same keys that lead to an understanding of ourselves can open new doors in corporate life. They are applicable regardless of the kind of organization involved. The challenge for task-oriented, excellence-oriented people in a bottom-line environment is this: ***How do we achieve relationship excellence?*** People are not human doings but human *beings;* therefore we have to understand their needs. Our need to love and be loved is at the top of God's list. If we are able to connect with one another on a personal level and create a sense of community in the workplace, we will find that people are more productive because they are getting some of their God-given needs met. If the leaders of an organization don't have a vision for this kind of corporate culture, everyone suffers. One thing is certain about vision: "If you can't see it you can't do it."

GOD'S PRIORITIES FOR US

This scene from a Franklin Covey training session[3] I attended speaks volumes to the issue of priorities:

One day an expert was addressing a group of business students.

To drive home a point, he used an illustration those students will never forget. As this man stood in front of the group of high-powered overachievers he said, "Okay, time for a quiz." He pulled out a one-gallon, wide-mouthed mason jar and set it on a table in front of them. Then he produced about a dozen fist-sized rocks and carefully placed them, one at a time, into the jar. When the jar was filled to the top and no more rocks would fit inside, he asked, "Is this jar full?"

Everyone in the class said, "Yes."

"Really?" he asked. He reached under the table and pulled out a bucket of gravel. Then he dumped some gravel in and shook the jar, causing pieces of gravel to work themselves down into the spaces between the big rocks. He asked the group once more, "Is the jar full?"

By this time the class was onto him. "Probably not," one of them answered.

"Good!" he replied. He reached under the table and brought out a bucket of sand. He started dumping the sand in and it went into all the spaces left between the rocks and the gravel. Once more he asked the question, "Is this jar full?"

"No!" the class shouted.

Once again he said, "Good!" Then he grabbed a pitcher of water and began to pour it in until the jar was filled to the brim. Then he looked up at the class and asked, "What is the point of this illustration?"

One eager beaver raised his hand. "The point is, no matter how full your schedule is, if you try really hard, you can always fit some more things into it!"

"No," the speaker replied, "that's not the point. The truth this illustration teaches us is: If you don't put the big rocks in first, you'll never get them in at all."

Ω

Stop for a moment and think about the "big rocks" in your life that should be top priorities from God's perspective. *What are they?*

God's priorities for us may seem completely different from what we would expect. His love for us is at the top. In His love God desires to be in relationship with us. This necessitates our dependence on Him. But there's a paradox in that dependence: *The more we abide in Christ, the more we become who we are truly meant to be.* To be fully human and mature is *not* to be independent of God but exactly the opposite. Our first and foremost priority is our relationship with God. He breathes life into our entire being.

Next on God's priority scale is our family relationships—under siege today as never before in history. Our extended community relationships follow, then our calling or profession. Have you noticed how this order contrasts with our current cultural thinking? On the whole, our society teaches us to live upside down. It trains us to prioritize our jobs and what we do first. Then relationships come second and if we have time we squeeze in some God time. Prioritizing life according to God's priority scale is essential if we are going to meet our God given needs and realize the abundant life.

God's Priorities	Our Needs
• Connecting with God	• To live
• Our Family	• To love and be loved
• Our Community	• To experience variety
• Our Calling and Profession	• To feel important

God planted needs within us that closely reflect the priorities He designed us to have. According to noted psychologist Dr. Murray Banks, we need to live, to love and be loved, to experience variety, and finally, to feel important. You will find that wise people prioritize their lives to meet these needs in their respective order.

It is in our relationship with God alone that all of our needs can be met; that is why we prioritize our relationship with God above all others. Second, in our relationships with those closest to us, God can teach us to love and be loved. Some of you may have noticed that these closer relationships take more work than mere acquaintances. *Exactly.* They are fashioned to deal with our issues and drive us to

God for help! John Paul Jackson has said that when we get to Heaven, one of the first questions we'll be asked is, *"Have you learned how to love?"* Our broader sphere of relationships will offer us an experience of variety, and in our callings of servanthood as we let God work through us to influence the world, we have the opportunity to experience significance and feel important. Our main sense of importance is first derived from our status as children of God; our *calling* is to flow out from that identity.

GOD'S VALUES FOR US

Values are defined as those things that really matter to each of us; the ideas, beliefs and attitudes we hold dear. Our values reveal how we believe things "should be." The more we hold them up, the more they define how we travel through life. Caring for others, for example, is a value; so is the freedom to express our opinions. In our culture, for example, we've seen a drastic shift away from family values toward careerism and entertainment. Not only that, but the way in which those values are passed down has shifted too. Parents used to be the prime nurturers of values, with school, church and even media reinforcing those values. Now the media has a bigger microphone. The toxic nature and sheer volume of the media now all but drown out godly influence. The result is a very opposite message to what would support the health of our society.

Imagine you are driving down a long highway and see no road signs. Even if you have a map, you have no way of knowing if you are on the right road. Imagine now that you see road signs that are actually *wrong*; they lie and aren't the right signs for that road. Same problem only worse, because you believe the sign and don't know that you aren't on the right road. This is the scenario we have with the values in our culture. The values are like road signs that help us stay on the right road, unless of course they are misleading us. Many of us have "should-be's" that are strong opinions but leading in the wrong direction.

God has given clear road signs for us, values to live by. We do not have to navigate from scratch. But we do have to navigate using His road signs if we want to "get there," to live a fruitful life. Furthermore God's values are intended to be lived out in and through community. Interesting that roads are not designed to exist for their own sake but lead from one community to another. There might be lonely stretches at times, but we were made for connection and teamwork.

As I did in the last chapter, I've listed for you the *Seven G's, Values for Abundant Living*. Whereas the first listing showed our human perspective of these values, this list describes God's perspective. This list represents a consolidation of God's wisdom gleaned from my own training as a disciple and through training and mentoring others regarding God's values.

Ω

Again, you can use the list as a workout session: You may feel the "stretch" as you compare your current life with the blueprint that God has designed for you. I will present them briefly below and then we will expand on them in several of the following chapters as we look at how to apply them to our lives.

SEVEN G'S: SEVEN VALUES OF ABUNDANT LIVING
(GOD'S PERSPECTIVE)

GUIDANCE is necessary in order to carry out God's will.
We depend upon God's leadership (or guidance) through the Holy Spirit. We all need regular devotional and prayer times to connect with God and His guidance in solitude. We pursue the will of God through committed relationships in prayer, Bible study, circumstances, the Church and spiritual mentors. We acknowledge the reality of spiritual warfare, where the battle is raging in the heavenly realms, and commit ourselves to praying so that God might use us to battle against the forces of darkness (*Ephesians 6:12*). We show our need for God and our desire to grow our relationship with Him and others when we pray. Pray for yourself, your family, your community, people in authority over you, the sick, the poor, the crippled, the needy, etc. Through prayer and the guidance of the Holy Spirit, God uses our

lives to influence others.

We respect those God has placed in positions of authority and servanthood in our lives. They help lead, guide and shepherd us along our journey of faith. As we commit to seeking out their guidance as well, we're engaging in the principle of maximum connection to God. It is through embracing God's guidance for our lives as His sons and daughters that we will find our most powerful connection to Him.

GRACE is God's bridge to us and our bridge to others.
We are saved by grace through faith in Jesus Christ—and this not from our own works—so that no one can boast (Ephesians 2:8). Christ followers receive Christ's saving, sustaining, and enabling grace. Our focus is on the resurrected Christ and His Spirit who saves us, is at work changing us, and empowers us to do God's will. Therefore, we are gracious and patient with the people around us who, like us, are on a journey of faith. As God's ambassadors, we reach out and share His grace with people and help them grow in faith. We believe in relational evangelism and believe that the Gospel is best shared person to person through the power of community. This includes the principles of authenticity and being real, for it is only in a relational environment of grace that we can be truly authentic and real.

GROWTH is a process toward full maturity in Christ.
We recognize faith as a process and are committed to challenging ourselves and others to grow to maturity. Maturity means taking hold of all that is Christ *(Philippians 3:12)* and through His enabling Spirit, doing works of service that move us toward the goal of life. This goal is the fullness of Christ in us, *(Ephesians 4:12)* pleasing Him in every respect *(1 Thessalonians 4:1).* We need to surround ourselves with mentors and partners who will love, challenge, and provide guidance to us as we grow in faith. As diligent students of Scripture, we allow God's truth to be pressed through the fabric of our lives. We look at our lives holistically, and allow the mental, emotional, physical, spiritual and social dimensions of our lives to be transformed by the Holy Spirit into Christlikeness.

As we mature in our faith and God entrusts people to our care, we will strive to be good mentors to the people in our lives who look to us for discipleship training. Leaders who believe in Growth will strive to be submitted to those they lead and have regular discipleship and accountability times with their mentors. This includes the principle of reproductive discipleship chains. Growth from God's perspective is maximized as we are engaged in being discipled by God through others and allowing God to disciple others through us.

GIFTS of divine empowerment are given to all believers to grow God's Church.

We are committed to discovering our spiritual gifts and passions and using them to serve and build up the Kingdom of God. Like our Master, we don't come to be served but to serve, and to give our lives for one another *(Mark 10:45)* in love *(John 15:12)* and unity. We do this so that the watching world will believe that Jesus, the Savior, really did come *(John 17:23)*.

God calls us to use the gifts, abilities and resources He has given us to help build up His Church. We are all called to serve in general and specific ways. Our general calling of servanthood includes getting involved in service projects with our community and striving to model Jesus Christ's life of servanthood. Our specific calling of servanthood is where God has uniquely gifted us to build up His Church. We are all created for a purpose, and God empowers us all to make a supernatural contribution to the building of His Church.

GLORIFICATION of God is the goal of our lives and our church.

God calls us to be a royal priesthood of believers who go to Him for guidance and empowerment, and we will be held accountable for the way we live our lives both personally and corporately *(1 Peter 2:9; Hebrews 4:13; Romans 14:12)*. We lead lives of worship and bring glory to God in all we do when we humbly follow the guidance He provides. As God's saints, we will strive to live lives of submission to God and identify our lives with Him. This includes the principle of being before doing. Being connected to God and filled with His love allows the Holy Spirit to bear fruit through our lives that brings Glory to God. As He miraculously loves others through us He will bring glory to Himself and we will bear testimony to the true source of love and power in our midst. We will participate in regular times of worship where we can submit ourselves to God and refocus our lives on His Lordship.

GOOD STEWARDSHIP is the reasonable response to our gracious God.

We understand our relationship to God and this world as that of stewards or managers of our whole lives. Christ-followers realize they have been bought with the price of Christ's blood, and everything they are and have belongs to Him. In light of this, we live as stewards of all that God entrusts to us. We view our time, abilities, relationships, resources, etc. as precious gifts that need to be faithfully managed according to God's will, principles, priorities and promptings. In response to Christ's abundant giving, we increasingly submit our lives to His Lordship and display a spirit of generosity and cheerfulness in supporting His work in the world as He leads. This includes following God's priorities for living and managing our lives in wise and God-honoring ways. Where our treasure is, there will our hearts be also *(Matthew 6:21)*.

As God leads, we will accept and strive to faithfully serve in leadership positions within the body of Christ. People are God's most precious resource and the pinnacle of His creation; therefore, we take the corporate stewardship responsibilities in our lives seriously. We strive to serve the Kingdom of God and lead and guide others with gentleness and respect as good stewards of His community.

GROUPS of Biblically functioning community provide the optimal environment for life change.

We are committed to living our lives together in groups where both the vertical (you and God) and horizontal (you and others) components of the Christian life are lived out and growth is optimized. Christ calls us together as a people belonging to God, *(1 Peter 2:9)* a new creation,

(2 Corinthians 5:17) established in true righteousness and holiness, *(Ephesians 4:24)* who in community are to show forth His praises *(1 Peter 2:9)*. God desires that we learn from one another's diversity. Therefore our groups should be willing to be diverse in every way: ethnic, racial, cultural, sociological, economic, etc. Differences and diversities easily divide, but we are called to follow the Master in our microcosm of His Kingdom.

We are commanded to live lives of humility, patience, love, and forbearance *(Ephesians 4:2)* as Spirit-led people through whom His fruit will be seen in community. The fruit of the Spirit cannot be seen apart from community *(Galatians 5:22)*. We all need to become a member of a local fellowship (local expression of the family of God, local church). By entering into covenant relationship with others, we are placing ourselves in the optimal environment to experience life change. We will strive to live out the "one anothers" of Scripture together as God's family. This includes the principle of unity in diversity. God has created us all different by design. It is only as we are corporately submitted to God and living in unity that the fullness of God can be released through us to a watching world in desperate need of God's love. As Jesus said "they will know you are my disciples by your love for one another."

GOD'S IDENTITY ROLES FOR US

You may have heard the expression, "putting feet to your faith." Many sincere Christians understand only a small piece of their faith. They may intellectually grasp the theological foundations of the faith, but they don't know how to *live* it. God wants us to not only understand but also act in accordance with His plan for us. That's where the feet—our identity roles—come into play. That's how we walk out what we believe.

God gets to define these identity roles for us. (Remember? He's the owner, we're the stewards.) For example: One of my identity roles is that of father to my four children. It is obviously my God-prescribed task to guide and discipline them. But now, with God's top priorities in mind, the most important thing I can do in my role as father is to model the love that my Heavenly Father has shown me. It is only through God's vision that I have seen the importance of this in my life. We reproduce who we are, not who we *think* we are. Without God's intervention, the best parenting that I could hope to provide to my children would be what my parents gave to me. Make no mistake about it, much of the parenting my children receive is exactly what I received. Unless we come to God and ask Him to re-parent us, we will never be able to parent our children with a greater experience and expression of God's love. You can't give away something you haven't received.

In Chapters 5, 6, 7 and 8 I have laid out 14 Identity Roles that are clearly defined for us in Scripture. As we look at those we'll also put them together in priority with the Identity Roles Diagram. **The basic assumption for us is that we don't know who we really are until God reveals it to us.** The world, our parents, our friends and other authority figures have given us a sense of self, but we will not truly understand who God created us to be until we come to Him and ask *Him* to tell us who we are. Once you decide to embrace God's identity roles, the next step is to discern His vision for you in each role. Then, seeing God's plan for you in each role, you will better understand God's genius. You will live out your identity in Christ more completely.

A THEOLOGY OF INTENTIONALITY

Picture a happy childhood birthday or Christmas. Every fiber of that child's being is focused on the gift. He or she wonders what's inside the wrapping, examines the size and shape, shakes the box and listens, anticipates, lives for the moment when it's time to tear off the ribbons and see what the present is. That is what I call intentionality.

And from the days of John the Baptist until now the Kingdom of Heaven suffereth violence, and the violent take it by force. (Matthew 11:12 KJV)

Many people balk at this translation, finding the word "violence" to elicit images of war, strife greed and all manner of evil. Another quote doesn't comfort much either: 14th century author Thomas à Kempis wrote in *The Imitation of Christ*, "Unless you do violence to yourself, you will not overcome vice."[4] Neither use of the word violence is meant to condone harm done to another or oneself. Rather, this violence is the kind of determined intentionality that will do away with other things of lesser importance and overcome obstacles such as habits and attitudes that are not life-giving or honoring to God. It's a tearing open of the awesome package God has provided for us. Some parts of the package are easily opened with a single pull; others take quite a bit of wrestling and work. Either way, without intentionality we'll only see the wrapping, while the whole time God intends for us to receive the gift inside. The present has already been given to us; our opening of it is in the asking, seeking and knocking.

Here's where the gift goes beyond our imagination: God Himself, the Giver, IS the gift. As we begin to "open the package," we find that what we're given is not mere information. It is not even mere manifestations of God's power such as joy, freedom, self-discipline, etc. Yes, we find those things, but the main thing we find is that Jesus Christ died to become that fullness of life for us. As we seek Him for Himself, He becomes manifest in those ways through our lives. He is that joy, freedom, self-discipline; He is that and so much more. *Christ in you, the hope of glory (Colossians 1:27) is* not a flowery statement but a massively transforming declaration. That one line encapsulates the revolution God has started. The life of Jesus has gone deeper than just saying, "God gives us peace." He incarnated the reality that God IS our peace. He died to *become—in us—*what the Father wants to provide. But again, the abundance inside that package doesn't become available to us until we open it: *Intentionality* is key.

Now picture Christmas every day (without the shopping hassles.) The opening of the gift, *Christ in you,* is not a one-time thing. Your experience of the abundant life will be progressive and cumulative. Like the leaven that Jesus spoke of as filling the loaf of bread, it will fill every part of your life, growing over time.

And so we know and rely on the love God has for us. God is love.
Whoever lives in love lives in God, and God in him. (1 John 4:16)

Love is who God is. It is the most important part of life. Everything
in the Bible is given to us to show us how to love God and one another
better. As we look at managing our time and lives better, we will be
following the scriptural command to live lives of love. We will begin
to become love. That is a gift worth tearing open.

ON MISSION WITH GOD

In my secular consulting, it's not my role to lead people to Christ but
rather to ask them where they want to go and then help them get
there. By contrast, in my Christian work, I encourage people to set
aside where they presently want to go and open themselves to God's
leading. At first, many are intimidated by the word *mission*. They
may think that if God had His way, He'd send them to a place they
don't really want to go. But for those who are willing to take a chance
on God, what they find is that they are on a journey to places more
meaningful and exciting than any human journey could ever involve.
Discovering God's exciting mission comes from being willing to ask
the questions, **"Who do you want me to be, how do you want me
to relate and what do you want me to do with my life?"** No matter
what the setting, the Law of Abundant Life operates in the same way.
When we really choose God's mission to be our mission and intentionally
pursue it, we begin experiencing the abundant life.

I sum up God's mission for our lives with 4 C's: **C**onnecting in
real, loving relationship with God through Jesus **C**hrist in the power
of the Holy Spirit, with others in contagious Christian **C**ommunity,
and with our **C**alling of servanthood in the world.

**God is inviting you to *Connect* in real, loving relationship
with *Christ, Community* and your *Calling*.**

52

NO LONGER IN CHARGE

When I started into Christian ministry I was thrust into leadership right away; I was asked to take over the Campus Crusade for Christ ministry at Brown University as a volunteer, start a church in Providence, join the staff of another church plant in Boston as their Senior Pastor and then transform the disciple-making culture of another church in Greenwich, CT. One of my mentors said something to me years ago that hit me like a lightning bolt: *"Wouldn't it be interesting,"* he said, *"to see what life would be like for you if you weren't in charge?"* That statement was like a grain of sand in my mind; it was placed there to develop into a pearl of wisdom.

Becoming a leader or being "in charge" is what our culture in America has identified as the be-all and end-all. In the career of a professional clergyperson, ironically, it's even more that way. Everyone who attends seminary is groomed to be a pastor and eventually the senior pastor, even though many people have neither the gifting nor the calling for that role. Seminary is one of the least likely places where one could learn to *follow God's lead.* That must be caught, not just taught.

It is only when we let go of self-leadership that we can begin to understand what God's leading is all about. God is the overseer of events in our lives, the one who has built a particular road for each of us to travel. In my case, He provided me with the mentors and partners in ministry who could lovingly hold me accountable and coach me toward Christlikeness and God's mission. I shudder to think what my journey would have been like if my entrance into ministry had been the more typical path of many pastors and leaders today who exist apart from any real accountability or mentoring in their lives. Of course, the answer to my mentor's question is that my life is infinitely better when I'm not in charge but have God leading and empowering it!

ARE YOU ON MISSION WITH GOD?

Most people think they're on autopilot, but really they are on self-leadership pilot. People just want to do what they want to do, and rarely slow down to listen for God and choose His mission. If and when people do try to slow down, it is not usually to listen or to seek God's direction. Most of the time it's to escape the pressures and "tune out." Instead of true mission and true rest, we humans split off into overdrive and escape. But once you recognize that abundant living comes only as God is guiding and empowering your life, you'll no longer want to escape but tune in. You'll want to slow down *and* listen for His guidance regarding how to reach each next step.

What is the picture that comes to your mind when you hear someone mention "the good life?" The typical scenario has you reclining in a beach chair with a cool drink on the side, palm trees swaying nearby in the balmy breezes. Nothing against vacations, but the fact is we humans were made for a mission. Just as a car was made to run and dies when it's not used, we too are made for a very clear mission. Have you noticed that without that sense of meaningful accomplishment that we find in meeting a challenge, there's no sweetness to the rest? Once again I did not say workaholism; God's mission is perfectly balanced for us and His challenges are not to be equated with our striving. The true "good life" is one that has you on the mission that God chose for you.

Ω

Put the following question to yourself right now: *Do I or don't I want to live the abundant life?*

As Paul wrote in Philippians 3:10, *"I want to know Christ and the power of his resurrection."* That was part of Paul's own mission statement. There is powerful torque in making this decision consciously, and then reminding ourselves of it frequently. If we don't make that decision to know and grow, it simply may not happen. When you're experiencing the abundant life, your mission is the same as God's mission for you. Your perspective and God's perspective then start to work together; you are following His internal compass and letting it drive you even though you don't always understand where you are going.

THE NEXT STEPS

Here's what the training plan is for the next few chapters: First, together we'll be looking at each element of your mission, taking the pieces apart to see them more clearly. Then we'll reconstruct these elements in a way that will help you use them as spiritual power tools for your life. After that first step, you'll have a sense of where your life is right now.

Following the "You Are Here" assessment, I'll be working with you on goal setting and encouraging you to allow God to infuse His perspective into each of those elements of your life. For this you will have to simply let go, much the way a drowning person needs to allow the lifeguard to do the rescuing instead of trying to help. When that letting-go happens, you'll see your life goals take on a whole new significance, you may notice new life goals come into view, and life dreams will seem more attainable. This is not Heavenly hype but the way God works; it's His nature to be supernatural!

For with God, all things are possible.
(Matthew 19:26)

You're on your way along the tremendous road of transformation, moving from the meaninglessness of the self-centered life to the abundance of the God-centered life. You have engaged in the reality that you are a steward, not an owner, of your life. It is my hope and prayer that you are now ready to get on mission with God. As you do, you'll begin to tap into the true source of light and power in the universe, and you will know the joy of being used for the mighty purpose that dignifies our lives beyond our imagining. There is no higher calling, no deeper meaning, than to be on mission with God. Lived in God's way, life is truly good and filled with greatness. You're ready for the next step in our journey.

CHAPTER 4

How Do You See?

LAW 4

The Law of Perspective: *Having a biblical worldview and seeing life from God's perspective is essential if we are going to experience God's abundant life. If you can't see it, you can't do it!*

By now you know that I throw the discus. I trained for two separate Olympic games (1992 and 1996) as a discus thrower, learning quite a bit about human performance in the process. Have you ever seen "Discobolos," the classical icon of a discus thrower from Ancient Greece? I am convinced that the reason it's used as a symbol of the Olympics is because throwing a discus is the most unnatural act that you can do with your body. I have no proof of this, mind you; this simply makes sense as to why discus throwers have been so admired.

"IF YOU CAN'T SEE IT, YOU CAN'T DO IT"

One of my favorite discus coaches used to drill this mantra into us: *"If you can't see it, you can't do it."* He knew that to train the body to do something it's not naturally inclined to do takes enormous visualization. We used to study hours of tape showing great throwers. We'd compare it to tape of ourselves to find strengths and weaknesses in our technique. Under the pressure of throwing in competition, if you wanted to throw far, it was imperative that you had a clear picture of the various positions that you would have to move through in order to properly transfer the maximum amount of power to the discus.

The unnatural nature of this action is a great metaphor for living the abundant life, because we don't *naturally* want to follow God's guidance for our lives. We need to watch God's tapes first. We need to study the "great throwers" in Scripture, Jesus chief among them, to understand how God desires to coach us to desire, feel, think and act in life. If we can begin to see that, then we can do it! Furthermore the discrepancies we find between God's tape and ours need not be a source of discouragement, but can be useful for training. Seeing the difference will help us to chart a wise course of training in order to close the gap between God's vision and our reality.

GOD'S-EYE VIEW

God has a perspective for your life. His view is immensely broader and richer than any that you could have ever dreamed up for yourself. Remember, He is neither Heaven's bellhop rushing to fulfill your every selfish whim, nor is He the cosmic killjoy waiting to blow the whistle on you the moment you start having fun. He created you to undertake a noble mission, and if you choose that mission, it will become a pathway to the kind of overcoming you have longed for but haven't yet tasted fully. The question is, how to tap into His perspective?

Consider the training tapes again: In order to improve, I first had to admit that my technique was different from the world champion's. My technique felt "right" to me; it was familiar. Doing something new is not familiar, and at first it may not feel "right." But if it is right, I need to make the adjustment. Just so, God's perspective isn't the same as ours:

> *"For my thoughts are not your thoughts, neither are your ways my ways,"*
> *declares the Lord. "As the heavens are higher than the earth, so are my*
> *ways higher than your ways and my thoughts than your thoughts."*
> *(Isaiah 55:8-9)*

Not only are we prone to assuming that God's ideas for our lives aren't as applicable as our own, but we are also likely to think that God doesn't care about many of the little details of our lives…or that He only cares about the "religious" aspects of life. Nothing could be farther from the truth.

REAL LIFE WITH A BIBLICAL WORLDVIEW

Let's take a look at Larry. Larry has a couple of habits he'd like to shake some day. They aren't menacing to society in a major way, he reasons, but he's been meaning to work on these things for some time now. Larry's habits have begun to reinforce his perspective; he's gotten *used* to these habits and come to believe, in spite of himself, that it might just be the way he is. Of course if Larry's wife would only stop trying to help him change, then maybe he'd be able to buckle down and do it his way. And then his boss would help, too, if he ever noticed Larry enough to give him the raise he needed.

Notice that Larry's worldview has been created by the combination of these—and dozens of other—perspectives on life. As we've described in the previous chapters, this worldview has been reinforcing itself in cycles of perspective, belief and behavior that lead to more sin and frustration. At this point in Larry's life he has come to believe that if only his wife and boss would change, then he'd be able to make the transformations necessary; that's a victim worldview.

Now what if Larry encounters some feedback from a counselor who challenges him to let go of the victim mentality? Let's say Larry doesn't like it, but begins to take responsibility for his own behavior instead of putting himself in subjection to the actions of his wife and boss, then blaming them for his choices. That one move alone begins to break up the old worldview. Larry then has a chance to receive more grace. The grace was available to him all along, but he couldn't access it as long as he wasn't admitting his own limitations. That moment of lining up with God's view is like the alignment of a key in a lock, and the door begins to open as soon as that turning takes place. Multiply that moment and a new cycle is created, one that guides Larry into experiencing greater freedom from the old habits, not to mention new love and respect for his wife and boss.

Without a biblical worldview it is impossible to live God's abundant life. If you can't see it, you can't do it. But just one peek through the lens of God's perspective and you can see it. By His grace you can do it, even if it's not a popular trend. As it is with discus throwing, to adopt a biblical worldview today is to go against the grain. But you'll be choosing rightly, as God is the only one who *does* "hold a corner on reality." By the way, that should not be seen as an occasion for self-righteousness or criticism of others who choose differently. Smug intolerance is not a fruit of the Spirit. What it does mean, however, is that we can feel strong and secure in the knowledge that we need not flounder in a sea of subjectivity.

A WORKOUT STEP

How do we begin to make changes? What's involved in lining up our perspective with God's? The first step is to take stock of our various perspectives on life (what we do see), bring them to God and declare to Him that we are blind. Like Larry, we all have areas where we don't see how we've kept ourselves stuck. When we do admit our blindness, it is then that God can fill our lives with *His* perspective as we ask Him to give us eyes to see. Once we have gone through this process with God in a few areas of our lives, we will be convinced of our natural inability to see life from His perspective. Yet we will also be overwhelmed by the sheer genius, beauty and simplicity of supernaturally seeing life His way. *"So are My ways higher than your ways and My thoughts than your thoughts."* Isaiah 55 goes on to speak of great fruitfulness, of God's word not returning void. That fruitfulness will be manifested in our lives too as we expand the borders of our minds toward the amplitude of God's perspective. As we continue to examine other areas of our lives for similar transformation, we'll rise to a new reality. Instead of repeating old patterns and blaming others or ourselves for the problems, we'll become people who have eyes to see and ears to hear what the Spirit is doing and saying.

Ω

Consider asking yourself: *What outlooks or perspectives do I have that may be hindering me from making progress? In what ways have I slipped into a victim mentality instead of seeing ways God might help me change? Where in life have I been making the same moves over and over instead of seeing God's tapes?*

OUR IDENTITY, NOT OUR ACTIVITY

Take a look at the following diagrams, and see if you can identify where you are. The two cycle illustrations show the upward spiral we can experience toward grace, contrasted with the downward spiral toward sin and grief. These opposite perspectives or worldviews about life are adapted from James Lawrence, a trainer with Arrow Leadership Ministries.[5]

In the first diagram, the cycle of grief, I find my identity in what I do, my acceptance in success. In the world's way, we're accepted by doing. If I perform, my acceptance goes up; if I stop performing, my acceptance goes down. Hence more activity, more acceptance, more activity, and around and around we go. We live more like human doings than human beings. This is a very dangerous way to live. I like to say it like this: "If I am what I do, when I *don't*, I'm *not*." Having experienced the down side of this cycle myself and mentoring some of the wealthiest and most successful people in America, I can tell you that this cycle of perspective, belief and behavior leads to grief, insecurity and fear.

Cycles of Grief and Grace

1. Achievement and Activity

2. Identity   **The Cycle of Grief**   **4.** Acceptance

3. Drivenness

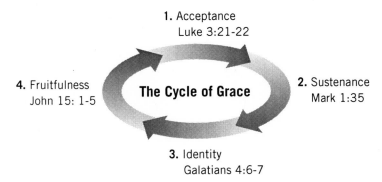

If we jump off the merry-go-round, we can enter the cycle of grace (see second diagram.) It's crucial to get a hold of this primary truth: **Without doing anything, you're loved by God.** Yes, He created you for an awesome mission, but first comes the certainty of His radical love. You can see this at the beginning of the ministry of Jesus, where full acceptance came first, not last:

When all the people were being baptized, Jesus was baptized too. And as he was praying, heaven was opened and the Holy Spirit descended on him in bodily form like a dove. And a voice came from heaven: "You are my Son, whom I love; with you I am well pleased." (Luke 3: 21-22)

He hadn't *done* anything yet! Stop a minute and let that sink in: *Before he began* His public ministry, Jesus had the love that cannot be earned. And He is the firstborn among many—you and me—who are to follow the same pattern.

Again, not that *doing* in and of itself is wrong; it's the underlying motivation and identity we're looking at. To the extent that the doing comes from the need to be accepted or "okay," it will lead us around the cycle of grief. When our doing flows from our *being*—our inner knowing that God unconditionally accepts us—we're free, living in His grace.

I cannot overemphasize that *our inner striving will not achieve what God intended to achieve by grace.* We cannot merit His favor, although we can yield to it…

Very early in the morning, while it was still dark, Jesus got up, left the house and went off to a solitary place, where he prayed. (Mark 1:35)

We would be wise to follow the pattern of Jesus who daily recalibrated His life with His Father in Heaven and received His grace. If we neglect this vital discipline we leave ourselves vulnerable to our drift factor. God never tires of reminding us how much He loves us unconditionally. It is on this foundation that Jesus did what He did and we should do what we are called to do. Sometimes it's best to just sit in the lap of the Father and hear Him tell us He loves us, over and over. We will gain more sustenance from that than from any expressions of acceptance from others. The closer we get to Him, the clearer His perspective becomes. The closer we get to Him, the less likely we are to drift back into the perspective of so many around us.

Because you are sons, God sent the Spirit of his Son into our hearts, the Spirit who calls out, "Abba, Father." So you are no longer a slave, but a son; and since you are a son, God has made you also an heir. (Galatians 4: 6-7)

In this Scripture we see clearly who we are: His children. Don't let any identity take precedence over that one. Lasting productivity comes from our identity, not our activity. It lasts because God is the one who does it through us, and so our only goal must be to let go and let God lead and empower us to do whatever it is He wants.

"I am the true vine, and my Father is the gardener. He cuts off every branch in me that bears no fruit, while every branch that does bear fruit he prunes so that it will be even more fruitful. You are already clean because of the word I have spoken to you. Remain in me, and I will remain in you. No branch can bear fruit by itself; it must remain in the vine. Neither can you bear fruit unless you remain in me. I am the vine; you are the branches. If a man remains in me and I in him, he will bear much fruit; apart from me you can do nothing." (John 15: 1-5)

From the perspective of a branch, it is easy for us to lose sight of the fact that God is the Gardener; He controls the universe. The idea of merely trusting in Him can often seem like a head-in-the-clouds notion that simply overlooks the "daily-ness" of real life. But if you consider the Gardener's interest, you'll see that His actions are practical, down-to-earth, and directly linked to the well-being of that vine, branches included.

I know a woman from New York who loves to cultivate primroses. She attended one of my Omega Courses, and I also mentored her some. She had been struggling with financial difficulties while still trying to give some attention to her beloved primrose avocation. As she began contemplating this Law of Perspective over and over, God revealed His point of view to her in a dream, changing her whole experience of life:

"I woke up teary-eyed with joy. My perspective on primroses has overwhelmed me with the realization that God has created, in the far corners of the earth's temperate and alpine zones, beauties for His pleasure as well as ours. As each early spring day dawns, I marvel seeing little beauties, treasures to me from far off war-torn Iraq and Afghanistan, from the Alps, Alaska, and Canada, from India, Japan, China and Russia. And then, in addition to these, only God enjoys those growing in remote mountain crevices, beyond the footsteps of man."

Even before all her problems were solved, this woman's perspective burst wide open. It expanded, resized to include a glimpse of God's perspective. That kind of vision gives the kind of hope we need for life transformation. Notice that the revelation God gave to this primrose lover was tailor-made for her. It spoke to this woman of her Heavenly Father's love for her, and that love is what opened her horizon for other possibilities. The cramped, crimped, legally blind outlook that we normally have explodes into the Alpine expanse when we take God at His word. Promises spoken by Christ that seem "impossible" suddenly emerge in 3-D; we realize they belong to us since we are His children, His heirs. God who used to seem distant and unconcerned with our daily details starts "showing up" everywhere we look. In truth, He's been there all along; we just notice His fingerprints the more we seek Him.

THE PERSPECTIVE SHIFT
THAT SAVED MY LIFE AND MINISTRY

Have you ever met with someone whose presence gave you the feeling they could see right through you? Someone who gave you the sense that even if they didn't say a word, you were about to get slammed with a bigger picture that you'd bargained for? Christa Schoeber, one of my mentors, was that way with me. Before I share with you one of our pivotal conversations, the backdrop for this mentoring relationship is also relevant to our topic.

I met Christa through the Arrow Leadership Program, of which I'm a graduate. This program was founded by Leighton Ford, the brother in law of Billy Graham, to provide two years of mentoring to proven Christian leaders.

When you study the lives of great Christian leaders one thing stands out: **Mentoring. These great leaders continued to see the need for more and more accountability as their ministry responsibilities grew.** In contrast, those who isolated themselves from mentoring relationships soon failed. They used their leadership position to rise above accountability, and in that process shut themselves off from the main ingredient that leads to success. You see, many view respect for authority as equivalent to being an underling. They scorn the idea of standing on someone else's shoulders. But look closer: If we stand on someone else's shoulders, we'll then have the opportunity to see—and go—*beyond* them. Unfortunately, many people don't see it that way. They may start out great on their own, but without mentoring, they often fall tragically. And when that happens, the watching world is simply given more reason to discredit God and His church.

Arrow was begun to spark a mentoring revolution in Christian leaders' lives. It was designed to recalibrate them around a vision of leadership, mentoring and accountability that would set them on the right track and *keep* them on the right track as they grew. They knew that accountable relationships are key to long-term obedience and clear vision.

It was in this environment and with this in mind that I met Christa; she was assigned to me as my mentor during my two years with Arrow.

Christa is a deep woman of faith who is gifted in discerning
what is holding someone back in his walk with God. In our first two
meetings together, she asked a few questions… and I did all the talking.
At the end of our second meeting, she told me that at our next meeting
she would do the talking. This was encouraging to me, because up to
this point in time *she* had not said much. Like a wise sage, she wanted
to collect her data and properly diagnose the problem before revealing
her solution.

This is my best recollection of our third meeting:

Christa: *Well, I have spent time thinking and praying about you and
where you are with God, and I have a question for you. Before I ask my
question, let me say that I am well aware that God is using your life in a
mighty way and that you are diligently striving to serve His Kingdom.*

Me: Ok fire away.

Christa: *Do you realize the pace at which you speak when you
are with people these days? There seems to be an unsettledness about you.
So my question is, why are you so driven?*

All I can remember is feeling like someone put their hand inside
my body, grabbed my heart with their hands and began to squeeze.
I began to cry. God used this woman to lovingly challenge me at the
core of what was holding me back from experiencing a deeper life in
God. After about a minute of my crying and repeating the question,
she continued.

Christa: *I am aware that you teach this to others, but when is
the last time you have had a quiet time alone with God, and the picture
you've had in your mind was that you are a baby lying in the arms of your
Heavenly Father—and He is repeating over and over to you, "I love you,
I love you, and there is nothing you can do to make me love you more or
less"—and you let the reality of His grace-filled love and acceptance
fill you up?*

Jason: It has been a long time. The focus of my prayer life is so
mission- and ministry- focused.

Christa: *Those of us who have eyes to see can tell. You need to spend
more time receiving the love of your Father in Heaven, so that when you
are asked to minister to others in His name it is His freshly received love in*

you that is overflowing to those whom God calls you to serve. We reproduce who we are and right now you are functioning more like a ministry machine who doesn't want to let people down. You need to release yourself from this Cycle of Grief and pursue God's Cycle of Grace. The more you find your Acceptance, Sustenance and Identity in a grace-filled relationship with your Heavenly Father, through Jesus His Son in the power of the Holy Spirit, the more fruitful you will be for the Kingdom and the more you will enjoy the adventure of love. Does this make sense?

Jason: It absolutely does.

Christa: *Your homework is to spend time every day recalibrating your life around these truths and receiving the love of the Father into your life, sustaining yourself in this relationship above all others, embracing your identity as a powerless, dependent, child of God and allowing Him to bear fruit through you. Agreed?*

Jason: Agreed.

This breakthrough was the beginning of what remains a continual discipline in my life. **That time sitting in the Father's lap and receiving His love goes to the heart of what it means to submit to the guidance and power of God instead of slipping back into self-leadership and self-empowerment.** In fact, it involves more than discovering a good rhythm of work times and rest times; it involves learning how to let God stay in charge even when our personal efforts are at their most intense. One leads to the other; it is the set-apart times of rest that help us learn to live in that rest even when working. It is the fill-'er-up time that enables us to stay in the flow at all times.

Thomas Kelly, a Quaker writing in the 1930s, urged that we let life be willed through us. I think the Biblical David had this idea in mind when he walked out to face Goliath and declared, "The battle is the Lord's!" He knew perfectly well that the Lord had chosen to fight the battle through his skill with a slingshot, but that didn't mean that God was delegating His work—only that He was expecting David to be a clear channel through which His supernatural power could flow. David, despite his tremendous passion and world-famous victory, was not "driven." Rather, he had reason to be confident of being divinely guided and divinely empowered. This is exactly what we all need each day for battles great and small. From God's perspective, it is our depending on Him and trusting in Him that make it possible for His plan to unfold.

Many sincere Christians, having never come across this principle or been given the opportunity to put it into practice, have fallen prey to burnout or besetting sin. In my own case, I'm grateful that the Lord chose a wise mentor to point out something in my walk as a child of God that I had no likelihood of discerning without her help. We need mirrors and videotapes—wise coaching and feedback—to even begin to see our lives clearly.

CHOOSE LIFE

Throughout the coaching in this book, I'll be encouraging you to examine how God's perspective applies to your life in all its diverse aspects, from many different angles. God wants abundant life for you, perhaps even more than you do. But because God works with your free will, He awaits your daily choosing. Are you willing? Choose Life. It may seem complicated to examine your life from dozens of different angles to understand how God's perspective applies, but it's ultimately as simple as that. If we choose one, we get the other; if we choose God's governing mission and training for our lives, we'll begin to see from His perspective. Is it easy? No. Is it simple? Yes.

CHAPTER 5

Are You Fully Human?

LAW 5

The Law of Identity: *Abundant living comes from being who God created you to be and engaging your identity in Christ.*

You might think the question doesn't need to be asked. "Well *of course* I'm fully human!" you could protest, indignation rising. I'm not asking this question to imply insult, but to draw attention to all that is included in your identity as a human being. It is easy to overlook whole chunks of that identity. If you had asked me back in college if I was aware of my identity in Christ, my first answer would have been "absolutely." But later in this chapter I'll tell you how there was a whole piece of my life as a human being that I'd totally missed. It is ironic how easy it is for some of us Christians to miss even more of our identity than the average person; such great effort is put into being "spiritual" that the fullness of our humanity is often neglected. But Jesus was fully *human* as well as fully divine. And letting go of our old nature does *not* mean giving up being human, it means that we become fully human the way God intended.

HOW DOES GOD SEE YOU?

One ministry couple I know has helped many people hear from God during small group sessions and retreats. They conduct a simple exercise in which they hand out pads and pens and encourage everyone to get comfortable in a private spot. After a brief prayer, the group has about 20 minutes to write the answer they receive to this question: *"Lord, what do you think of me?"* Other variations are, *"Lord, who do you say that I am?"* or *"Lord, how do you see me?"*

Within ten minutes, half the people in the room are sniffling and blowing their noses. Most of them have been stunned to hear phrases they'd never have thought of applying to themselves. "This is far too awesome! I never would have said that about myself," they'll share afterwards. These are the same people who have spent years in church and have seen who the Scriptures say they are:

Child of God, joint heir with Christ (Romans 5:7)
Friend of Christ (John 15:5)
Citizen of Heaven (Philippians 3:20)
His Beloved (Song of Songs)
...to name a few.

Why are they so surprised? Did they not believe the Scriptures? You and I both know that it's possible to know something with your mind, yet not desire to pursue or feel the reality of it in your heart and soul. We also know that life gets busy, and our default is—you guessed it—to just keep going without stopping to ask, not only for directions but also for affirmation. But that is tantamount to not filling up your gas tank and expecting the car to run anyway. Just as it is with the Law of Perspective, whereupon we need to come to God and admit that we can't see, so it is with the Law of Identity: We need to come to God and **ask Him** *who we are.* Without His view of us, we'll never understand or reach our full potential.

The people who journaled for 20 minutes caught a small glimpse of what God had to say to them personally. In this chapter I'll be giving a more systematic illustration of what the Scriptures say about our identity. I believe it's important to receive this truth on both levels:

Study the Word the way you look in a mirror to see who you are; and also lean into your Heavenly Father's arms to hear that same truth in a more intimate way.

OUR IDENTITY ROLES

Remember the summary of God's mission for our lives that I gave in Chapter Three?

Connecting in real, loving relationship with God
through Jesus Christ in the power of the Holy Spirit,
with others in contagious Christian community
and with our calling of servanthood in the world.

In this statement I mentioned 3 C's, or three categories of roles that make up our identity: Christ Follower, Community Member, and Called Servant. Here they are in more detail:

Christ Follower

What would make fishermen drop their nets on the spot and follow Jesus? What would make a corrupt tax collector turn honest and want to pay back what he'd skimmed off for himself? These people had to have seen something in Jesus that was powerful and irresistible, compelling enough to make them want more. What did they receive that made them want to submit their whole lives to Jesus? The only way we'd "drop our nets" to follow Christ would be if we recognized in Him something of greater value than what we could find on our own.

Could it be that these first disciples received a love that was deeper than any other they'd known? Would they have wanted to follow Jesus without first experiencing His great love for them? In Deuteronomy 6:5 we are told to *"Love the Lord your God with all your heart and with all your soul and with all your strength."* Matthew, Mark and Luke repeat this as the greatest commandment, adding mind to the list, along with the second commandment, *"love your neighbor as yourself."* This is the main thing we are to do as Christ followers; it also gives a clue to as

70

to our human construction. I am convinced that being fully human involves freedom to love and be loved in each of these **four aspects of our identity: Heart, Soul, Mind and Strength**. We'll be looking at these four aspects in depth in this chapter. I am also convinced that in order to obey the command to love God and others, we need to first learn to *receive* that love from Him. It is only in our relationship with God that all of our basic human needs are met, love being the first and foremost.

Community Member

Notice what Jesus did after He called his disciples: He did not simply have them tag along, playing "Follow the Leader," watching Him perform solo. He talked with them, walked with them, ate with them, rested with them. He included them in His ministry, received from them and gave them all He had. This is the paradigm we're given for our roles as Community Members.

God is relational and made us relational. We will certainly have times when we'll need a moment to ourselves (like Greta "I vant to be alone!" Garbo) but it's in healthy community that several basic needs are to be met: **Loving and being loved, experiencing variety, and feeling important.** We're designed to contribute to community. Once we've received real love, God will move us to love others. Ideally, loving is not something that is supposed to deplete us; in God's economy, contributing to community fulfills both our vital needs and those of society. It's biblical that success is win-win, not a matter of stepping on someone else to get ahead. If we put the first commandment first, and don't jump into trying to love others in our own strength before we've gone to God, then we will have more than we need with which to participate in community. We'll look at the details of this role category in a later chapter, exploring **five kinds of relationships that make up what it means to be a Community Member: Inner Circle, Relative/Parent, Church Member, Mentee/Mentor and Ambassador/Friend.**

Called Servant

Observe the order here: First we are shown God's love and grow by connecting to Him with our heart, soul, mind and strength. *Then* we learn to love others and connect to them in the various roles we have as a Community Member. *After all that* comes the **opportunity to serve and do what God has uniquely gifted us to do in the world, in concert with others in His Church**. Have you noticed that the typical Christian tends to go after these three categories in reverse order? We jump ahead to the "servant" roles and gloss over the first two steps, which happen to be foundational and essential for truly successful serving. Again in a later chapter, we will examine this role category in greater depth and look at what it means to be **ministers of compassion, stewards of resources, empowered servants, calling mentee/mentors and working in professional roles.**

Here is a central question to ask yourself as you look with me at all these identity roles: **Does the Kingdom of Heaven—the abundant life that those disciples saw in Jesus—permeate all the roles that make up my identity? Does every aspect of my life show the kind of love that makes people want to "drop their nets" and go after it?** We have many roles, but are created to have one simple thing show up in each of these roles: the **love of God**. We have plenty of holy mysteries to explore, but really one great secret of the ages: **Christ living in us**. He lives to flow *through* us, not merely into us. We are not intended to be receptacles, but channels of love.

Now let's take a closer look at our role as Christ followers and delve into the aspects of heart, soul, mind, and strength that make us truly human. As we explore our new identity in Christ I will illustrate this new life with a diagram that puts our identity roles into perspective and in priority. I call it the Identity Roles Diagram.

Identity Roles Diagram - Being Human

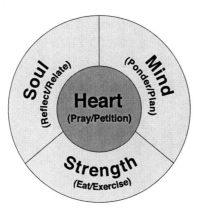

START WITH THE HEART

Do you spend much of your life just wanting what you want? Did you ever wonder what it would be like to truly want what God wants? That is precisely how He designed us…

Your heart is **the seat of your will, dreams, desires; it's the spiritual center of your being**. It is with your heart that you choose what you love or want. *As water reflects a face, so a man's heart reflects the man (Proverbs 27:19),* What you want will be reflected in what you do. No wonder the scriptures tell us: *Above all else, guard your heart, for it is the wellspring of life (Proverbs 4:23).* The heart can be a most wonderful place of freedom, but since the Fall, our hearts have been in great need of repair:

> *The Lord saw how great man's wickedness on the earth had become, and that every inclination of the thoughts of his heart was only evil all the time. The LORD was grieved that he had made man on the earth, and his heart was filled with pain. (Genesis 6:5-6)*

We can hardly fathom the pain God has felt. Consider parents who see their son or daughter choosing to do something self-destructive or harmful to others; what grief that brings to the parents' heart (because it is not what we want for them)! Multiply that exponentially and you have a taste of God's ache over all of us when we choose evil.

DIVINE HEART TRANSPLANT NEEDED

Fortunately, the Lord didn't leave us in that sorry state without recourse. He made a way for us to align our hearts with His. His desire is that we receive a new heart from Him, and He also intends to fill our hearts with His own Spirit. Certainly He has provided this amazing exchange through Jesus, but even in the Old Testament we see his promised provision:

"I will give you a new heart and put a new spirit in you; I will remove from you your heart of stone and give you a heart of flesh. And I will put my Spirit in you and move you to follow my decrees and be careful to keep my laws." (Ezekiel 36:26-27)

In other words, **God can give you the desire to desire His desires for you**. He can lovingly melt the hard shell around your proud heart, softening it and giving you the wisdom and humility to choose to submit to Him. As you learn to lean on Him, He can cause you to want what He wants—and see dramatic change happen in your life.

Trust in the Lord with all your heart and lean not on your own understanding; In all your ways, acknowledge him, and he will make your paths straight. (Proverbs 3:5-6)

Do you ever feel like you're going in circles or in a maze, meeting with roadblocks at every turn? Are you frustrated at times, wondering if you and God are "on the outs" and He's "mad" at you? God is not manipulative like we humans are:

When tempted, no one should say, "God is tempting me." For God cannot be tempted by evil, nor does He tempt anyone; but each one is tempted when, by his own evil desire, he is dragged away and enticed. Then, after desire has conceived, it gives birth to sin; and sin, when it is full-grown, gives birth to death. (James 1:13-15)

It is in His love for us that He established His boundaries so that we would be frustrated in the pursuit of those things that would not truly satisfy or bring life. He takes no pleasure in our frustration, but longs for us to have His life. When we do return to Him, we are immediately realigned with His miraculous Kingdom reality; it's like the kink in a garden hose; once it's untwisted, the love can flow freely again.

Now that you have purified yourselves by obeying the truth so that you have sincere love for your brothers, love one another deeply, from the heart. (1 Peter 1:22)

Not that we don't also experience challenges and roadblocks when aligned with Christ; He makes it plain that this world is indeed full of trouble and we're not taken out of it instantly. But with His guidance we do have peace in the midst of that trouble. We do see a difference, and we do see growth. We're not left groaning with the Apostle Paul in Romans 7:19, *"For the good that I would I do not: but the evil which I would not, that I do."* Or in Romans 7:24, *"Wretched man that I am! Who will rescue me from this body of death?"* We are given the power to move continually into the following verses, where we know there is deliverance: *"Thanks be to God—through Jesus Christ our Lord!" (v. 25)* and no condemnation *(Romans 8:1).*

We don't start out meaning to be wretched and self-centered and indifferent; the world around us helps to harden us. There's a post-it note out there that is especially popular with secretaries. It says, *"You don't have to be crazy to work here, we can train you!"* And the world does. But God is constantly offering us clear exhortation for re-training, just like a personal coach would:

Dear friends, I urge you, as aliens and strangers in the world, to abstain from sinful desires, which war against your soul." (1 Peter 2:11)

You might feel that life is a battle at times, and you are right. God knows even better than we do that we're in the middle of warfare. A big gun in the battle is choosing to let God give you His heart. Even if you are one of those people who learns the hard way, God will keep giving you opportunities to choose to submit your heart to Him, and each life lesson then has the potential to strengthen your will to align with God's—and give you a true taste of His goodness.

Ω

How is your heart? Do you desire what God desires? Are you willing to receive God's heart right now?

SOUL: NOT A SOLO SYSTEM

In this book I define your soul as the aspect of your being that is the **profound expression of your feelings, intuition, conscience, and your true personality.** As you go through life, interacting with people and experiencing events, your soul is constantly **regulating, correlating, integrating and processing** what is happening to you, often guiding how your respond. You have feelings and impressions about yourself, others, ideas and circumstances; these are all processed through your soul.

Your soul is to be led by the Spirit of God and not function in a vacuum. Your **conscience and intuition** are designed to be hard-wired to the Lord and work like a **divine central nervous system: feeling, sensing and discerning** not only what is right (good) and wrong (evil) but also sensing the difference between God and not-God. Your soul is the aspect of your being that is hard-wired by God to guide you to His life for you. Ideally, your soul is to express the image of God in you and reveal His awesome thumbprint. **Your soul is made to thrive when you have first submitted your heart to God and have chosen to do His will. Then His Holy Spirit breathes life into your soul.**

What happens when your soul is wounded, stunted, corrupted by other influences or shut down through pursuit of evil desires? Let's take another look at that driven athlete who didn't get to pursue his glorious goals.

MISSING INGREDIENTS IN MY IDENTITY

I'd graduated from Brown and was working in business. I'd dealt with the injuries that had re-routed my plans my senior year, and moved on—or so I thought. My heart was steadfast; I'd suffered some blows but I had regrouped and made new choices. There was no doubt in my heart that I wanted to honor God with my life, and as far as I was concerned I'd submitted to Him and continued to follow His lead as best I could.

But something wasn't right. The changes were harder than I'd expected, and I wasn't quite sure what I was missing. At this point, Jen encouraged me to talk to a counselor. Have you noticed that sometimes other people can see more clearly what we need than we can for ourselves? This was definitely one of those times.

As I met with my counselor, a Christian social worker in Rhode Island, he listened to me describe what was going on in my life. (You will recall that I was used to doing the talking.) Finally he said to me, "I think what you're dealing with is one of the hardest things anyone can face in life—the death of a dream." He kept asking me how I felt about all that had happened to me.

I couldn't really answer that; all I knew was that it was time to regroup and keep going. To give you an idea of how I was used to functioning in life, the Special Forces poster I'd had on the wall of my dorm room in previous years said, *"Kill 'em all and let God sort 'em out."* Nothing wrong with my determination!

"Yes but has your *soul* processed this loss?" he asked. "It's like your heart has moved on but your soul is left behind to hold the pieces. How do you *feel?*"

Again, I couldn't answer. I was coming up zero on that one, but he wouldn't let me skip the question. I saw him reach into his desk drawer and fish around in his files for a bit. I figured maybe he was looking for a more astute concept to share with me, perhaps the latest Harvard study that might help explain my situation. He pulled a piece of paper out and held it up for me to see.

The paper had pictures of faces all over it.

"Which face shows how you feel?" he asked me. They all had different expressions. It took me a while, but finally I pointed to the face marked "confused."

"We use this on three-year-olds," he explained.

You see, my *social* intelligence was well-developed; that wasn't the issue. I could excel in business, coaching, ministry, no problem.

My heart, mind and body had all been well-trained. But my soul or *emotional* intelligence had been shut down. You've heard the expression, *"if you don't use it you lose it"* as applied to muscles and intellect; the same applies to feelings. How many of us have grown up learning that it wasn't okay to express this or that emotion? God designed me with the full set just like anybody else, but with the combination of decisions I made during my upbringing and then later facing more cultural expectations, I was on the path to shutting down that whole aspect of my identity. The desires of my heart were warring against my soul.

So began another journey: That of becoming re-acquainted with my soul and learning to be more fully human. It's no accident that the word *psychologist* literally means, *"soul* doctor." In my case it was important that the counselor be a man; not only for me personally but also because our culture does not encourage men to get in touch with their emotions. But that flies in the face of God's plan for a man's success:

> *What does it profit a man to gain the whole world and lose his own soul? (Mark 8:36)*

FEELINGS AREN'T DANGEROUS; SUPPRESSION IS

The Scriptures also say, *"Blessed are those who mourn..." (Matthew 5:4).* The passage doesn't say, "Blessed are those who pull themselves up by their own bootstraps and move on." I'm aware that mourning may seem scary to some people. "What if I start crying and never stop?" you might be saying. "I can't just wallow in a pity party!" But I've learned that there's a difference between mourning and wallowing. When experiencing loss or grief of any kind, mourning is actually essential for moving on. You will find that you are more stuck when neglecting to acknowledge your feelings than you'd be if they had healthy expression.

Again, your soul is not supposed to lead or govern your decisions, but it's a full member of the team. Your soul is not "bad," and yet it can be corrupted or shut down, and *that* can have a bad effect. Consider this: Sociopaths don't *feel*. They have lost the ability to discern between right and wrong and have seared their souls to the point of numbness. Having a soul that is shut down can be dangerous. To the extent that we are out of touch with a healthy range of emotion and discernment, it could be said that the potential to become like Hitler is there for all of us. Our souls can be seared by our own sinful choices; they can also be seared through hurtful things that are done to us. Either way, we need the healing power of the Holy Spirit to address these issues.

If you have discovered that you're behind in clueing into your emotions like I was, do not blame yourself. The world system does everything it can to train our sensitivity to God right out of us. Furthermore, the thought of being open to pain is not encouraging. But I can assure you that it is ultimately more painful and more damaging to ignore your soul and miss out on that whole aspect of life.

Rejoice with those who rejoice, weep with those who weep.
(Romans 12:15)
Jesus wept. (John 11:35)
He will rejoice over you with singing… (Zephaniah 3:17)

These and scores of other Scriptures reveal that our God is a deep-feeling God who freely expresses emotion. He's not out of control; *He is slow to anger (Psalm 103:8)* and offers *self-control* as a fruit of His Holy Spirit *(Galatians 5:22)*. But He's in touch and expressive. This is how He made us to be. Where we've developed a hard shell of self-protection just to survive, God is offering *His* protection, which is in fact more effective than our hard shell.

The Lord is my rock, my fortress and my deliverer; my God is my rock, in whom I take refuge. He is my shield and the horn of my salvation, my stronghold. (Psalm 18:2)

Ω

What are you feeling? Are you aware of your emotions? Have you noticed areas where you have been either shut down or out of control? Why not seek help from a wise counselor who may be able to assist you in this area? You might also invite God's protection so you have a

safe place in which to experience your full range of human emotions...

A RE-DESIGNED MIND

"What's on your mind?" ... "The battle is in the mind."... "Mind over matter" ... "I'm losing my mind!" ... "She's back in her right mind."

You've heard some of these expressions. They give an indication of how much value we place on the mind in our culture. They also indicate how pervasively our minds are influenced by our emotions and our wounds. Yes, our minds perform a key role: They enable us to **process ideas, images and information with our ability to think**. From there we can then **discern what is true and organize a worldview** to accomplish a mission in life. With our minds we **form strategies and plan our lives**. Our minds also help us **move forward** and **evaluate our progress**. This clear, objective discernment and planning ability is an ideal.

With all of this powerful ability, however, the mind is only a part of the picture. You now know how important your heart and soul are, and also how neither functions properly without God's guidance and power. It's the same for the mind: It was **designed to thrive when submitted to God.**

DON'T THROW IT AWAY...

Some people, coming into faith for the first time and newly horrified at where their own thinking has led them, have leaned toward discounting their minds. Most classic "brainwashing" starts out in the form of people wanting badly to do the right thing and following a leader. The trouble begins when those people stop using what God gave them: their minds. That might even be a reason some are leery of submitting to God. But God doesn't require that we ignore our minds or check our brains at the door. He calls us to reason with Him:

"Come now, let us reason together," says the Lord. (Isaiah 1:18)

He also invites us to use our minds by thinking on what is good:

Finally, brothers, whatever is true, whatever is noble, whatever is right, whatever is pure, whatever is lovely, whatever is admirable —if anything is excellent or praiseworthy—think about such things. (Philippians 4:8)

And ultimately, He invites us into the **renewing of our minds**. Rigorous training of this sort couldn't be farther from the notion of brainwashing or devaluing of intelligence. When our minds are evaluating life in the light of God's truth, they are powerful tools for victorious transformation.

Do not conform any longer to the pattern of this world, but be transformed by the renewing of your mind. Then you will be able to test and approve what God's will is—His good, pleasing and perfect will. (Romans 12:2)

This verse is dynamite in your hands. In a nutshell, this Scripture sums up the process of replacing your "default" mission with God's; no less than letting go of old mindsets or worldviews that bog you down, then installing new ways of seeing, thinking and planning— like getting a brand-new hard drive with quadruple capacity already programmed for us!

ACT NOW

There is a catch, however: In order to have a renewed mind, you will need to take action. To be super-saturated with scriptural truth is excellent; to speak the truth is even more powerful. But for total transformation, you'll need to continually put what you're learning into practice. Then the truth-in-action will turn around and change you. That's why it says at the end of the passage in Romans 12, *Then you will be able to test and approve what God's will is...* Your mind will be that much freer of the old ways of thinking and planning, and you'll be transformed enough to be able to see that much more clearly who God is and what He wants for you. Many Christians think they need to "figure out" God's will perfectly first, then act. But in this

Scripture the pattern is laid out that we'll see God's will more clearly as we take action and allow ourselves to be transformed first.

FINDING TRUE WISDOM

Are we "there yet?" No. But as we act on what we have so far, it will expedite the renewing of our minds and access more of God's secret wisdom. This is not like the "wisdom" of the secret societies that take pride in their special codes and handshakes; this wisdom is born of life tests in which we've learned to put God's truth into practice and understood His ways. It is then that our minds can be fixed on things above while retaining a humble and practical outlook on everyday realities. We can recognize the tawdry nature of so much in our surrounding culture while maintaining our focus on the things that are noble, true, lovely and praiseworthy. The mind of Christ within us makes this possible.

> We... speak a message of wisdom among the mature, but not the wisdom of this age or of the rulers of this age, who are coming to nothing. No, we speak of God's secret wisdom, a wisdom that has been hidden and that God destined for our glory before time began... The man without the Spirit does not accept the things that come from the Spirit of God, for they are foolishness to him, and he cannot understand them, because they are spiritually discerned. The spiritual man makes judgments about all things, but he himself is not subject to any man's judgment: "For who has known the mind of the Lord that he may instruct him?" But we have the mind of Christ.
> (1 Corinthians 2: 6-7, 14-16)

There you have it: As with our hearts, God wants us to have His mind. He's not like some human leaders you may know who like to keep trade secrets to themselves. He gets more glory out of giving it away. He delights when we grow in power, intelligence, understanding and spiritual discernment.

SO PERCEPTIVE...

The father of a friend of mine loves to tell the story of an old village vendor who was being interviewed by the press after he'd witnessed a major town catastrophe. The villager's eyes were lit up and hands waving as he spoke. "I saw it coming," he said. "I *knew* something was wrong the minute that train went through the fruit stand!" There's nothing like possessing deep powers of perception.

There's nothing wrong with pursuing intellectual growth, either. But remember that it shouldn't be elevated to an end in itself, and spiritual discernment is not the same thing as intellectual acumen or academic prowess. Discernment between truth or deception is the fruit of a God-empowered mind. Your mind can help with that discernment at times, but these two are not to be confused. Furthermore the gift of discernment, or our ability to think, will be developed in us all the more as we depend on God more and more.

Again, notice that God's way is the opposite of our culture of independence. *Maturity through dependence* is a radical idea to most of us. Similarly, becoming who we're meant to be through submitting ourselves seems crazy to some:

The message of the cross is foolishness to those who are perishing.
(1 Corinthians 1:18)

For, as I have often told you before and now say again even with tears, many live as enemies of the cross of Christ. Their destiny is destruction, their god is their stomach, and their glory is in their shame. Their mind is on earthly things. (Philippians 3:18-19)

FOUR AREAS OF THE MIND

In his book *Renovation of the Heart*, Dallas Willard discusses four areas of the mind in which we need God's spiritual empowerment. The definitions below are taken from that book.[6]

Ideas – *"Ideas are very general models of, or assumptions about, reality. They are patterns of interpretations, historically developed and socially shared."* Some examples are freedom, education, happiness, the American dream, and the Kingdom of God.

"To change our governing ideas, whether in the individual or the group, is one of the most difficult and painful things in human life. In this way, genuine conversion is a wrenching experience."

You might think of spiritual growth or change in terms of a healthy immune system. Just as the good, healthy cells need to rout out the bad or unhealthy cells by way of recognizing them as *not-us*, so it is with our spiritual passage from darkness into light: We need to recognize whatever is *not-God* and replace those ideas with those that are godly. If we embark on this growth head-on, we'll be less likely to be forced into it later through more painful crisis or breakdown.

Images – *"Images are always concrete or specific, as opposed to the abstractness of ideas, and are heavily laden with feeling."* They are closely associated with the governing ideas of our lives. *"They mediate the power of governing idea systems by dialoguing with our soul and discerning how our ideas work in the real situations of ordinary life."*

On deliverance from destructive ideas and images, Willard writes: *"The process of spiritual formation in Christ is one of progressively replacing those destructive images and ideas with the images and ideas that filled the mind of Jesus Himself."* A great example of this process is found in inner healing: Often when people receive prayer for healing of painful memories, they report seeing an image in their minds of Jesus appearing in that memory. They may still have that scene as part of their life story, but the story takes on a whole different tone once they see Jesus' loving care for them in the picture. The image no longer triggers the old trauma, but instead reminds them of God's help in that situation. Another excellent example is the powerful effect our *seeing*—images in our mind's eye—can have on anything we do, as we discussed in Chapter Four. With everything from sports moves to creative projects to overcoming addictions to family reconciliations, seeing it is a vital first step.

Information – It is with our minds that we seek out, store and process information, both helpful and harmful. *"Without correct information, our ability to think is restricted....Without the requisite information, we may be afraid of thinking at all, or simply be incapable* *of thinking straight."* Having a robust knowledge base to draw upon is vital to knowing and doing the will of God in our lives. Especially important is our knowledge of God's already revealed will in the Holy Bible. When humanity cursed itself by choosing to eat from the tree of the knowledge of good and evil we cast our once pure minds into confusion and frustration. Since the introduction of evil thoughts into our conscious minds and into our world experience we have had to choose to filter out the evil thoughts and guard our minds from being exposed to evil knowledge. Those who do not heed the biblical caution to "take every thought captive to Christ" curse themselves by believing that there in nothing wrong with knowing about evil. We have been deceived by the same lie since the beginning. The reality is, we are better off not knowing the thoughts and lies of the Evil One.

Our ability to think – Thinking is *"the activity of searching out what must be true, or cannot be true, in light of given facts or assumptions. It extends the information we have and enables us to see the 'larger picture' —to see it clearly and to see it wholly."* Thinking is directly related to the issues we discussed in Chapter Four, "How Do You See?" Empowered by the Holy Spirit, our ability to think undermines false, misleading or evil ideas, images and knowledge. It is through a Holy Spirit empowered mind that we are able to discern truth from error, God's wisdom and plans for us from foolishness.

Ω

You might want to stop and reflect (that is, think!) at this point. Ask yourself: *What does my mind dwell on? What ideas and images come up often for me?* **You might even ask,** *What do I think of thinking?*

SUPERNATURAL STRENGTH

Strength refers to our **physical body, energy and abilities.** To remain strong physically, we need to find the **right balance or rhythm for the pace of our lives.** As you have seen with the heart, soul and mind, this aspect too requires submission to God. We have nothing but good to gain from the transaction. In fact, the Scriptures remind us that **our bodies belong to God in the first place:**

> *Do you not know that your body is a temple of the Holy Spirit, who is in you, whom you have received from God? You are not your own; you were bought at a price. Therefore honor God with your body. (1 Corinthians 6:19-20)*

So much for bargaining leverage! But remember, being owned by God has it privileges. **God designed us to be filled with His energy.** The Apostle Paul declared that God's energy worked "mightily" within him. That might sound like he was boasting, but it is actually one of the most humble statements he could make. To be a vessel for God's power flowing through him, Paul had to be submitted. Furthermore he noted that it was often when he was weakest that God worked through him most powerfully. In 2 Corinthians 12:9 God reminds Paul, *"My strength is made perfect in weakness."* Paul eventually got used to going with the flow:

> *"I know what it is to be in need, and I know what it is to have plenty. I have learned the secret of being content in any and every situation, whether well fed or hungry, whether living in plenty or in want. I can do everything through Him who gives me strength." (Philippians 4:12-13)*

IS IT WRONG TO BE STRONG?

You may have noticed that sometimes very strong, high-energy people encounter circumstances that put them out of commission. My athletic injuries are a great example of that. It would be wrong to conclude automatically that God was fighting me or didn't like my strength or was "trying to teach me a lesson." I wouldn't give the enemy all the credit either, though he certainly tries to thwart God's gifts in us from coming through. Rather, it might be useful to see these things as opportunities to develop a different kind of strength. Whether we see God work miraculous physical healing, learn to rest and receive or end up discovering a whole new kind of endurance that's beyond what we could muster, none of our difficulties are wasted in God's hands.

One friend of mine has spent many years training others in healing ministry. She is one of those high-energy types who loves to be around other people and seems to get even more energized as she goes along. She doesn't always need a lot of sleep, and when you stand talking to her, you sometimes get the feeling she's on a pogo stick. Is this natural, or supernatural?

She would say both. On the one hand, she will tell you that she works at doing those things that she knows will take care of her body: Eating healthfully, exercising, making time for rest and recreation, etc. But she will also share that she can't rely on that alone. There were many times when she'd be just about to teach a large group of people or lead a healing service, and out of the blue she would be hit with health symptoms. It drove her to prayer and desperate reliance on God. Yes, once in a while she would groan, "Lord, it would be so much *easier* for me to lead this group if I wasn't hoarse and deaf and lame!" But later, after the experience of ministering during a "low" physical ebb, she noticed that she had learned to tap into more spiritual strength or energy habitually; she was less inclined to rely solely on this or that physical regimen, which would amount to worshipping strength instead of God. I have found this to be true in my experience of God. As we submit to God, He releases His supernatural power in and through our lives.

Again, God made us to be healthy and strong. He takes no pleasure in our illness or incapacities. But the common thread in all these areas is our learning complete reliance on Him for all we need.

One of the quickest recipes for burnout is to try to minister in your own strength. It's not always easy to tell the difference, as we have different callings and some people are wired more intensely than others. What may be just right for one person may be total drivenness for another. Certain world-changers do seem to have an extra dose of divine energy: The great 18th-century evangelist John Wesley was so single-mindedly on mission with God that he rode on horseback between locations as he preached at least three times a day, every day, until he was more than 85 years old. Small in stature, he packed a spiritual punch that prepared the entire nation for the wide-sweeping social reforms that came in the wake of his ministry. Whether you are considered intense or mellow in personality, the mandate to rely on God's resources remains the same:

If anyone speaks, he should do it as one speaking the very words of God. If anyone serves, he should do it with the strength God provides, so that in all things God may be praised through Jesus Christ. To him be the glory and the power forever and ever. Amen. (1 Peter 4:11)

Ω

Ask yourself: Am I honoring God with my body? Caring for myself physically? Do I feel God's energy flowing through me?

"MY PEACE I GIVE YOU..."

"Peace I leave with you; my peace I give you. I do not give to you as the world gives. Do not let your hearts be troubled and do not be afraid." (John 14:27)

And the peace of God, which transcends all understanding, will guard your hearts and your minds in Christ Jesus. (Philippians 4:7)

How do we get that peace that passes understanding? One clue is right in front of our eyes in that verse: We need to remember that we won't always understand everything! If we could, there would be no need for that step of submission. Another clue is in the verses preceding Philippians 4:7. We are exhorted:

Do not be anxious about anything, but in everything, by prayer and petition, with thanksgiving, present your requests to God. (Philippians 4:6)

God wants us to be at peace. Yes, the world has plenty of trouble in it, but much of the reason for our trouble pertains to the fact that we need to be retrained, discipled into Christlikeness, and don't know what that means. We can't be at peace and attuned to God if our minds are stirred up with anxieties and our hearts filled with worldly desires. These things clog up our pipes and prevent God's love and power from flowing through us. Just as it takes some determined plumber work and cleaning to get water flowing through a clogged pipe, it takes submission to God and re-training as His disciple to experience the peace of God flowing freely in our lives again.

Later in the book we'll explore the importance of spiritual disciplines in greater detail. For now, I will simply list disciplines that correspond to each area in the role of Christ Follower. I would like you to see these disciplines as opportunities to keep your pipes clean. Or you might think of it as "lifting weights" and growing strong as a disciple of Jesus.

For those who appreciate memory devices, here's one that I created years ago to help me remember the basic spiritual disciplines that nurture my being. The acrostic I created is called P.R.E.P.² It helps me remember when I wake up to get properly prepared (or PREPed) for the day from God's perspective. Think of your routine when you start your day. What do you do? It is amazing to me that many Christians spend no time preparing themselves to live each day, knowing it was the custom of our Lord Jesus Christ to get up early in the morning to draw away to a solitary place where He could connect with His Heavenly Father.

$$\Omega$$

Here's the P.R.E.P.² that I like to practice daily so that all four aspects of my being are submitted to God and in Alignment with Him:
Pray & Petition = **Heart**
Reflect & Relate = **Soul**
Eat & Exercise = **Strength**
Ponder (God's Truth) & Plan = **Mind**

You can ask God to show you what area might need some immediate TLC. We think of "discipline" as hard, but it's also applying love and attention to certain areas of our lives that need restoring or developing. To start, you will find that simply becoming *aware* of these aspects of your life will begin to work some changes. Your focus begins to make room for each new thing God is about to do. Now when I ask you, "Are you fully human?" you can remember how confused I was as I looked at all those faces, and you can laugh with me at our blind spots. After all, we're "only human," right? That phrase makes being human sound like something shabby, but I believe that God meant for our humanity to be a marvelous and full-bodied expression of His image in us. Our being fully human is His divine plan for our lives.

CHAPTER 6

Can You Relate?

LAW 6

The Law of Community: *We need the love, fellowship, wisdom, and accountability of Christ-centered covenant relationships to keep us on track and growing.*

A MARKETING LEADER AWAKENS TO COMMUNITY

"Your wife has cancer and it has spread some... I'm sorry." On January 7, 2004, Mike Stallard heard those most sobering words from his wife's surgeon. Mike, one of my partners and founder of the Greenwich, CT consulting firm E Pluribus Partners, shares this story of how God used his family's experience of community to change his life forever:

"I stood in the waiting room of our local hospital. Thirteen months earlier, Katie had been diagnosed with breast cancer. Fortunately, it was caught early and treated through surgery and radiation. As frightening as breast cancer was, this diagnosis of advanced ovarian cancer left me stunned. Thoughts about life without Katie put me in a place I never imagined. I had hoped that a moment like this would never occur in my lifetime, but when it did, I found myself suddenly feeling alone.

That evening, I took our daughters, Sarah (age 12 at the time) and Elizabeth (age 10), and my mother-in-law, Bunny Harrison, to see Katie

91

in the Intensive Care Unit. She looked so pale and fragile that it scared the girls. On our way out of the ICU Sarah backed up against a wall and started to slide down as she fainted. A short time later, as we passed through the hospital lobby on our way to the parking lot, Elizabeth began to sob. I knelt down to her level and Sarah and I both wrapped our arms around her.

That night our hearts were broken. We all knew Katie was not well and her future seemed uncertain. I vividly remember the overwhelming feeling I had struggling to figure out what I should do to help Katie and our two beautiful young girls who had fallen asleep on their mother's pillow. I felt utterly alone. I prayed for wisdom. As I grew tired, my words were replaced with unspoken yearnings as I reached out to God for help.

After dropping the girls off at their schools the next morning, I returned to the hospital. Katie's mom had spent the night in her room so that she would not be alone when she awoke and the mental fogginess of the anesthesia had cleared. To my surprise, a close friend of mine, Jason Pankau was sitting at Katie's bedside too. I was surprised that he beat me to the hospital. At the same time, it comforted and encouraged me that Jason had rushed to our aid. It amazed me that even though I felt I was on my own, having had a focus on "me" for some time, many of those whom I loved still had "we" at the center of their lives."

FRIENDS NURTURED US FROM "ME" TO "WE"

"From that day forward, over the course of the next year, we experienced an extraordinary outpouring of affection and support from our community of family and friends. There were tangible gifts: beautiful bouquets of flowers; care packages of reading materials, lotions and blankets; an assortment of Ben and Jerry's ice creams; notes of encouragement—and the intangible yet very real gifts of love and prayer. One dear friend prepared a beautiful travel bag for Katie to take with her to the chemotherapy sessions. Inside the bag were gifts for passing the time such as a CD player and CDs and a book, as well as practical items such as band-aids and lotion. Another dear friend came to visit Katie in the hospital and offered to organize dinners to be brought in. And organize she did! A network of moms from our elementary school brought us dinners over a span of months. This friend made sure there was a variety of meals ("okay ladies, hold it on the lasagna this month") and even brought over extra food one week when stormy winter weather was forecasted. The food was so good I gained ten pounds! Friends chauffeured our girls to and from their after-school activities. We regularly had people stop by to see us. The visits weren't somber occasions though, quite the contrary. We talked and laughed and enjoyed one another's company.

Teachers and administrators kept close watch of our girls and reached out to say they were there for them if they wanted to talk. The principal of our elementary school surprised Katie when she visited her in the hospital and slowly walked around the hospital floor with her, IV pole in tow.

With each chemo treatment that spring, it took Katie a little longer to recover. On their own, Sarah and Elizabeth went through our family photos and pulled out memory-laden pictures, each selected because they knew it would touch their mother's heart. The pictures were assembled in a collage that the girls placed a few feet from Katie's side of the bed so that she could look at them while bedridden. Later, Katie tearfully told me just how much those pictures meant to her and how often she studied them.

A few times we took people up on their offer to "call me if you need anything." One evening, I remember having to rush Katie to the emergency room. While there, a call came in from home that Elizabeth needed Valentines cards for school the next morning. I called a friend of ours, who promptly picked up Elizabeth and took her to buy the cards.

When you experience difficult times, it's normal to have people share that they are praying for you. There were people praying from coast to coast and, we learned, as far away as Rwanda and Poland. These heartfelt expressions of concern and compassion were deeply moving to us."

LINKS BETWEEN COMMUNITY, FAITH AND HEALING

"We're certain that Katie's positive attitude and strong Christian faith combined with the support of our family and friends played a significant role in her recovery. Today, Katie is completely cancer-free and not expected to have a recurrence. Although there are many factors that affect the treatment of cancer, doctors recognize that the patient's state of being is extremely important. I recall reading the worst thing that could happen to a cancer patient is to feel isolated and alone. Fortunately, we were far from alone. People did what they could to help us, whether it was preparing a meal, helping take care of our daughters, or stopping by to visit. At times, I felt like George Bailey in the final scene of the classic movie "It's a Wonderful Life" when his friends rallied around him. With each act of kindness, the people around us lifted our spirits. As a result, we experienced something I wouldn't have expected: joy and hope. The love and connection we felt helped to crowd out my feelings of anxiety.

In addition to the connections we felt with others, staying spiritually connected helped us cope. There were times when helping Katie and our daughters on top of working, left me feeling numb by the end of the week. Attending our weekly Sunday morning worship service at Trinity Church in Greenwich was healing to my soul. I've thought a lot about what I've experienced on those Sunday mornings and concluded that it comes down to truth, beauty and goodness. I experienced the truth in my pastor's teaching, beauty in the music and God exalting worship, and goodness in the loving people I met and sacramental life we shared together. Although I don't pretend to understand the mystery of it all, I'm convinced that God began healing my soul during this season as I experienced His truth, beauty and goodness with new eyes. Each Sunday morning in the tired, 1950s-era middle school auditorium that Trinity uses for its services, truth, beauty and goodness washed over me like a river to refresh my parched soul and restore me for the week ahead."

THE TRUE CONNECTION

"Reflecting on all of these things gave me reason to pause and wonder what I had missed over the past few decades. My me-centered life had so often blocked out the love and prayers of others and for others. I came to a realization that transformed my life: **real joy—a genuine sense of gratitude and contentment—comes from staying connected to God and the people in your life**. These feelings of connection only come from developing a we-mindset that includes serving others and serving God rather than a me-mindset that focuses on serving yourself. An unexpected change came in the profound effect these experiences had on my thoughts about life today, including the workplace environment and how it can bring out the best and worst in people.

Earlier in my career I believed that it was wise to separate my personal life from my life at work. I was cordial and polite but kept an emotional distance from co-workers. Even though I was helping people at times, I wasn't really serving and connecting with them. In a sense, work became a stage for me. I didn't realize how relationally isolated I had become from being me-focused until I felt the joy that comes from being part of a caring community. Now I know that being authentic and serving others is best for me and, I believe, for the people with whom I work. Instead of compartmentalizing my life and thinking of people at work as rivals, I am focused on helping the people around me to achieve their personal potential given their talents and on achieving my personal potential given my unique abilities. It's a different mindset—a way of thinking that is much healthier because it encourages connection rather than isolation and loneliness.

In addition to compartmentalizing my life, I had become an "achieve-aholic" with my sense of self-worth too wrapped up in my job. This is common today. According to Gallup Research, a major sociological change has occurred in the past twenty years. At one time, Americans defined themselves by their family and community. Today, most people define themselves by their job, on the basis of their position's title and the brand image of their employer.

When you get so caught up in the status of your job and let achievement and competition totally crowd out time for relationships with others and staying spiritually connected with God, as I had done at times in the past, you will eventually regret it. I had become a human doing, not a human being. Like so many things in life, balance is key. Of course, there will always be seasons in our lives when we experience imbalance and those seasons may last for some time. If imbalance becomes the norm, however, a price will be paid someday.

After feeling the encouragement from faith and the genuine friendships that developed over the course of Katie's treatment, I knew I couldn't go back to a workplace environment where people are so focused on work that they are largely indifferent to one another. Instead I set out do something about it.

With the help of Carolyn Dewing-Hommes and Jason Pankau, two of the friends who had stood with us in our time of need, I wrote a book about connection in the workplace. It is entitled *Fired Up or Burned Out* and was published in 2007. We have had the opportunity to speak at leading companies, government agencies, and universities on this message of how important relationships are in life to people and organizations. God surrounded me with support from our community not only to bring our family through a crisis, as powerful as that was, and not only to bring my relational life into better balance. I believe He also wants the same for others, and the changes I made to be able to share this message more broadly are part of His larger plan."

CAN YOU IDENTIFY WITH MIKE'S STORY?

How many others do you know who are fine citizens, yet somehow isolated as Mike was before his family faced crisis? He would be the first to tell you that to seek community today is to go against the grain of our individualistic society. Not only do work-aholism and a competitive spirit fight community, but non-stop entertainment further isolates us. One study reports that the average American watches 14 hours of television a week. Another study reports that the typical father has 12 minutes of meaningful conversation with his son or daughter each week. 12 minutes *per week*. Gone are the days of a pick-up ball game in the neighborhood, as kids now retreat for hours to sit in front of a computer. The constant media connection has the *appearance* of community as we plug in to TV, phone or internet; technology is filled with talk of being "connected." But does it really help us relate?

Certainly God can use all this technology to help us connect with one another, but our mindsets need to be changed first. We need to move from "me" to "we" just as Mike did. If God had meant for us to do it alone, He wouldn't have created us to be a "we" to begin with. He created family and community, knowing that's where we would thrive.

"See how they love one another!" (Tertullian, quoting those observing Christians) That love is the main difference, the main proof of God's presence. It's not possible without community. It is through community that we learn how to grow, and it is through community that we learn how to love. Dependence on God and interdependence with one another is the essential precondition for both. What I describe in this chapter is a healthy, godly dependence that is free of the co-dependence so rampant in the relationships around us. The present-day Church is not immune to this co-dependence; in fact it's especially susceptible to it. However if we grow in the kind of love that God has modeled for us, the wisdom and discernment He gives us serves as an antidote to the imbalanced ministry motives and mutual manipulations that we see in some Christian circles. The fact that some communities have become codependent or corrupt should not prompt us to withdraw from community altogether. Rather, all the more reason to allow God to heal and reveal His true blueprint for a shared life.

ACCOUNTABILITY OF THE GOD KIND

"You'll be held accountable for this!" How many times have you heard that phrase and cringed? It is too bad that accountability has been associated with a sense of punishment for wrongdoing or at best, attempting to perform well for the good grade. In God's design, accountability is your best friend. It's designed for encouragement; where we tend to flag, those around us can bolster. One pastor I know is fond of saying, "Aren't you glad we don't ALL want to give up at the same time?" He's got a point. True accountability is one of us not giving up when the other might want to. It's a way for us to support one another in a positive light, joining our faith together to make sure His blessings come through. Accountability not only helps us with much-needed discipline; it also opens the way for us to glean insight from others who know and love us, and it gives God an open door to communicate with us in the way He has chosen to do it best.

Look at Mike's story again. What if, when he ran into his friends and neighbors and they asked him how he was doing one day, he had said, "fine, thanks," worried that they might think he wasn't performing well as husband and father if he didn't sound positive? Or what if Katie had refused visitors, not wanting anyone to see her suffer? The family might have missed a ton of blessing! Mike's daughter wouldn't have had her Valentines for the next day at school. Mike would have burned out. Katie might not have made it through if she'd been isolated. But as it was, they weren't isolated, they were honest about their need, and they learned to receive more deeply from others. That's true accountability. Doing life together gives life. One plus one equals more than two, because God's blessing is added into that equation.

When we *do life together* and not merely attend the same church service for a couple of hours each week, it's as though we join with God in creating a whole new atmosphere. God uses our mutuality and openness to increase the fullness of His blessing:

Oh, how good and pleasant it is when brothers live together in unity! It is like precious oil poured on the head, running down on the beard, running down on Aaron's beard, down upon the collar of his robes. It is as if the dew of Hermon were falling on Mount Zion. For there the Lord bestows his blessing, even life forevermore. (Psalm 133)

Elton Trueblood is referring to this kind of unity-substance when he urges us to cultivate the kind of faith "by which the potential glory of common life is liberated and revealed."[7] In glory, serving becomes more personal and less like volunteerism. The kind of service to humanity commanded by Christ has always been personal. In contrast, our society has turned philanthropy into something far more removed and bureaucratic. Instead of making disciples of all nations (Matthew 28:18-20), something that is a life-on-life process, our modern church version of serving has become programmatic. Shortly after Glasnost, some Russian children's camp directors invited missionaries to visit, but they had this request: "Please come show us love," they said. "We don't want programs. We've had enough programs. Please come show us love." They had it right.

SACRAMENTAL LIFE

If Christianity were only an inward, solitary relationship with God and didn't also take tangible form in a community setting, what do you think we would see? Not only that, but how long do you think it would have lasted? (If you answered, "not much" and "not long," you were being generous!) It's true that many of our outward forms of faith have degenerated to the point where they've become empty rituals. Humans have a way of corrupting the very thing they're trying to preserve through organization. But that's no reason to throw out the forms entirely; that would be like trying to have a body dance without bones.

Consider the sacraments. In the *Book of Common Prayer*, a sacrament is defined as *"an outward, visible sign of an inward, spiritual grace."* [8] That inward grace of God is central to our lives. How many times do we say, "by the grace of God," not even aware of how desperately we need that grace? It's like the air we breathe: so essential for life yet so easily taken for granted. Taking a fresh look at the outward, visible signs— the sacraments—may help us see the inward, spiritual grace with new gratitude for both God and community.

Baptism
Whatever your preferences or beliefs are regarding how to go about baptism, one common thread is captured in the phrase of Martin Luther, who affirmed that the disciples should be baptized "so that the new man should daily come forth again." The word *baptism* has at its root the meaning "to dip"—as a cloth is dipped in dye, becoming fully saturated with the color. We are "dipped" in the death of Christ and rise in His resurrection when we are baptized. The sacrament of baptism is designed as a public event not for show but for support:

To be immersed in the life of Christ is to also be immersed in community. That "new man" can't daily come forth without the help of the people around him.

Confession

Confess your sins to one another and pray for one another, that you may be healed (James 5:16). Again there are many ways people of different denominations go about confession, but there is a bottom line, which is that God urges us to do it because it's good for us. It's cleansing. When you are unburdened of guilt, do you not feel that floodtide of God's grace rush in to re-establish you in peace and healing joy? Furthermore there is something about confessing to a person; it establishes real witness and closure in a way that can't happen when we're alone. It also proves the unconditional love of the Father in a more tangible way. Keep in mind that confession is not to be confused with airing dirty laundry or exposing private issues to the public; it needs to be treated with discretion and discernment. The kind of bond formed in a mentoring relationship provides a safe place in which confession can happen rightly, in a way that builds character and releases healing, not shame.

Communion

This sacrament may be the most mystery-filled and powerful of all. Again, regardless of the specific ways you are accustomed to celebrating the Eucharist or Holy Communion, the main thing is that it's done together. Communion is by definition and nature *communing*, done in *community*. Some may have an occasional Eucharist alone with God, but so much of what Jesus said at the last supper (see John 17, for example) points to community. In 1 Corinthians 11 we are exhorted not only to enter into communion "in remembrance of me" (Christ) but also to be mindful of the quality of our connection with people in our world. We are commanded not to dishonor the Communion supper by harboring anger, unconfessed sin or disunity. We are to maintain our unity within the body of Christ. Communion is a regular reminder of the importance of our connection with God

and one another. In God's mind these aren't separated issues or
categories:

> *Therefore, whoever eats the bread or drinks the cup of the Lord in*
> *an unworthy manner will be guilty of sinning against the body and*
> *blood of the Lord.* *²⁸A man ought to examine himself before he eats*
> *of the bread and drinks of the cup.* *²⁹For anyone who eats and drinks*
> *without recognizing the body of the Lord eats and drinks judgment*
> *on himself.* *³⁰That is why many among you are weak and sick, and*
> *a number of you have fallen asleep.* *³¹But if we judged ourselves, we*
> *would not come under judgment.* *³²When we are judged by the Lord,*
> *we are being disciplined so that we will not be condemned with the*
> *world. (1 Corinthians 11:27-32)*

In remembering Jesus' death and resurrection we must never forget
His intention to connect us to God *and* one another in a dynamic, loving
and transformed community that changes the world. One dear sister in
Christ that I know shares that she often sees the word "remembrance" as
"re-*member*-ance;" it makes her think of all the members of the Body
of Christ and how one part can't ignore the hurt in another part. Those
who reached out to help Mike's family were acting on that reality.

> *"The King will reply, 'I tell you the truth, whatever you did for the*
> *least of these brothers of mine, you did for me.'" (Matthew 25:40)*

Volumes can be written on the amazing exchange provided for us in
communion, where we can tap into the life and healing of Jesus through
identification with His death on the cross, but for our purpose here, the
emphasis on community is made extra clear in communion.

BECOMING THE BODY OF CHRIST

How exactly are we to work out all those inevitable problems,
differences and irritations experienced in community? God specializes
in turning our more abrasive circumstances into community-building
moments as we look to his guidance:

> *Brothers, if someone is caught in a sin, you who are spiritual should*

restore him gently. But watch yourself, or you also may be tempted.
Carry each other's burdens, and in this way you will fulfill the law
of Christ. If anyone thinks he is something when he is nothing, he
deceives himself. Each one should test his own actions. Then he can
take pride in himself, without comparing himself to somebody else, for
each one should carry his own load. Anyone who receives instruction
in the word must share all good things with his instructor. Do not
be deceived: God cannot be mocked. A man reaps what he sows. The
one who sows to please his sinful nature, from that nature will reap
destruction; the one who sows to please the Spirit, from the Spirit will
reap eternal life. Let us not become weary in doing good, for at the
proper time we will reap a harvest if we do not give up. Therefore, as
we have opportunity, let us do good to all people, especially to those
who belong to the family of believers. (Galatians 6:1-10)

This passage is convicting on many fronts. It wastes no time pointing
out our need for one another in confronting sin and avoiding evil.
The exhorter in Galatians assumes we have a covenant community as
he instructs us how to live with one another in the church. We are told
that if we see our brother in Christ veering off track or caught doing
something wrong, those who are spiritual (that is, those humbly submitted to God and walking in the Spirit) should restore him gently. Very
few have experienced this kind of respectful correction. Why is that?
For one thing, we have not cultivated the kind of covenant community
lifestyle needed for this to happen; also, people have misinterpreted these
instructions in their woundedness and often "corrected" in a way that
has been abusive. In other words, confrontation is necessary at times in
the Body of Christ, but if it's done according to un-submitted human
perspective, it amounts to playing God and is not fruitful but harmful.
In contrast, when confronting humbly, with the power and love of God
moving through us, few things are more cleansing and liberating.

I believe our lack of understanding of how true covenant community
works is what is holding us back in many Christian communities. We
do not come to church expecting the other people around us to function
as change agents in our lives. If we knew how powerful a tool this set-up

is, we would jump at the chance. Not only are the people we admire marvelously suited by God to help train us, but also those who we don't admire—the ones who "bug" us—can be great refining tools in our lives. Just by being there, these people can reveal in us what God wants to heal and refine. They are like mirrors, showing us where the (often prideful) rash, bruise or inflammation is.

HOW MUCH DO WE HELP EACH OTHER?

As to carrying each other's burdens and our own load: Some clarification may be helpful with this exhortation. A burden is different from a load. A load is something only I can do, such as make my own choices as to how I will submit to God each day. A burden is something that can only be carried in and through community. The example of a disabled child, a grave illness such as we saw earlier in this chapter, a region-changing project are examples of burdens. Furthermore, as Lisa Leach writes in her book, *Feeling God's Heart Without Falling Apart: Confessions of a Burden Bearer*, the word "bear" in the phrase "bear [or carry] one another's burdens" actually comes from the Greek word "bastazo" which means "to lift, take up." This word is similar to the Hebrew word "nasa" meaning "lift off." We are to help others *lift off* their burdens, the way we might help them take off their heavy backpack on a long hike. In other words, we are not supposed to carry their entire burden ourselves but join together with God and others to make that burden lighter.

Again Mike's family is a great example of this "lift-off" concept: On the one hand, some people took on jobs that Katie may have done when she was well, and in that sense helped the family in very practical ways; they each carried a portion. But on the other hand, no one personally took on the illness that Katie was battling; that would have been preposterous. They certainly prayed for her healing, prayed for Mike's strength, prayed for the girls to have peace through it all; they also visited and encouraged and loved on them. In so doing they *collectively* helped lift the burden from the family. As God does the orchestrating, our giving ends up not being heavy but actually gives back to us in the process.

A friend's father used to preside as director of their local beach association. Every spring they would be faced with the task of getting the float from its winter perch on dry land down to the water, where people would swim to it all summer. A low-budget beach community, they did most of the work themselves and couldn't hire a crane or barge for such jobs. Obviously one or two men could not budge the heavy wooden structure. But they'd send out a notice to all the residents, and on the appointed day, *25-30* guys would show up to help. Stationed on three sides of the float, they easily lifted it and shimmied it down to shore. Not only that, but they ended up enjoying the gathering, staying to chat afterwards, catching up with one another after their shared hauling was done.

IT'S ALL ABOUT YOU

The word "you" in Scripture is usually plural. Much as we would like to self-help our way into focused Christian living, we are designed to be incapable of doing that alone. And that's the *good* news! The Great Designer of our lives made us into dependent beings. Therefore if you really want to rise to your potential, you will need to take part in covenant relationships so your roles and goals can be subjected to regular focus, evaluation, encouragement, coaching and prayer.

OUR IDENTITY AS A COMMUNITY MEMBER

Let me review with you the nature of *roles*. You may think that "being a Christian" is a role; it's not. Being a Christian is an all-encompassing way of life; it should dominate every role. If you look at every role you play in life, compare it to God's blueprint and invite him into that process, you will end up living with greater focus.

As your coach, that's what I'm going to walk you through in this chapter. We have already examined the four aspects or roles of being human: heart, soul, mind and strength. Let's look now at the five roles of being a Community Member: Inner Circle, Relative/Parent, Church Member, Mentee/Mentor and Ambassador/Friend—as we build the next layer of our Identity Roles Diagram.

Identity Roles Diagram - Community

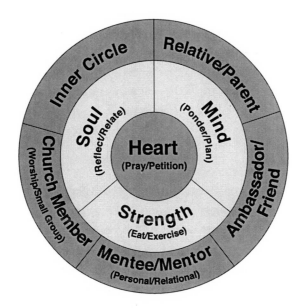

INNER CIRCLE

If you are single, your first role is found in an inner circle of great friends. If you are married, your role is to grow in relational oneness with your spouse. Our inner circle includes our most trusted and most secure relationships. Unfortunately these are the first relationships we are willing to neglect when life gets too busy. Ironic as it may seem, we tend to take for granted those closest to us. Remember that I shared about our "train wreck year?" I had gotten so busy that I neglected my wife Jen, and as a result, hurts added up over time. But like the "big rocks" illustration I used when talking about priorities, these close relationships are big rocks in our lives, second only to our time with God. After receiving good counsel, I began to invest more time in my marriage; we implemented date nights, took more time to talk. It was a healing time that wouldn't have happened if I hadn't adjusted my priorities. I had to approach my relationship with my wife with even more intentionality than I was giving other areas of my life.

When our close relationships are functioning well, these individuals are soul mates whom God uses to help us seek and find His greatness in our lives. They also become amazing people with whom we process our world, people who are willing to speak the truth to us in love. They mourn with us, serve us, celebrate us, love us and forgive us…and they let us do the same for them. This is our most intimate form of human community! They are our best friends in life.

THE MYSTERY OF MARRIAGE

Marriage is the ultimate covenant between human beings; the joining of man and wife is a picture of the relationship God desires to have with us. He wants nothing but the best for you, thus if He has called you to Christian marriage, He wants you to have a life partner capable of speaking His truth into your life, especially at moments of personal crisis. Some believe that a "marriage made in Heaven" is supposed to flow easily, without mishap, maintenance-free. This is a myth! Even the best marriages require hard work. If you're struggling, it is not necessarily an indicator that you've married the "wrong" person, for your spouse is God's number one refining tool.

"For this reason a man will leave his father and mother and be united to his wife, and the two will become one flesh." This is a profound mystery—but I am talking about Christ and the church. However, each one of you also must love his wife as he loves himself, and the wife must respect her husband. (Ephesians 5:31-33)

No small order, this challenge to love and respect! Again, let me say that our natural tendency is to neglect those in our inner circle and focus on those things that are more variable. But God's way is to focus on what is sure. Jesus set an example for us in how he surrounded himself with an inner circle. Throughout the Gospels we see him interacting with large crowds and teaching multitudes. Yet we also know that he spent much of his time focused on his small group of disciples. In Matthew we learn that Jesus took only his inmost circle with him on the mountaintop for a revelatory moment.

After six days Jesus took with him Peter, James and John the brother of James, and led them up a high mountain by themselves. There he was transfigured before them. His face shone like the sun, and his clothes became as white as the light. Just then there appeared before them Moses and Elijah, talking with Jesus. (Matthew 17:1-3)

If we dare to share at a deeper level on a regular basis with those close to us, then the power of God can pour more fully through everyone in that inner circle. We will grow in proportion to our willingness to know and be known in intimate community. Outside that group of close friends or your spouse, the level of sharing may be more selective, as others may not have the same core convictions as we do. Unfortunately relationships like this are rare in today's world and we are the ones missing out. Life was not meant to be done alone.

THE POWER OF COVENANT RELATIONSHIP

The word "covenant" means to define relational expectations. We overlook how powerful covenants were in early American history. Beginning with the Mayflower Compact in 1620 and including a number of church-based covenants by which many towns were established, these covenants were made in the presence of God to define relationships and responsibilities throughout New England. The Fundamental Orders of Connecticut signed in 1639 became the world's first true constitution. This covenantal approach to keeping social order is a godly form of agreement; it is one of the reasons the New England region prospered during the Colonial era, far more than regions where covenants didn't prevail.

To understand this at a personal level, it's helpful to think back to childhood or teenage years when many of us had at least a couple of friends with whom we went through difficult experiences. Even in the later years of life, it is possible to call those friends and experience the same emotion as long before, because they've earned the right to a special place in our lives. We made a spoken or unspoken covenant to be *there* for each other.

Ω

Who have these people been in your life? Has your inner circle changed over the years? Have you invested your time and attention in these close relationships lately?

RELATIVE/PARENT

In these relationships we are responsible both to and for—responsible *to* our parents and relatives and *for* our children (in old age this responsibility may be reversed):

- *Train a child in the way he should go, and when he is old he will not turn from it. (Proverbs 22:6)*
- *Fathers, do not exasperate your children; instead, bring them up in the training and instruction of the Lord. (Ephesians 6:4)*
- *He must manage his own family well and see that his children obey him with proper respect. (1 Timothy 3:4)*
- *Honor your father and your mother, so that you may live long in the land the Lord your God is giving you. (Exodus 20:12)*

Think about it: A parent is a child's first impression of Godliness. A child needs the blessing of a father, for instance. My own father spoke that blessing into me when I was a senior in high school and I walked into the room announcing that I had a scholarship to college and didn't need his help anymore. Instead of answering in kind, my father said, "I know that my discipline has been difficult for you to understand for these past few years, but I want you to know that I did it because I love you and believe in you. If that is the right school for you then great, but you can go to whatever college you want and we will figure out a way to pay for it." That was a blessing that made an indelible mark.

This blessing goes both ways:

- *Honor your father and your mother, so that you may live long in the land the Lord your God is giving you. (Exodus 20:12)*
- *I have no greater joy than to hear that my children are walking in the truth. (3 John 1:4)*

If you are a parent, you know what a difference it makes to see your children going in the right direction. Your blessing is over the top when your children see you with God's eyes and understand what God has given them through you. Furthermore, that joy is just a little taste of the joy God has over us when we begin to catch onto what He has in store for us.

WHAT HAPPENS WHEN FAMILY ISN'T VALUED?

In our era, as more people move away from the nuclear family, a fragmentation of personalities is taking hold. As a result, many people are left like ships without rudders. For example, business executives are taking jobs in other countries without adequate provision for their relational support. What they don't realize, often before it's too late, is that they're setting themselves up for relational failure. Even when families are physically living together, the higher value placed on work affects each person in the family. Each member grows more isolated, and another generation is raised without essential nurture.

Family *matters*. Even the enemy's attempt to destroy the family is an indication of its importance. Studies have shown that civilizations rise and fall in conjunction with the value placed on family. The strength that we can draw from a Christ-centered family is almost without equal this side of heaven; building these relationships needs to be a high priority in our lives. One way to think about how these relationships can and should connect to one another is to look at all of the *"one anothers"* found in Scripture. This wisdom found in the Bible can give us insight into how a Christian community can and should function. These *"one anothers"* define the relational expectations that lead to life in our families and in our churches.

We believe that the Holy Spirit officially commissions every believer into a ministry of caring for one another whether in our nuclear families or in the church family. After all, none of the following commands are restricted to a particular title (such as elders only) or a particular gender (such as men only).

1. *"... Be at peace with each other" Mark 9:50*

2. *"... Wash one another's feet" John 13:14*

3. *"... Love one another..." John 13:34*

4. *"... Love one another..." John 13:35*

5. *"... Love each other..." John 15:12*

6. *"... Love each other..." John 15:17*

7. *"Be devoted to one another in brotherly love..." Romans 12:10*

8. *"... Honor one another above yourselves" Romans 12:10*

9. *"Live in harmony with one another..." Romans 12:16*

10. *"... Love one another..." Romans 13:18*

11. *"... Stop passing judgment on one another" Romans 14:13*

12. *"Accept one another, then, just as Christ accepted you..." Romans 15:7*

13. *"... Instruct one another" Romans 15:14*

14. *"Greet one another with a holy kiss" 1 Corinthians 16:20*

15. *"... When you come together to eat, wait for each other" 1 Corinthians 11:33*

16. *"... Have equal concern for each other" 1 Corinthians 12:25*

17. *"Greet one another with a holy kiss" 2 Corinthians 13:12*

18. *"Greet one another with a holy kiss" 1 Corinthians 16:20*

19. *"... Serve one another in love" Galatians 5:13*

20. *"If you keep on biting and devouring each other...you will be destroyed by each other." Galatians 5:15*

21. *"Let us not become conceited, provoking and envying each other" Galatians 5:26*

22. *"Carry each other's burdens..." Galatians 6:2*

23. *"Be patient, bearing with one another in love" Ephesians 4:2*

24. *"Be kind and compassionate to one another..." Ephesians 4:32*

25. *"... Forgiving each other..." Ephesians 4:32*

26. *"Speak to one another with psalms, hymns and spiritual songs" Ephesians 5:19*

27. *"Submit to one another out of reverence for Christ" Ephesians 5:21*

28. *"... In humility consider others better than yourselves"* Philippians 2:3

29. *"Do not lie to each other..."* Colossians 3:9

30. *"Bear with each other..."* Colossians 3:13

31. *"...Admonish one another"* Colossians 3:16

32. *"...Forgive whatever grievances you may have against one another"* Colossians 3:13

33. *"Teach ...[one another]"* Colossians 3:16

34. *"...Make your love increase and overflow for each other"* 1 Thessalonians 4:9

35. *"...Love each other"* 1 Thessalonians 4:9

36. *"...Encourage each other..."* 1 Thessalonians 4:18

37. *"...Encourage one another..."* 1 Thessalonians 5:11

38. *"...Build each other up..."* 1 Thessalonians 5:11

39. *"Encourage one another daily..."* Hebrews 10:25

40. *"...Spur one another on toward love and good deeds"* Hebrews 10:24

41. *"...Encourage one another"* Hebrews 10:25

42. *"...Do not slander one another"* James 4:11

43. *"Don't grumble against each other..."* James 5:9

44. *"Confess your sins to each other..."* James 5:16

45. *"...Pray for each other, that you might be healed"* James 5:16

46. *"...Love one another deeply, from the heart"* 1 Peter 1:22

47. *"...Live in harmony with one another..."* 1 Peter 3:8

48. *"...Love each other deeply..."* 1 Peter 4:8

49. *"Offer hospitality to one another without grumbling"* 1 Peter 4:9

50. *"Each one should use whatever gift he has received to serve others..."* 1 Peter 4:10

51. *"...Clothe yourselves with humility toward one another..."* 1 Peter 5:5

52. *"Greet one another with a kiss of love"* 1 Peter 5:14

53. *"... Love one another"* 1 John 3:11

54. *"... Love one another..."* 1 John 3:23

55. *"... Love one another..."* 1 John 4:7

56. "... Love one another..." 1 John 4:11

57. "... Love one another..." 1 John 4:12

58. "... Love one another" 2 John 5

God has a way of making Himself clear in the Scriptures. Twenty-one of the fifty-eight of the verses above call for Christians to love! Scores of additional passages exhort all believers to love their neighbors as themselves, build up the Church, be involved in mutual edification, be like-minded, be of one accord, and similarly *"...do good...to those who belong to the family of believers" (Galatians 6:10).*

Do you find it easy to love? Sometimes it may feel like an impossible task. Remember that God's commands come with His provision and power to carry them out. He is Love, therefore as we tap into Him, we will grow in love. Here is another observation that will give you a powerful edge in learning how to love: Family members usually know how to push your buttons (a mentor of mine says that's because they installed them!) Loving your family is actually more challenging than getting along with other acquaintances. Thus if you can learn to love those closest to you, you'll be better off when it comes to those in the outer circles. Again, this is only possible as we let God's love flow through us.

$$\Omega$$

Ponder your own life for a moment: *How is your family doing? Are there strains in your family relationships that need attention? Are there certain relationships in which you sense God prompting you to come to Him for help and an extra measure of His love?*

CHURCH MEMBER

In this section I'll be covering some principles that apply to both Relative/Parent relationships and Church Member, so you might keep both roles in mind as you read on. It may come as no surprise that they are similar, as the Church is the family of God. For some people the family of God will actually play a bigger role in our lives than our nuclear families or our relatives. Following Christ together with other brothers and sisters in Christ in covenant community is essential for us to realize the love and variety God desires for all of us to experience. This is how Jesus lived:

> *While Jesus was still talking to the crowd, his mother and brothers stood outside, wanting to speak to him. Someone told him, "Your mother and brothers are standing outside, wanting to speak to you." He replied, "Who is my mother, and who are my brothers?" Pointing to his disciples, he said, "Here are my mother and my brothers. For whoever does the will of my Father in heaven is my brother and sister and mother." (Matthew 12:46-50)*

Clearly Christ is using this as a teachable moment to say that He sees his disciples as vital parts of His life. To Jesus, the community of faith He was establishing should function like family, the family of God. Do you relate to people in your church like that, or do they have the impression they are just the people you associate with on Sunday morning and have no further meaning in your life? If members of our family are in trouble, most of us would take the attitude that they wouldn't even have to ask before we move into action. If we don't take this same attitude toward members of our church community, we are the ones who are missing out. When the church loves one another according to the Scriptures, we become the kind of community through whom God can change the world. Actually, it is only through churches that live and love according to the Scriptures that God has *ever* changed the world. Are you willing to do whatever it takes to stay connected to God and His Church? If so, move forward with the conscious intention of forming relationships based on what you're going to give and not what you're going to *get*. By doing this, you will put yourself in a position for God to work wonders in and through your life. It's not that you give in order to get from God; rather, it's that in your giving, you are showing your great trust in His generous nature while also aligning your life with His right design for the Body of Christ. Furthermore, you can't out-give God!

THE SEVEN VALUES OF ABUNDANT LIVING AND CONTAGIOUS CHRISTIAN COMMUNITY

I'd like to turn your attention to a community that rocked with world-changing power and love. You will find it in Acts 2:42-47. Look at how these people in the first century of the Church related to one another; they were real people with real daily challenges, like you and me, yet they managed to tap into something awesome as they worked out their community relationships. To help us see the pattern, I've arranged each segment of scripture in this passage so that we can compare them with the Seven G's (or Seven Values of Abundant Living) that I introduced in the section on values. Many of the phrases reflect more than one value, and you will find that they do all overlap and work together. However I have offered a general correlation here to show the fullness of life in that Acts 2 community.

"They devoted themselves to the apostles' teaching"

Growth – Devoting ourselves to the Apostles' teaching means being devoted to growing in Christlikeness. This is the process of living what we know to be true and allowing the truth of Scripture to be pressed through the very fabric of our lives.

"and to the fellowship,"

Group – Devoting ourselves to one another in fellowship means honoring the value of Group and living in covenant community with one another.

"to the breaking of bread"

Grace – Being devoted to the breaking of bread means being devoted to the remembrance of Jesus' sacrifice for our sins and the grace through which we can now approach God and one another. A forgiven people we freely forgive one another and maintain our relational unity through the grace of God. The Church of Jesus Christ is a community with a deep commitment to the experience and expression of the grace of God.

"and to prayer."

Guidance – Being devoted to prayer means being devoted to God's guidance in our lives. Believers in the early church submitted themselves to the Lordship of Christ and believed He would speak into their lives by the power of the Holy Spirit.

"Everyone was filled with awe, and many wonders and miraculous signs were done by the apostles."

Gifts – Everyone being filled with awe, and wonders and miraculous signs being done by the apostles means they believed in the value of Gifts. God moved through them in supernatural ways so their experience (awe) and the expression of God's love in power (signs and wonders) was evident to all.

"All the believers were together and had everything in common. Selling their possessions and goods, they gave to anyone as he had need."

Good Stewardship – The way they shared their resources according to need shows how devoted they were to the value of Good Stewardship. Any real Christian family shares the resources God has entrusted to it with one another as He leads.

"Every day they continued to meet together in the temple courts. They broke bread in their homes and ate together with glad and sincere hearts, praising God"

Glorification – That they gathered together in a variety of venues with the express purpose of praising God, shows how committed they were to the value of Glorification.

"and enjoying the favor of all the people. And the Lord added to their number daily those who were being saved."

Grace – When a community vibrantly lives these values, the grace of God builds bridges of love to those who don't know Him. The Holy Spirit uses these bridges to draw people into the family of God.

It is clear that those in the early church submitted to God and to one another in a way that made it normative, not extraordinary. They were in the rhythm of God together, and their aim was to bring Him glory. Through grace God built bridges of love among humans with a sinful nature. When the church of Jesus Christ is working right, there is nothing like it on earth. By contrast, when the church is merely a reflection of the world through stained-glass windows, it can be the curse of the world and God grieves over it. God grieves because people who He created come into contact with these Church communities with the expectation of experiencing God and His hope for their hopelessness. Instead they find a religious organization which doesn't connect with them or help them connect with the supernatural life in God that they were destined to experience, and they leave wounded, never to return.

IS THERE HOPE FOR US?

On the whole, the Christian church over the centuries has taken the path of least resistance. The result has been more spectators than participants, passive religion more than disciple-making communities of faith. But the early Christians weren't spectators; what you see in the above passage is boldness, joy, close sharing and involvement. What you see is change happening wherever they went, too. They impacted their culture so that the area was not the same when it came in contact with this community. Christianity prevailed throughout the Roman Empire not so much because of the beliefs being expressed, but because of the power of love in that community. Do you think God would want any less for us today?

If we have any hope of changing our culture, which is often decadent in aggressive ways, we will need to make major changes of the "close encounters" kind! Our supposedly Christian culture in America—"afflicted by affluence," as pastor/author Bill Hybels puts it—will not be changed through worn-out evangelistic programs. It will be changed from the inside out, through changed lives and hearts and communities. Put simply it will be changed in direct proportion to our commitment to follow the command of Jesus to make disciples

The church needs to mentor and coach one another again. We need to gather in all different sizes of gatherings and commit to following the commands of Christ together in covenant community. In addition to gathering in large groups for worship services, we will need to have small enough groups to allow for growth in close relationships. Big gatherings are effective in inspiring and educating us, but not in holding us accountable to live our faith and be trained in righteousness. We need a place to be really heard, seen and known personally. Yes, there is hope, but if we don't implement this kind of godly design in our Church community life, we will miss out on His blessing.

MENTEE/MENTOR

You may think of mentoring as something reserved either for exceptional Christians (the mentor) or for Christians with exceptional problems (the mentee). But unless mentoring is perceived by every serious Christian as normal, we will not grow as we need to, nor will we influence our culture the way we're born to do. Everyone needs to have someone to "chase after" (someone wiser than we are) as well as someone who follows after us (to whom we give what we've been given.) Because of our sin we can't see ourselves objectively. We need others to help us to grow to spiritual maturity and greatness. We need the God-empowered guidance, training and encouragement of wise mentors. We need to regularly open up our lives before people who can probe into what is really happening in the deeper aspects of our desires, feelings, thoughts and behavior, and help us see our lives from God's perspective. When mentoring takes root as a way of life among Christians, the soil of discipleship will become so rich and our submission to His Lordship so deep that God can bear much fruit in and through our lives. Evangelism won't be an abstract, tired concept anymore; people around us will see our changing lives and want to know what's behind them. New seekers will find churches to be the healing and strengthening communities they had hoped for.

WHAT DOES REAL MENTORING LOOK LIKE?

Christian mentoring is an intentional relational process where someone is guided, empowered, and encouraged by God through another to embrace God's presence, steward their life from God's perspective and realize their potential through God's power.

There are four different kinds of mentors that you should have operating in your life at all times. We all need to be mentored and we all need to be mentoring someone. In looking at different Biblical characters and the roles that they played in one another's lives, you could say that we all need a Paul (intensive mentor), Barnabas (peer mentor), Peter (occasional mentor), Stephen (Passive Mentor) and Timothy (mentee) in our lives if we are serious about the great commission.

First, the intensive mentor. An intensive mentor functions like a Christian life coach in our lives. This is someone who is going to play an intentional role of discipleship in your life for an agreed-upon period of time. This type of mentor helps you to create and implement a personalized growth plan toward Christlikeness. When I function as an intensive mentor in people's lives we usually meet monthly face-to-face and touch base by phone in between meetings.

Second, the occasional mentor. This is someone we meet with for specific counsel and timely wisdom. It is usually someone we believe has experience and wisdom in a particular area of life. This person should be sought out as needed during different seasons of your life for good and timely perspective about particular issues in which you believe they can help you to discern God's will.

Third, the passive mentor. This refers to people who don't realize that you view them as mentors, but nonetheless you are watching them. They are usually the heroes you have read about in biographies or authors and speakers whose lives inspire you to make dynamic changes in your own. They are not "passive" people; rather, they are setting an example for you from afar, often unbeknownst to them.

Fourth, the peer mentor. These are friends and colleagues who offer support, perspective, collaboration, and networking. Peer mentors are at a similar stage of life journey and are learning similar lessons to what you are currently learning. These people function like training or workout partners for you in life.

The world wants to gradually take away our dreams, and it is our duty to rise in defiance of that influence on our lives. To do so, we must tell people how God is challenging us now, thereby giving others the ability to exercise God-empowered guidance in our lives and coach and train us in alignment with God's revelation for our lives.

Plans fail for lack of counsel, but with many advisers they succeed. (Proverbs 15:22)

When we're trying to discern and follow God's next steps we need more than general advice. We need specific guidance, and we need to test it by placing it in front of multiple lenses.

WHAT DOES MENTORING LOOK LIKE?

One mentor I know shares that he finds his own life stories popping up as he's meeting with mentees. He may not always understand why a particular story comes to mind, but he's learned that God has His way of using it. As he begins to share the story, usually their mouths will drop open. "How did you know I needed to hear that?" they will often say. "I didn't, but God did," he says.

Similarly one of my mentors, Jim Frost, is very skillful in guiding me to the Scriptures that I need to learn in order to properly view what I am struggling with from God's perspective. Great mentoring always uses Scripture to guide people and always challenges people to submit themselves to God's truth. For instance, after I had a disagreement with my wife, I didn't enjoy hearing his insight or the Scripture's obvious rebuke of my actions. In fact, Jim even advised me to apologize to my wife. Although this didn't sit well with my ego, I knew Jim was helping me see God's wisdom for my life, and I was grateful.

Beginning an active mentoring relationship requires a conscious decision. It is possible that you would "stumble" on a mentoring relationship in that it develops over time and catches you by surprise; you may not have previously had the language to describe what was going on. But it is far more likely that you set it up intentionally. Find those you admire and ASK. And be ready to BE ASKED by those who look up to you. I believe mentoring relationships function best when the mentee invites the mentor to work with him and then they sit down together and create a covenant of understanding about the nature of the relationship. This helps to get both parties on the same page and defines times for review and potential closure to the mentoring relationship. People should function as mentors in our lives for seasons at a time. It's also good to have multiple mentors that we are working with in any given season of our growth.

Leaders who realize the tremendous value of mentoring move into the next level of effectiveness. I mentioned earlier the studies showing the main difference between leaders who succeeded and those who fell into disrepute: mentoring. Those reluctant to be mentored, thinking they have arrived and need no more accountability, are setting themselves up for failure. Some leaders may be as reluctant to mentor others as they are to be mentored. Insecurity may cause them to feel threatened by the success of those following them. But wise mentors know that a mentee's success is their success too. They also know that the more they give away, the more they too will grow.

Ω

Reflect for a moment: *Have you had mentors? Who are they? Have you been a mentor? If you don't have mentoring in your life now, who would you like to ask? What do you admire in these people? Who is your Paul (intensive mentor), Barnabas (peer Mentor), Peter (occasional mentor), Stephen (passive mentor) and Timothy (mentee)?*

AMBASSADOR/FRIEND

If you are a follower of Christ, you are one of God's ambassadors. You aren't necessarily assigned to an island somewhere; you're simply called to share God's love wherever you go. You are made for mingling! Is this what you see among Christians around you? The tendency for so many when they become serious Christians is to lose close contact with all non-Christians within about three years. That is sad. It's the opposite of Christ's example. He didn't limit himself to interacting with only His closest friends. In fact He spent so much time with "sinners" that He was criticized for that by the religious leaders of the day. His response was, *"I have not come to call the righteous, but sinners to repentance" (Luke 5:32)*. It is good to spend time with like-minded people, but you must also have relationships beyond that so you can offer Heaven's flavor to those who haven't yet tasted it. Evangelism isn't to be a separate or stilted activity, but a lifestyle of growing in love and letting that love show up in relationships with those who are far from God. As a Catholic priest once challenged me, "Our conviction is that God is evangelizing all of us toward perfection, whether we're Christians or not, which is why we use the word evangelization instead of evangelism, suggesting a continuous process. There's always someone on the journey we can help."

So from now on we regard no one from a worldly point of view. Though we once regarded Christ in this way, we do so no longer. Therefore, if anyone is in Christ, he is a new creation; the old has gone, the new has come! All this is from God, who reconciled us to himself through Christ and gave us the ministry of reconciliation: that God was reconciling the world to himself in Christ, not counting men's sins against them. And he has committed to us the message of reconciliation. We are therefore Christ's ambassadors, as though God were making his appeal through us. We implore you on Christ's behalf: Be reconciled to God. God made him who had no sin to be sin for us, so that in him we might become the righteousness of God. (2 Corinthians 5:16-21)

When we are functioning properly in this role, we will be able to love people differently than the world loves them. As this Scripture states, we no longer love people from a worldly point of view. The world teaches us to relate to people for what we get from them, not for what we can give to them. The passage even goes on to say that we used to relate to Christ in this way. *How much of your motivation for loving Jesus is because of what you get from Him?* As we mature, we begin loving Jesus for who He is and because He is training us in the abundant life, not because we think He will give us what we want if we go to church and pray. God loves us without condition and as we mature in our experiential understanding of this grace we will also be able to love those in our lives who don't have a relationship with God and His life-giving grace.

MIND-BLOWING RECONCILIATION

Not only will we love others in a new way, we will be empowered to forgive in ways that never seemed possible before we experienced the grace of God. Forgiveness is one of the most powerful healing actions we can take. Reconciliation, requiring a process of restoring trust over time, takes that forgiveness a step further. There may be life situations in which it is not wise to trust again (such as abusive relationships). I'm not advocating a lack of wisdom or discernment that would lead to further danger. But I am aware that so many broken relationships can be healed when we let God love through us, and He is a wonder-working God who changes hearts in ways we could not imagine. Forgiveness makes us stand apart in this world; reconciliation blows people away.

It's astounding that God chooses to make His appeal to the world through us. Our task is to love one another in the church with such intensity that it spills out into our relationships with those who don't believe in God. Be aware that this kind of radical love will be met with resistance as the powers of darkness attempt to shut it down. Yes, we are in a war. But also remember that we win! God makes His (and our) victory very clear throughout the Scriptures.

Who is going to harm you if you are eager to do good? But even if you should suffer for what is right, you are blessed. 'Do not fear what they fear; do not be frightened.' But in your hearts set apart Christ as Lord. Always be prepared to give an answer to everyone who asks you to give the reason for the hope that you have. But do this with gentleness and respect, keeping a clear conscience, so that those who speak maliciously against your good behavior in Christ may be ashamed of their slander. (1 Peter 3:13-16)

NOT A DOORMAT BUT A BRIDGE

You may worry you'd become a doormat if you tolerate and forgive unjust behavior. That's a valid concern. But there is a difference between enabling or tolerating abuse (which God hates) and freely choosing to love someone past their negative response. The first involves no sense of identity in Christ, only a broken-down self that is wired to allow mistreatment; the second is a free choice with full understanding of our royal position in God's family. We can know that we are standing our post in God's army, remaining in God's perfect rule, allowing the Kingdom of Heaven to invade earth through us. We are not just ambassadors of forgiveness but also ambassadors of reconciliation and peace. We can be the bridge to a new way of looking at life by loving people, forgiving them, and, in the power of God, offering the opportunity for true reconciliation.

Ask yourself: Am I helping to change the world, or is the world changing me? Ask it of the Church also, and take a fresh look to see if you find the kind of dynamic, life-transforming love found in Acts 2 … or a living death that has everyone rushing through life without truly relating. A healthy Kingdom community needs to have several ingredients: *love, accountability, mutual edification, shared disciplines and a common commitment to God's mission.* This is a power-packed checklist, an inventory well worth taking. Are you willing?
Can you relate?

CHAPTER 7

Do You Know Your Calling?

LAW 7

The Law of Calling: *God has called and equipped each person to function interdependently with others in a concerted effort to express His love to the world.*

Kim is a highly educated specialist at a prominent university hospital. She's also a beautiful and compassionate young woman. A few years back, she had excelled in all her courses and was on track for a well-paid position in the medical profession. By all appearances, her life was going well; she also seemed to be well situated in a field known for its great service to humanity. Anyone looking at her would have said she had found her calling.

But Kim (not her real name) suffered a breakdown. There were many factors that contributed, overwork not the least of them, but she was deeply unhappy in her profession and unsure of what she was doing with her life. She also had a strong desire to get married, and felt embarrassed to admit that, as though it might be a shortcoming of some kind.

In a prayer counseling session, Kim shared some about her childhood, which had been pretty rough. Those who were supposed to care for her had abandoned her, and others treated her abusively. Something had kept her going through all that, and despite the abuse, Kim managed to stay hopeful and compassionate. "What helped you stay so determined to love and give, when you were treated so badly?" her counselor asked.

"I'm not totally sure," she admitted, "but I always had this sense that God was with me, even through all that. And I kept thinking there was some reason—some meaning to it all—that maybe I might help people one day. I don't know how I knew it; I just had this 'knowing' inside of me. But now, I don't feel like I'm there at all. Everyone says, 'Oh, you should be happy with what you have,' but I just know there's got to be something *more*."

Kim experienced some healing with the help of prayer, then a breakthrough came later when she attended a medical conference. It was a symposium with many presentations, and during one of them Kim heard another young doctor sharing about his work in third-world countries. Not only did her heart leap as she listened to his talk, but she also found that talking to him unlocked dreams in her that she'd left dormant for so long. It was like finding a key piece of the jigsaw puzzle. Later, sharing about this conference, Kim's whole countenance lit up; it was as though she was a whole different woman.

REMEMBERING HER PURPOSE

"That's what I long to do, help those who have really suffered; I feel like my own suffering prepared me for this! I see myself traveling, ministering to the poor... The family I have thinks I'm crazy, and they want me to make more and more money, but I have no interest in doing that. When I heard this man speak, it was like I remembered who I was for the first time in so long! And I keep picturing myself working with him there—I want to be a partner and not do it all myself. Granted, I don't know if he's 'the one' God picked for me to marry or anything like that, but something *happened*. Just seeing his heart gave me hope. Do you think that is too far-fetched?" she asked. "Do you think I'm just head-in-the-clouds wishful thinking?"

What lit up Kim's face was the reconnection with her life purpose, her calling. She already knew her general calling as a Christian, and she already had a compassionate heart willing to love others.She even had a profession. But what had led her into despair was losing sight of her calling, which also very likely included marriage as well as ministry. The after-effects of the abuse she had suffered certainly contributed to this loss of vision as well. Her healing has been a process of emerging from oppression. But a key factor that helped bring her out of despair was remembering God's calling again, nothing less than His best desires for her.

Studies of World War II concentration camp inmates showed similar results as we heard about in Kim's story. Viktor Fankl observed in his classic book, *Man's Search for Meaning*, individuals who retained a strong sense of meaning in life held a far greater chance of survival. That sense of meaning doesn't exist in a vacuum; central to it is an awareness of being called. When we are called, every little ordinary thing in life becomes connected to a larger scheme that is purposeful and tied to what God is doing in the world. God will use our calling to meet our final two needs: *to experience variety and to feel important.*

IMPORTANCE IS IMPORTANT

"It's Shake 'n Bake, and *I helped!*" This line comes from an old commercial in which a child boasts about her part in helping to prepare dinner. The advertisers may not have known this, but one reason the commercial was so memorable was that it reflected the way God wired us. We have a deep need to be useful and truly needed—important —in this world. Kids as young as teetering toddlers love to have a special "job" to do, a respectable part in the family scene.

Just as it is with the parents of that toddler, thinking of age-appropriate ways that their child can help in a very real way and feel important, so it is with God. He's not indifferent about any aspect of our lives. It's not control but love that prompts Him to call upon us to think and act in specific ways throughout our day in every role and circumstance. Our continued responsiveness to His calling will not only strengthen our relationship with Him, but it will also deepen our ability to hear Him.

God has designed us to have a sense of meaning or importance in our lives, a sense that our life counts for something even if it entails losing it in a cause or in dedication to others. We're called to a peace of mind that surpasses all understanding, a peace that is connected to the pursuit of a noble ideal even when that pursuit includes hard times. An old novel depicts one of its characters as having peace of mind "when he's had a good dinner and his pipe is drawing." For the follower of Christ, the peace of mind we experience is not reliant on comfortable circumstances. What does cause strain and inner turmoil is incessant slavery to self, comfort-seeking and the triviality that has become the hallmark of contemporary culture. We may never be free of the strain of life, but we can learn to live with zeal and peace in the *midst* of that strain. That zeal will come as we serve the world in the ways God has called and equipped us to do. Just as Kim's face lit up when she saw more clearly what she was called to do, so we will feel that "lift" when we are on track with His purposes for our lives. The peace of mind that comes from mere absence of strain is temporary; God serving the world through us lasts forever.

SPECIAL INSTRUMENTS SET APART

We are the Church, the "ecclesia," which means "those who are called out." We are called to be set apart, which is the original meaning of the word *holy*. "Holy" is often taken to mean being really, really "good." Yes, in our pursuit of holiness we are called away from sin, from missing the mark of His perfect will for our lives. But holiness is so much richer than trying not to sin. It's not so much about being "good" as it is about being *His*. It's about abiding in God. It is when our lives rest within His perfect rule that He expresses His transformational power *through* us. Again, this is not to say that we can only begin our calling after having obtained some high degree of moral perfection. Our potency in the call of Christ is directly related to our commitment to abide in Christ. It's a process. It's a messy and confusing process at times because different forces are always at work to derail our efforts. But like the people in Noah's ark, we'll find peace in following God's call on the inside even when the storm continues to rage outside. We will become more like Christ as we abide in Him. As we abide, the submitting and obeying follow more easily. We are His chosen instruments of expression. Does the pen strive in the hand of the writer? Or does the pitcher strive as water is poured from its spout? As we abide in the vine, God loves the world through us.

DEPENDENT AND INTERDEPENDENT

If you've followed me this far, you know that God's main plan for our lives is to experience and express love. The question of calling is not separate from that plan. You might consider the scene of an ice cream shop: Everything in there is ice cream, but there are dozens of different flavors. The main call of God is ALL love, ALL the time; the various ways that love gets expressed can be seen in terms of all the different flavors.

Furthermore we're not to go off on our separate mission as individuals but function interdependently. An ice cream shop with only one flavor wouldn't fare as well as one with a variety of offerings. In our personal journeys, we need to discern our specific 'flavor.' But then that flavor is confirmed and enhanced by those around us in community. God will orchestrate the connections in our lives, adjusting our specific gifting with the needs around us. He has prepared us for the world and prepared the world for us, but it's only in continued communication with Him and others around us that it all gets opened, scooped out and served up.

For it is by grace you have been saved, through faith—and this not from yourselves, it is the gift of God—not by works, so that no one can boast. For we are God's workmanship, created in Christ Jesus to do good works, which God prepared in advance for us to do. (Ephesians 2:8-10)

Our natural human tendency—our default option, if you will—

is to see what our natural talents and abilities might be and then to look around for an arena where they might be exercised. This passage in Ephesians brings this tendency up short. It states plainly that God has already prepared in advance the things that He wants us to do. There is no room for boasting about our ingenuity, such as how we took an unpromising situation and made it into something great, because if it's not something God prepared in advance for us to do, then it amounts to nothing. On the other hand, if we began walking down the path He has prepared for us, we will be amazed at how everything falls into place.

> *With this in mind, we constantly pray for you, that our God may count you worthy of His calling, and that by His power He may fulfill every good purpose of yours and every act prompted by your faith. We pray this so that the name of our Lord Jesus may be glorified in you, and you in Him, according to the grace of our God and the Lord Jesus Christ. (2 Thessalonians 1:11-12)*

What is it that makes us worthy of His calling? Simply put, it is a humble and contrite heart. It is submitting to His guidance and power for living and letting Him love others through us. It is proper alignment of our lives under His Lordship.

PROPER ALIGNMENT

When the rubber meets the road, your wheel alignment is important. If you've ever worn out a pair of tires prematurely due to poor alignment, you know what I'm talking about. Having the wheels just a little 'off' will eventually cause the tread to wear unevenly, and the side that's taking all the beating can get bald pretty fast. How much more is this true of our lives! Have you felt "worn thin" in places, and hardly touched in others? That is how Kim felt. On the one hand she was working very hard, yet on the other, she didn't have a sense of peace about her calling. She was restless, and God used someone at a conference to break through to her and touch her soul. She simply knew that this is what she needed to do. She felt the alignment in her soul and knew that this is what she was created to do. This is what God has called and equipped her to do in the world.

This passage in Second Thessalonians suggests there are barriers to the proper fulfillment of our calling. In the natural world we might think of barriers that pertain to our levels of education and experience, but from God's perspective it is sin and strongholds that hold us back from the fulfillment of His purposes for us. The blood of Christ provides the remedy for sin; the cross provides the remedy for strongholds or mindsets that need to be put to death. Confessing our sin is like getting our wheels realigned; it helps us get back on track with God. Repenting of wrong thinking (or letting go of old mindsets, also called strongholds) can even be like getting new tires altogether. It is not only about saying what we've done wrong and being forgiven, as monumental as that is; confession and repentance are also about declaring who we are in Christ. This is a joint work we enter with God; it is Christ who changes us and makes us new.

The next logical step after being realigned with His Lordship is to connect with community and the ministry teams with which God has called us to serve. We don't dare go forward alone or in our own strength. Remember, we are created to be dependent on God and inter-dependent with one another. As I mentioned in the last chapter, one plus one equals more than two, as God creates a whole new synergistic flavor out of our combined flavors when we come together.

SERVANTHOOD WITH SYNERGY

Some friends of mine described their wedding reception, which was held under a tent on their church property. Their caterer had hired a team of some 17 waiters and waitresses (it was a large wedding.) As the church kitchen was upstairs, these waiters and waitresses were constantly running up and down the fire escape with plates on their shoulders. The wedding couple was amazed at how cheerful they were; it was a hot day and most of them were smiling and singing as they worked. What started all this joyful energy? For one thing, their boss (the caterer) was a joyful woman, and she was singing in the kitchen as she prepared the dishes. No doubt, once one of them had caught the joy bug, it started getting contagious. Then wedding guests started responding to the servers with more joy, and before long no one could tell where it had actually started.

This scene is a great picture of true servanthood. We are to function together like a network of mutual joy. When we're continually learning from one another, continually catching a fresh dose of joy and spiritual food from the "boss," we'll not only keep ourselves buoyed up but we'll also keep each other encouraged. One might think that running up and down the stairs with one plate of food after another would be boring work. But that isn't accounting for all the delightful conversation and fellowship that was taking place behind the scenes. It's almost as though the work isn't the main thing. What God has in mind, as we serve together and help each other grow in truth and love, is our growth in Him. Yes, the work is important, but even more important is that we attain fullness of life and love in the process.

The world and the enemy will do all they can to draw us away from this fullness of life. That's nothing new. One pastor said it this way: "If the devil isn't in your face every day, you might want to recheck your direction and make sure you're not following him." But God, as He moves through us in His power, displays His authority to the principalities and powers in the heavenly places (Ephesians 3:10). For when we love God, one another and the world like this, God's purpose for creating humanity comes into full bloom and the world sees a community of love on full display. Love trumps the plans of the enemy. It is the only thing that has ever changed the world or ever will.

OUR IDENTITY AS A CALLED SERVANT

When our ideas about God's mission are clear and we've made the decision to go forward with it, we begin to feel the sense of 'lift' that life is supposed to have when we're really living. You could almost see that happening for Kim as she described her experience at that symposium. It's worth our time to examine different aspects of the

Law of Calling, as we'll clarify even further what God's mission for your life may be. Having examined the identity role categories of Christ Follower and Community Member, let's take a look at the roles that make up the category of called servant: Minister of Compassion, Steward of Resources, Empowered Servant, Calling Mentee/Mentor and Professional. By studying these five roles, we complete the outer layer of the Identity Roles Diagram.

Our Roles Diagram

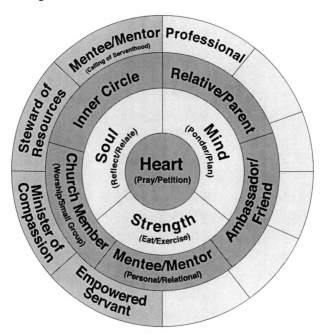

MINISTER OF COMPASSION

We are called to serve those in need among us. When we intentionally serve those less fortunate than ourselves, our compassion for people increases. So does our appreciation of God's blessings in our lives.

Several missionary teams from Connecticut visited children's summer camps in Russia during the 1990's. Returning, they weren't the same. In a matter of weeks they had fallen in love with the people they were serving, and voiced many times that they wondered who was really ministering to whom. People who were previously reserved wept openly as they shared about their trip. Many details of their lives were affected: After seeing the scarcity of paper in those camps, they could no longer bring themselves to tear off a large sheet of paper towel and throw it away after one small use. The same with food—no more waste. And clothing—they began to give away more clothes, for they had more than they needed. All their relationships deepened back home as a result of their encounter with the deep gratitude of their new Russian friends. It was not about Russia per se, though the people there are indeed a treasure. It could have been Mozambique, Guatemala, Myanmar or any other country where there would be an opportunity to give. What changed their lives was serving with their whole heart.

GIVE IT ALL YOU'VE GOT

We are called to serve with all that we are. Sometimes that means simply giving resources, and other times it means personally drawing alongside others to counsel them, love them, encourage them, help fix their house, whatever their needs may be. God can be very specific and practical as He prompts us to meet a need, and He doesn't set it up in a way that would shame others or deprive them of their own opportunities to grow.

The main thing we need to remember about serving is that we must get intentional. If we literally put ourselves into environments where poor people are, we are beginning to imitate Christ. Jesus regularly associated with all the different people in society, especially the less fortunate and outcast. God's vision of caring for one another was being violated at every turn in those days, and Jesus did all He could to model a different way of life. Again, as it happened with His attention to "sinners," Jesus was subjected to violent criticism and attacks from the religious elite of the day who did not associate with people they deemed to be unclean.

When you think of Jesus and ministry, it may be natural to picture it as more "godly" than human. After all, He came as God incarnate. But consider Jesus' full humanity also; He needed to serve as a Minister of Compassion just as we do, and for many of the same reasons. Yes, that identity role certainly tapped into His perfect godly nature; the very reason He came was to bind up the brokenhearted, set the captive free, heal the sick and so on. But Jesus also needed to keep perspective in life as we do. He needed to be kept humble and aligned with the will of the Father as we do. If it weren't so, Jesus wouldn't have gone off alone to pray so often. He too needed to be filled up in order to love.

THE GIFT THAT KEEPS ON GIVING

Praise be to the God and Father of our Lord Jesus Christ, the Father of compassion and the God of all comfort, who comforts us in all our troubles, so that we can comfort those in any trouble with the comfort we ourselves have received from God. For just as the sufferings of Christ flow over into our lives, so also through Christ our comfort overflows. (2 Corinthians 1:3-5)

This passage is probably the best definition of ministry ever written. It is also a great thing to think of when we have received comfort in a difficult time; it teaches us to go beyond merely thanking God to taking the initiative in sharing that comfort with others. Comfort is one of those things we can share with someone else without losing it ourselves; God designed us to receive more as we give more.

In *The God of All Comfort*, one of the Christian classics, author Hannah Whitall Smith writes persuasively about the fullness of life that is available to the Christian who trusts in God as a persistent act of the will. The result, she says, is "abiding peace and continual victory." The fullness of God—that sense of "Now I'm living!"—comes from the abiding relationship.

This is what the LORD Almighty says: Administer true justice; show mercy and compassion to one another. Do not oppress the widow or the fatherless, the alien or the poor. In your hearts do not think evil of each other. (Zechariah 7:9-10)

You may feel like you're not compassionate enough. That is fine; willingness is all God is looking for, and He will equip you and move through you. You may have heard it said, "God doesn't call the equipped, He equips the called." Furthermore He doesn't measure the effectiveness of ministry according to how you feel. You can put a stake in the ground and decide that you will be a Minister of Compassion. God can then make you an "instrument of His peace," as St. Francis put it. That won't happen without your being intentional, however. It has to reach the level of your day timer or Blackberry to actually move you out of the comfort zone into the adventure of God's comfort.

Ω

Have you had opportunities to serve, comfort, minister to others? If so, how has it affected your life? If not, are you willing to step out and let God use you?

STEWARD OF RESOURCES

Our second role as a Called Servant is that of a Steward of Resources —all of the various resources that God entrusts to us. As money is the second-most referenced topic in all of Scripture (after the Kingdom of God) we will discuss money in this section. The principles applied to money can also be applied to other resources in life such as your time and your gifts and talents.

We will expand this role and examine five aspects of being a Steward of Resources: **Diligent Earner, Generous Giver, Wise Saver, Cautious Debtor, and Prudent Consumer.** The definitions of these five areas come from Dick Towner, a friend and great disciple-maker, and his *Good $ense Budget* course. Again, if we engage God's training in our handling of money, we will also be training in wisdom that can be applied to the whole of life. For example, with regard to relationships, we learn to keep good accounts and to apologize when we are indebted to others after we've hurt them. You may also find that what you do with money provides you with a reflection of other aspects of your life. In many ways money mirrors what we value.

Diligent Earner. The diligent earner is one who works with commitment, purpose, and a grateful attitude. It's a role that must be taken seriously, while at the same time remembering that we are not called to be workaholics. Certain areas of the United States have a surplus of people whose motto seems to be "There's no place like work." Sometimes that is due to materialism or ambition and the earner's ego satisfaction of outpacing co-workers. In other cases, people may find work less stressful than home, especially if there are needs at home that seem harder to meet than those at the office. Whatever the reason, more time at work than at home creates a painful and dysfunctional family situation for which no amount of material reward can compensate.

The diligent earner shows commitment. Colossians 3:23 states: *Whatever you do, work at it with all your heart, as working for the Lord, not for men.* This can be one of the most liberating verses in the whole of Scripture. Regardless of whether or not you like your work, you can approach it knowing that God sees all your efforts and appreciates them. Even if you're alone, or your earthly boss and co-workers don't appreciate your work fully, God *does*. He is an awesome boss! Also, no matter what kind of work you're doing, at the office or at home, it becomes ennobled, sanctified, and enjoyable when you know that by doing the work you are pleasing God. Surveys have shown that 75% of American workers are disengaged from their work. Meaning, they are just in it for the paycheck. But when you know that your present employment is part of a larger scheme that God is using for good in your life, your work may take on a different focus and even become more enjoyable. In turn, your sense of commitment will rise more easily.

The diligent earner reflects purpose. *If anyone does not provide for his relatives, and especially for his immediate family, he has denied the faith and is worse than an unbeliever.* First Timothy 5:8 is a serious warning against idleness and self-indulgence that must be taken to heart in an era when we're flooded by advertisements and other exhortations to please ourselves, amuse ourselves, and flatter ourselves. We are given family as our most precious opportunity on earth to experience and express love. If our own family members are going without their spiritual, emotional, and material necessities being met and we are doing less than our best to correct that, then we are worse than an unbeliever.

The diligent earner reflects a grateful attitude.

You may say to yourself, "My power and the strength of my hands have produced this wealth for me." But remember the LORD your God, for it is He who gives you the ability to produce wealth, and so confirms His covenant, which He swore to your forefathers, as it is today. (Deuteronomy 8:17-18)

This theme is restated again and again in Scripture: God's power and not human effort achieves worthwhile results. God consistently chooses the "weak" or unlikely candidates of this world to do His work. Think of Moses, Gideon, and Jesus himself. If we suppose that we can prosper without God's light and power, we are embracing the grandest illusion of them all. The Scriptures say to remember the Lord your God, because it is He who gives us the ability to go to work, and, as a matter of fact, He can take it away if that is important to our growth.

Generous Giver. The generous giver is one who gives with an obedient will, a joyful attitude and a compassionate heart. The giver is empowered to change lives, to be God's vessel of timely blessing. We are created to give, and if we aren't giving in all areas of our lives, we begin to die. Consider the Dead Sea: A salt lake located between Israel and Jordan, the Dead Sea has no outlet. It is a receptacle rather than a channel, and as nothing flows out of it, life cannot survive in it. We become like that Dead Sea when we simply store up and hoard God's blessing in our lives without giving it away. Have you ever had a time in your life when everything seemed to be "stuck," then when you made a decision to reach out and do something, give something, suddenly everything began to flow again? That's because we were created to be channels, not receptacles. Hoarding is actually more dangerous to us than giving. Furthermore, as channels or stewards of God's resources we can give without fear of running out, because God is a limitless source of love and blessing.

Why God wants us to give:

- **To be responsive to His goodness.**

The closer we draw to God the more we partake of His nature, which includes His goodness or generosity. The thing we are most commanded in Scripture to do is to praise and thank Him; this praise follows easily as we increase in our awareness of His goodness. That gratitude is like a pump that releases more of God in us in turn. When we enter a cycle of goodness, others can begin to partake of God's nature as they encounter His goodness in us.

- **To focus on Him as our source of security.**

The natural drift of the human soul is toward resting places that are false. Our sufficiency can only rest in His sufficiency, and He has to pull the rug out from under us to show us time and again, so we will only rest in Him. He is the only solid point in all the relativities of the universe. For many, the hesitation to give is based on fear that personal security will be threatened, but once we become experientially aware of God as our only source of security, we can give freely and cheerfully.

- **To help achieve economic justice.**

Jesus found fellowship among the poor, and there is nothing in Scripture to support the common predilection toward associating with the wealthy and finding our self-affirmation in that way. Reducing the role of government and achieving economic justice in our country is an achievable goal if Christians simply do what God tells them to do. Some of my acquaintances are even doing a reverse tithe, that is, giving away 90% of their income and living on the remaining 10%. One of these, with whom I've been in a mentoring relationship, told me, "I've come to the conviction this is a practice that leaves me in the right dependent place on God and still able to enjoy His provision."

- **To bless others – blessed to be a blessing.**

If we have been blessed by God in material things—and Americans are well into the bonus, compared with the other 95% of the world—God has had a reason to bless us, and His reason is that we might ourselves be a blessing. Once we begin living with that in mind, we learn quickly that being a blessing becomes itself a blessing greater than anything we have received. We are lifted into a joy that we've never thought possible.

- **To break the hold of money on our lives.**

One of the most common misconceptions in life is implied in that phrase "financial freedom." We imagine that if we could only become financially independent and thereby free of a certain boss or of worry about material sufficiency, then we would be as close to the reality of freedom as any that could be imagined. What many don't realize until it's too late is this: If they achieve financial freedom, they're in danger of entering a slavery far more onerous than the one they think they left behind. This is one of the meanings of the saying that it is impossible for a rich man to enter the Kingdom of Heaven. When you live as an owner and not a steward of your resources, if you insist that your life is your own, it is impossible to enter the Kingdom of Heaven. Until we properly align ourselves as stewards of all God brings into our lives, we cut ourselves off from living the abundant life. Jesus followed up that declaration by stating, "With God all things are possible." It is clear He has given us an escape from this kind of slavery, and that escape is through giving. The more we give in obedience to His guidance, the freer we become.

Jenny and I had an experience that reinforced many of these giving principles. We were living in Boston and planting a church at the time. I hadn't been paid for two months. My wife was looking at me somewhat skeptically by then, wondering whether I knew what I was doing and also expressing the natural desire of a parent to feed the family. Then one day, we received a support check in the mail. The amount was for the exact amount that we needed—to the penny! Our breakthrough came at the eleventh hour, when everything seemed just about lost. It was a breakthrough so significant that all we could do was stand in astonishment and ask, "Why did we ever doubt?" It is in moments like that one—times when you serve and give obediently and trust that where God guides, God provides—it is in those moments that He builds your faith. If we do our best to hear God, there is no guarantee we will hear Him correctly, but over time, if we persevere, we will find Him true to His promise to give us wisdom.

Wise Saver. The wise saver is one who builds, preserves, and invests with discernment. The Scriptures clearly show that it is wise to save but sinful to hoard. Proverbs 21:20 states *"In the house of the wise are stores of choice food and oil, but a foolish man devours all he has."* Consider also this parable told by Jesus about a rich man whose land produced so many crops he ran out of room to store them:

> *"Then he said, 'This is what I'll do. I will tear down my barns and build bigger ones, and there I will store all my grain and my goods. And I'll say to myself, "You have plenty of good things laid up for many years. Take life easy; eat, drink and be merry."' But God said to Him, 'You fool! This very night your life will be demanded from you. Then who will get what you have prepared for yourself?' This is how it will be with anyone who stores up things for himself but is not rich toward God." (Luke 12:18-21)*

We see two fools—one who consumes all he has and doesn't save; the other who stores up his goods for himself and doesn't share. The wisdom of Scripture sets a middle course between the self-indulgence of unbridled consumption on the one hand and the opposite form of selfishness, which is hoarding.

The foolishness of self-indulgence is easy to see, whereas the opposite extreme can be harder to detect, probably because there is often a patina of wisdom in the idea that a good thing like saving can never be overdone. How then can we know when saving is being pushed over into selfish hoarding? God's wisdom guides us to believe it is wise to save for an unexpected hardship but foolish to stockpile beyond our foreseeable need. I know people who have several lifetimes of resources piled up, and I've noticed it's a challenge for them to give a tithe of their income or pray.

One Connecticut family received a modest inheritance that they used to buy their house, send their kids to college and make several much-needed improvements and repairs. They were generous givers before the inheritance, and delighted in being able to give more when they had more. Then both husband and wife were laid off in the same year, with several years of college yet to pay for, and they didn't have income for quite a while after that. They dipped more deeply into their remaining savings than they had anticipated, and began to wonder if they were foolish to have spent it so easily. God allowed them to come to the end of their resources again before they experienced a refill. It is not that God delights in "torturing" us; rather, He is weaning us off our dependence on anything but Him.

The illusion of self-sufficiency can loom so shiny and strong that our ability to listen to God can grow dull and weak. The command of Jesus to His disciples is, "Come, follow me." How do we do that? Not by a set formula; then we are back to control and self-sufficiency again. We learn to follow by the experiences we have as we continue on the journey and continue to watch for God's lead. There is no formula for how much to save, and so we've got to listen and look for the promptings of God in order to do what He set forth for us to do.

Cautious Debtor. The cautious debtor is one who avoids entering into debt, is careful and strategic when incurring it, and always repays it. Did you know that there is not one positive Scripture verse about debt in the whole Bible. That is because debt has a number of spiritual dangers.

First, debt presumes on the future. James 4:14 reminds us: *Why, you do not even know what will happen tomorrow. What is your life? You are a mist that appears for a little while and then vanishes.* We need to understand the claim that lenders have on our lives: We become slaves to lenders. In fact, Americans in general may well be entering a very dangerous time in our history. Statistics show that we now borrow more per capita than we save, and someday the debt bubble will burst even more dangerously than it already has at the time of this writing in October 2010. The average American household has $10,000 in credit card debt.

The biggest issue stopping missionaries from going on the mission field is debt. Those wanting to enter the mission field are now having to wait until they have paid off their debts. The agencies don't want missionaries serving two masters and having to run side businesses. Even mortgage debt can be dangerous for some people these days if they have to sell their house in a down market and do not bring in enough to pay off their mortgage. Things can change in regard to what we owe relative to what we have.

Second, debt denies God the opportunity to teach us something. One of the hardest things for any of us to do is to learn the kind of discipline that can come only from self-denial. The experience of parenting is instructive here. There's a saying that, "It's better to prepare the child for the road than prepare the road for the child."

One couple I know was hounded by their teenage son who wanted them to co-sign a loan so he could buy an extra car. They refused, explaining that they didn't want him (or themselves) shackled to that kind of debt. He was furious and acted like they were being stodgy and stingy, as though they were shackling him worse than the debt would have. Months later, they found out that the car he first wanted had all kinds of problems, and the owner was not entirely honest. By this time their son had saved enough to buy his own car free and clear. He was far prouder for having worked for it; he had waited for the right one, which happened to be a much better deal, in better condition and almost a gift from a family friend. This same son who was so cranky before now admits it was a good discipline to wait and not get what he thought he wanted right away. He is beginning to see a difference among his friends who have been given everything without that discipline.

God wants above all to teach us how to trust in Him and depend on Him, and that is the reason for most of our difficulties in life. In fact, where we encounter difficulty in life it is spiritually beneficial to us to learn how to say, *Thank you God. I will depend on you more.* Luke 12:31 says *But seek His Kingdom, and these things will be given to you as well.*

In America, we have roughly six percent of the world's population consuming roughly 35-40% of the world's resources. Two-thirds of the world's population, four billion people, live on less than two dollars a day and one billion don't even have that. One way or the other, God will teach us the things we need to learn so that we depend on Him more, but the avoidance of debt is one of the instruments at His disposal. We need to live within our means, especially when those means are beyond our basic needs. Going into debt simply to feed our cravings for more will only end up leading to continual discontentment and we might be missing out on an opportunity for God to grow our character and teach us something that will bless us for the rest of our lives.

Third, debt fosters envy and greed. Most people go into debt to get what they want. This has a ripple effect by fostering a community in which everyone is supposed to own a Lexus. Individual greed becomes a community project and the levels of greed spiral upward. In Luke 12:15 Jesus gave this warning: *Then He said to them, "Watch out! Be on your guard against all kinds of greed; a man's life does not consist in the abundance of His possessions."*

Prudent Consumer. The prudent consumer is one who enjoys the fruit of one's labor yet guards against materialism. A healthy kind of financial freedom could be defined as the contentment we experience as we faithfully manage our financial resources according to God's purposes, principles, priorities, and promptings. As a prudent consumer, it is our charge to listen for God's voice when making financial decisions and to use financial decision-making as a training ground for life stewardship.

The application of the principles we've covered under Steward of Resources is worth examining for yourself. Since we don't have the space to do that in this book, I will summarize by reminding you that God wants us to keep two principles in mind at all times as we move out into our financial worlds:

First, *beware of idols. "You shall have no other gods before me. You shall not make for yourself an idol in the form of anything in heaven above or on the earth beneath or in the waters below" (Deuteronomy 5:7-8).* This exhortation is so crucial that it is one of the Ten Commandments that God gave to Moses for all of the Israelites to know. Some may consider consumerism to be idolatry merely in the symbolic sense. However, observing people caught up into the cult of materialism— and it can happen to any one of us—it is easy to see that an element of the demonic is likely to be involved. You can see how materialism controls their inability to experience and express the love of God in their lives by keeping them consumed with money and stuff. To these people, money has become their god and they are not able to properly connect with the one true God until this is rooted out of their life.

Second, *be content.*

I know what it is to be in need, and I know what it is to have plenty. I have learned the secret of being content in any and every situation, whether well fed or hungry, whether living in plenty or in want. I can do all things in Him who strengthens me. (Philippians 4:12-13)

In this familiar Scripture, we learn about the interesting relationship between contentment and power. Being content in life is not as easy as it may seem at first. In difficult circumstances or in situations where we don't have what we want, contentment may seem quite beyond our reach. The supernatural power of God is necessary to achieve it. Then, once we do enter a degree of contentment, we find it has a power of its own over sin; it is difficult to tempt a supernaturally content person with illicit allurements. Contentment with gratitude for what we have is the antidote for greed and envy, and we find this combination is a strong preventative against other evils. It is worth noting that money problems are the second largest cause of divorce.

Money is fickle; it takes wings. Job was wealthy and God allowed Satan to take it all away. But because Job had conditioned himself to steward his life wisely, he wound up saying it's God's to give and God's to take away. That's a true stewardship perspective. If we are abiding in Christ, as the branch abides in the vine, living in and through His power, then we are prospering. That's our lot in life as Christians. We have the assurance wherever He guides, He also provides. *He* is our sufficiency.

In the next chapter we will continue looking at our Calling roles and dive deeper into that subject by examining the Law of Servanthood.

CHAPTER 8

Are You Slaving or Free?

LAW 8

The Law of Servanthood: *In serving one another with our lives, we become free and express significant transforming love.*

Have you ever wondered if it is possible to serve others without feeling like a servant? That is, without feeling downtrodden, worn out and hardly recognized for your contributions? A pastor I know has said, "You know whether you have a servant's heart by how you respond when *you're* treated like one." How true. I don't believe that God is honored by our allowing ourselves to be trampled upon and worn out. He came to set us *free!* Why would He want us enslaved again? I have no doubt that human slavery is the opposite of His plan for us. However I also know that He empowers us to serve others: freely and with joy, not out of obligation but giving from our position as a member of His royal family. I've seen many instances in which God has allowed us to serve in our own strength and ability alone until we've had enough, then He shows us what it's like to do it in *His* strength and ability. What a difference! This book is full of those instances in my life; here's one in which I got my first taste of God's supernatural power.

BLINDSIDED AT A BIBLE STUDY

As I mentioned in the Foreword to this book, I attended a meeting of the Fellowship of Christian Athletes when I was a high school student in suburban Chicago. Other students had invited me to this Bible Study; several of them were football teammates of mine. I had said I would come, but my intention was to forget about it. By the grace of God, these students just wouldn't give up on me. "You said you were coming!" they'd say. "Where *were* you?" Finally they cornered me in the locker room. Just short of a tackle I said, "Okay, okay, I'm coming."

I've already described my first impression of Mike Swider, the Olympic coach who gave a powerful talk at this meeting. In his talk, Swider took all the loose ends of what I knew about God and faith and tied them together, winding up with a question: "Who wants to commit his life to Christ?" I raised my hand, and my life has never been the same since.

Six months later, the leader of the group was organizing an outreach to junior high school students. He approached me and said, "I want you to come and speak at a gathering of our youth group."

"No, you don't," I replied. I was recalling a catastrophic effort I'd once made at public speaking when I was a sophomore… Everyone was required to give a speech in one of my classes that year. When my turn came, to say I was a little "anxious" would have been a gross understatement. As I went to the front of the class, paper in hand, then turned around to face the class, I gave them a look. The look said, "I *dare* you. *Nobody mess with me*, or you're going to be dealing with me after school." But then as I tried to give my speech, I began to shake. I shook so violently that the paper I was holding tore in half. Again I gave them the *look*. As I sat back down at my desk, I remember vowing, "I will *never* do that again!" If you hadn't already noticed, I was not fond of feeling nervous and humiliated. So when that speaking request came a couple of years later, I was convinced I was doing all of us a favor when I told the Bible study leader, "No way."

But he persisted. He assured me that everything would be okay, and God would give me the words to say; there would be nothing to worry about. So I prepared for the talk. I put together a few thoughts on perseverance, had a couple of Winston Churchill quotes in mind, and I was ready to go. Or so I thought.

When I arrived at Willow Creek Community Church and looked out at 900 kids in the youth group, my mind went *blank*. And I mean blank. All I remember is sitting in the front row in a lathered-up sweat, thinking that I was going to make a complete fool out of myself. I was praying earnestly for a means of escape. A sudden structural weakness in the floor beneath me, perhaps…

Then my friend who had invited me turned and said, "Let's welcome Jason Pankau up here." I stood up and walked to the microphone.

The Holy Spirit must have completely taken over my mind, because to this day I have no recollection of what I said to them.

After I sat down, people came up to me with words of gratitude about how I had really encouraged and inspired them. I was elated, but also profoundly confused and disturbed. I knew it wasn't me who had just encouraged people to seek out God in their lives, and I also knew I would never again be able to just "give it the old college try." I had now experienced something completely *beyond* me – a power not my own! I knew I could never go back to just working hard and doing life in my own strength. I had tasted the *Kingdom of God*. God revealed a whole new potential for me to consider and choose for my life. This new world had a completely different path for me to take. On some level I knew then that God would get all the glory for it, as He would be loving others through me.

Over the course of the next four years, God began to show me the difference between living in and through *my* strength for *my* glory and living in and through the power of God for *His* Glory in the world. Every day that I live, I am so grateful that God gives me the strength to choose His path, for it is a life far richer than I could have foreseen. Having God's miraculous guidance and power is not only possible; it's what God has *planned* for us. Many people tend to go to God as a "last resort" when their best effort doesn't pan out. But His abundance is Plan A, *not* Plan B! It is my fervent hope and ongoing prayer that you too will tap into this power of God in increasing measure.

That profound podium experience became a lesson I'll always take with me. When it comes to needing the power to encourage and inspire, there's nothing more effective than that place of total abandonment; the abundant life just doesn't work any other way.

GREATNESS CALLS YOU

You and I have the privilege of being called to greatness. That Bible Study leader knew I was called to greatness before I did. God used him to give me a glimpse of how I might be used in service of others. Now as your coach, I can confidently tell you the same thing: There is greatness in you. Most nominal Christians leave this life without ever giving expression to the greatness within them. That might be because their greatness is designed to be expressed in the form of servanthood. Jesus remained emphatic and explicit on this subject, and as He spoke to His disciples about it, He included himself first: *"The Son of Man came not to be served but to serve" (Mark 10:45).*

In the legend of Camelot, the knights sat at a round table because it was a symbol of the equality of all human beings. Etched into the center of the table was a motto: "In serving each other we become free." It's a motto that rings true from the standpoint of the Bible as well as practical psychology. When people truly serve one another, they stop worrying about everyone else's motives. Relationships are no longer a weary chain of quid pro quos. Instead they become more like the relationships God intends for us. He loves us whether we like it or not. We, in turn, can decide in advance to take on an attitude that says, "You *can't stop* me from loving you!"

God's Kingdom may not look like Camelot, but it prevails far longer and with greater glory than the "one brief shining moment" of that legendary kingdom. If we want to advance God's kingdom, how much more do we need to begin to express the kind of "knightly" serving that brings freedom! Once we have made this choice to adopt that kingdom mindset, it is then our duty and privilege as fellow servants to serve one another with our lives. That is how it works in the Kingdom.

The word "duty" may have a stiff and military sound to it. However, the reality is actually bright and encouraging because it instills courage. Duty strengthens the backbone when we are inclined to shrink back from some form of service that is intimidating. Duty lifts our spirits. Duty implies that we are part of something bigger than ourselves. And whenever we adopt a bigger vision, we receive bigger enablement to carry it out. Above all, a sense of duty helps us to serve even when no one is grateful and when the circumstances are not so glorious.

WHOM DO WE SERVE?

Servanthood means that we are doing everything "as unto the Lord." And here's a paradox: If everything is done in submission to the King, we too can reign in power. People tend to think of submission as bowing to oppression. But that is when they are submitting to a tyrannical or controlling ruler. Submission to God, the King of Kings, is not oppressive because His rule is perfect and not subject to human shortcomings. St. Augustine said, "Service is perfect freedom." His quote reflects an intimate knowledge of the Living God who is not an oppressive ruler.

Doing everything as unto God also gives us freedom when we have to serve human "masters" who are difficult, or when we have to perform tasks that we consider to be drudgery. At the very moment someone is behaving toward us in a dictatorial or petty manner, we can remind ourselves that it is not that person but the King of Kings and Lord of Lords we're serving. That understanding lends new meaning to the idea of speaking to the Manager! Not only that, but this positional perspective is the key difference between "enabling" (that kind of codependence that keeps someone else irresponsible, which God is not advocating) and true serving. It is the difference between slavery and freedom.

Eugene Genovese in his book *Roll, Jordan Roll* documents the lives of slaves in the American South in the 1800's.[9] One of the striking things he discovered was the resilience of many in the face of oppression and brutality. Looking deeper at their lifestyle, he found evidence that their deep faith and submission to God not only gave them strength to endure but also put them in a spiritual position that actually trumped their masters' authority. Certainly in their humanity they suffered deeply and didn't sail through life without trouble; moreover many of the slaves were kept down through a regime that portrayed Jesus as "The Great Massa"—a regime that was wrongly justified through distorted use of scripture. But the slaves' reliance on God bolstered many of them beyond human ability. If we are secure in our positional authority in God's Kingdom, earthly authority is no longer an issue; we can obey without chafing and bristling, knowing God sees every injustice and has a bigger plan.

WHY DO WE SERVE?

It is service that brings us into the fullness of God. When we act with purposes nobler than self, the Spirit expands within us, breaks through boundaries, and fills us with God's own life. Service is also like spiritual super-glue. When the context of service is the community of faith, the synergy of serving together becomes one of the adhesives holding that community together. If you were to try to serve all on your own, you would disconnect yourself from the fullness of God. You would also be headed for burnout. God designed us to divinely *empower* us, and it is the purpose of the church to bring glory to God by loving one another in this divine empowerment. If your car runs on gasoline, you won't dare pour iced tea into your gas tank and expect it to run. Yet we ask that of ourselves every day when we try to run on our own steam. God's power working in and through community is our fuel. That said, there is a difference between our cars and our spiritual lives, and that is the price of gas. When we drive our cars, we use up the gas and need to pay to refill our tanks. But in God's Kingdom, when we serve in the context of community and in His power, it creates yet *more* power. Imagine having more gas at the end of a 200-mile trip than you had at the start—that's what I call fullness! Even if we do get to the point where we are totally poured out in service, our "refills" are free for the asking. This is the kind of overflowing lifestyle we saw in the previous chapter when we looked at the people in the book of Acts. It seemed they couldn't get enough serving, their joy was so full.

HOW DO WE SERVE?

Look at this example of Jesus serving in John 13:1-17:

It was just before the Passover Feast. Jesus knew that the time had come for him to leave this world and go to the Father. Having loved his own who were in the world, he now showed them the full extent of his love. ²The evening meal was being served, and the devil had already prompted Judas Iscariot, son of Simon, to betray Jesus. ³Jesus knew that the Father had put all things under his power, and that he had come from God and was returning to God; ⁴so he got up from the meal, took off his outer clothing, and wrapped a towel around his waist. ⁵After that, he poured water into a basin and began to wash his disciples' feet, drying them with the towel that was wrapped around him. ⁶He came to Simon Peter, who said to him, "Lord, are you going to wash my feet?" ⁷Jesus replied, "You do not realize now what I am doing, but later you will understand." ⁸"No," said Peter, "you shall never wash my feet." Jesus answered, "Unless I wash you, you have no part with me." ⁹"Then, Lord," Simon Peter replied, "not just my feet but my hands and my head as well!" ¹⁰Jesus answered, "A person who has had a bath needs only to wash his feet; his whole body is clean. And you are clean, though not every one of you." ¹¹For he knew who was going to betray him, and that was why he said not everyone was clean. ¹²When he had finished washing their feet, he put on his clothes and returned to his place. "Do you understand what I have done for you?" he asked them. ¹³"You call me 'Teacher' and 'Lord,' and rightly so, for that is what I am. ¹⁴Now that I, your Lord and Teacher, have washed your feet, you also should wash one another's feet. ¹⁵I have set you an example that you should do as I have done for you. ¹⁶I tell you the truth, no servant is greater than his master, nor is a messenger greater than the one who sent him. ¹⁷Now that you know these things, you will be blessed if you do them."

This is a mind-blowing scene. Here is Jesus performing a menial task that even the lowest servant wouldn't relish. Yet it didn't detract from His greatness, only enhanced it. Jesus portrayed the greatest security anyone could have in this world: knowing that He came from God and would be returning back to God. When our fulcrum is firm, we can exert leverage. We can operate from the solid point, the unassailable fortress, where we can say, "I'm going to love and serve you regardless of whether you ever love or serve me." We can serve from this Heavenly position, firmly grounded in our identity in Christ. Remember God's guidance through the Apostle Paul in the book of Philippians.

Your attitude should be the same as that of Christ Jesus: Who, being in very nature God, did not consider equality with God something to be grasped, but made himself nothing, taking the very nature of a servant. And being found in appearance as a man, he humbled himself and became obedient to death—even death on a cross!

Therefore God exalted him to the highest place and gave him the name that is above every name, that at the name of Jesus every knee should bow, in heaven and on earth and under the earth, and every tongue confess that Jesus Christ is Lord, to the glory of God the Father. (Philippians 2:5-11)

One woman shares that she was reading these verses in Philippians when God gave her a whole new understanding of them that she'd missed for years. "Most people refer to this passage when they are talking about being obedient and humble, and the picture we get is of a really low position, Jesus being obedient to death and so on," she says. "If we're really honest, we'll admit that we don't *want* to go that low; it sounds kind of scary or martyr-like. But then God drew my attention to the beginning of the verse. What was Jesus' starting point? It was equality with God! He wasn't groveling in obedience; He was freely choosing to go that low. Then God reminded me of all the other passages about our position as Christians: We're seated with Christ in the Heavenly places! He showed me that our starting point, too, is way up there with Him—Wow! Then I remembered the passage from *Hind's Feet on High Places* [Hannah Hurnard's allegory] and the way the waterfall took great joy hurling itself down to the valley where it would be more useful. That whole picture just changed my whole attitude toward serving in one day!"

We see Jesus being exalted after bowing low to serve, and we think, "Oh, that's because He was Jesus." We put a barrier between Him and us when we think like that. In truth, He did what He did as an example and forerunner to us. He's the "first-born among many brothers," and made provision for us to do everything He did by His power. Notice the verse, *Humble yourselves, therefore, under God's mighty hand, that He will lift you up in due time (1 Peter 5:6).* This shows a matching pattern to the passage in Philippians. Our path to greatness is directly intertwined with Jesus' model of servanthood, which is not gloomy but glorious. Reform Jewish scholar Claude Montefiore said that this exaltation of servanthood into the status of greatness was just about the only thing unanticipated by the ethics of the Old Testament.

Invest your life in serving others and your success will turn into significance of the eternal kind. We are commissioned by Jesus to "wash one another's feet" in many different ways. If we recoil from that invitation, thinking it beneath us, we'll miss the awesome opportunity to grow in greatness and fellowship and joy.

EMPOWERED SERVANT

Being an Empowered Servant means you receive a "divine enablement"— God showing up through you by the power of the Holy Spirit. We are called to use not only our original abilities but also our spiritual gifts to build the church. We say "gifts," and there are an abundant variety of gifts, but in actuality there is only one real gift: The Holy Spirit. Imagine the most multi-talented, best educated, most broadly experienced and wisest person you know, at your disposal 24/7 for everything you truly need. Even that person pales in comparison with the Holy Spirit, who is offered to us as a life-gift. It's God giving us Himself as a gift! That personal aspect is important to remember so we don't limit the power of God who can manifest Himself in whatever way He chooses. God can place us in service roles far beyond our comfort zones or normal serving routine.

Here's an example of one man's journey beyond the routine: A gentleman greatly gifted in teaching was on his way home one night when he spotted a car accident. It was a lonely road, and he didn't see anyone else stopping. He couldn't just pass them by. When he pulled over, he found that the accident had involved a young toddler, and the mother was crying hysterically as her baby was unconscious and beginning to turn blue. Once he called 911, this teacher found himself moved beyond his normal emotional range. On the one hand, he'd never felt very confident praying for healing, and usually his prayers were mild requests based on scriptural teaching. Nothing wrong with that, but suddenly those types of prayers seemed anemic in the face of this urgent need. He found himself laying hands on the child and crying out, LIVE! BREATHE in the name of Jesus! *LIVE*!" In his mind, he was thinking he ought to do CPR, yet in his spirit he was being prompted to pray first, like he'd never prayed before. And this prayer was accompanied by weeping, a great outpouring of compassion beyond what our mild-mannered teacher was used to. The toddler woke up. When the ambulance arrived, the EMTs couldn't find anything wrong with the baby. Meanwhile the teacher felt like a mighty river had just rushed through him. "I always believed in healing, but I just thought that my gift was teaching and God would use somebody else with a 'real' gift of healing to do the heavy-duty miraculous stuff," he said. "This one night changed all that. I now know God's power is there waiting to be released to do whatever He wants to do, through whoever is willing. There was nobody else at the scene that night. And His gift of healing wasn't about me, it was for that little baby."

We are carriers of divine power. The flow of that power will depend on our willingness to let it happen and not quench the Spirit (1 Thessalonians 5:19). Thank God that teacher was willing to let God use him in a way that didn't make sense to him at first. As a result, not only was the toddler saved, the teacher was released to a new level of freedom and countless others may receive healing through him as well as the others who were encouraged by his actions.

SOME POWER BASICS

In my experience, people have many questions about the spiritual gifts. I'd like to go over some basics here to provide greater clarity for anyone who might be new to this arena. In short, we're talking about God's power. We use power everyday in our homes, and hardly think about it, until of course there's a storm and the power goes out. Power can be dangerous if misdirected or used improperly, but most of us don't consider that reason enough to refuse the help that power offers us. The same is true of supernatural power. It can be misused, but if we understand God's plans and protocols for its use, we will find we won't want to live without it. I've spoken about God equipping each of us for our specific callings in life; He also chooses to equip every believer to move in the fullness of His spiritual gifts in general.

SO...WHAT IS A SPIRITUAL GIFT?

A spiritual gift is a distinctive ability given by the Holy Spirit to every Christian according to God's grace and design for the purpose of building up the Body of Christ and revealing God's heart to those who haven't yet encountered Him. It is a God-given, supernatural capacity enabling you to do an effective ministry.

WHAT DO THE SCRIPTURES SAY ABOUT SPIRITUAL GIFTS?

You will find not only lists of various gifts in *Romans 12:3-8* and *1 Corinthians 12:1-31*, but you'll also find a balanced framework for understanding how the gifts (and each of us) are to work together. See also *Romans 12:9-21* and *1 Corinthians 13 and 14*. If we remember the way a physical body functions, each part distinct yet also relating to the other parts, we'll have a better grasp on the way the Body of Christ functions: full of variety yet designed to move in harmony. *Ephesians 4:7-16* gives an excellent description of this body-part design, and *1 Peter 4:7-11* offers another emphasis on the importance of our right attitude of love in all we do. I strongly encourage you to mull over all these passages if you haven't already.

The three-chapter stretch in 1st Corinthians is worth examining not only close-up but also from a larger perspective. Chapter 13, commonly known as *"the love chapter,"* is located smack in the middle of the two other passages on spiritual gifts. That placement is no accident and serves to emphasize God's main desire. If spiritual gifts are divine enablements, then they are expressions of God's love in its various forms. Where there is no love involved, then no matter how august the moment or superlative the achievement, it's our own performance, not a wonderful move of God through us. This chapter makes clear that though service is the key to greatness, service without love is not much more than noise. Walking in love, being filled with God's love, *becoming love*, will keep us in the "sweet spot" of walking in God's will.

HOW MANY SPIRITUAL GIFTS ARE THERE?

The primary Scripture passages list 20 gifts and there is Biblical support for at least 12 others. Here is the list that I use in my coaching of others, and which I teach in the Omega Course: Prophecy, Knowledge, Hospitality, Stewardship, Faith, Missionary, Teaching, Healing, Intercession, Miracles, Craftsmanship, Exhortation/Disciple Maker, Giving Discernment, Music/Worship Leader, Leadership, Helps/Service, Creative Communication, Apostleship, Pastor/Shepherd, Mercy/Compassion, Wisdom, Tongues, Interpretation of Tongues, Evangelist, Deliverance, Administration, Martyrdom, Celibacy, Voluntary Poverty, Encouragement, and Community Builder.

How Hungry are You?

 Further explanation of these gifts and a spiritual gifts inventory test can be found at www.lifespringnetwork.org.

WHAT IS THE DIFFERENCE BETWEEN SPIRITUAL GIFTS AND ORIGINAL (NATURAL) ABILITIES?

The Holy Spirit is the one who helps us make a lasting spiritual impact. Eternal impact is one of the main differences between the natural and the supernatural. Even the word "temporal," referring to the things of this earth, gives us a clue and sounds more *temporary* than "eternal."

Think of the natural realm for a moment: We tend to be impressed by good speakers, the person up in front of the congregation who is holding everyone spellbound. The spiritual difference, however, could be going on in the prayer room downstairs in the basement, where the more hidden members of the congregation are calling Heaven down to Earth and praying for that speaker to have the guidance and power of God. The speaker may be naturally gifted, and that's fine. But those intercessors may make the difference between "That was a really good sermon" and "Lord, change me—I need your help!" A response like that will transform a life, and a life transformed means lasting impact.

Another difference: The gifts of the Spirit also provide the most dramatic evidence that all things are possible for those who believe. There are some things that cannot be explained with reference to natural abilities alone. Astonishing things! The fact that some people have tried to manufacture or manipulate miraculous healings or revelations doesn't detract from the existence of God's very real Holy Spirit power; that only confirms it, for where there is a real, there is a counterfeit. I've witnessed truly miraculous healings; I've heard words of prophecy spoken into the lives of others regarding matters that they couldn't have known about in the natural realm. There is no way to read the Gospel without seeing that it is filled with signs and wonders done by the disciples in the early Church. Those disciples were amazed that they were able to do the same things that Jesus did, for they were all "regular" people like us. No naturalistic factors can account for these things.

DIVINE DOWNLOAD

God gives all of us original (natural) abilities when we are born.

In our journey as Christians, these abilities do play an important role and I believe God delights in them. Yet another way God uses these abilities is through contrast. For example, one musician I know was trained as a drummer. He played the drums for years, but then one day someone in a band needed a person on the keyboard. He had never played the keyboard, but when he sat down, he was able to play it as though he'd had many years of lessons. Dumbfounded, he knew it had to be God. He laughs to tell me that now he's in a band with other musicians who had the same thing happen; his drummer never had lessons on the drums, but was trained on the keyboard. It makes us wonder if maybe God is having some fun with this! Certainly He wants us to give Him the glory for those wonderful downloads of supernatural ability from Heaven, but I think He might also be enjoying His own creative ways of helping us take ourselves more lightly.

GOD THE SURFER

Another way He might use our abilities is by "surfing" on them. This term was coined by commentators to describe the way God can surfboard on our natural abilities with His supernatural abilities. For example, the Apostle Paul's profession as a tentmaker lends itself very well to the spiritual role he had as a builder of the Church. So too with Peter being a fisherman and later a "fisher of men," captivating the large audience with his story of Jesus on the day of Pentecost. If God wired me as a coach, for example, He has also taken me beyond the natural realm and "surfed" on my personality as He's used me to exhort people in their spiritual growth. I couldn't do any of this without His supernatural aid, any more than I could have given that talk to those 900 students by myself that night at Willow Creek.

WHAT IS THE DIFFERENCE BETWEEN SPIRITUAL GIFTS AND THE FRUIT OF THE SPIRIT?

The fruit of the Spirit, like natural fruit, takes abiding and cultivation. By contrast the gifts are just that—gifts! (All the more reason for us not to boast when we see them in our lives.) The fruit of the Spirit does not necessarily emanate in the form of signs and wonders, but they are true evidence of the Holy Spirit living in and through us.

> **Whereas Spiritual Gifts describe what the Holy Spirit does in and through our lives to serve others and build up the Church, the Fruit of the Spirit describes how the Holy Spirit serves the world through us.**

The fruit of the Spirit—*love, joy, peace, patience, kindness, goodness, faithfulness, gentleness, and self-control (see Galatians 5:22-23)*—are qualities that need to be nurtured through spiritual disciplines that help us abide and grow in Christ. These qualities can and should be exhibited by every Christian in the ordinary course of life and in every situation possible. The fruit proves that a person is indeed abiding in Christ, for a branch that has been broken off will not bear fruit. Like the seed Jesus spoke of when describing the Kingdom, fruit grows organically and becomes the visible manifestation of God's Kingdom within us. Spiritual fruit is the universal expression of *how* God does what He does through us.

If you look at the passage in Galatians, you will see that LOVE is at the top of the list; you may remember that in 1 Corinthians it is highlighted as being greatest of all. And again the emphasis on love shows us what kind of relational character needs to be developed in us. Without that love and strength of character, the gifts of the Spirit come across like a lot of noise. With them, we are strong vessels for God's power and will not break under pressure.

It is ironic that many people gravitate to what *appears* to be more powerful and dazzling, and focus on the gifts more than the fruit. But God gives both for a reason and intends for us to live in proper balance. The fruit also packs a powerful punch in the long run. This is not to say that we should disregard the gifts. Far from it! But just as signs and wonders point to the reality of God's existence, the fruit too will let people know you're the real deal. *"Thus by their fruit you will recognize them,"* Jesus says in Matthew 7:20. There are imitations of signs and wonders everywhere we look; there are also imitations of the fruit. You may have met people who have the appearance of being joyful, kind or loving but underneath they are not genuine. Either way, the fact remains that no one can imitate a transformed life. You cannot force fruit to appear, nor can you force truly spiritual qualities to show up in your life. You might be extremely enduring, engage in great efforts and even flow in all kinds of spiritual gifts, but the addition of the fruit of the Spirit will add that sweet aftertaste and make for lasting impact in people's lives. Similarly, there is no shortcut past the abiding in Christ that needs to happen for this fruit to grow.

Ω

You may want to ask yourself questions like these: *Am I striving, or abiding and allowing God to develop the character of Christ in me? In what ways has God used me, and what gifts have I seen manifested in my life? When I have served, has it been unto God, or have I felt oppressed and grumbled under authority? What kind of fruit is showing up in my life?*

CALLING MENTEE/MENTOR AND PROFESSIONAL

The final two roles are Calling Mentee/Mentor and working in a profession and functioning in Professional roles. These two roles are fairly self-explanatory. They need to be categorized individually based on the different roles each of us play in our professions. Many of us will spend the bulk of our waking lives working in professional roles to earn resources to live on and support our families financially. I highlight the role of Calling Mentee/Mentor to distinguish it from the personal and relational Mentor/Mentee that we discussed previously in the Chapter Six; we all have different kinds of mentors that can help us grow and process our lives. In the case of the Calling Mentee/Mentor, these are people who help us process and grow in the "doing" side of our lives. Usually they are people who are more experienced than we are but perform similar tasks, and we can therefore learn from their modeling and instruction. This is true in every role within the calling category from being Ministers of Compassion, Stewards of Resources, Empowered Servant, Calling Mentee/Mentor or Professional. In all of these roles we can and should be mentored into deeper levels of excellence and godliness.

SERVICE IS LOVE MADE VISIBLE

What about those who don't enter into serving but allow those around them to do it all? How do we treat them? We're told to disassociate ourselves from people who claim to be Christians but do not focus their lives in that way. We are also to warn those brothers and sisters in Christ that they are drifting from life to death again, and then hold one another accountable to honoring our commitment to love and serve:

> In the name of the Lord Jesus Christ, we command you, brothers, to keep away from every brother who is idle and does not live according to the teaching you received from us. [7]For you yourselves know how you ought to follow our example. We were not idle when we were with you, [8]nor did we eat anyone's food without paying for it. On the contrary, we worked night and day, laboring and toiling so that we would not be a burden to any of you. [9]We did this, not because we do not have the right to such help, but in order to make ourselves a model for you to follow. [10]For even when we were with you, we gave you this rule: "If a man will not work, he shall not eat." [11]We hear that some among you are idle. They are not busy; they are busybodies. [12]Such people we command and urge in the Lord Jesus Christ to settle down and earn the bread they eat. [13]And as for you, brothers, never tire of doing what is right. [14]If anyone does not obey our instruction in this letter, take special note of him. Do not associate with him, in order that he may feel ashamed. [15]Yet do not regard him as an enemy, but warn him as a brother. (2 Thessalonians 3:6-15)

Think about what speaks to people's hearts as they observe Christianity in action: Do you think some people would be questioning the viability of the faith as they see behavior that is slothful? We've already pointed out the issue of drivenness and workaholism in our culture, involving so much focus on work that relationships are neglected. That is one kind of sloth in that we are not investing our time according to God's mission and priorities for our lives. (We will discuss more about sloth in later chapters.) But here is a different and equally damaging problem, that of refusing to work or become accountable. This is a more obvious form of sloth. There may be underlying reasons for a person's stagnation of this sort; all the more reason to engage in mentoring and grow stronger in your own ability to discern, warn, exhort and encourage as the Lord leads. The Scripture makes clear that you are not responsible *for* the one who will not work, but you may be responsible *to* him. Your response and conscientious refraining from bailing them out may be the very thing that helps them turn around. Furthermore it's possible that as you engage in mentoring, both guiding others and learning from those who are wiser than you are, you may be helping to prevent the downward spiral described in the above passage, whether it's your own or someone else's.

As to those who are not able to produce financially due to disabilities or poor health, it is part of the training of God that we take care of them. Amazingly enough, as we serve those who are in need, God ends up serving us through them. If any of you are handicapped, disabled or in poor health, do not think God can't use you! It has been my experience that people with these challenges can be some of the most powerful instruments of God on the planet. Love on them in the power of God, and you will understand what I mean as you see God touch your soul. Service is love made visible. The earliest Christians loved. They took care of those who didn't have the power to care for themselves, and others were drawn to that. "Look how these Christians love one another!" they said.

Have you considered that everything in your life to this point may have been preparation for greatness that still remains to be demonstrated? Even the most difficult and seemingly unnecessary hardships or seemingly trivial inconveniences can be used by God as training for the "good works he has prepared for you to walk in." Maybe you regard your life so far as "good enough." Or maybe you are inclined to seek a path that is easier. But I challenge you to embrace the truth that you are called to the Christian greatness of transcendent servanthood.

If you serve the Lord – and others – with gladness, entering into everything you do as an act of service to God with His guidance and in His strength, you are promised an inheritance beyond all that you can ask or imagine.

CLARIFYING GOD'S MISSION FOR YOUR LIFE

As I mentioned in the previous chapter, you need to categorize your professional roles for yourself. I have included the current version of my roles diagram (as of this writing) for you to have an example to look at:

Jason Pankau's Roles Diagram

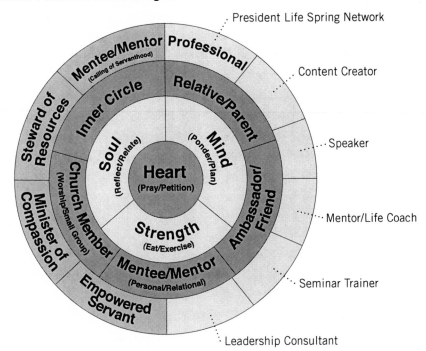

Writing a mission statement helps us define who we are and what want to see happen in our lives. In a sense, it defines the target. By defining each role (identity in Christ) in our lives, we gain a holistic perspective of our new lives in Christ. In these last two chapters as we have gone through each role, we have uncovered another layer in understanding our mission. Now we can more completely write out God's mission statement as:

To CONNECT in real loving relationship, with God through Jesus CHRIST in the power of the Holy Spirit (Heart, Soul, Mind, and Strength), with others in contagious Christian COMMUNITY (Inner Circle, Relative/Parent, Church Member, Mentee/Mentor, and Ambassador/Friend), and with my CALLING of Servanthood in the World (Minister of Compassion, Steward of Resources, Empowered Servant, Calling Mentee/Mentor and in my Profession as:

_____.)

To make your mission statement come alive and to help you better understand what you are striving for in each role, I would recommend that you write vision statements for each identity role. This should be done prayerfully, listening for God's feedback and direction as you ponder each role.

A Vision Statement is a description of your understanding of who you would like to become in each role. It is your expression of what you believe to be ideal and worth aiming for in your life.

Continuing to think through the various components that make up your Mission Statement will help you to live it.

- **Vision:** What does it mean to experience and express love in each area of life? Continue to expand and revise your vision statements for each role of your life.

- **Priorities:** Regularly review how you are investing your life, and discern roles upon which you may be over- and under-focusing. This helps to adjust your decision-making, put areas of your life in proper relationship to one another and invest your time wisely and holistically.

- **Values:** Pray the 7 Values of Abundant Living into your life and ask God to guide the hows and whys of what you do.

- **Identity Roles:** Use the Identity Roles Diagram to organize the various areas of life, set goals and as a framework for pursuing holistic Christlikeness.

How Hungry are You?

 For examples of vision statements and other tools to help you in clarifying God's mission for your life, you can visit our web-site: www.lifespringnetwork.org or take the Omega Course.

SECTION 2

Living Out God's Mission

CHAPTER 9

Are You Ready for the Journey?

LAW 9

The Law of Transformation: *We must choose to submit ourselves to God's mission and His transforming power if we are going to experience more abundance in life.*

With this law you move to the next level in your Life Focus Process. It's time to gain traction! First, let's take a hard look at what it means to make a true commitment to transformation. Now that I've spelled out the details involved in God's mission for our lives, we need to look at how to make that mission come alive for you. That means the journey starts here. You may have already begun to see changes in your life or your perspective if you've dug into several of the questions in previous chapters. If so, I commend your bravery! If not, you can fasten your seat belt now.

DIVINE MAKE-OVER

From what I have seen, the average Christian is used to being educated or inspired through his or her church experience, but is less familiar with the idea of being transformed. Yet transformation is the main salvation journey for all of us. When the Scripture says, *Work out your own salvation with fear and trembling (Philippians 2:12)*, it's talking about the transformation process. The "fear and trembling" is not about wringing your hands wondering if you'll get to Heaven; it's a statement that reflects full understanding of the ongoing leaps of faith you face in order to be healed and transformed. Does God's offer to radically remake you from the inside out excite you? I hope so! It should prove to be even more amazing than any of the make-over ads or TV shows you may have seen out there.

You are being invited to live a life beyond what you've thought of so far. The main condition is that you allow every experience you have to deepen your dependence on God. With each foray into an aspect of your life where He hasn't been allowed in yet, you will experience the discomfort of yielding control, but *then* the influx of His abundant life will so much more than make up for it that you'll be eager to take the next step on the journey. Imagine that you are a mansion with many rooms; you could say that you've invited Jesus into your home, but He hasn't yet been ushered into every room. Transformation is like working with Him to re-design and re-furnish every room, even the nooks and crannies.

Norma Dearing of Christian Healing Ministries gives us another illustration: She asks, **"Where is Jesus in the car of your life?"** She points out that some people may not have asked him into the car yet but are "driving around the block, seeing him standing there on the corner." Others have him "stuffed in the trunk—or maybe the back seat." She says you may even be letting him drive, but you're hitting the imaginary brake pedal while you sit in the passenger seat. As soon as you hear the question, you usually know where He is, and that lets you know where you are in your trust level, too. These pictures may help you understand the process of gradually letting God have more control over your life. Again, because He's good, that kind of submission is a good thing. And because life is not static, it's not just about sitting in the car but also *going* places! You are not to settle for a mere pittance of Eternal Life. Allowing God into every corner of your life will unlock His greater riches to be released to you. We're not to be merely informed or inspired. That's fine, but only to a point. Full transformation involves full renovation.

Did you know that simply "knowing about" God is possibly barking up the wrong tree? The "Tree of the Knowledge of Good and Evil" (found in Genesis chapter 2 and 3) is about human head knowledge and control. Many climb very high on that tree. But is it the right tree? In contrast, the Tree of Life is about relationship—relationship first with God and also with one another. The word "know" presented in Jesus' invitation to know Him refers to intimacy; that kind of knowing is the same as the closeness between husband and wife.

God will hold us accountable for what we know and what we did with our knowledge. If we continue to pile up inspirational experiences and education about the faith but are not engaging God's journey of transformation, we are building a false sense of what it means to be a Christian and possibly even climbing the wrong tree. On the other hand, if we seek the Kingdom, seek relationship with God and pursue opportunities with an eye toward transformation, we will find that it takes place by the renewing of our whole being. Renewal leads to a transformed life, and God will be so delighted to see us accepting His invitation to walk with Him each day.

"Seek first His kingdom and His righteousness, and all these things will be given to you as well." (Matthew 6:33)

This verse is about Kingdom living, not just your ticket to Heaven. Everything else flows from your relationship with the King and your closeness to Him.

AUTHORITY, SUBMISSION AND SQUIRMY SACRIFICES

The central realities of Christian living are embodied in the words *"authority"* and *"submission."* We make the choice of submitting to the Kingdom of God personified in Christ as King. By extension, we submit to the great themes of Scriptural promise, namely *guidance, love,* and *provision* of everything we need for life in Godliness. The great paradox here is that when we do this, God can use our lives to exercise authority over anything at variance with the Kingdom of God within us and around us. In other words, God can *exercise* authority in and through our lives to the degree that we are *under* authority.

In choosing to submit ourselves to God, we are choosing to be like clay on the potter's wheel, and we're saying to God, "I don't know where you're taking me, but wherever it is, I want to go." That's trust. That is when God, the Master Potter, can make us more like Jesus.

Therefore, I urge you, brothers, in view of God's mercy, to offer your bodies as living sacrifices, holy and pleasing to God—this is your spiritual act of worship. Do not conform any longer to the pattern of this world, but be transformed by the renewing of your mind. Then you will be able to test and approve what God's will is—his good, pleasing and perfect will. For by the grace given me I say to every one of you: Do not think of yourself more highly than you ought, but rather think of yourself with sober judgment, in accordance with the measure of faith God has given you. (Romans 12:1-3)

In other words, we can say to God, "I come to you without reservation and submit my life to your guidance; remake me as you see fit." So many people take these verses to mean that we need to somehow fix ourselves up to please God. They see the "sacrifice" part and assume there has to be some kind of cleaning up of their act. But God is inviting us to first offer ourselves to Him AS-IS. He says coming to Him like that, engaging in the act of submission, is holy and pleasing to Him. He *then* helps us to be transformed. Worship is not only about singing praises; it's a whole lifestyle of offering ourselves to God. It is a cooperative effort, not a performance. It is a process. We submit our old desires, feelings, thoughts and actions to God to be remade in His likeness. As long as we keep our lives on the potter's wheel, He can have His way with us…but we have an awful tendency to jump off the wheel and move back into our old habits. This is the wrestling match that rages in our inner beings between wanting our will to be done and wanting God's will to be done. It is important to understand that God is patient with this wrestling process and is used to seeing us jump off the potter's wheel. He knows we'll have a lot of starts and stops along the way. However, He doesn't give up on us. We need to remember that He's the steady one, and we are the ones who wriggle off the potter's wheel.

"God, I don't feel very close to you right now!" a young man prayed.

"Oh?" replied the Lord. "Who moved?"

Anyone with children understands this dynamic. One day you are able to make tremendous progress in training your children how to really live. They seem to be rightly aligned, humble and teachable. Then the next day they're surly, independent, un-teachable…and they see *you* as the one with the problem. Are we not like that with God at times? Through it all, He is constant. Here's a stanza from a hymn that says it well:

Oh to Grace how great a debtor daily I'm constrained to be!
Let Thy goodness like a fetter bind my wandering heart to Thee.
Prone to wander, Lord I feel it; prone to leave the God I love—
Here's my heart, Lord, take and seal it; seal it for Thy courts above.
("Come Thou Fount" lyrics by Sara Groves)

"Prone to wander" indeed. Not only do we get squirmy in our human nature, but we also have an evil adversary to deal with who wants nothing more than to see us cut off from God. We'll look at this issue in more detail when we come to the Law of Reality, but suffice it to say now that the more you submit that human nature to God, the less the enemy has of you to devour.

Putting our lives on the altar of God is a revealing experience. It is like looking in a huge mirror, and a true one at that. God's thoroughly objective judgment shines into our lives so we can begin to see the real us. For some, the idea of surrendering like this and letting God see all is a fearful thing. They may find this a stumbling block and not want to open up in this way. As if we could hide! What is ironic about this hesitancy is that God sees all anyway and still He loves us. Our earthly fathers may have been imperfect, but God is a loving Heavenly Father who can be trusted and need not be feared. He wants to transform His creation (you!) into true greatness.

BETTER THAT WE DON'T KNOW IT ALL

Years ago, when I first began putting these concepts together and submitted them to a few theologians, a couple of them said, "Why do you put making a commitment to transformation so early in the process here? Why not clarify what people have to know before asking them to commit?" That may sound logical and natural, but if God revealed to us everything that needed to be changed, we would shrink from it. We are in for a life of constant reformation until we die; just when we think that there can't be anything else, God brings something into our lives that requires us to hit a new level of dedication. We are therefore better off committing first and then letting Him decide the areas in which He wants us to grow.

In an article entitled, "No Room At the Inn," Lisa Leach describes a family jaunt to pick out a Christmas tree. They had a small house at the time, so she and her children searched the fields for a small enough tree. Once they'd found one and brought it home, the tree seemed to have doubled in size. "It had looked so cute and manageable out there in the snowy field, the sky beyond it so big and expansive, just like our hearts felt. Just like those moments in life when you spread your arms wide and shout, *'Lord, make me into the person you want me to be!'*

"But then, back home, we had to rearrange all the furniture to fit the tree in the living room." In other words, what followed was the installation *process.* "There I was lying on the floor with pine needles down my neck, trying to screw the holders into the trunk before the tree tipped over. My fingers were covered in pine sap."

"'Mommy, is it Christmas?' my five-year-old said to me as I lay there sweating under the needles. *Oh yeah.* In that instant it hit me: *This is why we're doing this."* We never know, in that expansive, glorious moment in the field, how much stickiness or space-challenge we'll be facing later in the living room. But it's just as well. We invite Jesus in, and then down the road we can expect to "rearrange the furniture" to make more room for His presence in our lives.

By committing to transformation before God reveals to us all that needs transforming, we put Him in the position of leader and transformer of our lives rather than deciding on our own how we would like God to help. The whole point is trust. We don't "commit" based on knowledge of the journey but based to God's character. It's *Who*, not what. Remember your first love? When you really love someone, you don't mind much where you are as long as you are *with them.* That is what commitment to the journey with God can be like. **Maturity along this journey could be described as becoming more and more comfortable not knowing where you are going, hence, more and more responsive to the guidance and power of God.**

But whenever anyone turns to the Lord, the veil is taken away. Now the Lord is the Spirit, and where the Spirit of the Lord is, there is freedom. And we, who with unveiled faces all reflect the Lord's glory, are being transformed into his likeness with ever-increasing glory, which comes from the Lord, who is the Spirit. (2 Corinthians 3:16-18)

Again: it's a process, going from glory to glory. If we go along with the mundane flow, we have no hope of closing the gap between our current experience and God's vision of perfection for every aspect of our lives—marriage, friendships, parenting, talents, finances, work, and so on. But in closing the gap we escape the false freedoms that characterize our everyday whims and self-centered desires. We rise into the true freedom of the Spirit of the Lord. The poet T.S. Eliot, who spoke so trenchantly of modern emptiness in "The Wasteland," commented that most people imagine they are becoming free when in fact they are only becoming unbuttoned. The mass media is quite capable of filling our imaginations with attractive people enjoying various forms of false freedom, while a glance at page one of a supermarket tabloid should be enough to convince us of the miseries that come as a consequence of these false freedoms in the lives of those very same attractive people.

THE ROAD OF LIFE

As the journey of transformation is so important to understand, I have used a diagram called the Road of Life to give people a better sense of life from God's perspective. It is designed to help us all understand what God has done and provided for us so we can be transformed and live the abundant life. I'll show you this picture one piece at a time so we can all understand what is being offered to us by God.

"Enter through the narrow gate. For wide is the gate and broad is the road that leads to destruction, and many enter through it. But small is the gate and narrow the road that leads to life, and only a few find it."
(Matthew 7: 13-14)

The Wide Road to Destruction

First, we are all on a journey and we all have decisions to make along that journey. The road of life is difficult because we have an enemy who tries to distract us from finding the abundant, balanced, Spirit-led life for which we were created. The wide road reflects the world's system that ultimately leads to destruction. In this graphic the enemy is depicted as serpents lining the road leading us down the path to destruction.

For our struggle is not against flesh and blood, but against the rulers, against the authorities, against the powers of this dark world and against the spiritual forces of evil in the heavenly realms. Therefore put on the full armor of God, so that when the day of evil comes, you may be able to stand your ground, and after you have done everything, to stand. (Ephesians 6:12-13)

The Narrow Road to Eternal Life

Before we accept Christ, we are all moving along the path toward destruction. Some are farther along the road than others. Christians are people who have come to the reality that we are the problem and are in need of God's grace to help us find our purpose for living. When we ask Jesus Christ to come into our lives and be our Lord, we die to our old lives, repent (or turn) and begin to follow God. In other words, where in the first drawing we were going down in the same direction as the snakes, our repentance turns us in the opposite direction and we embark on the narrow road that leads to eternal life.

To Eternal Life

The Wide Road
to Destruction

The Turning Point

After we put ourselves on to the potter's wheel of God, we find we
are empowered to wrestle with the reality of evil in the world, meaning
not just the Evil One but our own corrupted nature. As we invite
God to have His way with us, He is faithful in making the "narrow"
life into a cornucopia of promised blessings. The way of the cross, if
we choose it, is the way of grace and hope on which God is walking
with us while working on us. The way is narrow, and we will be
discarding worldly baggage along the way. He relieves us of our
unneeded baggage, helping us to be less encumbered by the things
of this world. The former yearnings of our old destiny fall away
as He flings open the gates of eternity and begins remaking us from
the inside out.

The Role of the Church

On the road to eternal life, there exist off-ramps that we may be tempted to take. These off-ramps may take the form of distractions, burdens, (seeking to keep our own or take on others' baggage) or the influence of the Evil One. The love and nurture of the church can help bring us back to God and strengthen our resolve. The Evil One loves to get us to try to do it all on our own because when we're isolated it's easier to get us to choose an off-ramp. The good news is that God tells us that wherever two or three are gathered in His name, He is there in our midst and through Him we have the power to resist the temptations of the Evil One. The community of faith is the essence of this kind of corporate support. As God uses His Church to mature us, our lives will begin to look more and more like the life of Jesus. If we want to experience transformation, we will need to submit ourselves to the Church and to this process.

CYCLE OF RENEWAL

When mentoring people, I use a paradigm called the Cycle of Renewal to help them better understand how the process of transformation works in the church context. Jim Frost, a church planter with the Fellowship of House Church Planters in Rhode Island and one of my favorite mentors, was the first person to share this cycle with me.

This framework assumes that someone has entered into a covenantal community of faith and is seeking out the abundant life together with other members. Into that environment God begins His Cycle of Renewal, a cycle which will be repeated thousands of times in the lives of fervent followers of Christ who are serious and desire transformation as a way of life. This cycle is based on 2 Timothy 3:16-17.

All Scripture is God-breathed and is useful for teaching, rebuking, correcting and training in righteousness, so that the man of God may be thoroughly equipped for every good work. (2 Timothy 3:16-17)

1. **Revelation** – Revelation from God leads the process.
2. **Reproof (or rebuke)** – Reproof challenges our status quo.
3. **Repentance** – We can either agree with God and turn (repent) or disagree and, in essence, say "No. I don't think you know better. I think I know better." If we don't agree with God, our growth in this area of our lives stalls and is hindered by our disobedience. Sometimes God sends more revelation with higher voltage to get us unstuck or, if we are truly living in covenant community, others within our community of faith will notice something wrong and probe to find out what happened. You've already seen examples of both in the stories of

my life; God in His love has "zapped" me several times. Keep in mind that He may be gentler with you, depending on your personality and how teachable you are. In my case He knew it would take an occasional end-zone tackle! Assuming that we finally choose to agree with God and repent of our sin, then we need to go to the next step and learn how to change.

4. **Correction** – This decision to change is followed by figuring out the appropriate corrections needed. The Biblical term here is actually a medical term for resetting a bone. The belief is that through this process we heal stronger than we were before we "broke the bone" and actually grow in humility through the process. Once we have gotten right with God, it is time to get right with others in our lives who have been affected by our sin and make restitution or amends.

5. **Restitution** – To complete the cycle of renewal in our lives, some of us have to take an action that might be the most uncomfortable thing we have ever done, and that is to set things right with those we've wounded. God commands us in Scripture to confess our sins to one another so we may be healed or transformed. If we are serious about becoming like Jesus, then this becomes a daily process, even an hourly process, depending upon the nature of the problem. We make restitution for our sins by asking for forgiveness from those we have sinned against, asking what we can do to repay the wrong and behaving in accordance with God's new corrective path. The process of being trained in righteousness gets short-circuited if we don't submit ourselves to community and make restitution.

6. **Trained in Righteousness** – As we process the revelation of God in our lives by getting right with Him and others, we become trained in righteousness. This training dovetails with our ongoing healing process. If we find ourselves stuck or unable to progress with our training, it is an indication that a season of healing is necessary in which we would be freed up to engage in the training. After that our training will help us stay firmly established in our healing and walk in it. Without training, we will drift a totally different way: toward selfishness and decline. Once you get a taste of God's training, you'll desire it more and more.

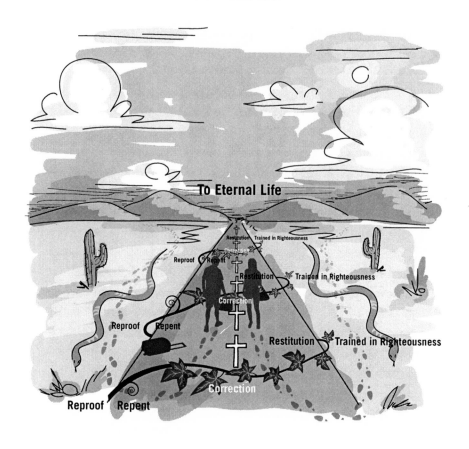

The Cycle of Renewal and the Road of Life

We go through several cycles of renewal as God grows us up in Him. We grow in our ability to experience and express love—this is the marker of our maturity in faith. Note in this picture the nature of a spiral: It does get somewhere, but goes around in a circular motion. How many times have you felt that you weren't "getting anywhere," but faced the same issues over and over? May I suggest to you that it's possible you're making *spiral* progress. That is, you can still see the same issues each time around, but you see them from a different level. One of the enemy's number one tools he tries to use against us is discouragement. Do not allow that discouragement to take hold, but keep looking up. Keep turning to God and He will bring you up higher with each turn. All along the way, it's nothing unusual that your growth process will be opposed by the Evil One and his influence in the world, so you should certainly be prepared for a battle. But it is a battle for which God equips us.

PUT OFF THE OLD NATURE...AND PUT ON THE NEW

In Christ we are new creations *(2 Corinthians 5:17)*. It takes time to learn to walk in this new life in Christ. It is a journey and a process of being trained in righteousness. Repentance is a normal part of life for Christians, not something grim and grief-ridden but liberating and joyful. It is part of the process of God living His life through us abundantly, as He declares, "I am the one transforming you. Depend on me to do it."

Transforming Culture

A group of ministers, regional leaders and state officials were gathered for a meeting to learn from some experts in prayer. They all wanted to discover ways to better influence their region for good. What would be the most effective way to bring transformation to each town? These leaders could plainly see the ills that were afflicting the areas they lived in, and they were ahead of the game in that they did want to see godly change. But it wasn't happening fast enough. They'd prayed, they'd studied and tried some new programs—but those things only seemed to scratch the surface. By the time they were seated in the meeting, most of them knew they were dealing with a higher level of spiritual warfare, and they wanted better weapons with which to fight it.

"What's the most effective thing we can do?" one pastor asked again after an entire day of teaching that had exposed the Enemy's tactics.

"Let God heal and change you personally," the speakers answered without hesitation. "Even the highest level of understanding in spiritual warfare is limited to the level of personal transformation you've allowed God to do in you." You could almost hear an audible groan in that auditorium. On the one hand, this answer is sobering. But then again, it's very encouraging: While our own personal lives are the only currency we have to work with in life and we cannot change another person without being controlling, those personal changes *will* have a powerful ripple effect around us. Others around you may not respond as much to your efforts to change them as they will to God's changes in you. That is how God intends to use you in transforming the culture.

God wants to equip us for a lifetime of discipleship and world-changing. This process must be in-depth, working from the inside out, with His living word that is infused into our innermost being. Many people may accept Christ, but for most of them the journey ends right there and they fail to engage God's training in righteousness. That is only a piece of the Gospel. God's intention is that the moment of accepting Christ not be the end of the journey but the *beginning*. Once a child is born, we don't leave that child to fend for him or herself! We don't consider our job done, not by a long shot. No, we nurture and raise that child into adulthood. How much more would that be true of the spiritual birth? God has no intention of leaving us to do it ourselves once we enter the Kingdom. His marvelous plan is for us to grow into such freedom of relationship with Him, such wisdom and love and power that we will be able to co-labor with Him and be a part of His world-changing work.

$$\Omega$$

Would you like to be part of the transformation of the culture around you? Are you willing to let Him change you? In what areas of your life do you sense the Lord wanting to do some rearranging? If you aren't sure, maybe you can start by asking Him to show you. Then perhaps you could invite Him into those rooms.

CHAPTER 10

Got Attitude?

LAW 10

The Law of Attitude: *Choosing godly attitudes brings focus to the journey of transformation and prepares us to experience and express love abundantly in any situation.*

STUCK WITH A HARD LIFE

A beleaguered young mother of a special-needs child stood in a line at church, waiting for prayer for herself and her son. It seemed that everyone was getting attention but her. (I'll call her Tess.) *Isn't this the way it always is*, she thought with a sigh. No stranger to being overlooked and overworked, Tess had grown up with alcoholic parents who either ignored or insulted her. Early on, she'd decided to take care of herself...and her younger siblings too.

After what seemed like another 20 minutes, a team came along and offered to pray for Tess and her son. They asked if it would be okay to lay hands on them, and she said yes. In a little while one of them spoke. "I sense God wants you to know He loves you so much; I also sense He's longing for you to let Him help you more. Disappointments have gotten in the way and it's like your heart feels closed off; it's been shutting out the help you long for. Does that make sense to you?"

185

Tess felt her face grow warm, and she wanted to cry, but she didn't. She gave a small nod of her head, thinking, *If He loves me so much, he'll heal my son.* A little more prayer followed, then they finished. Tess and her son left. She tried to feel glad that they'd gotten prayer, but for some reason she felt lonelier than ever, and a little angry. She'd been hoping for a miracle. Tess knew God could heal her son—or at least open the doors to bring in the practical help she needed. *Why can't He just do that?* she wondered. *Is that too much to ask?* The anger rose up fresh as Tess began driving home. She was exhausted from doing all the care-giving herself. Her husband drank, her neighbors shunned her. Was *that* her fault too? What was *wrong* with her? Every time she got prayer, it seemed it was *her* fault she had all these problems…and she felt so ashamed.

At this point in the story, let's pause to look at what Tess was told. Did they say it was her fault? No. But somehow she felt that way. Granted, at times prayer ministry can be quasi-abusive in that prayer ministers may overstep their bounds by dishing out well-meaning advice or judgmental remarks, or they might pray in a way that is not filled with God's love. But in this instance, it seems that the word to Tess was a fairly clear expression of God's longing to help her, and an acknowledgment of the disappointments she felt. Why didn't Tess feel encouraged? And why did she feel like all those problems were her "fault?" The answers are complex and have to do with healing on many levels. But this story gives us a strong example of how attitudes are formed and affect our lives.

GETTING UNSTUCK

Have you ever tried to help someone else see how much better his or her life could be? Sometimes it might feel like trying to describe yellow to a blind person. Where do you start? In my mentoring experience, I've noticed that an important way to start is by examining a person's attitudes. Not everyone likes the idea that they might need an "attitude adjustment." But if you recall from Chapter Four, our attitudes affect how we see, and how we see affects everything we do. So if this attitude examination looks challenging to you, hang in there—it's going to be worth it!

When you look at ads and motivational literature, you'll see that the writers know about attitude. They know that attitude is key, and they try to play it to their advantage. They even emphasize the attractiveness of "sporting a 'tude" as though it's desirable to be set in our ways. Unfortunately, they're often promoting bondage, not freedom.

An attitude is an advance decision about how we are going to desire, feel, think, and act (heart, soul, mind, and strength) in any given situation. We all develop attitudes that help to focus our lives and prepare us to experience life. Our parents and significant authority figures have trained us to value certain *desires, feelings, thoughts,* or *behaviors* in given circumstances. In addition to the modeling of these authority figures, our life experience can also have a dramatic shaping effect on our attitudes. Traumatic events in our lives can harden us against ever trusting or serving others again. Failures can harden us to ever risking again. You get the idea. Once the attitudinal decision has been made consciously, it acts as an internal (or subconscious) stabilizer amid the storms of life and every outside pressure. It becomes a survival mechanism. In the case of Tess, her childhood experiences led her to survive by taking care of herself and everyone else too. A noble thing in many respects, and it may have helped her rise above. But along with the coping skills came several underlying beliefs:

"Nobody is going to take care of me, so I have to do it myself."
"I'm not important, or God would have noticed me by now."
"There must be something wrong with me that my life is such a mess."
"I've done all I can do, I'm tired of it always being my fault."

This list goes on. Notice that these beliefs are what underlie the attitudes. For example, the attitude that would accompany the first belief, *"Nobody is going to take care of me, so I have to do it myself,"* might be lack of trust in people as well as in God, keeping a distance socially and even resisting others' attempts to help, etc. Notice too that the attitude tends to reinforce the belief. It's usually easier to see someone else's underlying beliefs and their resulting attitudes than our own.

When it comes to our own lives, we tend to think we need to hold on tightly to a certain belief system, for we associate it with our survival and success. It's all we know up to that point. But in actuality, only godly attitudes truly stand up to the storms of life and outside pressures. God's Word states it plainly over and over:

Do not put your trust in princes, in mortal men, who cannot save. When their spirit departs, they return to the ground; on that very day their plans come to nothing. Blessed is he whose help is the God of Jacob, whose hope is in the Lord his God, the Maker of heaven and earth, the sea, and everything in them—the Lord, who remains faithful forever. (Psalm 146:3-6)

It is truly ironic that the attitudes people adopt to try to protect themselves and their freedoms are often the very things that harden them, hamper their freedom and leave them open to greater harm. But left up to our own devices, we will revert to what is most comfortable and familiar. Proverbs 26:11 states it like this: "As a dog returns to its vomit, so a fool repeats his folly." If we're looking for liberty, stability and the only sure protection in life, God is it. Fortunately, we have a choice. In the case of those who have been deeply wounded in life, they may feel so paralyzed that the freedom of choice may be much harder to discern and exercise. It may be buried under layers of oppression. They would need someone who is willing to pray for them and love them back to health to the point where they can begin to make godly choices on their own.

THE POWER OF ATTITUDE

The key to understanding the power of attitude is recognizing that through our choice of attitudes, we can set our lives on a trajectory in which we either thrive in our walk with God or hinder our own progress by locking ourselves into certain patterns. As the power of attitude cannot be understated, it is important we base the attitudes of our lives on a sure foundation. God would have us base our attitudes on His promises. When we do that, we put ourselves in a position to live according to His blessings, not our limitations. The story of the loaves and fishes is a great picture of the contrast between these two different attitudes or approaches to life.

Picture the scene with me: There's Jesus and his disciples after a looooong day of ministry to thousands of people. (The Scriptures list 5,000, but that was only the men. Very likely it was 10,000 or more when you consider the women and children present.) Everyone is tired and hungry, probably hot and thirsty as well. What would you do if Jesus told you to feed all those people? "But Lord!" I can just imagine them protesting. According to the Gospel of Mark, they were flabbergasted: *"That would take eight months of a man's wages! Are we to go and spend that much on bread and give it to them to eat?" (Mark 6:37)* Some of you might have also said to Jesus, "Are you *crazy*?" But Jesus was unperturbed. He collected the small offerings they had on hand—five loaves and two fish—gave thanks, broke them into pieces, and directed the disciples to serve the people. The supernatural multiplication of what little they had fed that crowd of thousands with plenty more leftover.

But look at what happens later in that same Gospel account: Immediately after witnessing that miracle, the disciples were in a boat on the Sea of Galilee when a storm came up. They grew terrified, and Jesus had to remind them not to be afraid before he caused the wind to die down. The Scripture adds, *They were completely amazed, for they didn't remember about the loaves, their hearts were hardened (Mark 6:51-52).* My question to you is, what did the loaves have to do with the storm? ATTITUDE. Their set of beliefs and expectations led to attitudes and hardened hearts that couldn't see the possibilities of God. All they saw was grocery shopping and possibly drowning in the storm. They saw no Heavenly multiplication, no power or dominion over the weather, no miraculous potential in their circumstances, because their attitudes were based on human experience, not godly perspective. This point is crucial for us to understand in our day. The world is at unrest; we face not only an increase in storms, unusual weather of greater intensity, but also political, religious and economic storms. Our attitudes will make or break us in such times.

CAN WE REALLY CHANGE?

You might feel as though you can't change your attitudes, especially if they've been there for many years. But I am here as living proof that with God, you can change. He's given us all the freedom to let go of old thinking and declare truth over our lives instead. The famous psychoanalyst Viktor Frankl said, "A human being is a deciding being." He also said, "Everything can be taken from a man or women but one thing: The last of human freedoms is to choose one's attitude in any given set of circumstances, to choose one's own way."[10]

In this chapter I'm going to lead you through some rigorous attitude-choosing workout sessions. The main things you'll be exercising are your freedom to choose...and your tongue. The tongue is a powerful tool, as we'll see in greater detail later in James chapter one. The power available to us as we align our mouths with God's truth is astounding. It's one reason we are to *speak to one another with psalms, hymns and spiritual songs,* singing and making music in our hearts to the Lord *(Ephesians 5:19).* It's not just about having a good time singing, or even only about giving God glory, though that's certainly central and great. We are encouraged to sing because God knows we'll then be aligned with Him and built up by declaring the truth. The old hymns are full of this truth proclaimed. **Therefore as you choose new godly attitudes, I would encourage you to declare them *out loud.* Something happens to your faith and your whole being when you do that. It's like the rest of you is indeed obeying what you are saying and adjusting your new life course, just as a ship is steered by the rudder.**

THE ATTITUDE OF JESUS: OUR STARTING POINT

As a man, Jesus chose attitudes for His life that brought focus to His journey and prepared Him to experience and express love in every situation. In the book of Philippians chapter 2 we are given insight into His attitudes. In examining this and other Scriptures, I found it interesting to see the pattern of the seven values of abundant living reinforced. Let's look at this Scripture together, pausing to align the insights with the seven values of abundant living and expand their meaning so we can apply these insights to our lives.

Philippians 2:1-11

*If you have any encouragement from being united with Christ,
if any comfort from his love, if any fellowship with the Spirit, if any
tenderness and compassion, ²then make my joy complete by being
like-minded, having the same love, being one in spirit and purpose.*

Grace – Here you can see Paul mining down deep to touch even
the hardened among us. We need to be reminded often of the grace
that unites us with Christ at the cross, the comfort that we receive from
His love and the empowering fellowship of the Spirit. We also need
to be spurred on to respond to that great gift. Paul begins to instruct
our attitude in this passage and challenges us to live as ambassadors
of grace.

*³Do nothing out of selfish ambition or vain conceit, but in humility
consider others better than yourselves.*

Group –A person with an attitude that honors other members
of his community purposes his life to serve them and care for them.
When we all put the needs of the group above our own needs, we
won't be able to out-give the group! We will experience God loving
others through us and God loving us through others. If we don't, we
won't, and the community will begin to erode.

*⁴Each of you should look not only to your own interests, but also
to the interests of others.*

Good Stewardship – God's Kingdom community will comprise
those who share the resources God has entrusted to them as there
is need. Looking out for the interests of others and helping them to be
wise overseers of what God has placed under their stewardship is a
powerful statement of love and togetherness. In this sense, we are our
brothers' and sisters' keepers.

*⁵Your attitude should be the same as that of Christ Jesus:
⁶Who, being in very nature God, did not consider equality with
God something to be grasped,*

Growth – Here he speaks to Jesus' attitude of growth; though Jesus was fully God, He laid aside His divinity while on earth and lived as a man who would need to be trained in righteousness. Therefore, He applied Himself to His training and depended upon God's guidance and power in everything. When we don't engage God's training in righteousness in our lives, it is as if we are saying that we don't need the training and are therefore equal to God himself. Hmm. To be deceived to the point where we believe we can guide and empower our own lives well is one of the most damaging deceptions of all time. Jesus dealt with this one right away and embarked on what was necessary to live the abundant life as a human man. Jesus is the ultimate example of Growth.

⁷but made himself nothing, taking the very nature of a servant, being made in human likeness

Gifts – To continue from our discussion on Growth: Here we see Jesus' attitude toward empowerment. He understood that as a man the only way God's purposes can be fulfilled through His life is through the power of the Holy Spirit. Therefore, He took the very nature of a servant who is commissioned and empowered by His master to serve. It is only when we understand that we can do nothing without God's power in our lives (John 15:5) that we submit ourselves fully to the power of the Holy Spirit. It is only then that He can live and love through us.

⁸And being found in appearance as a man, he humbled himself and became obedient to death—even death on a cross!

Guidance – Jesus' attitude toward guidance was complete obedience. He trusted His Father in Heaven so much that He was willing to follow wherever He was guided, even to the cross. It is interesting to note that Jesus humbled Himself and became obedient. You might think, gosh, if anyone wouldn't need to submit, be humbled and obedient, it would be Jesus! Wasn't he humble and perfect enough already? But remember: He came as one of us. We all have the capacity to choose the path of self-help and guide our own lives, and Jesus was tempted as we are. His example makes our path clear: In order to connect with the guidance of God properly, we have to humble ourselves and seek His guidance for our lives.

⁹ Therefore God exalted him to the highest place and gave him
the name that is above every name, ¹⁰that at the name of Jesus every
knee should bow, in heaven and on earth and under the earth,
¹¹and every tongue confess that Jesus Christ is Lord, to the glory
of God the Father.

Glorification – Jesus lived His life for one purpose: to bring glory to His Father in Heaven. Through His perfect life of grace, community, stewardship, training in righteousness, service and obedience, God was glorified and Jesus shared in that glory. It is important to note that His goal was not to be glorified himself, but rather to bring glory to the Father. It is then the response of the Father to share the glory with His Son. As we purpose our lives to bring glory to God, He will reward us in Heaven according to His riches in glory (Ephesians 1:18).

GODLY ATTITUDES ARE BASED ON GOD'S PROMISES

Now let's look deeper into how the seven values of abundant living are based on the promises of God. *You can consider this section to be a second set of "reps" in your spiritual workout. I'm going to encourage you to focus on certain verses that highlight God's promises and then make some personal declarations. (It's time to be BOLD! Look for them in bold alongside the main text.) As you freely choose them and give voice to these declarations, you will literally build faith muscle for your new attitudes.* Remember, attitudes have the power to set your trajectory in life, so choose wisely. Base your attitudes on the promises of God and they will guide you to the abundant life.

GUIDANCE: God promises His guidance to those who submit themselves to His Lordship and follow Him. First remember that God *wants* us to have His guidance. He promises it to those who follow Him. I'd like to offer suggestions about choosing attitudes that will expand your capacity to receive God's guidance. Mull over this Scripture in your mind for a few minutes:

This is what the LORD says— your Redeemer, the Holy One of Israel: "I am the LORD your God, who teaches you what is best for you, who directs you in the way you should go." (Isaiah 48:17)

> **Consider choosing the following godly attitude, repeating it and meditating on it on a regular basis going forward:**
> *I need God's guidance in every aspect of my life and I will live as His follower.*

Focus on that phrase, *"what is best for you."* It points to the unbreakable link between His guidance and our well-being. Everything He commands and everywhere He guides is for our well-being. Where He guides, He provides. When we're in the center of His will, even the most dangerous place is the best place for us to be.

One of the secrets in the "art of hearing God" is stillness. Straining and striving in our own strength will only hinder our ability to hear God. It may seem at first that trusting in Him is a passive experience. Far from it! Trusting or waiting on God is active and takes great intentionality, especially given the noise and distraction all around us. One of the great mystics, Julian of Norwich, said, "Trust mightily" in Him. Trust in God is a brave act of might and vigor!

Trust in the LORD with all your heart and lean not on your own understanding; in all your ways acknowledge him, and he will make your paths straight. (Proverbs 3:5-6)

> **In the area of wisdom choose this godly attitude:**
> *I will always ask God to show me His perspective before choosing a course of action.*

As with guidance, God wants to give us wisdom and will fill us with it as we focus on Jesus and God's truth. *If any of you lacks wisdom, he should ask God, who gives generously to all without finding fault, and it will be given to him. (James 1:5)*

Consider making the following decision and affirming it from time to time: *I believe that God wants to make His guidance available to me, and I will seek His guidance and acknowledge Him as Lord in every situation.*

GROWTH: God promises to train and transform earnest disciples in how to live His righteous life. As we seek to improve and be trained, the great temptation in the quest for godly self-control is to seize the reins of our lives with a great burst of willpower. But we face a paradox in that His control is our control, and it's *letting go* that gives us greater control. God promises to train and transform us. Our task is simply to embrace the training and guidance He is offering —by faith. That is, before we have it in our experience (otherwise it wouldn't take faith!)

Consider choosing the following godly attitude: *I will embrace God's training in righteousness for my life and be-lieve in the God–empowered self-control that I receive each day, and each hour of each day, to obey God and resist temptation.*

Character is a matter of training. We must depend on His promise that He will train us into good character, which produces hope that will not disappoint us. The fruit of the Spirit is self-control, so accept the self-control that He wants to pour into your life. Thank Him for it by faith even if you're not sensing it yet; thank Him for it by sight if you are. Stay in training/follower mode. Resist the temptation to disobey God by refusing or postponing obedience to what He has guided you to do. Don't lose sight of the immense opportunities opening up for you.

Through these he has given us his very great and precious promises, so that through them you may participate in the divine nature and escape the corruption in the world caused by evil desires. (2 Peter 1:4)

> **Where impurity, corrupt impulses or wrong desires are an issue in your life, choose this attitude:** *When I am tempted toward impurity or wrong desires, I will be still before the Lord, flee evil and wait for Him, remembering that I must depend on Him to keep me.*

As we respond to evil in this way, God will wash through us. Be clean! Accept His cleansing as a pathway to His power. Just as each breath has a cleansing effect on the body, the Holy Spirit wants to do that for our souls.

In today's society, the lack of self-control shows up in the form of sin. One list that I like to pray through in order to get an attitude check on where I am at any given moment in time are the seven deadly sins: lust, gluttony, greed, sloth, wrath, envy and pride. These are historically recognized weak spots where the enemy of our souls attacks and tempts us away from God's abundant life. When confronting them, we need to be firmly rooted and grounded in God. We need to renew our minds and train them in the promises. It's through this renewal of our desires, feelings, thoughts and behaviors that God will transform us toward full maturity in Christ.

Ponder the following Scripture:

"Do not let this Book of the Law depart from your mouth; meditate on it day and night, so that you may be careful to do everything written in it. Then you will be prosperous and successful. Have I not commanded you? Be strong and courageous. Do not be terrified; do not be discouraged, for the LORD your God will be with you wherever you go." (Joshua 1:8-9)

> **Consider affirming this attitude:** *I will live as a disciple, striving to become more like Jesus in every area of my life.*

In these verses, God is speaking to Joshua, the leader of a people who were just about to take possession of Canaan. It speaks to our condition as well. The "giants" that the Israelites faced in that land each represent the life issues we work through. Each Canaanite tribe's name (Hittites, Jebusites, Ammonites, Midianites, etc.) is literally translated as a word that corresponds to each of the sin attitudes we need to conquer: fear, greed, oppression, and so on. When the Israelites sought God's strategy for the battles they fought in Canaan, they won. When they didn't, their adversaries beat them. What clearer picture could we have as we seek to deal with our own personal battles? Overcoming takes courage. In choosing an attitude of growth, we become humble and teachable, receive that courage from God, and the previously unconquered areas of our lives can then be transformed.

Just as respiration has a continual cleansing effect on the body, the inspiration of the Holy Spirit has that effect on our entire inner being. He gives us the weapons for warfare against our sin tendencies and the temptation of the Evil One. When your desires, feelings thoughts and behaviors begin to move towards evil, take the offensive. Rise up against them and reengage your training in righteousness! Stay in spiritual condition.

For physical training is of some value, but godliness has value for all things, holding promise for both the present life and the life to come. (1 Timothy 4:8)

GRACE: God promises His forgiveness to those who repent and live as His ambassadors in the world. God alone is Judge, yet He alone is perfect in the surest evidence of love: forgiveness.

"I have swept away your offenses like a cloud, your sins like the morning mist. Return to me, for I have redeemed you." (Isaiah 44:22)

An all-merciful God has particular mercy on those who are humbly repentant and dependent on His grace.

The LORD is close to the brokenhearted and saves those who are crushed in spirit. (Psalm 34:18)

God cares for us like a loving father and can do His best work when we are in a state of humility and recognize our need. As I pointed out earlier in the book, when you are drowning, you need to let yourself be rescued; your attempts to save yourself may not only hinder your own rescue but nearly drown the lifeguard as well. Fortunately God is patient but will not give in.

The Lord is not slow in keeping his promise, as some understand slowness. He is patient with you, not wanting anyone to perish, but everyone to come to repentance. (2 Peter 3:9)

Do you believe in God's goodness and His promise to forgive? Consider choosing an attitude that expresses God's grace: *I will repent continually and confess my sins, receiving the forgiveness and strengthening of God to resist sin in the future.*

When you find yourself caught in a sin, repent immediately, keeping short accounts with God. Accept His forgiveness with thanksgiving. When you have been sinned against, live as a forgiven ambassador of grace and forgive those who sin against you. In doing so, you will be living out the attitude of grace which will help you get over how you feel about being wronged, remembering that you too have been forgiven much. God shows His love by always acting in a manner that blows the minds of most human beings: forgiveness. Remember that forgiveness and reconciliation are not the same thing.

An attitude you might consider is: *I will love and forgive those who sin against me even when my natural feelings aren't consistent with love.*

While we are commanded to forgive others, choosing to trust them is a separate issue. For example, it may not be wise to trust someone who is dangerous or likely to be harmful, but forgiving them is done

198

between us and God first, and usually in many layers. We can recognize God as Judge while also learning to be wise and discerning with regard to trust. As ambassadors of reconciliation, we can take it a step further when it's safe to do so; we can offer those who have sinned against us the opportunity to repent and change their ways in order to restore the trust that was lost. It takes time to build trust back where it has been violated, but we can always forgive another person before God regardless of whether or not they have earned our trust.

Someone with an attitude of grace says: *"I will receive God's grace for my life and live as His ambassador of reconciliation in the world."*

We need to be rooted and grounded in grace. Love in every way possible, directly or indirectly, overtly or in hidden ways. Grace is the supreme attribute of love and it is the paramount experience needed in the life of someone far from God.

GOOD STEWARDSHIP: God promises His provision to those who depend on Him and steward life wisely. First, remember that we don't own anything. Then remember that if we are not careful, the stuff of life can end up owning us.

Keep your lives free from the love of money and be content with what you have, because God has said, "Never will I leave you; never will I forsake you." (Hebrews 13:5)

Repeat this: *I've made a decision to accept the peace Christ gives me and not to allow my heart to be troubled or let it be afraid.*

What godly attitude might be appropriate for this kind of contentment and freedom? Second, He promises His peace of mind about our worldly possessions. Poor stewardship of resources has often been the result of choices made out of fear. God is a fortress, a rock—

something unshakable. Jesus said, *"Peace I leave you" (John 14:27).* The power of a decisive, godly attitude applies here also. Rest on the solid point, which is Christ Himself. He is peace personified, security in any situation.

> *This poor man called, and the LORD heard him; he saved him out of all his troubles. The angel of the LORD encamps around those who fear him, and he delivers them. Taste and see that the LORD is good; blessed is the man who takes refuge in him. Fear the LORD, you his saints, for those who fear him lack nothing. (Psalm 34:6-9)*

Third, we need to live as citizens of the Kingdom of Heaven who trust in the Lord's provision.

> *"So do not worry, saying, 'What shall we eat?' or 'What shall we drink?' or 'What shall we wear?' For the pagans run after all these things, and your heavenly Father knows that you need them. But seek first his Kingdom and his righteousness, and all these things will be given to you as well." (Matthew 6:31-33)*

> **Choose and affirm as often as possible this godly attitude, taking a few minutes right now to reflect on it and its potential application to your present circumstances:** *In any need I have – material or psychological – I will seek the Kingdom of God and his righteousness, trusting in him to provide for me and those I pray for and love.*

As children of the King, we can live knowing that God will make provision for our need even when we can't foresee how. John 16:23 states, *"In that day you will no longer ask me anything. I tell you the truth, my Father will give you whatever you ask in my name."* In my name meaning according to God's will for us.

GLORIFICATION: God glorifies himself through reverent worshippers who serve His purposes. Worship is about our whole lives. As we purpose ourselves to glorify Him, we should expect Him to use our lives to manifest His greatness. Believe that you have received the seed of greatness from God that only He can bring to bloom in the world for His glory. In addition, take some action such as engaging in His training in righteousness so that you will be prepared to act when He calls.

"I tell you the truth, anyone who has faith in me will do what I have been doing. He will do even greater things than these, because I am going to the Father. And I will do whatever you ask in my name, so that the Son may bring glory to the Father. You may ask me for anything in my name, and I will do it." (John 14:12-14)

Commit to this: *I will glorify God with my life and draw on His faith within me in every situation that challenges me.*

You may have heard "glory stories." Glory is often linked to hardship, whether on the playing field or the battlefield. God allows conflict and challenge for His own good purposes, and that will always be the case. Yes, life is a struggle. Nevertheless, it is one of the clearest themes in the Bible that God will fight for us. Take heart, Christ has overcome the world, and we can enter continually into His already-completed victories. It is through the cross that we became true children of God with whom He's chosen to share in His glory.

Now if we are children, then we are heirs—heirs of God and co-heirs with Christ, if indeed we share in his sufferings in order that we may also share in his glory. (Romans 8:17)

Even in the worst of circumstances, we can follow the example of St. Paul who made the choice to rejoice even while in the jail in Philippi. Joy comes into our lives when we know that we are on mission with God. Again, this is despite our circumstances. We may be called into situations where we'll be treated poorly. But because God guides and empowers us to love, we are able to have joy like Stephen did at his stoning. His face shone like the face of an angel because he was being guided and empowered by God in everything he said and did. Even though he was brutally treated, God received a lot of glory that day because of Stephen's response (Acts 6, 7). If we share in His sufferings, we will also share in His glory and experience the most exalted form of joy.

> **Make this affirmation for a full day:** *I will obediently submit to God's guidance and power in all circumstances and live with joy as more than a conqueror so that I might experience and express the Glory of God in my life.*

The grandeur of creation is the most visibly dramatic form of His glory, as it exhibits His limitless power. In our everyday life we tend to live so far beneath our potential that we miss this constant display of His glory and power. But you can make a decision to change that, and the glory of creation will teach you of God's glorious ways.

When I consider your heavens, the work of your fingers, the moon and the stars, which you have set in place, what is man that you are mindful of him, the son of man that you care for him? You made him a little lower than the heavenly beings and crowned him with glory and honor. (Psalm 3:3-6)

> **Consider these attitude decisions:** *All I have and all that I am exists for God's glory. If any greatness comes through my life and blesses others, it is God who does it, and I will direct all praise to Him for it. I have decided to live as a worshipper and glorify God in every aspect of my life.*

There is no limit to what God can do in our everyday lives. All things are possible to us as believers. Expect manifestations of God's power through your life when you are submitted and aligned with His purposes. Blow the doors off what you think is possible and submit to letting God love others through you in whatever way He sees fit.

GIFTS: God promises His empowerment and protection to those who submit to Him and serve through His strength. We can live every day as empowered servants, allowing God to express His love through us. The call of God is both general and specific. The general call is to be a servant expressing the love of God. Your specific call is a matter that you must ponder and pray about with the One who created you. Your specific calling will be a challenge, whether publicly visible or not, and you will not be able to fulfill it in your own power. Your need to depend on the power of God will be obvious to you.

> **A godly attitude for gifts would be the following: *Because God has called and equipped me to serve others, I will serve faithfully in His strength.***

Focus on the idea that God is enough for you. No matter what the situation, He is your perfection, everything you need, an inexhaustible storehouse of all that is best for you. This becomes your sure defense against sin, which is usually brought about when you are bored, frustrated, or otherwise dissatisfied. It is important to remember, as we noted earlier, that without God we can do nothing—but through Christ all things are possible.

> **You may be led to affirm something like the following: *I believe in and rely on the Holy Spirit, who lives within me, and I will allow Him to express the love of God through me and exercise His power against all temptation and evil.***

Look at what Christ said in *Matthew 17:20*: *He replied, "Because you have so little faith. I tell you the truth, if you have faith as small as a mustard seed, you can say to this mountain, 'Move from here to there' and it will move. Nothing will be impossible for you."* True humility is acknowledging God's power in you. It would actually be arrogant to assert our lowly opinion of ourselves above God's opinion of us, His own creation. It may seem strange at first to say that an attitude of available power is godly, but it is. As you declare his greatness in you,

you'll get better accustomed to the idea.

We should avoid reverting to self-dependence when the going gets rough. The greater the difficulty, the greater should be our dependence. Look at the attitude of David when the Lord delivered him from the hand of all of his enemies:

> *As for God, his way is perfect; the word of the LORD is flawless. He is a shield for all who take refuge in him. For who is God besides the LORD? And who is the Rock except our God? It is God who arms me with strength and makes my way perfect. (2 Samuel 22:31-33)*

An attitude of Gifts says, *"I've made the decision that 'I will trust in him and not be afraid,' (Isaiah 12:2) regardless of circumstances."*

Dependence involves trust, a word whose origins suggest a solid place to stand or lean against. To trust implies a willingness to do things with the understanding that God will act on our behalf. God has made the first move and also declared His faithfulness to us. When we respond to Him and do our part, we experience God doing yet more of His part, and our ability to trust Him is strengthened for the next challenge. If we thank and praise God for difficulties, our ability to trust Him increases and even helps usher in His good plans for our lives in the midst of those difficulties.

GROUP: God promises His love, peace and presence to members of His family. Jesus said *"All that the Father gives me will come to me, and whoever comes to me I will never drive away" (John 6:37)*. A sense of belonging and of being loved is linked closely to the Law of Community. We can accept people and live in God's acceptance of us. Seek community, rather than the assertive individualism so idolized in the contemporary world. Accept people as brothers and sisters worthy of your deepest respect. Bring out the best in them.

Consider making the following commitment: *Because God has empowered me for service through my faith in Him and His faith within me, I will consecrate my life to the service of God and others, abstaining increasingly from self-indulgence and self-centered motives. I've decided to make loving service my aim in life.*

Compassion is an attitude too, not merely a feeling. How much less charity would be expressed in the world if everyone waited for his or her emotions to cooperate? If we are indifferent to the suffering of others, even the probable suffering, we will not be honoring God's command to build His Kingdom and we will violate the value of Group. We need to be rooted and grounded in the love of Christ in order to transcend self and attain a consciousness of our oneness with others. Psalm 95:7 says, *For he is our God and we are the people of his pasture, the flock under his care.*

Consider this as an appropriate affirmation: *I will draw on and exercise the compassion of Christ within me in situations where I see need.*

The Great Commission is usually understood as one of evangelization, and surely that is part of it, but not the whole: *Then Jesus came to them and said, "All authority in heaven and on earth has been given to me. Therefore go and make disciples of all nations, baptizing them in the name of the Father and of the Son and of the Holy Spirit, and teaching them to obey everything I have commanded you. And surely I am with you always, to the very end of the age." (Matthew 28:18-20)*

Consider the following affirmation: *I will live in covenant community as a member of God's family welcoming in all who desire to join.*

The words "go make disciples" are important. That exhortation can only be properly accomplished through the establishment and growth of covenant community. This involves connecting with one another one-on-one, in small groups and in the larger church community in every way possible. Studying the Bible and praying together, worthy as those things are, cannot lead to the fulfillment of life's potential on their own. We need to add fellowship with the Holy Spirit, serving one another and growing together in covenant community to fill out the picture. This kind of community closeness is our greatest challenge because it involves committing ourselves to loving other imperfect human beings and sharing our imperfections as well. Yet it's also our greatest opportunity because we will grow so much more than we would by ourselves. Community is essential to unlocking the manifold wisdom of God (Ephesians 3:10) and to sharing it with the world.

CHOOSING TRANSFORMATION

What are the decisions you've made (or haven't yet made) that will determine your journey toward realizing the potential of your life? It is these decisions that will drive doubt from your heart and make room for God's power to give you victory in every spiritual battle. It is these decisions that will liberate you from wondering whether you can handle a stressful or tempting circumstance when it arises. If you've made the decision to submit to the guidance and power of God in anything you're trying to do or endure, God's faithful provision of those qualities will yield an abiding serenity of spirit for each day.

Remember the decisions that I shared about in earlier chapters? They changed the trajectory of my life.

When I first came to faith, I received God's **Grace** in large measure on that day. Then when I saw how God spoke through me to the students at Willow Creek, I experienced the power of Spiritual **Gifts**; it was also when I decided to begin learning how to serve in the Spirit. When I was holed up without a TV in my friend's apartment and ended up having an intense dialogue with God, the result of that time was my submission to His **Guidance** for my life. Later, when I was praying with my father-in-law and asked God to remove my pride, that attitude shift redirected my life away from myself and toward bringing **Glory to God** through my life. As a senior in college I entered into my first of many mentoring relationships with Campus Crusade for Christ director Jeff Hatton. Through this experience of training in righteousness I made a commitment to pursue **Growth** towards Christlikeness in every aspect of my life. Later, working as a financial planner, learning Biblical stewardship principles and through the mentoring of Bob Kalander, I learned that my life is a gift from God. I chose to be a **Good Steward** of my life and live by God's priorities, promptings and principles. Then it was at Bay Community Baptist Church in Massachusetts that I first learned about living in godly community. From there, as I experienced my first church plant, Power Street Christian Fellowship in Providence, Rhode Island, I made a commitment to **Group** and doing life together in covenant community.

My progress has been one of fits and starts and spurts of growth as with most people. However, as I've opened myself up to God's revelation more often, I've noticed that my attitudes have gradually begun to conform more closely to God's truth. He has a way of revealing just what areas need attention each day, and over time I've seen His influence on each of these seven core areas in my life. The decisions and declarations I've shared with you in this chapter are tools that can be useful to you too. They can help you make many great changes and course adjustments in the area of attitude. Instead of bench presses, I've been exhorting you to press into God's promises. But I'm certain of victorious results for you, because God is true to His promises and will fulfill what He began in you.

You might consider this chapter on attitude to be like the second leg of your commitment to transformation. Commitment means both feet in, and with your choice of godly attitudes, you are putting your life on a trajectory towards God's abundant life. It is a journey that will be resisted by our sinful nature, the evil one and the world we live in. We will examine this subject of resistance further in the next chapter.

CHAPTER 11

Conquering Resistance

LAW 11

The Law of Reality: *Our sinful nature combined with the influence of evil in the world co-conspire to lead us away from God, but God has provided all we need to stand against these forces and realize His abundant life.*

What do you picture when you think of spiritual warfare? Some may imagine earthly combat in the clouds; for others a stereotypical devil and angel arguing may come to mind. No doubt about it, there is a tug of war going on in the universe over our lives. The Enemy's goal is to steal, kill and destroy (John 10:10). He has no original creative ability, but can only try to mess with what God has done. As you know, God has come to give us abundant life, therefore the Enemy works in the opposite spirit. But what does this tug of war look like in daily life? And how do we know when it's the Devil or "just us?"

Imagine a Sunday morning, just before church. The family is getting ready to jump in the car, but you can't find your keys. Then the kids start squabbling over a toy. You and your spouse begin to argue over where the keys were last, and that leads to complaints of the disorder in the house. You both start yelling at the kids; one of them isn't dressed properly, and another just let the dog out by mistake. You catch every red light on the road, and by the time you get to church, you are fit to be tied. Then, not wanting to be a "bad Christian," you put on your friendly face and smile at those you see in the parish hall.

Is that you or the Devil? It's often both. The Devil specializes in insidious approaches and has no problem using those close to us to try to get us off track, especially when we're headed to worship God.

Let's go back to the Sunday morning scene and look at some of the possible ramifications. Fuming in the car, you're thinking, *God, all I want to do is take my family to church! Why does it have to be so hard?* Your spouse is feeling hurt, smarting after sharp words were exchanged, feeling angry and justified on the one hand, yet on the other feeling like a hypocrite for thinking up nasty retorts. The kids are whining that they want to stay home and asking why they have to go to church. Later, greeting people before the service, you're not as open as you would normally be, and they pick up on that. Wondering if they offended you, or maybe you don't like them after all. They notice the strain but can't put their finger on it, so don't dare ask.

INSIDIOUS M.O.

See how a subtle bit of infiltration can drive a little wedge in all your relationships and serve to discourage you from even wanting to deal with your family, let alone the church community? I picked this scene because it's so "normal." But yes, our adversary is real and lurks nearby, waiting to devour, especially on occasions where we might grow spiritually. And he seeks to deter our every connection with God and one another.

Here are some other examples:

- A gifted speaker gets a sore throat right before every speaking engagement.
- A spiritually sensitive little girl, one able to sense God in dreams, has terrible nightmares. She's so scared by them that she decides in her heart that she doesn't want to dream anymore.
- A young man makes a commitment to attend Bible Study. He finds himself getting really tired right before it's time to leave

and wants to stay home. The following week, a friend calls and wants to get together on that very night. On the third week, he's chatting online and loses track of time; he arrives late.

Do you see the pattern? At this point you can probably think of your own examples. It is plain that the enemy wants to deter us from our pursuit of God, whether directly or indirectly, acting from within or without.

WHAT IS HAPPENING BEHIND THE SCENES?

While the spiritual battle is real, let me emphasize that we need to see it in balance. Some people put undue focus on the devil and demons or promote needless anxiety; others dismiss the idea of evil and deny there's a war going on. Yes, there is an Evil One (also known as the Devil, Satan, or the Adversary) but he is no match for God's power. Our approach in this battle needs to be informed by God's perspective and understanding of our position in Him. Our coming into the Kingdom immediately makes the Devil our enemy, but it also puts God's resources at our disposal. *The one who is in you is greater than the one who is in the world (1 John 4:4).*

Remember that God is always the First Mover. He is the Creator. Therefore anything the Enemy can do is only a counterfeit, a counter-attack; a negative reaction to God's positive action. The Enemy tries to intimidate us and give the impression that we're on the defensive, but the truth is we're on the offense in the Lord.

That said, I want to examine with you the more subtle forms of attack. We know that Satan is not at all respectful and attacks in a blatantly vicious and destructive manner. He wounds without cause and seeks to cut off our freedom in every way possible. What we don't always detect are his more insidious moves. These are the kind that happen within us and actually feel like our own personal conflicts. The enemy can't read our minds, but he very often aims to infiltrate our thoughts by inserting half-truths in there, tossing them our way like potshot pebbles in a pond. He'll also emphasize our shortcomings and quote

Scripture with distorted emphasis to twist the truth. If he can't get us to act "bad," he'll try to discourage us by insinuating we're not being very "good." Meanwhile we have enough struggle letting go of old habits without dealing with these distortions from the Enemy. Look at this conflict Paul describes:

> For what I do is not the good I want to do; no, the evil I do not want to do—this I keep on doing. [20] Now if I do what I do not want to do, it is no longer I who do it, but it is sin living in me that does it. [21] So I find this law at work: When I want to do good, evil is right there with me. [22] For in my inner being I delight in God's law; [23] but I see another law at work in the members of my body, waging war against the law of my mind and making me a prisoner of the law of sin at work within my members. [24] What a wretched man I am! Who will rescue me from this body of death? [25] Thanks be to God —through Jesus Christ our Lord! So then, I myself in my mind am a slave to God's law, but in the sinful nature a slave to the law of sin. (Romans 7:19-25)

The inner struggle is clearly portrayed there. Slavery to sin can happen through our own poor choices and without initial Enemy attack. However, the Devil usually misses no opportunity to take advantage of that tendency. Let's look again at the basic M.O. of the Evil One, for exposing his tactics will give you an advantage in the battle. The Devil comes to steal, kill and destroy: I see a pattern of attack in this description of evil. First, Satan tries to **steal** life from us by tempting us to settle for less than God's best for our lives. Over time, this subtle seduction forms habits of disobedience toward God and submission to another. Often we are convinced that we're simply doing our own will, when we are actually doing the will of the Evil One who put the idea into our minds that swayed our desire. Once we have chosen to disconnect from God's guidance and power in our lives, we begin to die. There's the **kill**. When we are disconnected from God we are not truly living. If we don't repent and return to God before we physically die, this disconnection becomes permanent—and we are destroyed. That is the plan of the Evil One—to **destroy** all of humanity—and it runs right up against God's plan to save and redeem all of humanity. This is a very real battle; the stakes of victory and defeat are eternal life and eternal death.

In this battle we need to be conscious of our tendency to get in our own way. Our sinful nature is predisposed to want to cooperate with the influence of evil. When we are living "in the flesh" we are unwitting co-conspirators, leading ourselves away from God's abundant life. One pastor says that our human nature is the Enemy's "lunch." We don't want to feed the Enemy! But God has given us so much to help us in this fight. First, we have our soul (feelings, personality, conscience, and intuition.) God designed us with a divine central nervous system that is constantly giving us signals, convicting us of wrong and guiding us to God's divine life for us. Second, we have the Holy Spirit and the angels of God available to us. God's Holy Spirit has been given to continually help, guide and empower us to live abundantly when we submit to His lead.

COSMIC CHECKMATE

The teaching of Ed Silvoso has impacted me. In his book, *That None Should Perish*, he spells out how to reach and transform entire cities through prayer evangelism.[11] Silvoso shows how the book of Ephesians provides a roadmap of the heavenly places. He cites five references in Ephesians, each of them representing a move by God on a cosmic chessboard that leads eventually to checkmate. The battleground is the heavenly places, and whoever controls these places, wins. The Church must take its position in Christ, stand firm and defend against Satan's counterattack, which is aimed at fragmenting the unity of the Church through unresolved anger directed by members against one another. These unresolved conflicts create *jurisdictions* in the heavenly places for Satan to exercise the authority conceded to him by the Church. (You might picture openings or weak spots in a wall.) If unity is compromised, the credibility of the Church and the effectiveness of its message of love are diminished. Voiding those jurisdictions (or eliminating those openings for the Enemy) is the first step toward bringing the Church to full strength for the purpose of reaching any city for Christ. In other words, the Enemy doesn't have jurisdiction where, somewhere along the line, perhaps several generations past, people hadn't given it to him through their choices and actions. He continues to attempt to go where he has no right, but as we deal with every area where there have been openings for him in the past, we do systematically close off his access. We can have the same success against the enemy in our current relationships. When we work on dealing with those anger issues and seek God's unity, we're doing effective spiritual battle and advancing the Kingdom.

The first Ephesians reference has to do with the Father, in particular our adoption as His children:

Praise be to the God and Father of our Lord Jesus Christ, who has blessed us in the heavenly realms with every spiritual blessing in Christ. ⁴For he chose us in him before the creation of the world to be holy and blameless in his sight. In love ⁵he predestined us to be adopted as his sons through Jesus Christ, in accordance with his pleasure and will— ⁶to the praise of his glorious grace, which he has freely given us in the One he loves. (Ephesians 1:3-6)

Again, God the Father is the First Mover. He planned from the beginning to send Jesus to reconcile us to Him, and chose to freely give us everything we need for the abundant life. Our receiving this life and grace in itself is a great reason to give praise.

The second reference has to do with Jesus, with a particular emphasis on His authority:

I pray also that the eyes of your heart may be enlightened in order that you may know the hope to which he has called you, the riches of his glorious inheritance in the saints, ¹⁹and his incomparably great power for us who believe. That power is like the working of his mighty strength, ²⁰which he exerted in Christ when he raised him from the dead and seated him at his right hand in the heavenly realms, ²¹far above all rule and authority, power and dominion, and every title that can be given, not only in the present age but also in the one to come. ²²And God placed all things under his feet and appointed him to be head over everything for the church, [23]which is his body, the fullness of him who fills everything in every way. (Ephesians 1:18-23)

Jesus has altered the playing field in the heavenly realms. He now functions as the head over everything; He's crushed the power of evil and defeated it for good. He is the true head of the Church, which He has purposed to fill in every way with His abundant life. Our understanding of all these truths (as the eyes of our hearts are enlightened to them) gives us a powerful edge in battle. The stage is set by God and the constants are in place. Now let's look at the variables.

The third reference has to do with the Church, in particular how He has made us "alive with Christ:"

As for you, you were dead in your transgressions and sins, [2]in which you used to live when you followed the ways of this world and of the ruler of the Kingdom of the air, the spirit who is now at work in those who are disobedient. [3]All of us also lived among them at one time, gratifying the cravings of our sinful nature and following its desires and thoughts. Like the rest, we were by nature objects of wrath. [4]But because of his great love for us, God, who is rich in mercy, [5]made us alive with Christ even when we were dead in transgressions—it is by grace you have been saved. [6]And God raised us up with Christ and seated us with him in the heavenly realms in Christ Jesus, [7]in order that in the coming ages he might show the incomparable riches of his grace, expressed in his kindness to us in Christ Jesus. (Ephesians 2:1-7)

God has paved the way for us to exit the dungeon of sin and transgression by receiving His forgiveness for our sins and making Him Lord of our lives. The key phrases here are "with Him" and "with Christ." It is when we align our lives with Him that these realities come alive for us. Knowing *about* Him or knowing *of* Him are different from being *with* Him. Spiritual battle is not about just one moment of turning to Jesus but our daily following and aligning with Him. Spiritual battle is about relationship. If you remember that, you're in a better position to win the battle.

The fourth reference has to do with principalities and powers:

I became a servant of this gospel by the gift of God's grace given me through the working of his power. ⁸Although I am less than the least of all God's people, this grace was given me: to preach to the Gentiles the unsearchable riches of Christ, ⁹and to make plain to everyone the administration of this mystery, which for ages past was kept hidden in God, who created all things. ¹⁰His intent was that now, through the church, the manifold wisdom of God should be made known to the rulers and authorities in the heavenly realms, ¹¹according to his eternal purpose which he accomplished in Christ Jesus our Lord. ¹²In him and through faith in him we may approach God with freedom and confidence. (Ephesians 3:7-12)

One advantage of knowing that there are evil beings at work: It may help you understand people better and refrain from blaming (or expecting too much of) humans where other forces have played a part. This is not to give the Devil "credit" for everything or to absolve us of our human responsibilities, only to shed light on the bigger picture. Without neglecting responsible social actions we can take in society, we're wiser to take into account the spiritual forces *behind* society's structures as well.

> **It is God's purpose to train up communities of Christians who will connect in real, loving relationship with God through Jesus Christ in the power of the Holy Spirit, with each other in contagious Christian community, and with their calling of servanthood in the world. When we do this, the manifold wisdom of God will be on display for all the rulers and authorities in the heavenly realms to see that God can reproduce love in the world.**

Ephesians 3:10 is seen by some to be the mission or purpose statement for the Church. When we're in close relationship with God and with one another, it gives notice to the Enemy. When God gave the commandments to love Him with our heart, soul, mind and strength

216

and then love our neighbor as ourselves, He was not on some kind of divine ego trip. He was giving us a blueprint for our own protection and well-being in Him. *We* are the ones who tend to be preoccupied with ourselves. Getting self-centered, sinful people to choose training in righteousness, submit their independence and love God and one another is the ultimate expression of God's plan for humanity. If wisdom is "knowledge applied to life that makes life work the way it was meant to work," then we will truly see the wisdom of God show up when we live out His mission.

It is the Evil One's plan to stop this from manifesting in our lives and to rid the world of love. We must be on guard against Satan's weapons of lies, deception and anger triggered by unwholesome words.

> *Therefore each of you must put off falsehood and speak truthfully to his neighbor, for we are all members of one body. *[26]*"In your anger do not sin": Do not let the sun go down while you are still angry, *[27]*and do not give the devil a foothold. *[28]*He who has been stealing must steal no longer, but must work, doing something useful with his own hands, that he may have something to share with those in need. *[29]*Do not let any unwholesome talk come out of your mouths, but only what is helpful for building others up according to their needs, that it may benefit those who listen. *[30]*And do not grieve the Holy Spirit of God, with whom you were sealed for the day of redemption. *[31]*Get rid of all bitterness, rage and anger, brawling and slander, along with every form of malice. *[32]*Be kind and compassionate to one another, forgiving each other, just as in Christ God forgave you. (Ephesians 4:25-32)*

When we get angry at each other and deprive each other of grace, we invalidate our testimony. The trigger is usually unwholesome words. We therefore need to do everything possible in our strength to reconcile with one another. This is not about "stuffing" the anger either but recognizing it and taking it to God for help first. Unless we quickly apply grace to our anger, we will fall victim to the Devil's schemes and allow him to divide us. We also need to be able to humbly ask for forgiveness when we wrong someone else, and we need to accept the apologies of those who wrong us.

When we have a humble heart of unity and seek reconciliation through grace, God is able to deliver us from the Evil One. Unity, forgiveness, truth, grace and love are what make the Church truly powerful and able to rule the heavenly realms, where the battle is raging for the souls of humanity.

The Evil One seeks to establish what are often called "strongholds" in our lives. Strongholds are mindsets, outlooks and strong opinions. They can also be beliefs based on traumas. They are simply footholds in us that enable evil to occupy more and more of our lives. Strongholds are the places within each person by which Satan can gradually gain control. They are what people rely on to protect their way of looking at the world, which often reflects the vulnerability of their damaged souls. You may be seeing even more reason now for our focus on attitudes in the previous chapter. It is by means of strongholds that the Evil One is able to have a devastating impact on the Church. Surprisingly, strongholds are often made up of thoughts that seem good, such as the seemingly justified understandings that lead to disunity in congregations and marriages. Similarly, a stronghold can develop through overconfidence in a natural ability, leading to a spirit of independence from God. Most often, however, a stronghold is a defense mechanism that grows out of a traumatic experience, an experience that God must heal in order for us to move beyond it. It's as though we "climb into" our own makeshift strongholds to seek protection from those things that have hurt us in life. We may have needed it at the time, but our walls of self-protection later become the same walls that shut out God and others.

Our response to the presence of strongholds must be to exercise the authority that has been delegated to us as adopted sons and daughters of God. God's chosen vehicle for that is prayer. One of the most powerful forms of prayer we can undertake for dealing with strongholds is the form of prayer called "binding and loosing," which has been advocated forcefully by Liberty Savard in her book, *Shattering Your Strongholds.*[12] A counselor friend tells me that she uses these prayers with her clients regularly. As they re-align themselves with God by praying the prayers out loud, then also verbally destroy any alignment they've made with the Enemy, they report feeling an immediate release. Old bitterness falls away; they feel less fretful and suddenly see more clearly how God is *for* them.

One of the reasons we get in our own way is we all tend to have experiences of woundedness from the past, unresolved conflicts that leave a residue of resentment and fear. But prayer releases power from within us, rivers of water from our innermost being, and this is the key to demolishing every hindrance. Now in Christ, we can stop the work of the Evil One in our lives and in the lives of those around us. We can be restored, encouraged and emboldened to desire, feel, think and act as God does again. It is through the power of prayer, forgiveness, repentance and training in righteousness that we can forgive one another and maintain our unity in the family of God here on earth. Repentance and forgiveness are two of the most powerful and effective weapons of warfare against the Enemy's influence in your life.

The stronghold image pertains not only to evil but also to God. He is a good stronghold! "A mighty fortress is our God," begins the famous hymn by Martin Luther. We are under siege all the time; the arrows are coming in unceasingly, but they don't have to penetrate. Our opportunity is to take ourselves, our loved ones, and everything that is of value to us into the fortress of God—into His Presence— for safekeeping. So long as we don't wander out of the fortress of His will again, but rather trust in His power to protect and provide, we will find that our trust is honored beyond all we can ask or imagine. We're safe in the place where He is training us, and we don't have to wonder any more what will happen to us.

The fifth reference has to do with the struggle between the Church and Principalities and Powers, a struggle that must be waged through prayer.

Finally, be strong in the Lord and in his mighty power. [11] *Put on the full armor of God so that you can take your stand against the devil's schemes.* [12] *For our struggle is not against flesh and blood, but against the rulers, against the authorities, against the powers of this dark world and against the spiritual forces of evil in the heavenly realms. (Ephesians 6:10-12)*

The Church has the potential to rule where the Prince of the Power of the Air has ruled. But to do so, the Church needs to engage in battle and retake the heavenlies in the name of the Lord. This action in the heavenlies is also reflected in the reclamation of territory on earth; the eyes of those still being held captive by Satan will be opened. When I speak of territory, I do mean land, but I also mean people. In the Scriptures, we believers are often likened to the land of Israel. Just as the Israelites had yet to occupy all of the land they were given, so too we have yet to let Jesus occupy every area of our lives. It is our lifelong challenge to partner with God in the reclamation of this territory within us as well as outside of us.

Satan's only option is to try to deceive the Church, God's agent on earth, into yielding to him what has been entrusted to our care by God. You may recall that he did the same thing to Eve, and then to Adam, in the Garden of Eden. Like Adam and Eve, we may be tempted to rationalize our behavior when it goes awry. However, when we do that, we don't claim God's truth for our lives, and we allow Satan jurisdiction over our testimony.

EQUIPPED TO OVERCOME

In the sixth chapter of Ephesians, Paul goes on to describe the spiritual armor God has given us to fight this battle.

Therefore put on the full armor of God, so that when the day of evil comes, you may be able to stand your ground, and after you have done everything, to stand. ¹⁴Stand firm then, with the belt of truth buckled around your waist, with the breastplate of righteousness in place, ¹⁵and with your feet fitted with the readiness that comes from the gospel of peace. ¹⁶In addition to all this, take up the shield of faith, with which you can extinguish all the flaming arrows of the Evil One. ¹⁷Take the helmet of salvation and the sword of the Spirit, which is the word of God. ¹⁸And pray in the Spirit on all occasions with all kinds of prayers and requests. With this in mind, be alert and always keep on praying for all the saints. (Ephesians 6:13-18)

I've lined up each of the pieces of armor with one of the Seven Values of Abundant Living; this connection may help you remember how to "wear" each piece in your everyday life. In the previous chapter, we discussed the impact of choosing godly attitudes. When we do that, we are also putting on our spiritual armor which equips us to overcome the influence of evil.

> *¹³Therefore put on the full armor of God, so that when the day of evil comes, you may be able to stand your ground, and after you have done everything, to stand. ¹⁴Stand firm then, with the belt of truth buckled around your waist, (verse 13-14)*

Belt = Guidance – The belt is a key piece of armor as it secures our clothing and provides a place to hang our weapons. When we live by God's perspective and according to His guidance, our lives will be bound to His will which is "good, pleasing and perfect" (Romans 12:2). We will not be embarrassed by the fruit of a foolish life, but rather reap the secure reward of wisdom. We'll also be properly clothed in our most vulnerable area, and will have a firm place to attach the Sword of the Spirit. Without the guidance of God, our lives and our armor fall apart in the stress of battle.

> *with the breastplate of righteousness in place, (verse 14)*

Breastplate = Growth – The breastplate of righteousness protects the vital organs of our chest cavity and abdomen, heart and lungs playing a major part in life-supply to the body. The chest cavity is also where we digest food and drink, distributing that nourishment to the rest of our bodies. When we engage God's training in righteousness and pursue the path of growth towards Christlikeness, we are properly digesting the nutrients and exercising the muscles that fuel the Heart, Soul, Mind and Strength. The breastplate also covers all of the connecting tissues of our midsection that tie the parts together, helping them work in harmony with one another. The path of growth does these same things in the life of a believer.

¹⁵and with your feet fitted with the readiness that comes from the gospel of peace.

Shoes = Grace – Shoes are an important part of any armor. The speed with which we can move in battle is often tied directly to the quality of the footwear that we have. In football, spikes are worn in order to gain traction when running on grass. The shoes God is calling us to put on are the shoes of grace. Living out the attitude statement "you can't stop me from loving you," we are ready to run into our relationships with grace. We are prepared to love the unlovable and forgive any offense that might come against us. In this way we become agile people of love in a dog-eat-dog world.

¹⁶In addition to all this, take up the shield of faith, with which you can extinguish all the flaming arrows of the Evil One.

Shield = Good Stewardship – When we live as good stewards of our lives and manage our lives according to God's principles, priorities, plans and promptings, we are truly living by faith. When you raise up your shield of faith you are not able to see forward, for you are protecting yourself from the arrows that are coming. Hebrews 11:1-2 states, *Now faith is being sure of what we hope for and certain of what we do not see. This is what the ancients were commended for.* An arrow is a weapon shot from a distance. Symbolically, arrows are like the Evil One trying to get us to worry about our future, trying to make us anxious so we will hoard and stockpile based on fear rather than share and steward our resources as God guides. We are people who are called to live one day at a time, by faith, stewarding this day's bread and trusting God for future provision.

¹⁷Take the helmet of salvation

Helmet = Glorification – A helmet protects the most vital organ in our bodies, our brain. A soldier's helmet would have the insignia of the army displayed on the side; thus the helmet of salvation is a good reminder of the One for Whom—and with Whom—we're fighting. It also reminds us that when we received God's forgiveness and made Him our Lord, we repurposed our lives to bring Him Glory.

For we are God's workmanship, created in Christ Jesus to do good works, which God prepared in advance for us to do." (Ephesians 2:10) "and the sword of the Spirit, which is the word of God. (verse 17)

Sword = Gifts – The sword of the Spirit is the only offensive and defensive weapon in this list of armor. This represents the recorded word of God in the Bible, but more literally represents the living word of God. This piece of armor, which sits on the belt of truth until drawn, I tie with gifts of divine enablement that God manifests through our lives. When we are living in and through the power of God, our lives become the living word of God as God communicates His love through us in its various forms. St. Francis of Assisi said, "Preach the gospel always; if necessary, use words." By submitting to the power of God in *our* lives, He can use us to cut through the sin and evil controlling *others'* lives, helping them in turn submit to the power of God.

[18]And pray in the Spirit on all occasions with all kinds of prayers and requests. With this in mind, be alert and always keep on praying for all the saints.

Prayer = Group – An army is usually weakest when being attacked at its flanks (sides) or from behind. How can you defend against an enemy coming at you from all directions? This vulnerability is especially noticeable if we are fighting alone. That is why we are called to do life in covenant community with other believers, watching one another's backs. How do we watch one another's backs? Mainly through prayer for each other. Prayer is the most powerful discipline that we can engage in when fighting the spiritual battles of our lives. When we pray for one another, it is as if we are standing back-to-back, able to handle the attack of the enemy coming from any angle.

BINDING AND LOOSING

Liberty Savard's prayer method of binding and loosing can help us to make this practical and is very effective when dealing with the forces of darkness in the world. First, let's look at the process of binding ourselves to God and one another. Savard describes the binding in terms of binding ourselves to God like a papoose is bound to the mother; we want to be wherever He is, as our sustenance is in Him. In her words, "I bound my days and nights, the work of my hands, and nearly everything I could think of about myself to the will of God, all in the name of Jesus Christ.... As I worked with the simplest form of binding myself to something of God, I began to feel a gentle steadying throughout my day. I had a sense of lining up with God's will more than I ever had before, experiencing a new balance and surefootedness in my spiritual walk." Her prayers of binding led her to bind herself and others to the truth of God, which yielded victory over the deceptions of the Evil One, and also to the blood of Christ with its power to cleanse and protect. This binding process is similar to choosing godly attitudes towards life and living into them.

Second, loosing *(from the Greek word luo: To loosen, break up, destroy, dissolve, melt and put off)* is destroying any wrong patterns in our lives that are out of alignment with the will of God, including attitudes, ideas, desires, beliefs, habits, and behaviors learned from ungodly sources. This loosing too is done through prayer in the power and name of Jesus. The shrapnel from our old patterns needs to be carefully removed and our wounds healed by God. As this is done over time, the prayer of binding ourselves to God continues, reordering and renewing our lives in accordance with the perfect rule of His Kingdom.

The power of prayer begins on the personal level. This same aligning with God's will can also be organized on a citywide and regional basis. A collective repentance, or region-wide turning to God is all that much more powerful and will displace the powers of darkness as it ushers in God's presence in greater measure.

SUNDAY MORNING REDEEMED

Let's take one more look at our Sunday morning scene sketched earlier in this chapter. What would be some of the positive ramifications as one or more family members caught themselves in the middle of their reacting and turned to God instead? And how would that little family drama possibly reach a whole city?

At the moment the family discord hits and begins to evoke an irritable reaction, let's say you catch yourself at it and take your frustration to God. You ask Him for help. (It could also be your spouse who makes the first move; one helpful rule of thumb here is that whoever considers him or herself to be more mature should be the first to repent!) As you begin to pray for God's help, you sense that He sees your predicament. You also get the impression that it could also be the Enemy trying to aggravate the family (remember that *divide and conquer* is his M.O.) and discourage everyone from wanting to go to church by stirring up negative associations with Sunday mornings. You say something like this: "Okay guys. I'm sorry I just got really cranky. Please forgive me." That alone would reverse the negative spin and begin to change the atmosphere at home. If your other family members are with you in the faith, you can take it a step further and include them in some follow-up prayer. If you're the only believer in your household, your "prayer flag" is between you and God.

Following up, you might say, "I'm getting the sense that this isn't just us having a hard time. I'm guessing the Enemy doesn't want us to go to church or get along as family, so I want to stop just a moment and pray right now, okay?"

Ω

You might pray something like the following:

"Father, I know you see the stresses and strains we're dealing with; I submit our cares to you now. Please send your angels to minister to each member of my family. I command any contentious or controlling spirits to depart from me and my family now in the name of Jesus; report yourselves to Jesus for Him to deal with. Holy Spirit, come refill us now. And Lord, I also invite you to continue

to bring down my strongholds; I loose their influence on my life today. I repent of striving, trying to make it happen my way, trying to look good instead of loving each member of my family. Please fill me with the love I need for them. Help us start over today and keep our eyes on you. Oh yes, and God? Would you help us find our car keys? Thank you Lord!"

You may notice a subtle shift in the atmosphere as you pray. Even if you don't, you've just realigned yourself with God by faith and invited Him to take over the day. Let's say the others in your family feel the change, including the children. They say, "Yeah, the Devil hates it when we pray to God!" or, "We're friends now! I let him hold my bear!" Later, as you arrive at church and begin to run into people, you happen to share how the Lord just helped you regroup when your family was about to lose it. They sense the Holy Spirit in you, helping you open up, and it gives them encouragement to open up to you in turn. Other people begin to come into this circle of influence as the openness creates more room for greater transparency church-wide. Even the kids share something in their Sunday School class about how God helped their family, and a few other children go home and say to their parents, "We should pray to God!" In other words, in your simple turning to the Lord in one small moment, you've created a ripple effect that has far-reaching impact.

SUMMARIZING SPIRITUAL WARFARE

Before we move on to the Law of Consequences in the next chapter, let me summarize the reality picture of spiritual warfare:
- The battleground is the heavenly places.
- Whoever controls the heavenly places, wins.
- The Church must take its position in Christ in the heavenlies and defend against Satan's counterattack.
- Satan's main counterattack is aimed at fragmenting the unity of the Church through misperceptions, judgments, expectations, unresolved anger and wrath, etc. among those in the Church Body.

- This creates jurisdictions in the heavenly places for Satan to exercise authority conceded to him by the Church.
- If unity is compromised, the credibility of the Church and the effectiveness of its message are diminished.
- Voiding those jurisdictions is the first step toward bringing the Church to full strength for the purpose of reaching everyone for Christ.
- The battle is waged with all the pieces of spiritual armor and the prayer strategy of binding and loosing.

By following the path laid out in Ephesians, we have no reason to believe we will lose the battle. In fact, we are promised every spiritual blessing in Christ, so long as we stand firm. He is the Head, we are His Body; we are in line as long as we're not running off without the Head. If we remain obedient and place ourselves under His Name that bears complete authority over the power of evil, the tremendous provision of God's blessing becomes available to us. What in each difficult moment appears to be a vicious attack on our Christian walk can then become the stepping-stone for greater transformation as we turn to God for help. We are on the offense, God's winning team, and He can so redeem every assault of the Enemy that it becomes the very means by which He advances His kingdom through us.

CHAPTER 12

Blessings and Curses: The Choice Is Yours

LAW 12

The Law of Consequences: *Actions taken and words spoken have profound consequences on our journey of transformation, either blessing or cursing our lives and the lives of those we touch.*

"Whatever you do, don't confuse the salt and the sugar!" These were the last instructions given by the seventh grade science teacher before the class broke up into teams of two for their doughnut-making assignment. The whole point of this lab session was to practice following directions. "Now you might think this is easy," the teacher had said, "but so much of life is remembering to obey and follow, most of us don't want to do that. We think we know better. So this is more important than you think!"

Lab partners Trudy and Beth were giggling over a note they'd just shared. Beth had heard the thing about the salt and the sugar, but she figured they'd know the difference. At the lab counter, she and Trudy took turns measuring their ingredients, laughing as they mixed them together. Trudy went to the main counter and came back with a full cup of white granules.

"Wait, is that the salt or the sugar?" Beth asked.

"Who cares?" Trudy chortled.

Beth was going to suggest they taste it first, but she didn't want to appear to be too uptight around Trudy, so she laughed too and said, "Right, who cares?"

When the cooking was done, the kids in the class got to eat their doughnuts. Trudy and Beth's batch came out looking less fluffy than the others; their "doughnuts" were hard as a rock. Beth tried to bite one; her face scrunched at its bitter taste. Far from a doughnut, it was more like a stale pretzel, only much too salty.

CHOICES AND CONSEQUENCES

A simple juvenile scene, this story might sound like it wouldn't apply to the "real world" of adult life. Just doughnuts and pretzels and kids goofing off, right? But think again. Everything we do in life has consequences. Some more serious than others, but the basic principle is the same. It is a small step from that seventh grade science class to the work force where a young executive ignores the faint voice of his conscience and switches figures around to his monetary advantage. Or the home of the recovering rage-aholic: He's gotten a little help, begins to feel better, and decides he can "handle it" without counseling. Or the staff party where everyone has been drinking and one wife begins to flirt with her husband's co-worker. These are all examples of situations in which choices are being made to disregard a guideline. You can easily fill in the blank and predict some of the consequences these people will be facing.

There are times when we naturally chafe at the idea of consequences, thinking that rules are only there to spoil our fun or impinge on our freedom. But God gives us guidelines that will protect us and bless us with life and greater freedom. Not only will living outside those guidelines not be fun; it may also cut our freedom and our lives short.

"See, I set before you today life and prosperity, death and destruction.
[16]For I command you today to love the LORD your God, to walk in his ways, and to keep his commands, decrees and laws; then you will

live and increase, and the LORD your God will bless you in the land you are entering to possess. ¹⁷But if your heart turns away and you are not obedient, and if you are drawn away to bow down to other gods and worship them, ¹⁸I declare to you this day that you will certainly be destroyed. You will not live long in the land you are crossing the Jordan to enter and possess. ¹⁹This day I call heaven and earth as witnesses against you that I have set before you life and death, blessings and curses. Now choose life, so that you and your children may live ²⁰and that you may love the LORD your God, listen to his voice, and hold fast to him. For the LORD is your life, and he will give you many years in the land he swore to give to your fathers, Abraham, Isaac and Jacob." (Deuteronomy 30:15-20)

CHOOSE LIFE

The pathway to the abundant life is not hard to figure out. In fact, it is something we can simply choose. In the passage above, Moses laid the choices out very clearly as he addressed the Israelites: Life or death, prosperity or destruction, blessings or curses. He exhorted them to choose life. If we don't choose life and intentionally act upon that choice, the default pathway will automatically be chosen *for* us in accordance with our fallen human nature. Does that sound like freedom? That path leads down toward destruction.

God wants to release us into His good plans for our lives. Yet because of our free will, it is within our power to thwart His desire for us, just as it is within the power of children to be disobedient to their parents. Many people become trapped in a pattern of frustration, when the means of liberation is fairly simple. *Choose life. Submit to God, the Giver of Life.* By now you have seen the paradox: We have greater self-control (ability to do what is right and good for us) when we submit to God, and He is guiding and empowering our lives.

Within that larger choice to submit, there are our smaller daily choices. The Law of Consequences is proven on both levels, and operates in a straightforward, cause-and-effect manner. It involves understanding the power of what we say and do. When I say this law is straightforward, I don't mean it's necessarily easy to swallow. Submission is a simple act, yet we resist it. One great hurdle for us human beings is that we are creatures of habit, our main habit being our tendency to please the self (the sovereign self, a tyrant that can never be satiated.) When we live in a society that reinforces these values, we tend to influence one another away from God's life of blessing and even inadvertently curse one another with our disobedience. Look at how easily Beth caved in to Trudy's defiance of the instructions; then that small choice resulted in a ruined recipe as well as a rebellious attitude reinforced. Part of what we're examining in this chapter is how to create new habits to align with God's ways. We are challenged to retrain our habitual nature, or *what we do*. The other challenge we have is in our mouth; it concerns *what we say*. We tend to underestimate the power of our own words. I'd like to point your attention to some wisdom God gives us about this power.

THE POWER OF THE TONGUE

Consider these verses:

- *Through the blessing of the upright a city is exalted, but by the mouth of the wicked it is destroyed. (Proverbs 11:11)*
- *Reckless words pierce like a sword, but the tongue of the wise brings healing. (Proverbs 12:18)*
- *Do not let any unwholesome talk come out of your mouths, but only what is helpful for building others up according to their needs, that it may benefit those who listen. (Ephesians 4:29)*
- *When we put bits into the mouths of horses to make them obey us, we can turn the whole animal. ⁴Or take ships as an example. Although they are so large and are driven by strong winds, they are steered by a very small rudder wherever the pilot wants to go. ⁵Likewise the tongue is a small part of the body, but it makes great boasts. Consider what a great forest is set on fire by a small spark. ⁶The tongue also is a fire, a world of evil among the parts of the body. It corrupts the whole person, sets the whole course of his life on fire, and is itself set on fire by hell. ⁷All kinds of animals, birds,*

reptiles and creatures of the sea are being tamed and have been tamed by man, ⁸but no man can tame the tongue. It is a restless evil, full of deadly poison. ⁹With the tongue we praise our Lord and Father, and with it we curse men, who have been made in God's likeness. ¹⁰Out of the same mouth come praise and cursing. My brothers, this should not be. ¹¹Can both fresh water and salt (bitter) water flow from the same spring? ¹²My brothers, can a fig tree bear olives, or a grapevine bear figs? Neither can a salt spring produce fresh water. (James 3:3-12)

The tongue is also a power tool. It needs to be plugged into the right circuit and used properly. And like that tool, it can be used for very creative purposes or very destructive. Most of us are far more destructive with our mouths than we realize; we say more negative things about others and ourselves than we'd be comfortable admitting. If we find ourselves cursing, it may be an indication that we're not abiding in the fullness of the Holy Spirit. It's time to stop, take stock and plug back into God's presence before we do further damage.

Some people hear the word "curse" and think of a witch's hex, a shaman's ritual or something from the dark corners of another culture. They may also think of what we call "cussing." Yes, those are all forms of cursing, but curses also exist in our everyday language:

"Oh, she's ugly."

"I can't believe how dumb he is."

"You're lazy, just like your father!"

You get the picture. This kind of cursing is needless negativity that we can and should choose to filter out of our lives. If we don't they can become self-fulfilling prophecies.

Lisa Leach describes how she used to abstain from talking one day each week. Her children were school-aged then, and she called it "Mom's Mum Day," using gestures and notes to communicate when necessary. She found that being quiet was actually restful; it was also humbling and caused her to notice all the things she would have said if she'd been talking. To her dismay, many of those unspoken remarks were negative. No wonder the silence was so restful!

The power of the tongue should humble us all and remind us to guard what we say. It should also remind us to filter through God's truth everything that is said to us. This is especially important when speaking with or listening to people with whom we are in close authority relationships. For example, a parent speaking to a child is a highly charged situation in which much blessing or cursing can take place; the expectations of that life-giving dynamic are sky-high. The closer someone is to us, the more potential impact they can have on our lives.

WORDS & IDENTITY

Carole (not her real name) grew up in a well-to-do home that looked great to all who passed by. Her parents attended church, and her mother was especially interested in keeping up good "Christian" appearances. Carole's father was preoccupied with his work, except when he drank. Then he became taciturn and sometimes explosively angry. When he exploded, Carole's mother retreated and denied that anything was wrong, trying to keep things looking smooth.

One day when Carole was about five years old, she went to ask her father something. She doesn't recall now what it was; all she remembers is being in the wrong place at the wrong time. "You IDIOT!" he screamed. "What do you think you're *doing*, asking me? You're just like your mother, *always in the way!*" He swiped at his little girl and missed, throwing his huge frame off balance. Carole looked on in horror as he fell and knocked over some precious heirlooms. She assumed it was her fault he was angry and her fault the heirlooms broke.

In another scene from Carole's young life, she was sitting in a meeting at school while her teacher and her mother went over her academic progress. It didn't sound good. By this time Carole tended to cower and try to disappear, lest she get in trouble again. So she didn't raise her hand much in class, and she found it hard to focus on the subject anyway.

"Carole's grades are lower than average, and her performance is

233

slipping," the teacher explained. "She's now reading below the acceptable grade level."

"She's easily distracted at home," her mother added, embarrassed. "I have to ask her three times before she obeys."

The teacher sighed as she looked over her papers. "It's possible that she is just one of those who will never really amount to much in life."

Carole, now in her 50's, remembers those childhood incidents vividly. She spent most of her life feeling stupid, assuming she was asking too much or taking up other people's time needlessly. She was also convinced that she wouldn't amount to much in life. Where do you think she got those ideas? We don't have to strain to figure that one out. But in actuality Carole is smart, thoughtful, funny, loving and giving. She still has the potential to go far in life, yet she's been held back a long time by that distorted image of herself.

In those childhood scenes you see a clear example of the power of the tongue. That power is magnified in those moments when a person of authority—a parent or teacher, for instance—is speaking to (or about) a child. It's a crucial, formative moment, like a sharp tool hitting the wet clay as it spins on the potter's wheel. What could have been done differently to help Carole? And now, years later, is it too late? Can the power of blessing override those years of damage and usher Carole into a better life than she's had so far?

THE PRINCIPLE OF AUTHORITY

An awareness of the principle of authority is indispensable to understanding the power of the tongue. The words and predictions that authority figures speak into our lives do not need to be our ultimate authority. Instead, we can hear God's perspective and receive healing for those wounding words. Christ lives in us, and He stated during His ministry on earth that all power has been given to Him in heaven and earth. When we exercise our rightful authority in the name of Jesus—which is to say in the *authority* of Jesus—then what we say and do helps release that power into ourselves, our circumstances, and the lives of others.

When Carole went to a prayer counselor for help, she heard for the first time some of the wonderful things God had to say about her. The truth found in Scripture acted as an antidote to the many years of poison lodged within her by those old negative words. Carole also learned that she could even bless herself by declaring those truths out loud and telling God that she received them. She learned to break off negative words that she'd spoken over herself, too. How often do we make agreement with lies that others have tossed our way, not realizing it's like swallowing something toxic? As Carole received the truth, the curses were displaced and her whole countenance changed. She became lighter, bolder, more confident and joyful. Her actions began to change more easily once she was transformed on the inside. It's an ongoing process, but still a miraculous thing to see.

Like that prayer counselor, we all have the privilege and the opportunity to release the authority of the name of Jesus into the lives of others so that it takes hold within them, whether it is to pronounce a blessing or rebuke a curse. Gaining mastery over the tongue can be a master key to healing. When you make affirmations based on the promises of God, you are in a position to liberate both yourself and others from sin, sickness, and self. By contrast, the continual voicing of victimhood, resentment, and accusation has led to incalculable harm. Nothing is more illusory than the idea, "Words will never hurt me." They do hurt. But fortunately, they can also heal.

BLESSINGS AND CURSES

Both blessings and curses are impartations of spiritual power—one for the positive and one for the negative. There are a few examples of cursing that you might consider as having a positive effect: Cursing the root of a disease or demolishing an old stronghold are each instances in which someone's healing or well-being is the result. In that case the power tool is aimed at their shackles, not at the person. The basic thing to keep in mind is that both blessings and curses come into our lives by way of words and actions. As words are reinforced and modified by actions and vice-versa, it may be hard to discern which came first; our lives involve an interplay between the two that has a far-reaching effect.

The influence of blessings and curses can also be of a generational nature. For instance, Carole was not only affected by direct words spoken when she was young; her mother and grandmother both had the same shame and poor view of themselves that she had. We may not know where or how it started, but these things are passed down through our family lines as well as in our present lives. Just as we inherit genetic characteristics through our families, we also inherit dispositions and inclinations. There is a constant interaction of nature and nurture at work in our lives, and this interaction includes spiritual components as well. There is much that comes down to us through our forebears. Even so, *God is our ultimate parent!* It is His will that our experience of being parented not stop with our own parents but be completed by Him. He can nurture us and help us break the power of curses in our lives so we can move toward his blessing.

How do we access greater blessing? In addition to verbal blessings being spoken into our lives, we can also enter into blessing by stepping into the revealed will of God through obedience. That obedience begins by letting in the love of God. It also, by its very nature, ushers in a greater experience of His love. It's not that God loves us better when we obey; He loves us unconditionally. Rather, our experience of His love is *unlocked* as we obey. Time and again, people share their amazement that God could love them so much. "How could He be so pleased with me when I've fallen so far short?" they say. Part of it is that He sees you with His pure heart, not as you see yourself. The more time you spend receiving that love and aligning with His blessings, the more likely you will *be* a blessing.

Most of us have what you might call a tape-recorder identity. Like Carole, we might play over and over in our minds some of the negative evaluations that have been made about who we are and what we can do. Through the power of God we can record over these tapes and replace them with tapes of the truth of God and what He says about us: who we are in Him and who He made us to be.

He lifted me out of the slimy pit, out of the mud and mire; he set

236

my feet on a rock and gave me a firm place to stand. He put a
new song in my mouth, a hymn of praise to our God. Many will
see and fear and put their trust in the Lord. (Psalm 40:2-3)

I believe that the new "tapes" might be what these verses are
talking about. Once we find ourselves transformed, lifted out of our
old, muddy way of seeing things, we can't help but stop moaning
and start praising.

SEEING, BELIEVING AND SAYING

What are you believing for your future? If you accept and declare
something negative about it, you may find you're a prophet in an
unintended way. The common phrase "self-fulfilling prophecy" can
be shockingly real. There can be actual evil power in what we say
and do (to others or ourselves), despite the fact that we are not God
or any other supernatural being. To give an extreme example of what
I'm talking about, in Australia the aborigines have a practice called
"pointing the bone." If someone commits a serious offense against
the tribe, the witch doctor will take the bone of a bird and point it at
the person. Invariably the offender dies in a very short period of time.
We may think this is far from our experience, but think of the scene
at your typical doctor's office. "You have six months to live," a doctor
might say to one of his patients. It could be an accurate prognosis,
but then again, no doctor can perfectly predict the hour of a person's
death. How many times does that pronouncement function like a
curse, especially when the patient believes it?

Everyone has a kind of faith; the problem is that unless we are alert
to God's point of view, we will tend to focus our faith on the *problem*
rather than faith for the answer. We will be affirming the problem so
often that we become the problem. However, if we can begin affirming
what God wants us to have, affirming the answer and not the problem,
then we are on the road to God's solutions to our problems. This is
not merely the "power of positive thinking." This is a total change in
outlook from our small view to God's reality. It's becoming people

of faith who focus from God's perspective on what is rather than on what *is not*. We need to press into that reality in our lives, even if we can't see it.

FROM FEAR TO FAITH

One pastor, Canon Jim Glennon of Sydney, Australia built a worldwide preaching ministry based on this principle. According to him, it was the urgency of his personal circumstances that forced him to practice this in what he called his "own fear-ridden life."[13]

From earliest childhood, he had reacted to everyone with fear and defensiveness. Later, he reported, "What a tremendous relief and release it was to know that I could stop affirming the problem and start affirming the answer; and to find, not all at once but as time went by, that it worked for me." The first thing he had to do was face the fact that he was always reacting to stress by being afraid. Then he turned in the opposite direction, over and over, to what God has already provided. One answer that really stood out to him was the promise found in 2 Timothy 1:7 (KJV): *God hath not given us the spirit of fear but of power, and of love, and of a sound mind.* Over time, Glennon experienced victory. So encouraged by these results, he then began to exercise this same kind of faith for other problems with yet more amazing changes. Now with his ministry, Jim Glennon is a great example of how God can change others in proportion to the transformation we allow in our own lives.

$$\Omega$$

You might stop here to ask: *What kinds of things do you say often? Are there old tapes or reactions in you that need to be replaced with God's truths? What is the first one that comes to mind? Can you find what the Scriptures say in answer to that issue?*

OBEDIENCE IS POWER

Blessings come into our lives through obedience; curses through disobedience. You might object that you don't have the power to reject bad habits and accept the things that are right for you. This is where faith in the promises comes into play. You accept the promises of God by a decision of your will. If a father says to his child, "I'm going to bring you a present when I come home," that child will eagerly anticipate that present, provided the father has been consistent in fulfilling his promises thus far. That's faith based on relationship. The child's obedience in this case is simply believing the father and being ready to greet him and receive that present when he comes home. The child is also acting in faith when she says, "Daddy is bringing me a present when he comes home!" And if someone other than her father tries to give her something that is not that present, she refuses it, knowing the difference between her daddy and that impostor. Sometimes we treat obedience to God more like slavery than close relationship and grateful anticipation, perhaps because we are not used to His goodness.

Given that truth about our relationship with our Heavenly Father, we can begin a healthy discipline based on the words "choose" and "refuse." Remember the discussion regarding the Law of Attitude? How powerful it can be to make key decisions in advance regarding how we can and should desire, feel, think and act in every situation. And what more powerful decision could we make than the one presented to us through Moses earlier in this chapter: *"Choose life!" (Deuteronomy 30:19)* As a practical matter, we can only choose life by being very intentional about it; also by continually refusing the lure of those things that are *not life*. If you are expecting a certain package, and one arrives that was not one you ordered, you write "refused: return to sender" on that package and send it back. It's the same way with life and not-life. Some of the things you will need to refuse are the occult, gossip, negative self-talk, and prayers that are accusatory or manipulative. You can make what is called the "Great Exchange:" the casting away of everything outside of your best interest in exchange for God's gift of life, which is the precondition of every other blessing.

I would add here that the first step is in the *choosing*. Each time we choose life, that life *displaces* the not-life. When we are in relationship with God, those things we need to refuse fall away much more easily.

Just as that little child could proclaim the goodness of her daddy when he was still out of town and she didn't yet have the present, we can exercise the discipline of proclamation and praise even when we can't yet see all of God's promises fulfilled in our lives. This proclaiming is even more powerful in adverse circumstances. If we praise God in our troubles, even giving Him thanks for allowing them to occur in our lives, these praises are converted into affirmations of faith which in turn release God's transformational power into those very troubles. It's not that we're glad to see difficulties; rather, it's that God's character and our relationship with Him is solid in the *midst* of those difficulties, and our turning to Him activates His redemption of them.

Here is an example of a Scripture-based prayer of affirmation: *"Father, I believe that Jesus is the Son of God and the only way to God. I believe that Jesus died on the cross for my sins and rose again from the dead in victory. I repent of my sin and rebellion and I submit myself to you as my Lord. I lay my sins before you now and confess that I have relied on my own ways instead of Yours; I've cursed myself through disobedience. I ask you to forgive me for my waywardness and heal me of my sinful ways. Release me also from the consequences of my ancestors' sin. By a decision of my will, I forgive all who have wronged me, just as I want You to forgive me. I renounce all contact with anything of evil origin, and I cancel any agreement I've made with oppression, lies or discouragement. Lord Jesus, I believe that on the cross you took on yourself every curse that could ever come upon me; it is through your resurrection power and the help of your Holy Spirit that I can live the abundant life. Therefore it is in your name, Lord Jesus, that I render null and void every curse over my life. It is in your name that I am released. I commit myself to walking in obedience to your will. I also commit to repeating this process whenever I sin, that I might be trained in your righteousness. By faith, I now receive my release and I thank you for it."*

240

CONSIDER THE SOURCE

Remember the contrast of kingdoms we saw in chapter 10? *"The thief comes only to steal, kill and destroy; I have come that they might have life and have it to the full." (John 10:10)* This explanation from Jesus is now amplified against the backdrop of the exhortation to choose life. When facing a choice of attitudes, remember that *you* are the variable in this equation. For the Evil One to accomplish his plan to destroy your life, you would have to acquiesce to him and move away from God. No matter where you begin, your choices will, each moment, bring you either closer or farther away from your Source of Life. While you do have a choice, the choice is quite stark; the authority available to you comes only from God. The Author of all Life, who sits enthroned above all things, is the only one who should be trusted as the author (or authority) of your personal life. You would be deluding yourself to think you are the authority in your personal life; it would be like saying you formed yourself in your mother's womb.

Ω

Take a moment to reflect: *What is your source of power and authority? From whom are you accepting packages or taking commands—from evil disguised as self-leadership, or from God?*

CURSES OF DISOBEDIENCE

Here are ten areas of disobedience to God that result in the cursing of our own lives as we engage in them. You may notice that several of these are the direct opposite of many of the Ten Commandments. The first seven areas are mentioned in Deuteronomy 27:15-26.

[15]"Cursed is the man who carves an image or casts an idol—a thing detestable to the LORD, the work of the craftsman's hands—and sets it up in secret." Then all the people shall say, "Amen!"

1. Idolatry
Idolatry in ancient days referred to the worship of carved images,

but those images have been replaced in our day by anything that we worship and look to for guidance and strength in our lives besides God. Whether it is money, sex, power, prestige or the affirmation of a loved one, there are myriads of idols competing for our attention. Our challenge is to cut through all the false gods and worship the one true God—Father, Son and Holy Spirit.

[16]"Cursed is the man who dishonors his father or his mother."
Then all the people shall say, "Amen!"

2. Disrespect of Parents

Our parents are the first human authorities in our lives. How we relate to them will be reflected in how we relate to authority in general. Even if our parents have been abusive, we can still honor them for giving us life. Disrespect for authority has become the hallmark of our era, defiant self-assertion the standard fare of our culture, starting with the situation comedies of TV and extending to social and political realms. We can reverse that trend by asking God how to begin to honor our parents and all those in authority.

[17]"Cursed is the man who moves his neighbor's boundary stone."
Then all the people shall say, "Amen!"

3. Dishonesty and Greed

Dishonesty and greed in an atmosphere of financial turmoil has become the object of constant dispute: however, the focus has been on specific news items such as bankers, bosses, politics and special interest groups. The more important issue hasn't been addressed: Widespread dishonesty and greed, even though hidden within opaque financial instruments, will boomerang badly to the impairment of the whole economy. We need to return to living as good stewards who will have to give an accounting of our stewardship to God who sees even our desires and secret thoughts.

[18]"Cursed is the man who leads the blind astray on the road." Then all the people shall say, "Amen!" [19]"Cursed is the man who withholds

justice from the alien, the fatherless or the widow." Then all the people shall say, "Amen!"

4. Harming the Helpless and the Weak

All through Scripture God's message is clear: We are to love and care for one another, bind up the brokenhearted, care for the less fortunate, and share His blessings equally in His Kingdom. Justice from God's perspective is very different from worldly justice, because His standard is perfect. Harming the helpless and weak has taken many forms in our society, one of the most grievous being child neglect and abuse. According to the National Council on Crime and Delinquency, rates of child abuse have risen sharply during a recent 20-year period. As for neglect, a book entitled *There's No Place Like Work* by Brian C. Robertson details the rise of careerism as the focus of fulfillment, leaving many children to believe they are far down on the list of their parents' priorities. God is calling us to live as a community of people who look after one another and protect those who are weak and helpless in our midst.

[20]"Cursed is the man who sleeps with his father's wife, for he dishonors his father's bed." Then all the people shall say, "Amen!" [21]"Cursed is the man who has sexual relations with any animal." Then all the people shall say, "Amen!" [22]"Cursed is the man who sleeps with his sister, the daughter of his father or the daughter of his mother." Then all the people shall say, "Amen!" [23]"Cursed is the man who sleeps with his mother-in-law." Then all the people shall say, "Amen!"

5. Sexual Immorality

Sexual immorality is prevalent at the foundation of every ancient form of paganism. It is also found to precede the fall of every great civilization in history.[14] Nothing destroys the close ties of family, to the point of wrecking it, more effectively than this one. The specific references may seem bizarre, and yet the examples today of what is being offered as acceptable, including polygamy, can move well into the realm of bizarre. British journalist Malcolm Muggeridge, a late-in-life convert to Christianity, expressed it in his typically direct manner: "The orgasm has replaced the cross as the focus of longing and fulfillment." Sexual immorality is quite simply anti-community and anti-intimacy, destroying the fabric of love that God intended for building in the world.

> [24] *"Cursed is the man who kills his neighbor secretly." Then all the people shall say, "Amen!" [25] "Cursed is the man who accepts a bribe to kill an innocent person." Then all the people shall say, "Amen!"*

6. Hatred and Murder

Hatred and murder, the most obvious of the self-destructive, curse-laden activities, might seem far from the experience of the average person. However we need to see that they are the end result of a sequence of other self-oriented behaviors. The rise of fatherlessness in America, for example, is correlated closely with violent crime; leading to that we also see the tolerance of deviant sexual behavior (e.g., premarital sex and adultery) as powerful influences leading to fatherlessness. But Jesus brings the point home to us all when He says that we commit murder simply by harboring hatred in our hearts. The Apostle John captured this same thought in 1 John 3:15: *Anyone who hates his brother is a murderer, and you know that no murderer has eternal life in him.*

> [26] *"Cursed is he who does not confirm the words of this law by doing them." Then all the people shall say, "Amen!"*

7. Hypocrisy and Disobedience to the Word

Hypocrisy and disobedience to the Word are the twin causes of curse among those who either recognize the authority of the word or openly disdain it. We will sometimes see those who respect the Word, and even spend time spreading it, living secret lives of sin. These are the ones who might have avoided such scandal if they'd stayed in accountable mentoring relationships. Disobedience to the Word is most common among those who simply don't recognize its authority, but it is also to be expected among those who call themselves believers yet trust in their own power to remain obedient. Our trust in God must extend past mere belief in His existence and His authority and be applied to our daily walk with Him. It needs to extend to His ability to *keep us;* that is, help steer us away from those things that would hinder us from doing what we believe. The antidote to this curse is to constantly pursue God's training in righteousness, repent without fail when sin is revealed, and engage His new path of correction.

> *This is what the LORD says: "Cursed is the one who trusts in man, who depends on flesh for his strength and whose heart turns away from the LORD. ⁶ He will be like a bush in the wastelands; he will not see prosperity when it comes. He will dwell in the parched places of the desert, in a salt land where no one lives." Jeremiah 17:5-6*

8. Pride

Pride is often seen as the most serious of the sins because of its ability to give rise to all the others. So many sexual sins, for example, occur not because of a desire to gratify physical urges but a desire to appease the demands of the ego for admiration and conquest. Greed can arise from the desire to "keep up with the Joneses." People who have decided to lead their own lives in their own strength pursue self-glorification and are driven by pride. The curse pronounced here accents the ironic result of all that "keeping up:" *"dwelling in parched places...where no one lives" is the last thing a person of pride would imagine themselves doing. "There is a way that seems right to a man, but in the end it leads to death" (Proverbs 14:12).* Dependence on God is the answer we continue to see for each of these sinful tendencies.

> *All who rely on observing the law are under a curse, for it is written: "Cursed is everyone who does not continue to do everything written in the Book of the Law." ¹¹ Clearly no one is justified before God by the law, because, "The righteous will live by faith." ¹² The law is not based on faith; on the contrary, "The man who does these things will live by them." ¹³ Christ redeemed us from the curse of the law by becoming a curse for us, for it is written: "Cursed is everyone who is hung on a tree." ¹⁴ He redeemed us in order that the blessing given to Abraham might come to the Gentiles through Christ Jesus, so that by faith we*

might receive the promise of the Spirit. (Galatians 3:10-14)

9. Religion

Religion, defined in the narrow sense as the mere observance of rules and rituals, contains one of the most radical curses in all of Scripture. Seen from the standpoint of life stewardship, we have to bring ourselves up short and ask whether we are living in our own strength or in the strength of God for the consequence of self-empowerment is a curse! We are not intended to go to God for His guidance only to have to live it out in our own strength. Yet this inclination is rampant in the Church. Its resulting self-righteousness sneaks up on us; we may need correcting often in this area, especially if we are zealous to honor God. Even Paul had to be taught a severe lesson along these lines:

> *We do not want you to be uninformed, brothers, about the hardships we suffered in the province of Asia. We were under great pressure, far beyond our ability to endure, so that we despaired even of life. Indeed, in our hearts we felt the sentence of death. But this happened that we might not rely on ourselves but on God. (2 Corinthians 1:8-9)*

10. Unrighteous Stewardship

When we live as owners and not stewards of our resources, we curse ourselves. When the love of money takes over, regardless of whether we are rich, poor or somewhere in between, our sense of self-dependence cuts us off from the guidance and empowerment of God. Many serious Christians place their work and financial lives into a separate compartment where the principles and priorities of God are a mere afterthought, if considered at all. They are rarely content, and they rob God by their failure to give tithes and offerings. Hence they fail to experience the blessings of obedience in this area and instead subject themselves to a curse. God's promise of blessing when we do put Him first is unmistakably clear and steady. However, when our dependence is on Him, we will not lack but overflow with abundance. That abundance may or may not take the form of material wealth, depending on God's purpose for our lives. The main point is to partake of that freedom that comes only when our trust is in His care.

*"Is it a time for you yourselves to be living in your paneled houses,
while this house remains a ruin?"* *⁵Now this is what the LORD
Almighty says: "Give careful thought to your ways. ⁶You have planted
much, but have harvested little. You eat, but never have enough.
You drink, but never have your fill. You put on clothes, but are not
warm. You earn wages, only to put them in a purse with holes in it."*
(Haggai 1:4-6)

*"Will a man rob God? Yet you rob me. But you ask, 'How do we rob
you?' In tithes and offerings. ⁹You are under a curse—the whole nation
of you—because you are robbing me. ¹⁰Bring the whole tithe into the
storehouse, that there may be food in my house."* *(Malachi 3:8-10)*

THE SEVEN VALUES OF ABUNDANT LIVING
AND THE CURSES OF DISOBEDIENCE

As we wrap up this section, I want to share how the ten different
categories for curses of disobedience line up with the seven values of
abundant living so we can see not only what not to do, but also be
reminded of how obedience in these areas is consistent with God's
mission for our lives.

Guidance deals with *idolatry* in that it asks us the question:
"Whom are you following?"

Group relates to *disrespect* of parents and sexual immorality because
of the way that those attitudes and actions have a disintegrative impact
on families and the wider community.

Good Stewardship relates in obvious ways to *dishonesty, greed,*
and *unrighteous stewardship* in general; each is a failure to adhere to
God's principles of stewardship.

Grace stands in opposition to any *harming of the helpless and weak*
as well as *hatred* and *murder*. Grace is God's free gift, His unmerited
favor, and in extending grace to others, we are reflecting what God
is extending towards us. People of grace have made a decision to love
everybody, especially the helpless and weak.

Growth is relevant to *hypocrisy* and *disobedience to the Word*, because these are among the principal things that hold us back in our journey with God. They block Him from developing His nature within us. They are signs that we have disregard for God's training in righteousness.

Glorification is, of course, a reference to *God's* glory, not our own, and is therefore the antithesis of *pride*. Following the founder of their religious order, Ignatius of Loyola, Jesuits have a tradition of starting everything they write with AMDG ("ad majoram Dei gloriam" in Latin, meaning "to the greater glory of God") showing the need to discipline ourselves against the natural drift toward pride and self-glorification.

Gifts refer to His spiritual gifts given for His purposes, which He alone has empowered us to fulfill—the opposite of *rule-focused religion* with its emphasis on following God's guidance through our own power. God's distribution of gifts also stresses the interdependence of Christians, because we act with maximum power when all the gifts are being exercised in a concerted way.

CONFRONTING SIN IN THE CHURCH
(GOD'S COVENANT COMMUNITY)

With a clear understanding of blessings and curses, we hold the key to the renewal of the entire Christian church. Not only do blessings and obedience unlock the power to heal us individually, but as we allow God's truth to displace the lies in our culture, it too stands a chance of being filled with the love and power God intended.

We must begin to confront the reality of sin in the Church. Yet the subject of sin has become so touchy, the taboo so strong against perceived "judgmentalism" or "intolerance" that we are now treading on dangerous territory to face the issue at all. However, we can deal with it: (a) through persistent prayer where we know there's a problem; and (b) through confrontation in the sensitive and confidential context of covenant community.

Confrontations about personal sin are best done according to the pattern set forth in Matthew 18:15. In some cases, dealing with sin in the Church refers to specific offenses between and among members. In this passage, Jesus has provided us a model for confronting one another as we move toward healing, reconciliation, and peace:

> *"If your brother sins against you, go and show him his fault, just between the two of you. If he listens to you, you have won your brother over. [16]But if he will not listen, take one or two others along, so that 'every matter may be established by the testimony of two or three witnesses.' [17]If he refuses to listen to them, tell it to the church; and if he refuses to listen even to the church, treat him as you would a pagan or a tax collector. [18]I tell you the truth, whatever you bind on earth will be bound in heaven, and whatever you loose on earth will be loosed in heaven. [19]Again, I tell you that if two of you on earth agree about anything you ask for, it will be done for you by my Father in heaven. [20]For where two or three come together in my name, there am I with them." (Matthew 18:15-20)*

By moving through this process with one another, we can reverse the effects of the curse that has been brought to bear on our lives through one another's sins, help one another pursue God's obedient path of blessing, and maintain the unity of the Church through forgiveness, healing and restoration of trust.

This Scripture assumes that the confronting is being carried out within the covenant community of the church, with an understanding that it's the Holy Spirit's job to convict people of sin. It also assumes that those doing the confronting have an attitude of loving humility. If someone remained unrepentant after this multi-layered process, that would be a signal that they are not yet open to the Holy Spirit's influence in their life. Therefore, we need to treat them as we would an unbeliever. That is, not shunning them as people, but understanding that they are not yet submitted to God. We need to put the discipleship process on hold at that point and shift back to evangelizing them toward a real understanding of a relationship with God as Savior and Lord.

If they are open to that, we can help them build a new foundation for their faith and be properly welcomed into the family of God as

His disciples.

When a church doesn't understand and honor these principles for creating and maintaining the covenant community of the church, our light begins to flicker. Given time, it will go out. Remember, we don't drift toward anything good! If we are the hope of the world but don't properly build and maintain God's transformational community by training one another in righteousness, the world will suffer. It is through a covenant community of faith, which sees discipleship as *normal* for every member, that the Kingdom of Heaven can advance. Only then will we be the blessing we are called to be.

Ω

Have you invited in the love and discipline of the body of Christ into your life? Is there anyone in your close (covenant) community whom you need to lovingly confront because they have sinned against you? In order to honor your part of the covenant, how do you envision yourself humbly challenging them to turn and be retrained in righteousness?

CHAPTER 13

Know Yourself & Stretch Your Limits

LAW 13

The Law of Potential: *Having an objective awareness of our obedience to God's mission, character and purpose is essential to realizing life's potential.*

Do you know your potential? Not many people do. With this Law of Potential we move to the third level on the Life Focus Process, which is entitled *Know Thyself.*

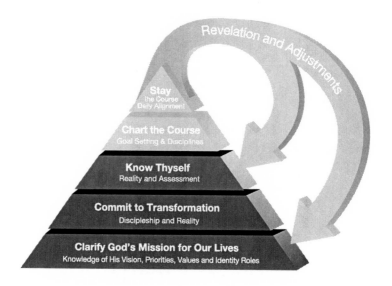

When I speak of potential, I'm not only talking about your human capacities. Factored into the equation is ***Christ in you***. Having Christ in you adds an explosive power to your already tremendous potential. God doesn't make junk! Look at what God has to say about your potential:

"All things are possible to him who believes." (Mark 9:23)

That doesn't sound like much of a limitation, does it? Or how about this:

"If anyone says to this mountain 'Go, throw yourself into the sea,' and does not doubt in his heart but believes that what he says will happen, it will be done for him." (Mark 11:23)

That too is an amazing claim that applies to your potential. On balance, keep in mind that God is not a heavenly vending machine. The mighty power within you can only be exercised after you have placed yourself onto the Potter's wheel. When you get God's perspective, you become like clay that He can mold for His awesome purposes. The double reality of our intrinsic weakness and His gigantic strength within us is revealed to our astonishment as He molds us into greatness.

252

Your life—every life—has been endowed with specific core strengths. These are meant to be enjoyed and exercised, but not as mere subjects of self-congratulation. In the Body of Christ, they correspond to the weaknesses of others (as *their* strengths correspond to our weaknesses) so that we can act with strength through cooperation. Remember Ephesians Chapter Four? We are each a part of Christ's Body and we're designed to work harmoniously together. Nothing is coincidental; all is part of His great plan for us, "to give us hope and a future" (Jeremiah 29:11). In this chapter, we will delve into the diverse forms of strength with which we have been blessed. My aim in highlighting these strengths is to help you mobilize them toward full realization of your potential, both as an individual and as a member of the Body of Christ.

MOVING BEYOND GOOD ENOUGH

Let me give you an example of God's potential stretching in my life. As you've heard, He blessed me with physical ability and strength, which I worked very hard to develop. By the time I entered Brown University, I was one of the strongest athletes in the school, so there weren't a lot of role models to look up to, strength-wise. Even so, I applied myself diligently and worked out six days a week for three to four hours a day. During the summer of 1991, heading into my senior year at Brown, I was invited to spend a month at the Indianapolis Colts training camp as an assistant strength and linebackers coach. Part of the deal was that I would help out at the camp; in return, the strength coach and the linebackers' coach would train me. I was not able to pad up and participate in drills, but every day I would be trained by one of the strongest men in the world and the coaching staff would be able to evaluate me.

I will never forget my first workout with Tom Zupancic, the strength coach. Looking back on it now, it is clear that God created a divine ambush and was going to teach me a lot about potential. Coach Zupancic, or "Super Zup," as we called him, wasn't one to mess around. With one look at me, he knew I could be pushed much harder than I had been pushing myself. Tom bench-pressed 675 pounds and I think he still holds the world record for the neck lift. He was quite the formidable man, with a keen intellect to match. He told me we would begin working out together after dinner at the end of a long day. We were to meet out on the field, where the workout facility had been set up under a tent, and he would train me. I was told we would begin with a lower body workout and that I should be prepared for pain. I have lifted a lot of weights in my life, but I must admit, nothing I had ever experienced prepared me for that hour.

Before the work out, Coach Zupancic asked what a difficult squat workout would look like for me. I mentioned I would usually end with 500 pounds and do it five times. With this information, he told me we would do five sets of 20 reps beginning at 135 pound and add 90 pound per set until we arrived at 495 pounds. I was a little nervous at the prospect of this training routine, and then he added the kicker. He told me that instead of the normal three minutes between sets that I was used to, I would only be allowed the time it took me to put a 45-pound plate on each side to rest between sets. At this I actually started to mumble a bit. Then he looked at me and began questioning whether someone from the Ivy League belonged anywhere near an NFL training camp. He said it more colorfully than that, mind you, but he definitely got my attention. He is a master motivator; he knew I was a bit afraid to attempt such a workout. I was afraid of what you might expect: failure, getting hurt and the pain that would be involved. But when he got in my face and basically challenged my manhood and athleticism, my fear evaporated in the heat.

I began the workout and progressed nicely through the first three sets. It is important to note that he was looking for 20 good, full squats and didn't hesitate to point out when they looked too shallow. The fourth set felt like my legs were on fire; I figured they were filled with so much lactic acid that they were going to burst. But I finished all 20 and racked the weight. Seeing that I was losing my initial burst of motivation created by his challenge to my pride, Coach Zupancic shot a few more intense challenges across the bow as I began to load the weights for the fifth set. I eyed the enormous weight before positioning myself underneath it. That was when I spoke to him for the first time since starting the sets. "I don't know if I can even move right now—and you want me to do 20…"

The next thing I knew, pain seared into my spine as he slapped me with an open hand right in the middle of my back. Once I finished recoiling from the blow, he came over my shoulder and screamed, "USE IT."

Pressing through the next 30 seconds was a blur to me. I was so angry and scared that I just did it. Remember, I was all alone in the middle of a football field with one of the strongest men in the world who was hitting and screaming at me. I picked up the weight and just began squatting. I was out of my mind for the first twelve. The pain of going into the 13th rep got my attention, but I just kept going. I was bound and determined to finish that workout.

It was then I noticed something different. There was a focused purpose to his genius, which up to that point had looked to me like an out-of-control moment. On the 14th rep, and for the concluding reps all the way to 20, I felt him right behind me, spotting my every move. Amidst the fear and the pressure, I also felt cared for and protected from harm. His presence there felt like a loving father who knows it is his job to bring the best out of his son: He has to discipline him, but he is never far away and will not allow him to be harmed.

It would be an understatement to say that when I finished all 20 reps my legs hurt terribly. I stumbled out of the squatting cage, and Coach Zupancic fired again. "Now jump!" I proceeded to jump as high as I could (which was about four inches) and then I collapsed on the floor. To this he said, "Good, two minutes rest and then leg press." This torture lasted through leg press, leg extensions and calf raises. At the end of the workout, I was completely exhausted. Coach looked at me and said, "Clean up, and I will see you tomorrow for upper body." He left me there in the weight tent all by myself. I will admit that I lay on the ground for a good 15 minutes before getting up again. It took another half hour to clean up the weight tent, and I didn't dare imagine what the next day would bring.

That night changed my life. Being alone at night after those workouts, God met me in profound ways. As I took stock of the feats of strength Coach Zupancic would coach me to accomplish for the rest of that month, I was truly amazed at how much potential I had never used before, simply because I was never coached by greatness.

I learned two valuable lessons from my time of training with Coach Zupancic. First, *nobody gets great without great coaching.* In any area of our lives in which we want to realize our potential, God has designed life to work best when other humans who are more mature in their understanding of that area coach us into greatness. Second, *we don't drift into greatness.* Nobody gets there without intentionality and focus. Furthermore, the *intentionality* and *focus* that we need for breakthrough has a tendency to plateau; we achieve a certain level and get used to the comfort there. But we need to grow to truly live. Is it easy? No. One leader put it this way: "Plateaus have ends. They're called cliffs." Is it worth the leap? Absolutely. But I'd use a parachute if I were you, for we can't take that leap alone. Whether it is old habits that need to be broken, the fear of stretching beyond what we think is possible or simply our sinful nature that resists growth, we need to put our lives under the authority of people who desire to bring about God's best in and through our lives and submit to their training. As we need that parachute, we need the help and authority of coaches and trainers.

KNOW THYSELF

In order to grow, you need to begin by finding out where you are. Even in a mall we are provided with a map: "You are here." How much more vital is it to know where we are in life! **In the Law of Potential, the first "coordinate" on that map is an objective awareness of our obedience to God's mission**. The great coaches and mentors I have had the privilege to work with throughout the years all began with me in this way. They knew it was important to get a snapshot of what my current lifestyle looked like. They took a holistic view of life as they probed into all of the various roles and aspects of my life. From there they could discern where I was strong and where I was weak, in need of a season of strengthening. Great coaches and mentors know that everyone has a unique potential in life and they strive to coach us right up to it.

This need for a snapshot is the reason I created the Roles Diagram to guide us. As we look holistically at the various roles we play in life, we'll see more clearly how obedient to God's revealed mission we are living. Whether we like it or not, the largest aspect of reaching life's potential is engaging God's plan for training us in righteousness. When we choose to get on mission with God, engage in His training and disciplines as well as seek out wise coaching and training partners, we live out Romans 12:1-2:

> *Therefore, I urge you, brothers, in view of God's mercy, to offer your bodies as living sacrifices, holy and pleasing to God—which is your spiritual worship. [2]Do not conform any longer to the pattern of this world, but be transformed by the renewing of your mind. Then you will be able to test and approve what God's will is—is good, pleasing and perfect will. (Romans 12:1-2)*

The promise is this: when we are obedient to what God has asked us to do, we will see that His will is good, perfect and pleasing. When some hear that phrase, "the will of God," they assume it's a price that has to be paid, an unpleasant task that has nothing to do with their well being except as a means of avoiding God's wrath. It's a surprise for them—maybe for all of us—when we come to realize that His will encompasses such things as our peace and our joy. "His good, pleasing and perfect will" is good, pleasing and perfect for us as well as for God.

At every point in our journey, it is essential that we deepen our knowledge of ourselves, both our strengths and weaknesses. If you know yourself, you can more easily recalibrate when you begin to veer off the path God intended. Furthermore your honesty with yourself and God will accelerate your progress. Can you imagine how someone would be able to improve if they couldn't admit they needed adjustment to begin with?

A little boy had been throwing rocks into the water, and he boasted to an older gentleman nearby, "I'm *strong!*"

The gentleman agreed, admired his throw, and added playfully, "I'm strong too!" He threw a rock in the water also, and it landed short of the boy's throw. Then he mused, partly to himself, "But of course we all have weak spots."

The little boy examined himself, checking both arms and peeking under his shirt at his belly. Then he pulled himself up to full height and glared at the older man. "I don't have ANY weak spots!" No doubt that boy was imagining literal "spots" and of course he could boast truthfully along that score. But his outrage at the thought does mirror our own indignation, and maybe you can identify. However, the benefit of growing to full potential far outweighs the humbling experience of honestly examining our weak spots.

God wants us to be fully mature, which means developing every role of our identity in Christ, not just the roles (or strengths) toward which we naturally gravitate. Until we understand who we really are, it is difficult to set appropriate goals for our growth. I recommend getting 360-degree feedback on your life by asking trusted people to give you their insights regarding how you're doing in your various roles. Ask them how they think you could improve. The concept of 360-degree feedback simply means you will be asking for this assessment from people who are related to you in a variety of different authority relationships. First, there are mentors and leaders who are over you in authority; second, there are peers who are equal to you in authority; and finally, there are mentees or followers over whom you have authority. It would be wise to have people who function in all of these ways evaluate and assess your obedience to God's mission and your character.

In addition to 360-degree feedback, it can also be helpful to take objective assessment tests. These give you various snapshots of things like your passions, spiritual gifts, personality types and love languages. They may not tell you everything, but each gives a glimpse of the whole picture. The better you can "know thyself," the better you will be able to chart a wise course for growth in your life with the help of mentors. **When we begin along the path of developing all of the God-ordained roles in our lives, we'll discover the wonder and genius of God as He grows us in roles in which we didn't even know we**

were capable of functioning. Sometimes God will shine the brightest through us as we grow in these new roles because that's when we'll be depending on His strength the most. As Paul wrote in Philippians 4:13: *I can do everything through him who gives me strength.*

If you were to buy a several-volume set of books and found when you got home that two volumes were missing, what would you do? Most of us would go back to the store and make sure we received the full set. Then why would we settle for missing volumes in our lives? Working on our weaknesses is a way of making sure there are no gaps in the set. Do you see roles in your life that you're neglecting? You may be unnecessarily limiting yourself. For example, God may be calling you into a role you're not naturally accustomed to, such as being an ambassador of Christ among people you see every day. It's true some people have a special anointing and gifting to function as evangelists, but all of us are called to be witnesses to those around us. (If your style is more intellectual, God will use your life to share with those people who would not respond as well to someone with a more emotional style. Or a former gang member is more likely to reach those who are street-tough. And so on; God knows very well how to put people together.) That's one example of a role that you may develop.

You may remember from our previous chapters that it is through our servanthood that God will change the world. Now, as you interact with other people and find out from them how you're doing in various roles in your life, you have an opportunity to increase the "flow" of Christ in you in that servanthood. As we all grow towards His potential for each of us as individuals, we will also be growing towards a new corporate potential to extend the Kingdom of God here on earth.

THE 24 CHARACTER STRENGTHS

After finding out how your life lines up with God's mission, the next coordinate is an objective awareness of your character strengths and weaknesses.

In a book titled *Character Strengths and Virtues* by psychologists Christopher Peterson and Martin Seligman, the authors affirm that positive character strengths are essential to mental health[15]. Their mission is to transform social science to support virtue, positive emotion and positive institutions. The results of their worldwide study revealed 24 character strengths that have been celebrated by religious thinkers and moral philosophers throughout history. These are then organized around six virtue categories. The character strengths are derived from many sources including Christianity, Judaism, Islam, Confucianism, Taoism, Buddhism, Hinduism, and Athenian virtues (e.g., by Aristotle, Plato, and Socrates). Also considered were previous efforts such as the values of Boy Scouts and Charlemagne's Code of Chivalry, as well as the works of Erik Erikson, Abraham Maslow, and others.

I have used the basic framework of the 24 character strengths, which I believe paint a clear picture of the character strengths of Jesus, and I've re-categorized them according to the Seven Values of Abundant Living. These character strengths empower us to live out the values under which they are categorized. I've listed a primary association between the strengths and the list of values, but I'm aware that the various character strengths can help to empower more than one value. I've slightly adapted and amplified these character strengths to bring out their Christian roots, while staying as close to the original definitions of the character strengths as possible. **For now, consider how your life reflects these character strengths. Make special note of the weaknesses you discover, for that could very well be the next area where God will be showing up strong in your life.**

Character Strengths of GRACE

1. FORGIVENESS AND MERCY
2. HOPE (optimism, future-mindedness, future-orientation)
3. HUMOR (playfulness)

Character Strengths of GROUP

4. LOVE (valuing close relationships, sharing and caring)
5. KINDNESS (generosity, nurturance, care, compassion, altruistic love, "niceness")

6. SOCIAL INTELLIGENCE (emotional intelligence, personal intelligence)
7. CITIZENSHIP (social responsibility, loyalty, teamwork)

Character Strengths of GROWTH
8. LOVE OF LEARNING
9. PERSISTENCE (perseverance, industriousness)
10. INTEGRITY (authenticity, honesty)
11. SELF-REGULATION (self-control, self-discipline)

Character Strengths of GIFTS
12. CREATIVITY (originality, ingenuity)
13. BRAVERY (valor)
14. VITALITY (zest, enthusiasm, vigor, energy)

Character Strengths of GLORIFICATION
15. HUMILITY/MODESTY
16. APPRECIATION OF BEAUTY AND EXCELLENCE (awe, wonder, elevation)
17. SPIRITUALITY (religiousness, faith, purpose)

Character Strengths of GUIDANCE
18. CURIOSITY (interest, novelty-seeking, openness to experience)
19. OPEN-MINDEDNESS (judgment, critical thinking)
20. PERSPECTIVE (wisdom)
21. LEADERSHIP (encouraging and organizing group activities)

Character Strengths of GOOD STEWARDSHIP
22. FAIRNESS (equal treatment according to notions of fairness and justice)
23. PRUDENCE (careful about words and deeds)
24. GRATITUDE (aware of good things that happen, thankful and giving thanks)

How Hungry are You?

 For more description of each of these character strengths and how they fit with God's values, you can refer to our website at www.lifespringnetwork.org. The rich material there offers a great opportunity for reflection and godly self-examination.

Our world is saturated with therapeutic approaches to transformation. Some have even offered mentoring and discipling of the kind I've been describing in this book. However, transformation should not be relegated to healing ministry alone, nor should healing be limited to those who are struggling. Given the current offerings in the Church, this emphasis on character development is a game-changer. And yet, mere strategies for the deliberate cultivation of character are destined to fail unless those seeking to improve their character submit first to the guidance and power of God. Christlike character strengths are not simply achieved but received and developed. It is God's will for us to possess them, and if we pray and obey persistently in alignment with His will, we will emerge into a new level: people of strong Christlike character. It must also become crystal clear that character building is less likely to take place in a human vacuum than in a nurturing environment. In a landmark study called *Hardwired to Connect*, the YMCA, Dartmouth Medical School, and the Institute for American Values produced massive scientific evidence that the deteriorating mental and behavioral health of children cannot be improved apart from what they call "authoritative communities." These are *"groups of people who are committed to one another over time."* This is a secular report, but it should be obvious that the church functioning as a mentoring network is the ideal group and fits that definition. Development of godly character, by necessity, means that God will transform our lives from self-centeredness to God-centeredness, which will in turn be reflected in our serving one another. The secular forces favoring selfishness and the other enemies of character are so strong that we, like soldiers in battle, must move forward with an attitude of unity and proactive training in righteousness in order to prevail.

UNDERSTANDING YOUR P.U.R.P.O.S.E.

We have looked at how important it is to have an objective awareness of our obedience to God's mission as well as an objective awareness of our character. Now for the third coordinate on our "You-Are-Here" map. The final area we'll be examining in light of realizing our full potential is having an objective awareness of our **purpose**.

You have been on an odyssey of discovering the *real* you. One simple test to determine a person's true identity is the fingerprint. No two are alike; what a wonderful picture of the unique creation you are! This next section might be best described as a close look at **God's fingerprints** in your life. Again, no two people are alike, so even though we're looking at God's fingerprints, there is an infinite number of different combinations in all our different lives. Looking at each of the following areas (I've used an acrostic: **P.U.R.P.O.S.E.**) may reveal more signs of His handiwork in your life:

Passions

Upbringing

Resources

Personality

Original abilities

Spiritual Gifts

Experience of Love

Understanding your **P.U.R.P.O.S.E.** will help you understand how God has formed you on purpose to experience and express His love. Over the years, I have found that exploring each of these seven areas (in the acrostic) offers dramatic insight into your specific purpose in God. He has designed you with so many unique touches, and the way His life is to be lived through you is unlike any other. Are you operating in the sweet spot of God, in other words, in the middle of His will? If you are, then the waves of abundant life have begun to flow over your being in all its aspects. With a sense of purpose, each of our little lives can know something of the tremendous and triumphant plan by which God has created and sustained the universe.

By "purpose" I am referring to both our general purpose in life as Christians and our particular purpose in life as unique individuals. Ideally, these two dovetail and harmonize with one another. Sometimes God gives us very specific revelation about our purpose. At other times it's difficult to know and understand our particular strengths and weaknesses, capabilities and blind spots, areas of insight and areas of confusion. It is hard to tell how much of us is nature and how much is nurture. It's also hard to tell the degree to which we may not be operating in our original personality because of things that have happened to us. For instance, one woman spent the first 39 years of her life thinking she was an introvert. She was shy and spent lots of time alone. A counselor gave her a personality test (shown later in this chapter) revealing that the woman was an extrovert. She was amazed. "How can that be?" she asked. Together, she and the counselor discussed how it was the woundedness that had caused this woman to go against her nature and keep so much to herself. As she received healing, she grew stronger and was restored to her originally intended personality. She was freed up to enjoy people much more. With the aid of certain tools such as that test and assessment aids that have been developed in recent decades, we can now come to know ourselves with a specificity that was not available to previous generations. I will also line up each aspect with one of the seven values of abundant living and provide insight into how they relate to each other.

Let's look at each of these areas in more detail:

P: Passions

We each have different passions that have been placed in our lives by God. Passions seem to be a combination of nature and nurture, and usually involve three things:

- People – a passion for working with or helping certain people.
- Place – a passion to spend time or invest yourself in a location.
- Action – a passion to do a type of work or activity most important to you.

I like using a list that a former ministry partner of mine, Jeff Caliguire, and his co-author, Tom Siciliano, created in their book, *Shifting into Higher Gear*. This engaging list is entitled "10 Ways to

Recognize It's a Passion." [16]

1. Your face turns red and you become animated when you talk about it.
2. You typically find yourself curious and seek to learn more about it.
3. You don't get tired when actively engaged with it.
4. You could stay up late talking about it or doing it and wonder where the time went.
5. You wouldn't need to get paid to invest time or energy in it.
6. Others seem interested in speaking with you about it.
7. You sometimes wonder why others are not as passionate as you about it.
8. If you had a day off, you would enjoy engaging in it.
9. If you had all the money, time, and freedom in the world, you would be involved in it.
10. If you were in a bookstore, you might easily gravitate toward issues that relate to the topic of your passion.

What comes to mind as you read through these descriptions? It's not hard to notice, is it? That's the nature of passions. Keeping in mind our need to experience and express love, the next question becomes: How can we love God in that passionate area of our lives? Here are some examples: I love talking to people about spiritual growth and mentoring them toward God's plan for them. When I'm engaged in that activity, I'm energized rather than drained. My wife, on the other hand, enjoys talking to children about their lives and helping them to overcome traumatic experiences that have scarred them. Jen is almost tireless in this role. She is a trained social worker, and we had the privilege of running some foster homes for children years ago before we had children of our own. It was amazing to me to see the zeal and energy that flowed through her life into the lives of those children and the staff who worked with us. That is what it is like when you see someone working in the area of his or her passion.

• **Passions & Grace** – Your greatest passion will flow out of your greatest pain, wound, need or where you have received Grace.

English author Samuel Johnson observed that life held "more to be endured than enjoyed." However, our worldly thinking may reject certain experiences as mere unpleasantness to be endured, while God's intention is to use them for His great purposes. When you consider the great passions of your life, look back and consider the experiences that have left their mark on you and which have ignited God's passion in you for making a difference in the world.

U: Upbringing

When looking for aspects of God's handiwork in your life, it can be helpful to examine your upbringing, or even the upbringing of your parents and previous generations. This is not to limit you to the usual determinative attitude that some analysts may bring to that kind of discussion; rather, it helps you understand the ways in which you can welcome the true parenthood of God in your life. On the one hand we can see evidence of blessing that has come down through generations, but we may also see evidence of negative characteristics, even curses, from which we now, as children of God, have the opportunity to be set free.

You may want to develop a genogram of your family tree in order to trace certain family patterns. A genogram is a pictorial display of a person's family relationships. It goes beyond a traditional family tree by allowing you to visualize hereditary patterns and psychological factors that punctuate relationships. It can be used to identify repetitive patterns of behavior and to recognize hereditary tendencies. You don't have to know every last detail to make a genogram or discern a family pattern. Just put in what you do know, and it can provide a general sketch. Looking at my genogram has enabled me to see patterns of blessings and curses in my own family line. I can be thankful for the blessings, and I can seek God's re-parenting and help with break-through when it comes to the curses. This is the miracle of knowing that God knew who our parents would be. Even though nobody parents perfectly, there is a reason for the upbringing that we all had that can only be fully understood when we are living in Christ. Many have discerned negative patterns from the past, affirmed their true nature as redeemed children of God, and then broken through into positive new futures that contrast dramatically from the past. It's an awesome privilege to be entrusted with the understanding in the Lord that helps establish new freedom and increased blessings for the generations after you. By constructing your genogram and spending time reflecting on the relatives who have affected your life, you will be able to better know yourself and see patterns in your family. You will discover how and why God placed you in your family, on purpose. You have been given an inheritance of unique relationships, character strengths, influence, a good name, relational patterns, and more—all of which God can use to build His Kingdom.

- **Upbringing & Growth** – How have you been trained by your life? Even seemingly trivial, forgettable occurrences in our lives are part of God's great training program, which works on us more effectively than any formal training we ever receive when we submit to His parenting of our lives. Understanding the growth patterns and trajectories of someone's life will greatly inform your ability to help him change his ways and chart a new course for growth towards Christlikeness.

R: Resources

God has resourced us for a reason, and it is our duty to listen carefully to His leadings so we understand what that reason is. We are told in Scripture that God gives different amounts of resources to us all, as He determines. Taking stock of the resources God has entrusted to your stewardship is an important aspect of how he has created and blessed you to build His Kingdom. That is why we are called to be good stewards, so that we don't squander the resources that He intended to use to provide for our immediate families, enabling us to live in a certain place and live generous lives.

In the area of money, more than any other, we tend to compartmentalize our lives. Is your service to God in one airtight compartment and your service to money in another? Some think that somehow the issue of money isn't "holy" enough to concern God. But by now

I trust that you see otherwise. God is interested in *every* nook and cranny of our lives. To overcome this compartmentalizing, we must seek to become fully yielded to God's leading in the financial area of our lives. Then and only then will we begin to experience the blessings of a fully yielded life.

To achieve this "yieldedness," it is important to examine the various components of our earning, giving, spending, saving and investing. God's wisdom for us is to experience and express love, and that *includes* our money. How we handle our money reveals where our priorities lie. We are commanded to be content with our lot in life and also to avoid creating any idols. Our job is to be obedient, especially with our resources, and He provides us with the guidance for accomplishing that. There are few things that are more disillusioning to non-Christians than to look at the lives of some Christians and wonder why they are not more at peace with their lot in life.

We are also expected to be good stewards of our material blessings. God wouldn't give you these blessings without the power to do well with them, and it is to God's standard to which we will be accountable. As we are faithful with what God has entrusted to us and He deems us capable of proper stewardship of it, He might decide to entrust us with more resources to steward in order to extend His Kingdom. It is awe inspiring to me how, as we are faithful, God resources us perfectly to provide for our families, pursue His passions for us and serve according to His calling.

- **Resources & Good Stewardship** – Resources are entrusted to you. As I've discussed previously and cannot emphasize enough, the most important thing to be stewarded is our life in its entirety. Financial resources serve as the training ground for whole life stewardship. Managing our resources according to God's plan for our lives will help us to realize our life's potential. Poor stewardship of the resources God has blessed us with holds back a lot of people with good intentions from pursuing God's greatness. Many people have become slaves to their lenders and are not freed up to serve God. In contrast, good stewardship of our resources not only trains us in good life stewardship, but keeps us well supplied and ready to serve when we are called. Remember that we will be held accountable for stewarding what God has blessed us with, nothing more and nothing less.

P: Personality

As I've said, it's easier than ever these days to find tools that help you discover your natural temperament. These can be useful in determining the personality God gave you versus what you have developed based on your reactions to your environment. After the onset of puberty, our adult learning begins to overlay our core personality, which is when the blending of nature and nurture becomes more evident. For some people, this serves to strengthen what is already there. With others it produces multiple facets of personality. Discovering this innate core of yourself is part of the journey of using a personality test to enrich your life spiritually.

Are you an extrovert or introvert? This depends on where your most natural energy orientation lies and where you're likely to focus your attention, that is, on the outer world or the inner. Are you sensing or intuitive? This depends on whether you automatically perceive things in terms of the present and concrete, or in terms of the future and possible. Are you the thinking type or the feeling type? This depends on whether you naturally go about deciding things according to logic and objective analysis, or according to values and subjective evaluation. Are you the judging type or the perceiving type? This depends on whether you deal with the outside world according to organized, settled procedures, or whether you're more inclined to be flexible, spontaneous, and open about options. A reliable tool for making these determinations is the Keirsey Temperament Sorter.

There's no right or wrong in this analysis; we have been given different personalities by God—you guessed it—on *purpose*. He knows what He is doing and how your personality will mesh with the other personalities that He has created. I believe that He even knows the names and personalities of those He is going to guide you to serve with. In addition, as we all know, opposites attract; particular men are attracted to particular women based partly on opposite personality characteristics and the need for that balance of opposing characteristics for fullness of life. We're talking here about your natural state, not learned skills. Certain behaviors and situations recharge us, and others drain us, depending on your personality type (think of an extrovert and an introvert entering a roomful of new people). Some of us, including myself, need reassurance we're not alone.

- **Personality & Guidance** – Understanding personality types provides insights into how we prefer to give and receive guidance in our lives. Different people receive guidance in different ways, especially when it takes the form of serious correction. When we understand our core personality and that of our friends. we will better be able to "submit to one another out of reverence for Christ" (Ephesians 5:21). And as God uses our lives to guide one another in covenant community, it will be helpful to understand the various categories we covered in the Keirsey Temperament Sorter. You will find that talking with someone with one type of personality will require a completely different approach than another type, and these tools will help you adjust your mentoring accordingly.

O: Original Abilities

It would be false to say that our original abilities or the lack of them determine our destiny, because research has shown repeatedly that many of the greatest achievers manifested little promise in youth. (Case in point: Basketball superstar Michael Jordan, after joining his high school basketball team, was cut from the team after his first year. Another great example is the genius Albert Einstein, who didn't always do well in school.) But it would be equally false to assume that such abilities are irrelevant to our destiny, because God placed those within us for a purpose. It is wise to take stock of your original abilities and the skills and talents that you have developed using your original abilities, as you discern how you can best serve the Kingdom of God.

- **Original Abilities & Glorification** – Nothing caters to our pride and self-satisfaction more than the conspicuous exercise of some ability that draws admiration from those around us. It is vital that we submit to God's glory those things we've always been able to do on our own. This is the freest and in some ways most difficult aspect of living a life that glorifies God, especially if we have always been able to do these things and we are tempted to live entitled lives of recognition-seeking rather than grateful lives that glorify God.

S: Spiritual Gifts

As we have noted earlier, a spiritual gift is a distinctive ability, given by the Holy Spirit to every Christian, according to God's grace and design, for the purpose of building up the Body of Christ. More commonly, the phrase "spiritual gift" is used to refer to a God-given supernatural capacity that enables an individual to have an effective ministry. The concept of spiritual gifts, together with common questions asked and a listing of 32 spiritual gifts, is discussed in Chapter Eight, where we covered the Law of Servanthood. Understanding our spiritual gifts and identifying how the Spirit is manifesting himself through you will obviously help you to understand how He is calling you to serve in His Kingdom.

- **Spiritual Gifts & Gifts** – This one is an easy match, operating in our spiritual gifts and letting God serve others through us. As we have mentioned before, because of the power of God which is able to work in and through our lives to express the love of God to the world, our potential for being used as conduits of God's power is without limit when acting in accordance with His will. If we abide in God and submit to living in and through His strength, we will experience and express the love of God made manifest in the resurrection power of Christ.

E: Experiences of Love

People are naturally inclined to express love in several different ways. Most significantly, the typical couple is composed of a man and a woman with different "love languages." The failure to understand that and to adjust accordingly can lead to serious discord, whereas a good mutual understanding of each other's preferences can promote a deeper harmony. The following is a basic description of these (based on

Dr. Gary Chapman's book *The Five Love Languages*)[17]:

• **Words of Affirmation.** Verbal appreciation speaks powerfully to people whose primary love language is "Words of Affirmation." Simple statements such as, "You look great in that suit," or "You must be the best baker in the world! I love your oatmeal cookies," are sometimes all a person needs to hear to feel loved. Aside from verbal compliments, another way to communicate through "Words of Affirmation" is to offer encouragement. Here are some examples: reinforcing a difficult decision, calling attention to progress made on a current project, or acknowledging a person's unique perspective on an important topic. If a loved one listens for "Words of Affirmation," offering encouragement will help him or her to overcome insecurities and develop greater confidence.

• **Quality Time.** Quality time is more than mere proximity. It's about focusing all your energy on your mate/close friends. A husband watching sports while talking to his wife is NOT giving her quality time. Unless all of your attention is focused on your mate, even an intimate dinner for two can come and go without a minute of quality time being shared. Quality conversation is very important in a healthy relationship. It involves sharing experiences, thoughts, feelings and desires in a friendly, uninterrupted context. This involves "active listening" to assure the other person knows you are truly listening. Many people don't expect you (or even want you) to solve their problems. They need a sympathetic listener. An important aspect of quality conversation is self-revelation. In order for you to really communicate with another person, you must be in tune with your inner emotions. It is only when you understand your emotions that you are able to share quality conversation and quality time with another person. Another important aspect is doing quality activities together. Many people feel most loved when they spend time together, doing activities they love to do. Spending time together will bring you closer, and help you build a memory bank that you can draw from in the future.

• **Receiving Gifts.** Some people respond well to visual symbols of love. If you speak this love language, you are more likely to treasure a gift as an expression of love and devotion. People who speak this love language often feel that a lack of gifts represents a lack of love from his or her mate. Luckily, this love language is one of the easiest to learn. If you want to become an effective gift-giver, you might have to learn to change your attitude about money. If you are naturally a spender, you will have no trouble buying gifts for that person. However, people who are used to investing and saving their money may have a tough time adjusting to the concept of spending money as an expression of love. These people must understand you are investing the money not in gifts but in deepening your relationship with the other person. The gift of self is also an important symbol of love. Sometimes all a person desires is for you to be there for him or her, going through the same trials and experiencing the same things. Your body can become a very powerful physical symbol of love. These gifts need to come every week or even every day, but they don't have to cost a lot of money. Free, frequent, expensive, or rare, if that person relates to the language of receiving gifts, any visible sign of your love will leave him or her feeling happy and secure in your relationship.

• *Acts of Service.* Acts of service can bring about a great sense of feeling loved for those for whom it is a love language. In a marriage relationship or within a family, sometimes simple chores around the house can be an undeniable expression of love. Even tasks such as doing the laundry and taking out the trash require some form of planning, time, effort, and energy and will be appreciated. Just as Jesus demonstrated when He washed the feet of His disciples, doing humble chores can be a very powerful expression of love and devotion to your loved one. It is very important to understand what acts of service another person most appreciates. Also of importance is to engage in these acts of service out of love and not obligation. Someone who does chores and helps out around the house out of guilt or fear will inevitably be communicating resent-ment rather than love—he has the right love language but not the right dialect, as it were. It's important to perform these acts out of the kindness of your heart. Sometimes demonstrating acts of service can mean stepping out of the stereotypes. Acts of service require both people to humble themselves into doing some chores and services that aren't usually expected from their gender. However, these little sacrifices will mean the world to the other person, and invite a happier relationship.

• *Physical Touch.* Many people feel the most loved when they receive physical contact. For someone who speaks this love language loudly, physical touch can make or break the relationship. Sexual intercourse makes many mates feel secure and loved in a marriage. However, it is only one dialect of physical touch. It is important to discover how your partner not only physically responds but also psychologically responds to these touches. Sometimes little acts such as touches on the cheek, on the hand, or the shoulder can really make a difference. All marriages will experience crises. In these cases, physical touch is very important. In a crisis situation, a hug can communicate an immense amount of love for that person. A person whose primary love language is physical touch would much rather have you hold him or her and be silent than offer any advice. It is important to remember that this love language is different for everyone. What type of touch makes you feel secure is not necessarily what will make your partner happy. It is important to learn each other's dialects.

• **Experience of Love & Group.** To experience and express the love of God properly in relationships, it is helpful to understand people's love language(s). Jesus said, *"All men will know that you are my disciples if you love one another" (John 13:35).* Our experience of love is often one-on-one, of course, but there is a corporate dimension as well, in which we sense the unity of the family, the small Christian group, the church congregation, and the wider society. Heaven itself, the communion of saints, is a vision of God and also of the full, unhindered love that will prevail among those who have submitted themselves to Him during their lives on earth. If we are going to live as His Kingdom ambassadors here on earth, we need to become experts in love—for *God is Love (1 John 4:16).*

Ω

Just reading about all these ways to get to know yourself better, are you finding new insights pop up? *What aspects of yourself stood out to you in the preceding descriptions? Any surprises? Any relief that it's okay to be who you are? What strengths and weaknesses did you notice, and how do you see God helping you to develop weaker areas? Invite Him into those areas in your life now...*

Some people think it's selfish to focus on themselves. They are rightfully concerned that they don't become prideful in that focus. But consider this: There's a difference between prideful obsession with the self and humble awareness with an attitude of openness to godly transformation. Not only that, but knowing yourself just might be the least selfish thing you could do, for it will unlock your full potential to love and give as never before.

How Hungry are You?

 If you want more on the seven areas covered in the P.U.R.P.O.S.E. paradigm and assessment tests you can use with your friends or mentors, you may go to our website: www.lifespringnetwork.org or take the Omega Course.

CHAPTER 14

Believing is Seeing

LAW 14

The Law of Belief: *Your behavior is a reflection of what you truly believe will best meet your needs and provide you with a life of abundance.*

You've heard the expression, "seeing is believing." But in life, it plays the other way around: What you believe will influence how you see —and what you do. Remember from Chapter Four: We established that the way you see affects everything you do. This chapter deals with the beliefs underlying all of that and how our beliefs are created and changed. You may have already noticed that one of my recurring points has to do with the importance of letting God redo our inner "wiring" (or our beliefs.) This submission to His deep inner work is far more effective than trying to do (or not do) this or that good or bad thing.

Our beliefs are formed in our being by processing the interaction of our true desires, feelings, thoughts and capabilities. Many of these beliefs are formed subconsciously, through our experiences in early years. Some of those beliefs may have arisen from incidents that were wounding to us, and because of that, these might lead us to maintain a distorted picture of the world. Other beliefs may be chosen consciously. In order to fully understand how beliefs are created in our lives, it is important to wrestle with this fact: In life we are always choosing what we believe will be the best possible way to meet our own needs based on the choices we see, whether we are choosing the godly path or choosing to believe (live by) the world's system of thinking in some area of our lives. When making decisions consciously, we do an internal pros-and-cons list. When our decisions are made sub-consciously, we may not be aware of all the pros and cons, but are generally reacting in a self-preservation mode. Either way, our true beliefs always manifest themselves in our behavior. It is also important to understand that the Evil One is able to put extra weight on that drive we have to get our needs met. He wouldn't miss an opportunity to manipulate and deceive us into believing in lifestyles that are less than God's best for us. So while our souls are designed by God to seek the abundant life, unless we are submitted to His guidance and power, we will not be able to distinguish truth from error and will go looking for love in all the wrong places.

When you think of *beliefs*, what comes to mind? You may be reminded of a certain set of ideas you have about life—neatly positioned off to the side in a place of honor, like a prize collection of books. But in reality, beliefs are always operating in our lives, whether we're aware of it or not. When the Bible uses the word "believe," it is not referring to an intellectual assent about something. To believe in something means that we rest in it and live by it.

> ...*if you confess with your mouth, "Jesus is Lord," and believe in your heart that God raised him from the dead, you will be saved.* [10]*For it is with your heart that you believe and are justified, and it is with your mouth that you confess and are saved. (Romans 10:9-10)*

To believe that *Jesus is Lord* means we have chosen to live our lives like He did, to do whatever He shows us to do and to serve His purposes with His resources. We've made a conscious choice to believe in and follow Jesus. We've also begun the process of inner transformation that involves daily choices and revelation of existing (often subconscious) beliefs.

GOD'S FAITH WITHIN US

The process of believing in someone or something with greater confidence takes time, as well as trial and error. I have adapted a model from Hyrum Smith to help illustrate how beliefs are formed in our lives and how they grow stronger or weaker over time. I have entitled this model the Belief Model.[18]

The Belief Model

Our beliefs are formed in our being by processing the interaction of our true desires, feelings, thoughts and capabilities.

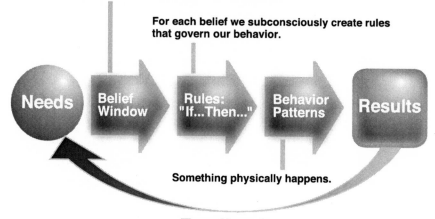

For each belief we subconsciously create rules that govern our behavior.

Needs → **Belief Window** → **Rules: "If...Then..."** → **Behavior Patterns** → **Results**

Something physically happens.

Feedback

If the results of your behavior meet your needs over the long haul, this feedback tells you that you have a correct belief or harmless opinion on your belief window.

Our beliefs are a combination of what is truly in our heart (desires), soul (feelings), mind (thoughts) and strength (capabilities). For each belief, we subconsciously create rules that govern our behavior. Then when we act on our belief, something happens. If the results of our behavior meet our God-given needs and bear godly fruit over the long haul, this feedback tells us that we have a correct belief on our belief window. This *belief window* can be defined as our ability to predict our future based on the consequences of our present beliefs. Regardless of whether or not our beliefs (desires, feelings, thoughts, capabilities)

278

are correct (in line with God's reality), incorrect (not reflecting reality) or simply matters of opinion or preference, we tend to assume that all of them are correct—and we behave accordingly.

Have you noticed that our noble inclination is to ask God to give us ideas and then ask for His blessing? That sounds like a very respectful, Christian approach. The real necessity, however, is to put ourselves onto the Potter's wheel and allow Him to shape us. If we do that, we can be confident He will fill us with the wisdom we need so we will ask rightly when we are praying.

"Have faith in God," Jesus answered. ²³*"I tell you the truth, if anyone says to this mountain, 'Go, throw yourself into the sea,' and does not doubt in his heart but believes that what he says will happen, it will be done for him.* ²⁴*Therefore I tell you, whatever you ask for in prayer, believe that you have received it, and it will be yours.* ²⁵*And when you stand praying, if you hold anything against anyone, forgive him, so that your Father in heaven may forgive you your sins." (Mark 11:22-25)*

Many Christians think this is simply too good to be true. But if we're trusting God, and have no doubts, then His miracle-working power becomes operative and mountains do begin to move. First, of course, we have to align ourselves with the will of God. And, by the way, that does include a life of continual forgiving; it's no accident that verse 25 follows the previous advice on asking and receiving. Forgiveness is a daily part of our aligning with God. If we are *living* in alignment with His will, we are more likely to have His *desires* that are in alignment with His will. Combine that with asking for His wisdom to fulfill those desires, and we can trust in His faithfulness to do just that. This is not a magic formula; it is a description of God's ways and our growth in understanding His ways. The more we see answers to prayer come through as a result of our alignment with God, the more reinforcement we'll have for our *belief* in Him; our confidence in Him will grow.

How do you shift from former beliefs to God's beliefs? It's a gradual process of transformation, just as we've seen elsewhere throughout this book. First, our beliefs change through experiencing God in new ways. God's beliefs are spiritually discerned. You can nudge the process along by asking God to reveal them to you, whether through reading Scripture, through prayer, through a word spoken to you or through circumstances that get your attention. As you progress in believing in God's ways, you will be doing what He says to do in Deuteronomy 30: *"choose life, so that you and your children may live* ²⁰*and that you may love the LORD your God, listen to his voice, and hold fast to him. For the LORD is your life" (Deuteronomy 30:19b-20a).*

As you saw in the chapter on the Law of Identity, when we live contrary to God's will for our lives and pursue evil desires, our souls begin to die and become scarred, our minds become corrupted and our strength becomes limited. Our own plans for our lives will not lead us away from this scarred-soul, corrupted-mind and limited-strength condition; they will only make it worse. Remember, everyone believes that what he or she is doing, however destructive, is good. *There is a way that seems right to a man, but in the end it leads to death (Proverbs 14:12).* Even drug addicts can become involved in a romantic view of their dissipated life, particularly if it's connected to any artistic endeavor. As we pursue God's beliefs for abundant living, however, we begin to move away from the emotional scarring, mental corruption and limited strength into God's plan for us. This takes time; we have expectations of an immediate and dramatically different life, but we underestimate the time it takes to unlearn and heal from our old beliefs. Therefore understand that the journey may get worse before it gets better. When we continue to abide in God, however, our hearts, souls, minds and strength *will* come alive more and more each day and this *will* reinforce our ability to choose God's beliefs for our lives.

What do we do with bad habits and areas where we struggle with self-control? Where to begin? These can be examined in light of our existing beliefs, then followed up with appropriate, spiritually discerned disciplines to help us form healthy habits. Once we start down the path of God's discipline, we will learn how "His knowledge applied to life makes life work the way it was meant to work." As you may remember, that is my definition of wisdom.

If any of you lacks wisdom, he should ask God, who gives generously to all without finding fault, and it will be given to him. ⁶But when he asks, he must believe and not doubt, because he who doubts is like a wave of the sea, blown and tossed by the wind. ⁷That man should not think he will receive anything from the Lord; ⁸he is a double-minded man, unstable in all he does. (James 1:5-8)

You can't stop a belief; if people believe something, they're going to go forward with it. As we saw earlier, strongholds include very strong beliefs. This is why complete transformation is critically important. To change the roots of a tree is to change the whole tree. To believe in Jesus is to be *rooted and grounded in love (Ephesian 3:17)*. The evidence may take some time to appear 'above ground' in our lives, but the effects are lasting and complete.

ONE WOMAN'S BELIEF CRISIS

A young mother of three (I'll call her Maryanne) found herself running ragged trying to live up to her idea of loving parenthood. Her kids were screaming as she tried to talk on the phone. *How ironic, she thought; here I am trying to get prayer so I can be a better mother, and they won't even let me talk!*

"MOMMMMM!" her son yelled. "I want my SNACK!!"

"Just a minute, honey, I'm coming," she called, feeling torn while she tried to focus on the phone call. Maryanne had grown up neglected by her parents, and she was determined to be a better mother than she'd had. She wanted to make sure her children's needs weren't ignored, and the last thing she wanted was to have her kids grow up feeling deprived and end up hating her. But lately it seemed that the harder she tried, the more they screamed. And now the school was concerned about her two oldest ones; they were resisting the teachers' discipline and showing disruptive behavior. This made Maryanne feel even worse than she already did. "I've tried so hard!" she cried on the phone to her mentor. "Now this teacher makes me feel like I'm *flunking motherhood!*"

Let's pause our story at this spot and pan out to a more objective observation point. Maryanne's children are beginning to act "spoiled" and are sorely in need of some good discipline. Maryanne didn't intend on raising tyrants, but that's what she's got on her hands. An otherwise intelligent woman, she seems to have a blind spot when it comes to her own children and parenting technique. What are some of the beliefs that could be operating here? A conversation with her mentor revealed these underlying beliefs:

1. [The opposite of parental neglect is serving the children all the time.] *"I need to avoid neglect at all costs. This means I need to give the children everything they want."*
2. [Discipline is the same as abuse.] *"If I discipline my children* (make them stop screaming, wait for something or do it themselves, for example) *"I'm a 'bad' parent."*
3. [Wants are the same as needs.] *"If the children want something, they need it in order to feel loved."*

These are a few; you may discern even more. The important thing is that she sees how some of her beliefs may not be God's best for her. She also needs to see her own need for healing of childhood hurts, and be open to God's re-parenting even as she is learning to parent. The crisis comes when the behavior (her hopping to her children's every whim and her resistance to disciplining them) is not bringing about the desired results (teacher calls, kids not behaving, mother feels even worse, etc.). That's when there is an opportunity for change, beginning with finding out what God has to say on the subject. In Maryanne's case, there is hope in that she has chosen to look to God for guidance and also has a mentor willing to pray with her. If the relationship is good and full of love and trust, that mentor can continue to ask Maryanne more of the questions that may reveal underlying patterns; she will also have the favor to pray for Maryanne's healing and even make suggestions in line with Scriptural principles of child-rearing.

Now let's look at beliefs underlying the children's behavior. Maryanne's children may or may not be interested in change. "Mommmmm!!" is the scream that routinely seems to result in their "needs" being met.

The scream continues until she relents, and her giving them what they want is a pretty simple illustration of reinforced beliefs based on getting one's needs met. Of course it's disputable that those wants are all legitimate needs. On the surface, Maryanne may appear to be humbly serving her children, acting as a Christian example. But her kids need to learn an attitude of humble service, too, and will not if they are not given the opportunity and training. Discipline is one of their true needs that is not being met.

As the children's mother learns different habits, she'll be re-training her children in different habits as well. "You need to wait until I'm done talking on the phone," she might say. "And I will not respond to you if you're screaming. You need to ask politely." Or, "You may get your own snack, provided you clean up after yourself." Mom and teachers can work together to begin to make the necessary changes. It may feel like trying to pull off a fourth-quarter rally, and they may have to get creative as they hold the line and come up with consistent and reasonable consequences for the children. But the basic picture will reveal a change in the children's beliefs. They will shift from, "If I scream loud and long enough, Mom will give me what I want" to *"I'll need to behave respectfully both at home and at school in order to get what I want."*

THE TOTAL MAKEOVER

Let's look in detail at that process of moving from sinful habit to realignment with God. You'll recognize the actions Maryanne will have to take as you read through the steps below. You may even be thinking of an example from your own life. Basically, these five steps outline what's needed to change your belief window:

1. Identify the behavior pattern that is not producing the desired results.
2. Identify possible beliefs and the root desires, feelings, thoughts and actions driving the behavior.
3. Predict future behavior based on following those beliefs.
4. Identify alternative beliefs that may produce better results.
5. Predict future behavior based on the new beliefs.

Ω

You may be thinking of an example from your own life. *What are some behaviors that are not producing desired results for you? Can you identify some possible beliefs that are underlying these behaviors? Ask God to show you His alternatives, and also His healing, where applicable. Receive and declare His truth in place of your old beliefs.*

We can open the process up even more deeply and look at beliefs in the light of our human make-up in Chapter Six. See how the four aspects—heart, soul, mind and strength—help us understand both our sinful human nature and the godly nature we're destined to have.

God's aim is to train us to believe in Him. We can't do that fully without His life in us! We need His help to begin to:

- *Desire* what God desires for us,
- *Feel* right and wrong, joy and sadness the way God feels,
- *Think* clearly about truth and plan accordingly, and
- *Act* out of our true capability in Christ.

The four aspects of our being also interact with one another. This interaction moves us in one direction or the other, that is, either into God's abundant life or into sin. Here are four examples of how heart, soul, mind and strength might interact with one another to bring us either closer or farther from God's life:

- *Heart to Soul* – You might have desires that war against your soul, inhibiting you from experiencing your true self and feeling God's promptings in your life or connecting with the feelings of others.
- *Soul to Heart* – You might have feelings or wounds that disable you from desiring to move towards intimacy in relationships. For example, if you have wounds from past relationships that have not been properly healed by God, they can hinder your desire to move toward deeper intimacy with people in your life and rob you of a deeper experience and expression of love with others.
- *Mind to Heart* - Your understanding of truth or your plan for

your life influences your desire to pursue something or someone. For example, if you have a false understanding about someone, it could hinder your desire to move towards that person who could be part of God's plan for your life.

- *Strength to Heart and Mind* – Capabilities that you believe you have lead you to try various activities, then if you are successful in them, to create understandings about what is possible for you. Similarly, if you have never been able to perform a task, such as speaking in public, you might believe that God could never use you to perform such a task.

SIN TENDENCIES

It's essential to be clear about the nature of sin. The Biblical term for sin means to miss the mark. The bull's eye, or mark, is God's glory. When we align with God's ways, we partake of God's abundant life and even catch a taste of His glory. When we choose to desire, feel, think and act in ways that are contrary to God's will for our lives, we miss the mark. Sin begins in our inner being, so that is where we need to begin to examine our lives, trying to figure out what is really happening in the core of our being.

An insightful definition of sin comes down to us from the mother of John Wesley, the 18th-century theologian who, along with his brother Charles, founded the Methodist movement. (I've added the italicized words to Susannah Wesley's definition to make the connection with the four aspects of our being.) I first heard this story from my friend Tony Cimmarusti: When John Wesley was a boy, he asked his mother, "What is sin?" His mother, who had no formal theological training, replied:
"Whatever weakens your sense of reasoning *(Mind)*,
impairs the tenderness of your conscience,
obscures your sense of God *(Soul)*,
or takes away your relish for spiritual things – *(Heart)*.
In short, if anything increases the authority of the flesh over the Spirit *(Strength)*,
that to you becomes sin, however good it is in or of itself."

That says it all, doesn't it? What I love about this definition is that it highlights how *personal* sin is and how our sin tendencies will all be different. That should also help us refrain from jumping to conclusions or judging others. It is the Holy Spirit's job to convict of sin, and we can usually be the best help to others as we allow God to work on our *own* lives. The key is, as we discovered in the Law of Reality, to understand how the evil in us and the evil in the world are co-conspiring to lead us away from God. That understanding will help us more quickly repent and follow the Cycle of Renewal.

THE CYCLE OF RENEWAL AND BELIEVING

A great way to summarize these reflections on sin and righteousness is to use a tool we looked at before in regard to transformation (Law 9). Seeing it again here will help us better understand how to view the sin in our lives and be trained in righteousness.

Believing in the Lord Jesus with all our Heart, Soul, Mind and Strength means that we:

1. Embrace the revelation or feedback that God brings into our lives which convicts us of our sin and need for Him;

2. Change incorrect or negative beliefs through holistic repentance: agreeing with God's will (Heart), receiving healing of wounds (Soul), learning His truth (Mind) and calling upon His strength (Strength); and

3. Embrace God's new correct beliefs (Desires, Feelings, Thoughts and Capabilities) for our lives by making amends or restitution to those we have wounded and engaging our new training in righteousness.

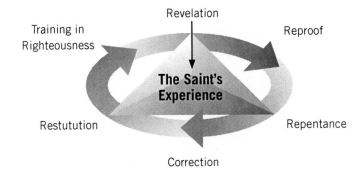

All Scripture is God-breathed and is useful for teaching, rebuking, correcting and training in righteousness, so that the man of God may be thoroughly equipped for every good work. (2 Timothy 3:16-17)

If you consider these steps as they apply to Maryanne's situation, we could describe them as follows:

1. The feedback Maryanne receives from her mentor begins to open the way for God to highlight her sin; she *thought* her sin was in being a "bad mother" or "not giving enough" to her children; in reality it lay in *wrong beliefs about herself and her children,* resulting in neglected discipline. The underlying sin might also be in not forgiving her parents for the neglect *she* received.

2. Maryanne begins to open up to healing of her own hurts (soul); also begins to forgive her parents and other authorities. As she learns of God's principles for her life (mind), she can start agreeing with and declaring His truth regarding His love for her and her children (heart), and then enter into His discipline as she learns to re-train her children in God's strength (strength).

3. Along with embarking on new habits at home, Maryanne may also find herself taking further steps, such as asking forgiveness from those in her family or circle of friends for the way she has lashed out at times of frustration, or the times when she judged

them or couldn't recognize their show of love. These actions may depend on the willingness of others to engage in open dialogue. If they're not open to it, Maryanne's further action would take place between her and the Lord, then between her and others in a Christian community.

THE SEVEN DEADLY SINS

You won't find this actual "list" of the seven deadly sins anywhere in Scripture, although they are all there. This is a list that, through the centuries, the Church has agreed are the main areas of opposition or temptation that we face during the journey of discipleship.

Do not love the world or anything in the world. If anyone loves the world, the love of the Father is not in him. [16] *For everything in the world—the cravings of sinful man, the lust of his eyes and the boasting of what he has and does—comes not from the Father but from the world.* [17] *The world and its desires pass away, but the man who does the will of God lives forever. (1 John 2:15-17)*

Ω

As you read through each of these descriptions, I encourage you to use it like another spiritual workout session. Look for the underlying beliefs in this list, for it's the beliefs that make up our sinful nature. The sinful actions are mere symptoms of that sinful nature. I have contrasted the sins listed with the opposite Virtues, for I want your main focus to be on God's plan for you, not the enemy's snare. I've also added some corresponding insights from our Seven G's list. By now I am sure you can easily make the connections between the Seven Deadly Sins, the Seven godly Virtues and the Seven Values of Abundant Living. After all, you've had a coach who keeps drilling you! Even so, I'm aware that each time we go over these things, we can see them from a new angle. Look for what stands out to you this time, and make a note of how the Holy Spirit may be prompting you to respond.

1. PRIDE

One definition of pride describes it as "a high and **exaggerated opinion** of one's qualities, attainments or estate or lack thereof." (I've emphasized the word *opinion* to draw your attention to the nature of that belief system.) Pride has traditionally been considered the root of all sin. As such, it is a disordered or excessive self-centeredness. It can be either a high or low opinion of oneself; the main aspect being the **focus on oneself and assertion of one's own opinion above God's view.** It results in isolation from God and fractures the bonds that link us to each other and the community. The obvious outcome of pride is a dismissal of the need to be in relationship with others. With this distance, hard-heartedness ensues, and compassion and empathy for human suffering are minimized. This holds not only for individuals but also for groups and even nations, as pride undermines both community and communion.

Pride is self-exaltation. In fact, pride is **preoccupation with self.** It places self at the very center of life. We are to love the Lord our God with all our heart, soul, mind and strength (Mark 12:30). Pride puts self in the center and loves self first. Ironically, the self isn't truly loved with this kind of exaltation. There is little room for God when we are full of ourselves, and therefore little room for real love.

Pride also destroys faith. We can't believe two opposite claims at the same time. It is impossible to believe that the one who is happiest is the one who cares for himself first, and at the same time, believe the teaching of Jesus that the one who finds his life is the one who gives it away.

The Opposite Virtue: Humility

The virtue that is counter to the sin of pride is humility. The virtue of humility is a hard sell today (perhaps it always has been). The popular view is that humility makes us doormats for others. We do well to remember the teaching of Saint Thomas Aquinas that humility is "a praiseworthy depreciation of oneself." It has to do with **an accurate sense of self and others with a deep reliance on God** throughout the seasons of life. It is seeing yourself "neither higher nor lower than you ought." *God opposes the proud but gives grace to the humble (James 4:6).*

Teresa of Avila (1515-1582) expressed it this way:

"It is a most certain truth that, the richer we see ourselves to be—confessing at the same time our poverty—the greater will be our progress and the more real will be our humility." [19]

True humility understands that without God "we can do nothing" (John 15:5) while at the same time remembering, "we can do all things through Christ who strengthens us" (Philippians 4:13). When we live self-directed and self-empowered lives, true greatness will forever be out of our grasp, but when we humble ourselves before God and serve Him as our Lord, unlimited greatness lives within us.

Pride vs. Humility: GLORIFICATION

Humility is a precursor to the holy dependence needed for the Glorification of God. Pride holds us back from experiencing His life and elevates self above God, seeking to bring glory to ourselves.

2. ENVY

Envy is defined as "the painful or resentful awareness of an advantage enjoyed by another, joined with a desire to possess the same advantage." **It's a belief that others have it better and we don't have what we need.** In 1 Corinthians 13:4, the Apostle Paul describes envy as the opposite of love. Galatians 5:21 lists envy as the fruit of the "flesh." The letter of James (3:14-16) associates jealousy and selfish ambition with evil and chaos. According to Aristotle, envy grows naturally in relationships between equals (or apparent equals). Geoffrey Chaucer, the 14th-century author of *The Canterbury Tales*, described envy as sorrow at the prosperity of others and joy in their hurt. Saint Thomas Aquinas defined envy as sorrow over another's good.[20] Feeling so insecure, the envious person sees anything good in another as detracting from his or her own personal value. The sources of continual entertainment and variety that modern life affords us have produced a continual quest for novelty and an added capacity for boredom and envy.

Many of our age's cultural values fuel the sin of envy. In a materialistic, competitive society, it's difficult not to struggle against others or compare one's success in relation to other's failures. The more we have, the more entitled or privileged we feel. Success breeds arrogance and intolerance of others less fortunate.

The average worker does not compete with the corporate CEO as he would with a coworker. An envious one watches others with an eagle eye in order to make sure that nobody gets ahead or becomes "more equal" than the rest of the pack. As a sin among equals, envy has a profoundly negative impact on the members of any group. The Christian community also struggles with the demon of envy among its members; the only difference might be in the addition of envying people's spiritual things as well as material.

The Opposite Virtue: Contentment

The writings of Saint Thomas Aquinas remind us that envy is contrary to love, the source of the soul's spiritual life. Love rejoices in a neighbor's good, but envy grieves over it. The most powerful statement of love is, of course, Saint Paul's teaching in 1 Corinthians 13.

Contentment strikes many as something for weak or inferior people. But in reality it contains a power over sin and self that surprises us once we exercise it. In *Conjectures of a Guilty Bystander*, the 20th century monk Thomas Merton writes:

"Why can we not be content with the secret happiness that God offers us without consulting the rest of the world? If we are fools enough to remain at the mercy of the people who want to sell us happiness, it would be impossible for us ever to be content with anything. How would they profit if we became content? ... The last thing a salesman wants is for the buyer to become content. You are no use in our affluent society unless you are always just about to grasp what you never have." [21]

Contentment is wanting what you have, not having what you want.

Envy vs. Contentment: GIFTS

It is not uncommon for people to envy one another's spiritual gifts and the adulation that comes along with being used by God in mighty ways. Even though our motives might be altruistic, the competitiveness of envy causes people to lose sight of what God has given them. Contentment teaches us to steward our "lot" in life (it's a LOT more than we realize!) and be grateful for whatever we have in terms of time, talents, treasures, spiritual gifting, friendships, opportunities to serve God and so on.

3. WRATH

As an emotion or passion, anger is a *natural reaction* caused by someone or something that restricts our freedom to act or carry out our desires. Anger arises when we face obstacles, frustration of our plans, restraint of our activities, physical harm, insult or psychological injury. It can also result from real or perceived hurt, unmet needs and expectations, or attacks against us, usually by significant people in our lives, such as parents and family members, friends and working associates. *Anger is first an emotion and as such is a neutral messenger, operating like a nerve ending or warning signal. However, it becomes the deadly sin of wrath when it is allowed to fester or becomes inordinate. That is, when it is allowed to grow against reason, and is connected with the desire for revenge, damage or destruction against the perceived cause of our hurt.* Then it breeds **a belief that revenge is ours to take.** The Lord clearly addresses this issue and exhorts us to wait for Him: *"It is mine to avenge, I will repay" (Hebrews 10:30).*

In Ephesians 4:26-32, Paul instructs the community not to let the sun go down while they are still angry, and to rid themselves of bitterness, passion, anger, harsh words, slander and malice. Anger must give way to forgiveness. While this has psychological significance, the grace of reconciliation and union comes from the Lord.

My dear brothers, take note of this: Everyone should be quick to listen, slow to speak and slow to become angry, [20]for man's anger does not bring about the righteous life that God desires. (James 1:19-20)

Anger that is unacknowledged (or "stuffed") leads to destructive behavior. Many Christians, trying to be virtuous, find themselves unwittingly stuffing their anger instead of letting God address it. As the letter of James indicates, it does not lead to the building of God's Kingdom. Such anger is often expressed in indirect ways such as backbiting, gossip, sarcasm, scapegoating and passive-aggressive behavior. In many cases, sinful conduct that is consciously chosen is rooted in unresolved or displaced anger.

The Opposite Virtue: Meekness

Meekness is related to patience. It has to do with *an inner strength or grace that allows us to embrace and endure an injury without self-pity or having to retaliate in kind.* **Meekness is submission to God's strength, a result of trust in God's ways, timing and power.** It is part of the ability to maintain perspective in the stressful heat of injury. The virtue that takes the wind out of wrath is meekness. Humor and the ability to laugh at self, others, and the ironies of life can also help deflate wrath. Both "humor" and "humility" spring from the root of *humus*, which is Latin for "ground." Meekness keeps us grounded and ready to properly respond to the sin and evil in the world with grace and truth.

Meekness, far from being mere control over wrath, implies an ability to be a *channel of God's power.* Jesus' meekness appears in his desire to forgive his murderers in the midst of his crucifixion. The Greek root of the word implies that *a yoke be well-fitted, thereby enabling an ox to pull a tremendous weight. Meekness also implies a superior responsiveness to the promptings of the Holy Spirit.* The more we trust in God rather than ourselves and our own understanding, the more surely we are guided into paths leading to fruitfulness, peace, and joy. The more we are motivated by a spirit of service, the more we will be led into opportunities reflecting real greatness, even if these are not the showy and superficial modes of greatness prized by today's celebrity culture.

Wrath vs. Meekness: GRACE

Meekness is Grace in action. It is the only antidote to wrath. We cannot give away something that we don't have, so we need to first experience the grace of God before we will have the experiential knowledge that empowers meekness in and through our lives.

4. SLOTH

Sloth is popularly known today as laziness. The ancient Greek word was *acedia*, meaning a lack of caring, apathy, aimless indifference, and a lack of desire for anything. The deadly sin of sloth is an apathy of the spirit in the face of the effort required to attain a goal and sustain it. In addition to *acedia*, another aspect of sloth is *tristitia*, meaning sadness or sorrow. Sloth is a dissipation of desire for anything that entails energy or effort. It is like living with a malaise akin to a mild depression.

Theologian Bernard Haring describes sloth as **"a lack of zeal for things spiritual." It might be characterized by beliefs such as *"What's the use?," " "It doesn't matter," * or worse yet, *"I don't matter."*** Sloth has to do with choosing to live in a spiritual vacuum. Its symptoms include lack of interest in things of the Spirit, flight from worship of God and lack of interest or lack of care for others. It is having an indifferent will toward doing God's will for your life.

A sluggard does not plow in season; so at harvest time he looks but finds nothing. (Proverbs 20:4)

Deep down, however, slothful people fear God's will and the cost to be paid if they respond from the heart. *There might even be other underlying fears involved, such as fear of failure, rejection, disappointment and so on.* It is easier to hide in the malaise and reject spiritual support than to take a risk. According to St. Gregory the Great, some of the "children" of sloth are melancholy, malaise and despair. Far too many people chronically complain about what is tragic or wrong in life while failing to recognize its beauty, loveliness and joy. These negative patterns of thinking need regular confrontation or they will dissipate faith, hope and love.

The Opposite Virtue: Obedience (Pro-actively on Mission with God) This is the most overt form of choosing life. It is stewarding your life from God's perspective, knowing that it *does* matter. You are not an accident but were created on purpose and therefore can **respond on purpose, in His purpose.** Obedience is not just obeying an order;

godly obedience is entering into full cooperation with Him. It requires us to partner with God as we reflect on our life mission and the various roles we play. As we seek God's wisdom in these reflections and listen to His direction, we are more likely to allocate our time wisely in each role. He may lead us in ways that seem contrary to our logic. Our drift pattern is away from God's mission, therefore **focus and discipline** are necessary to get us "on mission" with God.

Nothing goes down harder than the idea of *obedience* in a culture of postmodernism, where self-assertion commands attention and respect. H.W. Smith said that "Perfect obedience would be perfect happiness if we had perfect trust in the one we were obeying"—that is, trust that He will bring us to our desired condition or circumstances.[22] God has a purpose for our lives, a mission that is important from His perspective, and nothing will make us freer or more empowered than to get on mission with God in a spirit of complete obedience. When we enthusiastically (the word literally means in God = en Theos) pursue God's mission for our lives we are choosing to live in God.

Sloth vs. Obedience: GUIDANCE

Obedience is the virtue that moves us to follow God's guidance. Sloth will constantly be working against our followership and will try to convince us to do something other than the will of God for our lives.

5. GREED

Greed is an inordinate love of money or material acquisitions and the dedication to—or even the obsession with – their pursuit. **The implicit beliefs behind greed are that more is always better, acquisition is the way to happiness, and financial savvy and success confer status and make a nobody into a somebody.** The economy is driven by these needs and beliefs. The deadliness of greed lies also in the fact that we are desensitized to those who lack the basic amenities of life: food, housing, clothing, etc. We are confronted in our communities with the continuing plight of poverty and the violence and hopelessness that it breeds. Yet it is interesting that as we seek the comforts of upper-class life, we are easily cut off from the neighbors who need us.

"Do not store up for yourselves treasures on earth, where moth and rust destroy, and where thieves break in and steal. But store up for yourselves treasures in Heaven, where moth and rust do not destroy, and where thieves do not break in and steal. For where your treasure is, there your heart will be also." (Matthew 6:19-21)

"No one can serve two masters. Either he will hate the one and love the other, or he will be devoted to the one and despise the other. You cannot serve both God and Money." (Matthew 6:24)

If our hearts are set on possessions because of greed, and if that which really motivates us in life is the accumulation of things, then our hearts are diseased. It's possible that they are infected with other underlying beliefs: **People are often greedy because they believe money and possessions bring security, that money will keep them safe from hunger or homelessness. We may also view greed as a lack of faith, coming out of a fear of not having enough.**

The Opposite Virtue: Stewardship

We all must come to terms with our radical poverty as creatures before God; however wealthy we become, **everything belongs to God**. This also calls us to a greater sensitivity to the poor, God's special people. Disciples must give themselves to the social ministries that care for the under classes of society and the world. This requires not only a Good Samaritan attitude, but a prophetic concern for all who lack the basic amenities of life.

The realization that we're not owners at all removes the principal motive for greed, which is really pride. We don't even own our very lives, let alone our possessions or any personal quality. There is a hidden benefit to this fact. It implies that the owner needs these things to be managed for purposes that are well beyond our own petty and personal desires. *In submission to God, we become part of a grand enterprise, and our lives become part of God's glorious plan.*

But the first step is to settle it in our minds that we don't own our lives. The 13th-century mystic, Meister Eckhart, said: *"All gifts of nature and grace have been given us on loan. Their ownership is not ours but God's... Treat all things as if they were loaned to you without any ownership — whether body or soul, sense or strength, external goods or honors, friends or relations, house or hall, everything. For if I want to possess the property I have instead of receive it on loan, then I want to be a master."* [23]

Greed vs. Stewardship: GOOD STEWARDSHIP

Greed obviously works against any notion of Good Stewardship because the pursuit of money and possessions becomes an idol or false god in our lives.

6. GLUTTONY

St. Thomas Aquinas defines the deadly sin of gluttony as an inordinate or immoderate appetite in eating and drinking. Medieval writers considered eating and drinking excessive when they were driven by the hedonistic need to satiate the palate or stomach. Eating disorders such as anorexia and bulimia are very common in our time, causing cycles of starving or binging, and swinging between food-related anxiety, depression and guilt and the pursuit of sensory pleasure in food "addiction." Professionals in this area have concluded that **beneath this symptomatic behavior is an inner sense of alienation from the depths of oneself. The corresponding beliefs would be rooted in that shame: the self is *"not okay,"* and pain is *"too much to bear."*** This inner brokenness is a sad and destructive reality. Indulging and purging are merely symptoms of this inner ambivalence or endless hatred of and flight from self. Peter DeVries said, ***"Gluttony is an emotional escape, a sign that something is eating us."***

Do not join those who drink too much wine or gorge themselves on meat... (Proverbs 23:20)

The Opposite Virtue: Temperance

Temperance is moderation in the enjoyment of food or drink. This includes the idea of sobriety which is the moderation in the use of intoxicating drink. This virtue is often a hard sell because it challenges our perceived need for immediate gratification. The rewards of virtue never come quickly enough. For those who are obsessed with getting what they want and getting it right now, postponement of gratification is not only unbearable, it is unimaginable. However, **moderation is made possible by a greater gratification: the fullness of God's love.** Without that fullness, the advice of wellness experts becomes another attempt at self-help. They remind us of what good common sense has always maintained: Good health is fostered by a balanced diet, adequate physical exercise, and a proper blend of work, rest or recreation. All very good advice. But the *immoderation in our lives needs to be addressed first with God's touch on that inner gnawing within us; He alone will satisfy.*

If we set our hearts on a high, worthy ideal, we will do better in matters of self-control than if we merely recognize the dangers of intemperance or establish an unworthy goal, such as looking better physically than we do now or better than others. A 17th-century French bishop, François Fenelon, said: *"The best and highest use of your mind is to learn to distrust yourself, to renounce your own will, to submit to the will of God, and to become as a little child. It is performing the most common actions with your heart fixed on God, and as one who is accomplishing the end of his being... You will be moderate at table, moderate in speaking, moderate in expense, moderate in judging, moderate in your diversions... **It is this universal sobriety in the use of the best things that is taught us by the true love of God.**" [24]

We need to give God space and permission to transform us. We must *taste and see that the Lord is good (Psalm 34:8)* and then decide that being filled with Him and receiving His self-control means more to us than the gratification of our lower natures. Our victory will yield a joy that takes us by surprise with its intensity.

Gluttony vs. Temperance: GROWTH

Sustained growth requires the virtue of temperance as we properly balance the intakes and outputs of our lives. We can learn valuable lessons about overall growth in our spiritual, emotional, mental and physical lives by submitting to God and asking Him to heal and grow us in godliness. As self-control is a fruit of the spirit, monitoring our eating, drinking and exercise habits can often serve as a good indicator for us in discerning how submitted to God's guidance, power, discipline and training in righteousness we are.

7. LUST

Lust might be considered sexual gluttony. It is a perversion of what is intended to be a healthy intimacy within the covenant of marriage. Lust is the inordinate need to experience sexual or genital gratification, with little concern about the persons or relationships involved. The deadliness of lust is akin to all the others. We were made in God's image for relationship and self-giving: to spouse, to others, to God. Due to our fallen human nature, we suffer from concupiscence (strong sexual desire) which redirects authentic sexual self-giving to another into self-satisfying pleasure at the expense of another.

As an obsession, lust can also be cruel. It can be linked to most of the forms of sexual assault reported in the daily news: rape, incest, sexual abuse of children and minors, and sexual activity outside the marriage bed. Genesis 1:27 shows the divine gift of sexuality, the ability given people to enter into relationship with each other and with God. This intimacy was damaged first in the Garden of Eden as Adam and Eve felt the need to cover their nudity. We are seduced and we seduce one another in many ways. We are seduced by beauty, virility, power and control. Without any moral sensitivity, seduction can become a way of life at the expense of true love and intimacy. Herein lies the deadliness of the sin of lust. **Lust is an anti-intimacy sin, believing lies concerning true relationship and short-circuiting God's plans for true gratification with the allure of poor substitutes.** We can use our minds to begin to turn our focus back to the best that God offers:

Finally, brothers, whatever is true, whatever is noble, whatever is right, whatever is pure, whatever is lovely, whatever is admirable —if anything is excellent or praiseworthy—think about such things. (Philippians 4:8)

The Opposite Virtue: Chastity

The virtue of chastity is greatly misunderstood and often dismissed as naive. Chastity orders human sexual desire toward a union of two persons. It would be helpful to explore more deeply the implications of chastity for authentic human friendships, not only in relationship to celibacy and religious life. Chastity correlates with the beatitude, *"Blessed are the pure in heart."* It sees human sexuality and intimacy as an integral dimension of God's call to love, and doesn't devalue our bodies which were given to experience and express this love. Whereas lust puts an emphasis on the physical yet has a cheapening effect on the body, **chastity is based on true spiritual intimacy and the understanding that what God made is good; chastity honors the physical as well as the spiritual.**

One of the most common illusions is that the attainment of worldly pleasure can lead to joy. It is far more often the opposite, all the more so if the pleasure is illicit. In fact, an illicit pleasure will drain joy from the soul as predictably as impure food will drain health from the body.

Søren Kierkegaard said, *"Purity of heart is to want one thing."* By cultivating the love of God, the craving for unchaste pleasure diminishes proportionately. Practice praise and thanksgiving. When we meditate on His gracious provision of life and hope and the multitude of spiritual blessings available to us, the craving for impure pleasure gradually loses its power. It is replaced by the joy and peace that comes from continuous believing. Intimacy is being able to know one another deeply and cultivate and encourage God's best in one another's lives. And sex in marriage is intended to be God's expression of intimacy in which we each become whole in Him and yet one flesh in mutual enjoyment of one another. There is no true wholeness apart from holiness.

Lust vs. Chastity: GROUP

Lust is an anti-intimacy and anti-community sin, being a perversion of God's design for close relationship. It destroys the proper relating patterns in God's family as we begin treating one another like objects of desire rather than brothers and sisters in Christ. The antidote for this anti-group sin is found in allowing ourselves to be transparent before both God and those close to us. Lust is a counterfeit of the true and holy baring of souls that God has ordained for us.

Ω

Are there any areas of your life that began to stand out to you as you read through these contrasting descriptions? *Take a moment right now to invite God into those areas and ask Him to wash you. You can also demolish old strongholds or beliefs that have been exposed, and declare God's corresponding truth in their place. Take time to receive His love, especially if you have become aware of underlying hurts and disappointments, fears or feelings of shame.*

Just as I had to receive a revelation of God's care for me in the last chapter when working out with Coach Zupancic, so you would do well to "lie on the ground in the workout tent" for a moment. This is a good time to reflect not only on your beliefs and the challenges you face as God adjusts those beliefs, but also on the way your Heavenly Father does indeed have your back; He is watching over you with love in the midst of the discipline.

CHAPTER 15

Discipline & Joy: Growing New Habits

LAW 15

The Law of Discipline: *You overcome negative habits by changing incorrect (negative) beliefs and engaging in spiritually discerned disciplines.*

You are picking up speed! We now move to the fourth level in the Life Focus Process, which is entitled Charting the Course. At this level, you take the insights that you've acquired so far and use them as a springboard for the kind of disciplined growth that is required in transformation.

BUSTING MYTHS ABOUT DISCIPLINE

Discipline gets a bad rap. Some people immediately think of having their knuckles whacked with a ruler, or their privileges taken away for the weekend for something they didn't do. Others think of failed attempts at self-discipline. Many have not had the experience of a parent's healthy balance of loving discipline; they associate it with anger or inconsistent punishment instead. But all these instances fall short of the true opportunity found in discipline.

The word *discipline* comes from the word *disciple*, or one who is learning. And with God as our Personal Trainer, that learning can be a joyful adventure. Quaker philosopher Elton Trueblood expressed it this way:

> *"There is no intrinsic conflict between Christian discipline and Christian joy. It is not only that the discipline and joy are mutually consistent features of the Christian life; the deeper truth is that the acceptance of discipline leads to new joy. This is because the inner control, the new bondage, is the secret of perfect freedom."* [25]

This is not to say that discipline is a piece of cake; only that it can be far more positive than we usually think. Not only that, it can usher us into greater joy.

Hebrews 12: 1-13 addresses the attitude we are to have about discipline:

Therefore, since we are surrounded by such a great cloud of witnesses, let us throw off everything that hinders and the sin that so easily entangles, and let us run with perseverance the race marked out for us. ²Let us fix our eyes on Jesus, the author and perfecter of our faith, who for the joy set before him endured the cross, scorning its shame, and sat down at the right hand of the throne of God. ³Consider him who endured such opposition from sinful men, so that you will not grow weary and lose heart. ⁴In your struggle against sin, you have not yet resisted to the point of shedding your blood. ⁵And you have forgotten that word of encouragement that addresses you as sons:

"My son, do not make light of the Lord's discipline,
and do not lose heart when he rebukes you,
⁶because the Lord disciplines those he loves,
and he punishes everyone he accepts as a son."

⁷Endure hardship as discipline; God is treating you as sons. For what son is not disciplined by his father? ⁸If you are not disciplined (and everyone undergoes discipline), then you are illegitimate children and not true sons. ⁹Moreover, we have all had human fathers who disciplined us and we respected them for it. How much more should we submit to the Father of our spirits and live! ¹⁰Our fathers disciplined us for a little while as they thought best; but God disciplines us for our good, that we may share in his holiness. ¹¹No discipline seems pleasant at the time, but painful. Later on, however, it produces a harvest of righteousness and peace for those who have been trained by it. ¹²Therefore, strengthen your feeble arms and weak knees. ¹³Make level paths for your feet, so that the lame may not be disabled, but rather healed.

RE-PARENTING BY GOD

God is the best parent we could possibly have. He has already marked out the race for us. He has given us the path to run, given us His Spirit to help us run, and given us free access to His power and guidance for the duration of the race. It is up to us to run it in the right way, but as the Scriptures say, *His divine power has given us everything we need for life and Godliness through our knowledge of Him who called us by His own glory and goodness (1 Peter 1:3).* John Ortberg said, *"A disciplined person is someone who can do the right thing at the right time in the right way with the right spirit."* [26] God makes available to us everything we need to run the race in that right way. It is not God's intention that we follow this course in darkness but that we seek His guidance the whole way. Of course our receptivity to that guidance will depend on our perspective; if we remember that God is our Heavenly Father who is training us as His beloved children, we won't get bent out of shape in the process of receiving discipline.

Our need for re-parenting can't be understated. We all need God to fill in the gaps for us, completing the parenting that was begun by our human parents. Our submission to Him opens the way for that re-parenting, and our hearts play a key role. We have to want to receive His guidance and persevere in our responsiveness to it. Yet we have to remember this is not just another way to "do religion." The way forward is not to strive but to submit, and we can do this for the joy that is set before us because we will be sharing in His holiness, His divine nature. Holiness is not the price we pay to receive other benefits; it is itself a benefit of obedience to God's discipline. That is the promise, but we can only know it as a certainty as we began to experience it, especially as we experience His training through difficult situations.

WHAT ABOUT HARDSHIP?

The world is full of hardship, some of our own making, some due to spiritual warfare, and some simply due to the accumulation of sinful patterns over many centuries. While God doesn't enjoy seeing us suffer, He will use the hardships we face as a form of training. Jesus said, *"In this world you will have trouble; but take heart, for I have overcome the world" (John 16:33).* He is training us to become overcomers, and as we turn to Him in all our trouble, He will strengthen us to know Him even better and emerge that much more victorious than when we began.

Again it's your choice, but when hardship hits, that's your cue to grow in dependence on Him. If you don't know the nature of the particular kind of reform He's urging you to undertake now, He will provide the appropriate discipline so you can understand it and grow. You will characteristically go into maintenance mode in one discipline and then God will give you a new discipline for another area of your life. Therefore even when in the midst of hardship or negative circumstances, it's a positive cycle: You receive a discipline, you submit to it, you depend on God more, you know more of His power, and then you move on to His next form of discipline for you.

BETWEEN GOD AND A HARD PLACE

Tamara (not her real name) found herself in a marriage to an abusive man. She still loved him, but his behavior grew increasingly violent and even began to extend to their children. On the one hand, Tamara didn't want to get a divorce and felt it was not God's best, but on the other, she knew it wasn't right or safe to tolerate that abuse. She felt torn, wanting help from others but also afraid to seek it lest her husband blow up in a worse rage at her.

While there were many factors involved, this situation can be seen as an obvious hardship. Did God say to Tamara, "You made your bed, now you have to sleep in it"? No, His heart grieved for her suffering. But neither did He reach down to pluck her out of the marriage or instantly heal her husband. The hardship went on for a while, and Tamara found herself desperate to know what God wanted her to do. She had tried to reason with her husband, but to no avail. This drove her more forcibly into God's "chest," as she calls it, so desperate was she to hear from Him. She read the Bible with increasing thirst, needing any wisdom she could find there. She began to fast and pray for breakthrough. She didn't want the fast to be like a "hunger strike," she just wanted to know God's will and see His healing come. She finally got up the courage to attend a Bible Study even though it made her husband mad when she went out. She tried to continue to honor him even when he was being unreasonable. Later, she also sought counseling, another thing that had scared her because of the risk of upsetting her husband. All these things ended up being forms of godly training for Tamara, though she didn't notice the enormous effect at the time.

Tamara's difficult marriage was not something God wished on her, but He used it so thoroughly that she looks back on that time now as a period in which she grew the strongest. The emotional pain and bewilderment was so severe that she didn't know she was growing. But in retrospect, Tamara is amazed at how her roots in God's faithfulness grew so deep. One of her favorite passages of Scripture has to do with the date palm that is able to bloom in season and out of season, because its roots have grown deep during times of drought. We as Christians are likened to that date palm. The hardships we go through provide the very thing that will strengthen us and help us stay sustained in the provision of the Lord.

RECEIVED, NOT ACHIEVED

The discipline involved in Christian commitment is wrapped in a paradox. As it's not God's will for us to glorify ourselves, the discipline we need isn't through an inner striving. An invigoration of the will is certainly necessary, but it is the Holy Spirit that must do that work within us. We choose to open ourselves to that work, and we move forward believing we have received it, obeying where He guides us. In the process we discover freedom and mastery.

Discipline in Christ is easier when it is received rather than worked up. *We haven't been given a spirit of fear but of power, love, and self-discipline (2 Timothy 1:7).* Notice the word "given." You can relax a little, because the burden isn't on you to generate or force things to happen; you've been given the self-discipline you need in God. Your job is to affirm what you have been given and release it. In other words, God will guide you to the disciplines that will best benefit your training in righteousness in each season of your life, then He will empower your training in righteousness (love) as you submit and obey.

DISCIPLINES: THE KEY TO UNLOCKING OUR POTENTIAL

Do you have areas where you struggle? Welcome to the human race! As you saw in the last chapter on beliefs, we can approach these areas of struggle first by examining our existing beliefs. Underlying our bad habits, we all have something that we have believed that kept those habits in place. After taking stock in this way, we can then engage in appropriate, spiritually discerned disciplines to help us develop new, godly habits. Focusing our efforts through daily, weekly and monthly disciplines is the key to good habit formation and personal growth in our lives. Remember, this is a process. Don't engage in a discipline in a way that is going to burn you out because it is unrealistic. You wouldn't dare start lifting 400 pounds right off the bat; you'd gradually work up to that weight. It's the same with spiritual disciplines; be patient with yourself and build up gradually and realistically.

THIRTY-SIX SPIRITUAL DISCIPLINES TO HELP YOU GROW

$$\Omega$$

Here is another personal coaching moment for you. I have organized 36 spiritual disciplines in two different ways to aid you in discerning which of these disciplines God is challenging you to pursue. You will find a brief definition of each discipline on the following pages.

How Hungry are You?

If you want to see a more in-depth description of these 36 spiritual disciplines, they can be found on our web site: www.lifespringnetwork.org; also through taking the Omega Course.

In the Omega Course, we take people much deeper into this area of disciplines by first grouping them according to the 14 roles in the Roles Diagram. That list will give you many options to choose from in your training—suggestions for how to grow in particular areas— all of which should be undertaken with the guidance of a mentor. Keep in mind, the disciplines that must be central to your life will be determined by the chief sins of commission and omission that entice or threaten you from day to day. It can be arranged as a personalized program just for you. You don't want to go into combat in a half-hearted way against the "Seven Deadly Sins" listed in the last chapter nor underestimate the destructive power these negative habits can have in your life. They call for a comparably hard-nosed response on our part, supported by infinite grace. Fortunately, our God is the Source of that grace.

The Four Types of Christian Discipline

I have also grouped the 36 disciplines into Disciplines of Abstinence and Engagement. Then I have further broken down the Disciplines of Engagement into three categories: God Engagement, God and Community Engagement, and Life and Wisdom Engagement. As you read through the following categories of disciplines, I pray you will feel the strength of God begin to pour into you. May His divine nature within you already start dismantling your old patterns of behavior and replacing them with His virtues. And may you have joy even as you begin to engage in the disciplines.

THE DISCIPLINES OF ABSTINENCE

The spiritual disciplines of abstinence reveal the nature of the battle between the flesh and the spirit. By abstaining from food, social interaction, or sleep, we are "exercising" our spiritual muscles against the lower nature. It is like lifting weights; silly in itself, but useful as preparation for real physical tests in the future. The things we abstain from in the spiritual disciplines are not evil; it is for the sake of the exercise that we deny ourselves; to prepare us for real temptation, be it tomorrow or the next day. The disciplines of abstinence give us much needed experience and insight into the spiritual battle going on within us, and the lessons learned cannot be taught any other way. As we go along, we will discover what is it like to say "no" to the lower nature and what tricks it will play. The ways in which desire, habit, distraction, and other factors affect you will not be the same ways they affect other people. You must learn through your own experience how to live in holiness before God.

The disciplines of abstinence are an opportunity to train in safety. This is when we refrain voluntarily to some degree and for some time from the satisfaction of what we generally regard as normal and legitimate desires. These include not only our basic drives or motivations, but also our desires for convenience, comfort, material security, reputation or fame. It is the best course for dealing with any habit or pursuit, harmless in itself, that is keeping us from God and sinking us deeper into the things of this world. According to Bishop Thomas Wilson of the Isle of Man, *"Those who deny themselves will be sure to find their strength increased, their affections raised, and their inward peace continually augmented."*

This quote highlights the way abstinence, while it is a form of refraining, is in actuality *adding* something to our lives. When we engage in abstinence of any kind, we are exchanging one taste for another. The inconveniences of the flesh more finely tune us to God's ways and the things of the Spirit.

I.   The Eight Disciplines of Abstinence

1. **Solitude**, or the practice of being absent from other people in order to be present with God, sets us free from the things that trap and oppress us. By bursting apart the shell of our securities, it becomes a gateway to the successful practice of other disciplines.

2. **Silence**, the shutting out of sounds so we can hear God's voice, helps us to listen to people and observe them and also to live with quietness and confidence. *"Be still, and know that I am God"* (Psalm 46:10).

3. **Fasting**, most typically the abstinence from food, is a practice that helps us to depend on God more, in particular for the ability to endure deprivation more easily and the ability to exercise self-control. It requires practice to be effective, since as beginners it consumes all our attention.

4. **Simplicity** presupposes an attitude that God is the real owner of everything we have. It means a life of contentment and the ability

to focus our minds on the reign of God in our lives and in the world, His Lordship in everything. Less is truly more as it pertains to engaging in this discipline.

5. **Chastity** means more than abstaining from sin in the area of sex; it means avoiding an inappropriate sexual dimension in our relationship with another. As Dietrich Bonhoeffer observed, *"The essence of chastity is not the suppression of lust but the total orientation of one's life toward a goal."*

6. **Secrecy**, or keeping our good deeds and qualities from being made known, means that we experience a relationship with God that rises above the opinion of others. It implies a desire for others to do well, even to do better than we do. Our focus is on obedience to God and receiving His "Well done." Not letting our left hand know what our right is doing.

7. **Sacrifice** implies such abandonment to God that we give of our time, talents and resources even after it hurts to continue giving. This goes beyond being frugal so that we can be generous, into giving up our comforts and wants so that others' needs might be met.

8. **Watching** means abstinence from sleep while seeking to watch and wait upon the Lord obediently in prayer and intercession for His will to be done.

THE ENGAGEMENT DISCIPLINES

Author Dallas Willard defines the spiritual disciplines of engagement as the routine Christian activities of prayer, study, and meditation that are especially powerful in combination with the disciplines of abstinence. They are often mentioned in combination in Scripture, as seen in James 4:17. These disciplines balance the Disciplines of Abstinence (the in-breathing and out-breathing of our spiritual lives) by entering into action. **Abstinence counteracts tendencies to sins of commission, while engagement counteracts tendencies toward sins of omission. Abstinence makes way for engagement. These disciplines focus on helping us to engage the abundant life.**

Very few disciplines can be regarded as absolutely indispensable for a healthy life and work, though some are obviously more important than others. Practicing a range of activities that have proven track records across the centuries will help to keep us from erring.

Before we examine the disciplines, here are a few verses that serve to remind us of the task before us and the importance of being active, not passive.

Here is my advice: Live your whole life in the Spirit and you will not satisfy the desires of your lower nature. For the whole energy of the lower nature is set against the Spirit, while the whole power of the Spirit is contrary to the lower nature. Here is the conflict, and that is why you are not able to do what you want to do.... (Galatians 5:16-17, Phillips Version)

So then, my brothers, you can see that we owe no duty to our sensual nature, or to live life on the level of instincts. Indeed that way of living leads to certain spiritual death. But if on the other hand you cut the nerve of your instinctive actions by obeying the Spirit, you will live. (Romans 8:12-13, Phillips Version)

If a man cleanses himself from the latter, he will be an instrument for noble purposes, made holy, useful to the Master and prepared to do any good work. (2 Timothy 2:21)

II. The Eight Disciplines of God Engagement

1. **Worship** means engaging our entire being with the greatness of God and glorifying Him with our lives. This means praising and basking in the presence of God wherever we are drawing on His nature and character, allowing ourselves to be transformed.
2. **Prayer** is communicating with God, which helps us to know Him, hear from Him, and depend on Him. Prayer rises to its maximum effectiveness when it is practiced together with several spiritual disciplines.
3. **Meditation** gives us the opportunity to dwell in a focused way on the goodness and perfection of our Lord. It is sensing and responding to the life and light of Christ.

4. **Singing** fills our minds with God's Word and in that way causes us to be edified. It connects His Word with our subconscious, printing it onto our innermost being.

5. **Surrender** is a daily discipline by which we overcome our prideful self and make our hearts available to be vessels for the abundant life to flow through us. It is abiding in the vine so we will bear much fruit.

6. **Study** involves reading and pondering the Word of God, especially the "great and very precious promises." *All Scripture is God-breathed and is useful for teaching, rebuking, correcting and training in righteousness, so that the man of God may be thoroughly equipped for every good work. (2 Timothy 3:16-17)*

7. **Pilgrimage** and sabbatical are emblematic of the chosen people questing in the desert for the Promised Land. Readers of this book, for example, have embarked upon a journey that will lead them deeper into the abundant life.

8. **Sabbath** refers to a time of rest, typically one day a week, for regaining perspective and worshiping the God on whom our value depends. Doing this in the context of community provides a further enhancement of its power.

III. The Ten Disciplines of God-Engagement and Community-Engagement

1. **Teaching** from the Scriptures, an endeavor to which all Christians are called, means admonishing one another with all wisdom and instructing one another in godliness. The more mature are called to teach the younger disciples in the power of the Holy Spirit.

2. **Celebration** means gathering with others to recognize God's faithfulness in our lives. We dishonor God as much by fearing and avoiding pleasure as we do by dependence upon it or living for it. As Richard Foster said, *"Without a joyful spirit of festivity, the disciplines become dull, death-breathing tools in the hands of modern Pharisees."* [27]

3. **Service** means giving of ourselves humbly towards the active promotion of the good of others and the propagation of our faith.

In addition to the good that our service may be, it trains us away from arrogance, possessiveness, envy, resentment, and covetousness.

4. **Fellowship**, which is typically in the form of common activities of worship, study, prayer, celebration, and service, reflects the fact that we cannot be whole persons without one another. It is in covenant community that we grow in faith.

5. **Confession** involves acknowledging our sins before God and others and thereby removing obstructions to spiritual growth. As we meet our responsibility, we can experience true forgiveness regarding our deepest weaknesses and failures.

6. **Submission** is engaging the experience of placing ourselves under those in our fellowship who are qualified (those in godly authority) to direct our efforts in growth. It means giving up our way in favor of someone else's, an essential attitude and action for redemptive communities. If we have discerned that those in authority are not submitted to God's word, we have the responsibility to confront them, and if they are unrepentant, to remove ourselves from under their authority.

7. **Friendship Evangelism** recognizes that our lives and our love are the only "Bible" most people we meet will ever know. It is accomplished when we allow the Holy Spirit to live and love through us. As our lives bear witness to God's greatness, we intentionally share our faith with people in our lives in response to their inquiry and as we are prompted by God to do so.

8. **Assembling** means that we commit to gathering with the covenant community for the sake of being better able to discern God's will for us. This is an important discipline, because the priesthood of all believers only comes alive when we gather under the Lordship of Christ.

9. **Hospitality**, especially in the form of showing kindness to strangers, is a blessing as well as a discipline. As we experience the mutuality of giving and receiving, we also experience God's presence.

10. **Intercessory Prayer**, as distinguished from prayer for ourselves, means asking and trusting God to act for the advancement of others. God wants us to ask with urgency, passion, and perseverance.

IV. The Ten Disciplines of Life and Wisdom Engagement

1. **Journaling** involves keeping a spiritual diary that includes our prayers, our thoughts, and our record of what we hear God saying to us. Part of its value lies in the ability we have to go back over past entries to see the ways in which we have grown spiritually.

2. **Earning** is a discipline with spiritual value when undertaken with commitment, purpose, and a grateful attitude. As we produce value, we grow in the remembrance that it is the Lord our God who gives us the ability to earn resources.

3. **Saving** as a discipline becomes another means by which God trains us in righteousness. He gives us the wisdom to save for unexpected hardship and also the wisdom to avoid stockpiling wealth beyond our need.

4. **Giving** with an obedient will, a joyful attitude, and a compassionate heart pleases God and gives us entrance into His blessing. The recommended training discipline for giving is the tithe or ten percent of our income.

5. **Frugality** means striving to stay within the bounds of the kind of life to which God has led us. It involves avoiding the frivolous consumption that corrupts the soul away from trust in Him. It implies the good stewardship of maximizing our resources.

6. **Guidance** implies both seeking and giving wisdom through mentoring relationships. It is the duty and the opportunity of Christians to sensitize themselves to the specific plan that God wants us to follow.

7. **Retreat** gives us a chance to step out of our usual way of life for a little while for the sake of opening ourselves to God's wider perspective on it. It can be done totally alone or with a small group of people who have a common purpose.

8. **Temperance** stresses control and restraint not only over personal conduct but also over the expression of opinion. It implies submission to the power of the Holy Spirit as we ascertain wholesome boundaries for our lives, including moderation in the enjoyment of food and drink.

9. **Planning** involves deliberately spending time to seek wisdom about how we should steward our lives from God's perspective. Christian planning differs from secular planning chiefly because it is intended as no more than a structure within which God can continue to guide us toward His preferred future.

10. **Exercise** refers to the need to engage in physical labor or service to maintain a healthy body. This continual cleansing of stress yields benefits to us personally and to others.

CROSS TRAINING

After engaging in certain disciplines for a while, you might experience a "plateau" effect where the journey becomes stale and worn. Any workout routine is subject to the same phenomenon. During seasons like this it is advisable to do some cross training with other disciplines that will continue to grow you in the areas God is challenging you to focus on and keep the journey refreshing and new. Discipline need not be heavy-handed; it's more like a light touch on the steering wheel when you drive a car. You keep adjusting here and there, making little changes so you stay on the road. Eventually many of your new habits will become second nature to you.

THE HOLY SPIRIT AND DISCIPLINES

One danger in studying the spiritual disciplines is that we might practice them without the leading of the Holy Spirit. People can be led astray in that they enter into these disciplines with the "spirit of religion" for the purpose of impressing other people, ourselves or God.

On the other hand, I suspect we often thwart the Holy Spirit's leading because we are ignorant of what is likely to be asked of us. How many times has God disturbed our sleep with someone in mind and we "count sheep" or take a sleeping pill instead of watching and praying? How many sermons have we heard that don't sit well with us and yet we ignore the Spirit's prompting to study God's Word and thus end up with a faulty knowledge of God? How many earnest prayers go unanswered because we refuse to practice the discipline of fasting? How many ugly things do we say to those we love because we are not being obedient to the Spirit's call to spend some time alone?

At that time Jesus said, "I praise you, Father, Lord of heaven and earth, because you have hidden these things from the wise and learned, and revealed them to little children. ²⁶Yes, Father, for this was your good pleasure. ²⁷All things have been committed to me by my Father. No one knows the Son except the Father, and no one knows the Father except the Son and those to whom the Son chooses to reveal him. ²⁸Come to me, all you who are weary and burdened, and I will give you rest. ²⁹Take my yoke upon you and learn from me, for I am gentle and humble in heart, and you will find rest for your souls. ³⁰For my yoke is easy and my burden is light." (Matthew 11:25-30)

The yoke of Jesus may indeed be easy, but we keep throwing it off! Our lower natures are in control and running rampant! This is not following Christ's way of living. Small wonder our growth is stunted and real holiness is an elusive dream. If the Spirit led Jesus and every "saint of note" to consistently practice the spiritual disciplines so they could live life to the full, shouldn't we expect the same leading if we are truly His disciples?

His yoke is easy because His guidance (spiritually discerned discipline) is perfect. His burden is light because He empowers us to obey and live the supernatural life of a disciple. As we are trained by God and walk daily in the Spirit, we will experience the abundant life, and our soul, which is guiding us to submit to God's guidance and power, will find rest!

SPIRITUAL DISCIPLINES AND SPIRITUAL PATHWAYS

A key to wise yoke-bearing and training in righteousness through spiritual disciplines is understanding your preferred spiritual pathways and walking in them. A spiritual pathway is the way we most naturally connect with God and grow spiritually. The combination of spiritually discerned disciplines and spiritual pathways creates a synergy and enthusiasm for seeking God that will keep your interest and motivation high.

John Ortberg has identified seven main spiritual pathways. They are the Intellectual, Relational, Serving, Worship, Activist, Contemplative and Creation Pathways. While each of us tend to favor one or two, it is good to explore all of them. There's usually at least one that feels very unnatural for us. The goal is to feel great freedom and joy using them. To make the most of your spiritual pathway, give yourself permission to be who you are in God and be willing to engage in activities that move you out of your comfort zone. Explore and develop the other pathways, but be careful not to envy someone else's pathway or to judge someone else because of his or her pathway. For each pathway I will also line up one of the Seven Values of Abundant living and provide some insights for application.

Seven Spiritual Pathways
(Adapted from John Ortberg's course
An Ordinary Day with Jesus)

1. Intellectual Pathway
As a thinker, you draw close to God as you're able to learn more about Him, especially by studying Scripture and theology. You have little patience for emotional approaches to faith. When you face problems or spiritual challenges, you approach them as a problem-solver. You tend to read great books, expose yourself to lots of teaching, and find like-minded people with whom you can learn. To develop this pathway, devote yourself to corporate worship and to private adoration and prayer, because if your learning doesn't lead to worship, you will tend to become all mind and no soul, which exhibits itself in relationships as being all truth and no grace. Engage in self-examination and 360-degree feedback to assess whether or not you are being loving. Engage in mentoring with others who will hold you accountable to living what you have learned. Remember, *Knowledge puffs up, but love builds up (1 Corinthians 8:1)*. **Guidance–Intellectual** People with the Intellectual pathway usually have a strong commitment to the value

of Guidance. They are stimulated by the world of thoughts, ideas and logic and tend to search the depths of Scripture to pull out the deeper meanings and connections found within. They connect deeply with God along the journey of seeking His truth and guidance.

2. Relational Pathway

Spiritual growth comes most naturally to you when you're involved in significant relationships. Small groups and other community life experiences are key, whereas being alone can drive you crazy. In key times of growth, God will often speak to you through people, as you are easy with opening your life to them. You tend to use your spiritual gifts to serve others. You pray with others in community, you learn in a class with other people or in a small group, and you use your network of contacts to further God's Kingdom. To stretch yourself, develop a capacity for silence. Study Scripture for yourself. Invite close friends and mentors to speak truth to you. **Group–Relational** People with the Relational pathway usually have a strong commitment to the value of Group. They are stimulated by the world of people and relationships. They connect deeply with God when engaged in covenant community with others who are pursuing Christlikeness as God's family.

3. Serving Pathway

God's presence seems most tangible when you're involved in helping others. You're often uncomfortable in a setting where you don't have a role, and you constantly look for acts of service you can engage in. You easily get plugged into a community and tend to look for glimpses of God's presence in the people you serve and in the execution of your tasks.

To develop yourself and avoid the pitfalls of overemphasis, balance your service with small group and community life. Learn to receive love, even when you're not being productive, and to express love not just through actions but through words as well. Prepare to serve first by praying so your service is genuinely spiritual service. Remember that God loves you not because you are so faithful in serving Him, but because you are His child. Don't confuse serving with trying to earn God's love, and be careful not to resent other people who don't serve as much as you do. **Gifts–Serving** People with the Serving pathway usually have a strong commitment to the value of Gifts. They are stimulated by serving others in need through the power of the Holy Spirit. They connect deeply with God when engaged in growing the Kingdom of God through servanthood.

4. Worship Pathway

You have a deep love of corporate praise and a natural inclination toward celebration. In difficult periods of life, worship is one of the most healing activities you engage in; you come alive and participate enthusiastically on a regular basis, including in your car. To develop yourself, engage in the disciplines of study and solitude, while remaining committed to your community of faith. Also, serve God in concrete ways as an extension of your worship. Be careful not to judge those who aren't as expressive in worship and guard against an experience-based spirituality that always has you looking for the next worship "high." **Glorification–Worship** People with the Worship pathway usually have a strong commitment to the value of Glorification. They are humble people who come alive in the process of testifying to the greatness of God. They connect deeply with God when participating in and facilitating environments that bring honor and glory to God.

5. Activist Pathway

You have a single-minded zeal and a very strong sense of vision. Challenges don't discourage you, and you love a high-paced, problem-filled, complex, strenuous way of life. You do everything you can to bring out the potential God has placed in other people, to work with them, and to accomplish things. To develop yourself, guard against going too long without pausing to reflect on what you're doing. Also be on guard against running over others or exploiting them. Spend time in solitude and silence, while cultivating a reflective discipline like journaling. **Growth–Activist** People with the Activist pathway usually have a strong commitment to the value of Growth. They are stimulated by the journey of training in righteousness and actively working out their salvation with fear and trembling. They connect deeply with

God when strategizing, leading, or participating in practical hands-on Kingdom-building efforts that see progress and change lives.

6. Contemplative Pathway

You love uninterrupted time alone; prayer and reflection come naturally to you. If you get busy or spend a lot of time with people, you feel drained and yearn for times of solitude. However, you have a tendency to avoid the demands of the real world. To develop yourself, follow the intuitions and leadings that come in your times alone with God and act on what you hear from God in the silence. Resist the temptation to consider your times of private prayer and solitude as less important than the more public acts of ministry performed by others. To balance out your contemplation, choose for yourself a regular place of active service and be sure to stay relationally connected, especially when those relationships become difficult. **Grace–Contemplative** People with the Contemplative pathway usually have a strong commitment to the value of Grace. They are stimulated by their inner world and inner prayer life with God. They enjoy connecting deeply with God's grace in their lives and helping others to make that connection as well. Many of the great evangelists of our day refuel themselves through the contemplative pathway. They connect deeply with God when engaged in the dialogue of connecting with God both privately and with others struggling to make that connection.

7. Creation Pathway

You respond deeply to God through your experience of nature, and being outdoors replenishes you. You're highly aware of your five senses, including the ways they can be used to perceive art. You tend to be creative. However, you may be tempted to use beauty or nature to escape people who are disappointing. Given that tendency, guard against the temptation to avoid church. Take Scripture with you into nature and meditate on God's Word. **Good Stewardship–Creation** People with the Creation pathway usually have a strong commitment to the value of Good Stewardship. They are stimulated by nature and caring for God's creation as stewards or managers. They connect deeply to God through beholding the genius of God's handiwork in nature and caring for His creation.

PUTTING IT ALL TOGETHER

What about when you're in a position to help guide others? As you discern which disciplines will be most beneficial for them to engage in during different seasons in their lives, it is wise to keep in mind the roles diagram to discover underdeveloped aspects of people's lives, the various types of Spiritual Disciplines in order to explain them to others, and the Spiritual Pathways in order to help others understand what motivates them. (In many instances, it's a matter of common sense.) After you've discovered how someone is functioning in the various roles in their lives, you'll have a better sense of roles which need attention and which disciplines would best help address those areas in the context of their preferred spiritual pathways. For those of you who don't think you are capable of mentoring, just remember these two things: First, we are ALL designed to have those who look up to us as well as those to whom we look for guidance. And second, everything you learn about mentoring others helps you to better understand your own journey of discipleship. We learn best as we are teaching, training and mentoring others. **To give you an example of how all this information is fleshed out in real life, here's a peek at some sample mentoring for two very different men.**

TWO GUYS

The first I'll call Hugo. Hugo grew up believing in God, but only recently asked Jesus to be Lord of his life. A construction worker, he's built strong and has a gung-ho testimony to match. His upbringing was full of violence; Hugo got involved in gangs and drugs, eventually wanting to do himself in before he experienced a miraculous encounter with God that turned everything around for him. Certainly not lacking for zeal, Hugo still had several things that distressed him. He was finding himself exploding at his girlfriend in ways he didn't want to do. Also, even though he was clean and sober, he still felt a strong pull at times to go back to drugs.

MENTOR: How's your relationship with the Heavenly Father?

HUGO: *He saved my life! I'm always going to be grateful for that! I want to do right by God; I always knew He was there, but I didn't know He cared so much. I thought He was too busy. I want to know that the Heavenly Father is pleased with me, but sometimes I just can't shake it, this feeling that I'm gonna do something to blow it. Then He's gonna be really angry with me for that big mistake. I just can't seem to shake that fear.*

MENTOR: How about your family? Your parents?

HUGO: *Well my dad, he would hit first, talk later. Or maybe not talk, just hit, you know what I mean? And my mom, she didn't like seein' things that way, but she couldn't do anything about it. Sometimes I knew why I was in trouble; other times it didn't make any sense.*

Going around and through the roles diagram with Hugo, it becomes clear that he doesn't have many close friends yet, as all his buddies are still in the old lifestyle. One older couple has been encouraging him, and it seems they fit the description of Hugo's first mentors; God is using them to re-parent him. His work is going great; He's a hard worker and recognized as such. Still, he's a loner, trying to stay clean when several other guys on the job are not. And sometimes his boss seems grossly unfair.

Hugo's girlfriend is also a believer but she has some issues to work on too. Hugo is terrified he'll lose it and hurt her like his dad would. He gets frustrated and wants to blame her, but knows he needs help too.

Which disciplines would best help Hugo at this point?

First, **guidance** stands out as a crucial one. Hugo needs both assurance and direction as he goes forward with God and it would be so helpful for him to have counseling and healing prayer as well as mentoring. That involves Hugo's **submission** to the process, another basic discipline. As he begins to experience and recognize more of God's consistent love, his fears will be routed out. *"Perfect love drives out fear" (1 John 4:18).*

Many of Hugo's difficulties were experienced in a group, therefore a healthy group would be beneficial, especially in his new faith. He's like a seedling that needs good soil to be rooted and grounded. Regular **fellowship** in a small group and accurate **teaching** are therefore recommended to him; he was church-hopping at first but seems to have found one where he feels accepted. Membership there is encouraged. Submitting to covenant community will be a vital step in creating a safe environment for him to grow. The truths found in Scripture will displace the lies Hugo was subjected to in earlier years. **Confession** will help in a powerful way, especially as Hugo meets with a safer authority figure and finds clarification with regard to true guilt and absolution vs. false guilt or vague worry about God being angry with him.

What about Hugo's spiritual pathways? He is too antsy to sit down and study and meditate, but he loves to pray outside while on the move. When he takes walks, he finds himself remembering who he is and marveling at God's beauty. He's very sensitive underneath the tough exterior. A great spiritual pathway for him is the **Creation Pathway.**

> **HUGO:** *I always felt safer outside growing up, maybe that's why I like it so much. Of course I was always gettin' beat up inside, so maybe it was my way of escaping. But God was there for me! I didn't know it at the time, but He was watching over me!*
>
> **MENTOR:** You might want to consider taking a CD or ipod with you when you go outside, so you can listen to worship music or the Word...
>
> **HUGO:** *Oh man, that's a good idea. I never felt like I was a good reader, but maybe if I hear it, it'll go in.*
>
> **MENTOR:** That's right. "Faith comes by hearing, and hearing by the Word of God." It will build your faith.

Hugo has a propulsive excitement about him; some of it might be hyperactivity, but some of it is a gift from God. He's a great talker, very relational (**Relational Pathway**) and his mentor can envision God using Hugo's testimony to encourage many. But he needs grounding, rest and healing first. One thing that might also help him is having times of **silence, solitude** and **meditation.** This kind of discipline is totally foreign to him, yet it will balance out the overdrive and usher him into greater peace. Once Hugo has allowed the healing to begin, encouraging him to engage in **friendship evangelism** and mentoring (**guiding**) others who are new to their faith will greatly enhance his journey of discipleship, as God uses him to introduce others to faith he will grow exponentially.

Our second guy we'll call Frank. Now in his 50's, Frank is a mature Christian executive whose wife has encouraged him to seek help. He's a good, faithful man who is very safe to be around. Yet for years, he's felt a sort of malaise. He thought that was just the way life was, but his wife thinks he's depressed. Frank doesn't have a wide range of emotional expression, but he's good for a few well-placed witty remarks in a crowd.

MENTOR: How is your relationship with God these days?

FRANK: *I go to church every Sunday, and I used to sing in the choir until it got a little too busy at work for me to attend the rehearsals. We have a Bible Study in our home every Wednesday.*

MENTOR: Yes but how's your relationship with God? Are you on speaking terms?

FRANK: *Uh, I guess so. We have a quiet understanding. [Slight smile] He knows I'm here, and I know He's there. Work has really taken up a lot of my time, and I can't say I've thought much of my relationship with God as being conversational per se. My wife is the real prayer warrior in the family.*

MENTOR: How's your marriage?

FRANK: *I love my wife. She's perfect for me, a real icebreaker. Lately we've felt a little more strain, if you will. She wants proof that I still love her—but I don't know what else to do. I would think that after all these years, she'd believe me! But I guess it doesn't work that way with women, does it? I'm not sure I know what I'm missing here.*

MENTOR: How about your kids? How's your relationship with them?

FRANK: *They're almost all on their own now. They're good kids. My wife sees them more often than I do.*

MENTOR: Do you have any close friends?

FRANK: *I go golfing a few times a month with guys from work. We talk…but mostly about work, sports and weather, actually. We kid around. Not too deep, just buddies.*

MENTOR: How about what you're called to do in life—Do you know what God has created you to be and do?

FRANK: *Gosh. That's way beyond me. I'm just getting by, trying to keep my family supported here, you understand.*

MENTOR: Yes, I understand. Has there ever been anything that you really loved doing, so much that you dreamed of being able to do that all the time? Anything where you felt the most yourself when you were doing it?

FRANK: *You know, back in college I loved inventing things. I'm an engineer by trade, and I was always making sketches and drawing up formulas to solve everybody's problems. I dreamed of patenting all these things, you know, like most kids dream. The training I had still comes into play at work now and then, but the finance aspect of the job has really taken over. No time for dreaming there!*

MENTOR: How do you feel about your career?

FRANK: *It's a living.*

With questions and answers like these, Frank's malaise begins to make sense. He needs to connect more with his feelings, for one thing. His heart and soul are crying out for development. His wife seems to be doing all the relating in the family, and Frank's focus on work has taken its toll on both his marriage and his relationship with his kids. Ironically, even with all the attention on work, Frank isn't happy at work either. He says "it's a living," but is he really living? He's not doing what he loves or following the dreams he had in younger years. But what if God put those dreams in there? And what would help Frank recapture his sense of purpose and bring him back to life? Encouraging Frank to begin **journaling** and **praying** about His walk with God and how He feels would be tremendously helpful. Confronting him on his attitudes toward his relationship with God, his wife, his job and his calling is vital at this point.

Frank would benefit from working with a mentor (**guidance**) on **planning**. On the one hand he's very organized and responsible already, and you might not think he needs to work on that aspect of his life. However, he's lost track of some valuable dreams and has neglected to "put the big rocks in first" regarding cultivation of his relationships. Until he seeks out and **submits** a mentor to disciple him and hold him accountable to growth he will continue to drift. He has been a nominal Christian leading his own life for far too long and needs a renewal season of **surrender** and discipleship training. He will need help setting new goals for his life that would include a way to make room for actual hearing from God, a revitalized marriage and inner-circle friendships (soul mates) and even time to invent a few things.

It would be excellent for Frank to take a proactive break from his routine, such as a **sabbatical (pilgrimage)** or **retreat**. He needs to do this alone as well as with others; the main thing is that Frank reconnect with God and others on a deeper level, without the usual demands and distractions. He also needs **celebration** to help put life into his dull existence. He loves to sing, and would do well to get back into that choir; **singing** counts as a discipline! It's also recommended that he get away with his wife and do something special that they both love to do. These things would be considered to be the disciplines of basic fellowship and also mutual **submission**. This kind of time away may also be a **sacrifice** as well for Frank; it might be spending more than he expected to spend on his wife or himself, in addition to taking time away from work. But that sacrifice speaks to the necessary shift in his values that he would need to have in order to balance his life out.

Frank is by nature a thinker and would gravitate to the **Intellectual Pathway**. This is fine for him, yet he needs to somehow make it more personal and go from the head to the heart and soul. The **guidance, fellowship** and **singing** may help keep this pathway leading Frank continually to **worship**.

Frank also has an inclination to walk in the **Serving Pathway**. He prefers to work behind the scenes and is aware of the practical needs of others. As he seeks God's face for new direction in his life, it would be awesome for Frank to be in a position to receive encouragement and activation of the spiritual **gifts** in his life. He needs to see beyond the practical into the realm in which God's power can flow through him. This might be brought about by opening his home to strangers and engaging in **hospitality** and **friendship evangelism** of a most exciting kind. What was once routine could become an active outreach, feeding yet more life into the original group.

Ω

Have you seen glimpses of yourself in these descriptions? Which Pathways do you prefer to walk in? Are you drawn to deepen your walk with the Lord and engage in some new spiritual disciplines? Which ones stand out to you, and which areas of your life will be addressed as you add these disciplines into your life?

As your coach, I want to make clear here that **you need not tackle the whole list of disciplines at once**. In fact, it's not advisable! Just as you wouldn't eat everything at a buffet in one sitting, you wouldn't be wise to try to engage in all these life tools in one fell swoop.

If this were a first mentoring session, I'd first go over with you how you're doing in your various roles, just as you saw in the sample mentoring sessions with Hugo and Frank. I'd then work with you to pick out three roles that we feel could use some focus in your life over the following three months, based on our conversation and on God's leading. Again, not all at once, but focus on three. We might then pick three disciplines to focus on as well. A wise coach will rely on God's discernment to help narrow down the choices from the lists you've seen in this chapter.

If we were engaged in a longer mentoring relationship, I'd walk you through the whole Omega Course. We'd work systematically through everything you've been learning about in this book: Your understanding of your mission and calling in life, your perspective, your attitudes, the whole nine yards. I want you to envision these sample meetings as you read, to make the process more tangible for you. Otherwise it's merely a truckload of information, sitting there waiting to be delivered. But when you take just a little bit of the information and apply it, you're in a position to receive God's wisdom!

If you have gotten this far in the book and have been pondering the questions as we go along, you have already been engaging in spiritual discipline on many levels! Keep on going for it and you will not be disappointed.

CHAPTER 16

Grow for the Goal

LAW 16

The Law of Growth: *Growth toward Christlikeness requires accountability, process, and perseverance.*

Did you ever wish you could go into a phone booth and come out transformed, just like Superman? We live in a culture that looks for instant gratification. If we could only grow in Christ as fast as we microwave our snacks! Or if only the Bible was a neat set of directions, whereupon we could master the formula and get on with life. Or better yet, we could download it, or deposit it like a check in the bank. But all of that would deprive us in the long run, for **the main point of "getting there" is our closeness to God. The nature of God's kingdom is growth and gradualness**, not magic or performance. Our lives are to develop and be nurtured from something small to something massive and powerful. It is a process, not a sudden acquisition. Therefore we have to be patient with ourselves and others on the journey with us. Also, there is no substitute for **perseverance**. We will sometimes take a step backward, but through living in covenant community and engaging in **accountable relationships** with our fellow Christians, those falters should only be momentary. They can even become like springboards for a leap forward.

Not that I have already obtained all this, or have already been made perfect, but I press on to take hold of that for which Christ Jesus took hold of me. [13]Brothers, I do not consider myself yet to have taken hold of it. But one thing I do: Forgetting what is behind and straining toward what is ahead, [14]I press on toward the goal to win the prize for which God has called me heavenward in Christ Jesus. [15]All of us who are mature should take such a view of things. And if on some point you think differently, that too God will make clear to you. [16]Only let us live up to what we have already attained. [17]Join with others in following my example, brothers, and take note of those who live according to the pattern we gave you. (Philippians 3:12-17)

You can clearly see from this passage that God is not finished with us; He has work to do and He wants to accomplish it together with us, in and through us. God's perfect plan is to give to us and make us greater in Him, therefore we have nothing to fear by submitting self-will to God's will—engaging in a complete, all-out surrender.

Pan out to God's overall goal: He wants to advance the Kingdom of God through us on earth as we experience and express love. Now zoom the lens back in and look within that overall framework: God wants to instill specific goals into our hearts, and our task is to listen deeply, so we develop a sensitivity to the Holy Spirit and His leadings. We have to believe that God wants to speak *to* us and *through* us. If we train our minds on the Spirit, the leadings will come. Then, if we wait for God's favor to follow, that is, wait to have a sense of His timing, we will come to experience His victories. In fact, as we experience consistent *small* victories, we will come to expect and experience His BIG victory in major difficulties.

I. Goal-Setting and Accountability

If you've ever done any time-management work, you know that the best thing to do is to build it on a base of a long-range vision. Then those goals are broken down further into shorter and shorter increments. How many times, when you've set a goal, have you tried to stab the whole thing at once, then gotten overwhelmed just thinking about it? You've bitten off more than you can chew in one bite. Sometimes the ensuing guilt and paralysis is brutal! It's not that you shouldn't think big. It's GREAT to think big! The issue is to be strategic, establish smaller goals within the bigger ones, and build yourself a system of accountability so you receive proper encouragement. Write down your goals and create a plan that you share with your mentors or coaches. The plan can serve as an objective form of accountability when you meet to review how you're doing.

A little girl I know was describing the route she takes as she walks home from school. "Sometimes it's long though," she said. "That's when I do the telephone-pole thing."

"The *telephone-pole thing?*"

"Yes. I pretend the next telephone pole is home, so I don't get tired and bored. It's only a little walk to the pole. Then when I get there, it changes to the *next* telephone pole!"

"And that helps?"

"Yeah! And then when my friends walk home with me, we race to the next pole, and we guess how fast we're gonna get there. We get home in like two seconds!"

This little girl has more wisdom about goal-setting than many of us adults. She devised a system of smaller goals so she wouldn't get discouraged on the long walk home. Then she shared her goals with her friends, and they encouraged one another to have fun as they went along. We, too, would do well to break our lives down into manageable chunks and have more fun going at it like our precocious telephone-pole hopper. We'd also do well to increase our accountability as we grow. Most people tend to think we need less as we get older; God's perspective is just the opposite. We are to become more accountable and more connected to community as we grow.

THE POWER OF A COACH

As you know, I have been privileged to train for two separate Olympic Games in my life. The first was when I was a senior at Brown. It was the 1992 Olympic Games, and that one was a real long shot. The other was 1996 games held in Atlanta, which was much more realistic. It was in my training for the discus throw for the 1996 Summer Olympics that I had an experience that changed my life forever.

At that time in my career, I was pound for pound one of the strongest and most explosive men in the world. (I know that sounds boastful but it was true.) The only problem I had was that I wasn't throwing any farther than I had four years earlier. Now, throwing the discus isn't exactly the kind of sport that produces a lot of endorsement dollars. Most of the throwers I knew had to work a job and train alone because they couldn't afford to hire a coach to help them. That was the situation I found myself in. I lived in Providence, Rhode Island on the campus of Brown University and the school graciously let me use the throwing facilities to train. As you may recall, that was the year I was working the night shift at a residential home for troubled youth, attending seminary and starting a church on Brown's campus while training for the Olympics. Because of this schedule and the lack of access to good coaching, I simply worked and trained as hard as I could, hoping to progress.

Early in the spring of 1996 at a meet where high school, college and Olympic hopefuls all competed together, I did something completely desperate. I had won handily, but still I was not throwing farther than I had as a senior at Brown. I was frustrated, to say the least. During the meet, I had noticed a man coaching his high school son in the hammer throw. His son was the best thrower in the country at the time; he was also an aspiring discus thrower with a lot of potential. I approached the coach and asked him if he would be willing to help coach me in the discus. He responded by telling me he really didn't know much about discus throwing. To that, I replied that I knew enough for the two of us, but I had not been able to translate my knowledge of discus-throwing into better performance. I told him I would be willing to coach him and his son in discus-throwing if he would be willing to be **a set of eyes and ears helping me to make progress**. All we had to do was sit down and watch some videotape of the best throwers in the world and I would point out to him the kind of technique I was trying to imitate. Then, during our coaching time together, if he would simply point out to me where I didn't look like the tape, that information would help me tremendously.

I will never forget the first training session with Coach Flynn. He sat back and watched for a long time. Then finally after one of my throws he exclaimed, "It doesn't look like the tape."

"Could you be a little more specific?" I said.

He went on to describe some ways in which my technique did not look like the technique I was trying to imitate. As I had hoped, he'd caught the information I was looking for and I began to make some progress.

One week later, I was throwing at a meet in California and experienced *a seven-foot increase* over my previous best in competition and the following week after that, a *15-foot increase* in practice, as I threw 207 feet. To make progress like this as a discus thrower is almost unheard of. Discus throwers usually make progress in inches. To make progress in big chunks like this was proof that I had a fatal flaw in my technique that I obviously hadn't been able to fix through self-help. This throw would rank me among the top seven throwers at the time and put me back in the hunt to realize my dream of competing in the Olympics and representing my country.

AN EXTRA SET OF EYES

There is only so much you can process about your performance in life through your own intuitive and sensing powers. It takes the focus and objectivity of others willing to watch and study your life to help you truly assess how you are doing and help grow you toward your intended goal. The day I began to move beyond self-help was the day I realized that **I am the perfectly wrong person to give myself advice. This is not an insult; it's just a fact of life.** Think of a guy asking his fellow player, "is there a bruise on my back?" This need for extra eyes doesn't mean there's something wrong with us. Everyone knows you need help to see your own back. Our whole lives are like that as well. We're constructed to need others to help us see. Coming to realize the importance of accountability, wisdom, and the perspective of others to help me grow was a lesson that transformed my life forever.

It was the impact of good coaching that helped me to make improvements. For many of us, our potential is sitting inside of us: dormant and in need of a mentor or coach to unlock it. Perhaps you need to hit the point of desperation before you will reach out for help. But why wait? You can be proactive and receive help *before* you're at the end of your rope. Often, the people who've had the most struggles end up surpassing their peers in spiritual growth. Why? Because they've had a head start in desperation. They are quicker to realize they need help, and that's what puts them ahead of the game. When you do finally get desperate enough to reach out, you will find the help that can unlock your potential forever. True greatness requires focus, perseverance and coaching. Nobody gets great without coaching —nobody!

Most people live under the illusion that the only pathway to greatness is to self-help their way through life. It won't work. God is the Coach, and He's also the Master Thrower on the tape. Submitting to His standard is like that moment when my coach watched the tape and he was able to tell me what the difference was. The answer to unlocking our potential is submitting ourselves to God and His training for our lives in the power of the Holy Spirit, with the help of mentors and coaches. As we reach out and invite people into our lives who are willing to provide objective feedback, hold us accountable to our agreed-upon training regimen and encourage our growth, we will be moving beyond self-help into the powerful world of what God can do through mentoring and coaching.

MENTORING AND ACCOUNTABILITY

As a reminder: I define Christian mentoring as an intentional, relational process where people are guided, empowered, and encouraged by God through another to embrace God's presence, steward their lives from God's perspective, and realize their potential through God's power.

Plans fail for lack of counsel, but with many advisers they succeed.
(Proverbs 15:22)

There is no process more helpful for the attainment of goals than mentoring. That's why I've chosen to pursue it with all my heart. Christian mentoring is focused on training in transformation toward Christlikeness. Transformation happens when we are helping each other to be trained in righteousness. But here's an interesting fact: As we have trained hundreds of people to function as Christian mentors, we have learned that the average Christian is intimidated by the idea of mentoring another in their faith. I know a husband and wife who regularly have speakers come to minister in their home. They greatly admire these leaders and do everything they can to accommodate them as well as all the people coming to meet and pray with them. When anyone suggests that they already have a *ministry*, they quickly dismiss the idea and insist that they wouldn't know what to do. But the fact is, not only do they minister through their hospitality, but they also minister directly by mentoring and re-parenting everyone who visits their home. They are so loving and safe, that alone ministers powerfully. But they are also wise, always learning from their speakers and able to impart far more in their own right than they realize. They are a good example of what I'm talking about. They are quite capable but don't feel confident in it. What I'm saying is the potential is right there in the Church, but our mindsets about mentoring need to change for us to move forward.

The ministry of the Life Spring Network was commissioned to radically reverse this trend of exalting "leaders" only. We've been working to make mentoring relationships *normal* in the church. As I've mentioned in other chapters, I believe that the church needs to function like a mentoring network if we are to realize our full redemptive potential. In Christ this is not only *possible* but it's also His *plan* for our maturity. At Life Spring Network we have spent a decade building and testing seminars, courses, resources and mentor training to truly equip the church to realize the necessity for transformation.

Christian Mentoring relies on the **relational priorities of Jesus**. By implication, that means an avoidance of neat formulas and pre-cooked answers in favor of engagement in **creative dialogue, probing questions** and, above all, **unconditional love**. Any reading of the Gospels reveals a Jesus who made himself available to people as unique individuals. He listened attentively and confronted boldly when the situation called for it. Like my discus coach who studied the tapes of great throwers and pointed out where I was not imitating them, in mentoring relationships we can do this for one another. Great Christian mentors are people who know Jesus experientially and through study, people who are willing to get to know us well enough to point out where we are not imitating the life of Jesus. They are God's extra mirrors for us.

> *Be imitators of God, therefore, as dearly loved children ²and live a life of love, just as Christ loved us and gave himself up for us as a fragrant offering and sacrifice to God. (1 Corinthians 8:1-2)*

The growth process simply doesn't work unless it becomes a very deliberate lifestyle. This means having a regular stream of mentors in our lives, coaching us into God's greatness. Here are some practices that are helpful when engaging in mentoring relationships: Define the mentoring relationship right from the outset; establish the desired level of accountability and the ways in which the mentee will receive feedback. Healthy boundaries are also important, including an established goal for the mentoring period, what topics are off-limits, what things must remain confidential, the frequency of the sessions, and the duration of the relationship.

The best kind of Christian mentor is one who is committed and submitted to the Holy Spirit, thereby able to discern and respond to His promptings. A good mentor has spiritual *"eyes to see," (Matthew 13:12)* ready for "God sightings"—ways God is visibly at work in both the mentee and themselves. It is crucial that the mentor operate *only* in God's power; in cases when the mentor is not, it is important for the mentee to filter the advice being received. God can use a non-Christian to mentor us in different aspects of our lives in which the individual has expertise, but it takes a Christ-follower to grow another.

As I said in my definition of Christian mentoring, it is *God* working through mentors, giving them voice. In the meantime, it can be helpful for mentors to prime the pump by reviewing the themes found in this book, coming up with questions based on those themes. The mentor should also be honest, adaptable and believe that God can move in the life of the mentee. That is, it's good to leave the mentee with steps for specific action and be prepared for differing outcomes.

You may recall from earlier in the book that there are different kinds of mentoring. Some forms of mentoring fall short of the intense and *intentional* role implied in the phrase "Christian life coach." It is possible to have *occasional* mentors, providing advice and prospective, passive mentors, such as speakers or writers who don't even know that they are being viewed in that way, and *peer* mentors, who are friends and colleagues who play an important role of support, perspective, collaboration, and networking.

How Hungry are You?

 If you are interested in learning more about Christian mentoring, you can visit our website (www.lifespringnetwork.org) and you will find information about our Omega Mentor Training and how it is used in conjunction with the Omega Course to equip you to mentor others.

II. Goal-Setting and Process

Even if you have an aversion to setting goals, everyone needs focus. As the saying goes, "Aim at nothing and you will hit it every time." Many people like to take a problem-solving approach, rather than a goal-setting approach. Either way, engage in the process. Find a strategy that works for you and stick with it! Persevere! God will reveal His plan for your life and will inspire you to set God-discerned goals. When He does, you need to "record the revelation" and begin to pursue it with your life.

Then the LORD replied:
"Write down the revelation
and make it plain on tablets
so that a herald may run with it.
³For the revelation awaits an appointed time;
it speaks of the end
and will not prove false.
Though it linger, wait for it;
it will certainly come and will not delay."
(Habakkuk 2:2-3)

The tremendous emphasis on the written word shows up all through Scripture. Not to mention that Jesus is called the Living Word. When He was tempted by Satan at the beginning of His ministry, Jesus rebuked him by declaring repeatedly, *"It is written."* All of which is to say there is something powerful about writing down your goals. An old adage goes, "There is little probability of *impression* without *expression*." Just as we tend to believe what we see in print, when we write down and re-read God's goals for our lives, the act of writing will imprint them on our minds, keeping us focused as we pursue the goals. We've already elaborated on the great power of the spoken word in previous chapters. If you declare aloud those same goals you've written, that only adds to your momentum.

Once you've written something down, you have something more specific to aim at and can more easily adjust your course in little ways each day to stay on track. Let's say you set the course of a sailboat, determining to land at a certain spot on the far shore. The fact that your destination is clear doesn't rule out **all the little adjustments on the tiller along the way.** (More on sailing in the next chapter.) Mentors can help with those little adjustments as well as the initial goal-setting. Discernment takes practice, but very often God uses mature believers to speak to us in a way that is clearly not just advice but wisdom from God. At those times, the Holy Spirit within you will confirm the rightness of what was spoken. Christianity is not for Lone Rangers. We are not intended to seek insights purely as individuals but to depend on others in the body of Christ to speak into our lives.

Listen, watch, wait for it, write it down, make it clear, speak it, adjust the course as you live it—all part of the PROCESS of growing and discerning.

USING PLANNING PAGES

Have you used planning pages to record your goals? With them you can remind yourself of your focus. Share your planning pages with your mentors, and use them as the basis for your discussions about how you are doing and the kinds of adjustments you might want to make. It is wise to first set general goals for all of the various roles in your life, and then focus on two or three roles God seems to be highlighting. A question I often ask in mentoring situations is one that I adapted from master mentor Bobb Biehl: ***What three roles is God asking you to focus on in the next three months?*** The roles God highlights become the focus of your disciplines and your personal growth plan for that period. Discerning the right roles to focus on, given the season of life you find yourself in, is crucial to wise training in righteousness.

HONORING THE SEASONS OF YOUR LIFE

Depending on your stage and place in life, God will challenge you to grow in different roles using different disciplines for each role. He will arrange the challenges to correspond to the roles and seasons you're in; He knows exactly how much you can handle.

God will not allow us to be tested beyond that which we can bear (1 Corinthians 10:13). It is important to attend to each season of training. If you decide not to do what you need to be doing during that particular season, it will only prolong the growth process. It is like running in a hurdles race and thinking we can go around (instead of over) the hurdles without penalty. In life it is not much different. If we run the race *our* way and not *God's* way, we are disqualifying ourselves from reaching the zenith of our potential in every area of our lives (1 Corinthians 9:24-27). We're settling for less than God's best for us and perhaps missing the opportunity to serve in important roles within His Kingdom. As my coaches saw greater potential in me than I did, your coaches or mentors may see more greatness in you than you do. Like an athlete, listen to your coaches and continue to receive your training in righteousness.

$$\Omega$$

Ask yourself: *Is it a lack of preparedness that keeps you from approaching a "hurdle" with confidence? Is it a mindset you acquired based on your past?*

Here's another example of our need to honor a season. It comes from watching the development of young children. At two years old, toddlers are natural linguistic geniuses. If they are around people talking several different languages, they're likely to pick them all up very easily, for that's their season for learning to talk. But let's say they are never spoken to during that time (God forbid!). It would be far more difficult for them to learn a language at a later age. It's considered abusive and neglectful to deny those toddlers normal exposure to adult conversation; they would be seriously stunted without the opportunity to develop language. Why should it be considered any less stunting when we are deprived of the normal mentoring process and miss the fullness of our destinies?

The sad possibility of missing out on life's full potential should be motivation enough for us to accept every challenge and training assignment that God brings our way, in the *time* that He brings it. However, if we try to skip out on some aspect of our growth in God, He simply moves the hurdle further down the track and invites us to go over it again. He doesn't want us to miss out! Because of His grace we are given "do-overs." But we can only learn so much so fast, and we do risk squandering the growth opportunities that God is bringing us if we shirk His timing. Just as the Evil One is pleased when the Church becomes fragmented and people get out of step with one another, he is also pleased when we as individuals are out of step with God. Why? Because both our unity and our transformation are a huge threat to his kingdom! For both, timing is very important. All the more reason to submit to God's promptings and not miss the opportunity to live out our true destiny in all its fullness.

There is a time for everything,
and a season for every activity under heaven:
²a time to be born and a time to die,
a time to plant and a time to uproot,
³a time to kill and a time to heal,
a time to tear down and a time to build,
⁴a time to weep and a time to laugh,
a time to mourn and a time to dance,
(Ecclesiastes 3:1-4)

God has a reason for every season of our lives. Sometimes if you missed the season, it's gone. People have been described as "zealous" in a way that has implied their enthusiasm is embarrassing, but zeal is an honorable and praiseworthy emotion. We should develop zeal for more life, and go for everything that God wants for us! If we dedicate ourselves to being followers, honor the various seasons of our lives and submit to God's training, we will live *the life that is truly life* *(1 Timothy 6:19)*.

III. Goal-Setting and Perseverance

Sometimes doing the will of God will not "feel" like fun, any more than running a race feels fun while doing it. But when we complete the course, a sense of accomplishment and growth at the end make it all worthwhile. Again, our current culture has made us flabby when it comes to perseverance. We think if it's hard, it's not good for us. But that can be a deceptive reflex. God's path is good for us and it's not always easy. The yoke He gives us is easy due to His power working through us, but still our deciding to keep turning to Him is not the path of least resistance:

Watch your life and doctrine closely. Persevere in them,
because if you do, you will save both yourself and your hearers.
(1 Timothy 4:16)

You need to persevere so that when you have done the will of God, you will receive what he has promised. [37] For in just a very little while, "He who is coming will come and will not delay. [38] But my righteous one will live by faith. And if he shrinks back, I will not be pleased with him." [39] But we are not of those who shrink back and are destroyed, but of those who believe and are saved. (Hebrews 10:36-39)

These are not verses that speak of a little float down the river! As we have mentioned all through this book, God is inviting us to a life of greatness, but because of the nature of reality this side of the grave, the journey will be uphill all the way, thus perseverance will be needed. How do we stay motivated? In part, the abundant life itself is ongoing reward; we get to partake of the "carrot at the end of the stick" as we go along. Another strong motivation is remembering our effect on others. One way or another, for positive or negative, your life has impact. Why not make that a *positive* impact?

A friend of mine had a grandmother who lived to age 96. This feisty grandma would get up early, make her bed, make breakfast for herself and her grown granddaughter and great-granddaughter who lived with her, fill her days with sewing, oil painting, letters to family, luncheons with friends, and caring for her great-grandchild. Her life was rich in many ways. When asked her secret to a long life, she replied, "I think it's all the people in my life, especially my great-granddaughter now. She is really keeping me going, I'll tell you! She needs me, and that's why I get up in the morning. What I do matters!" Grandma knew her life had impact, and it was a powerful motivation.

PERSEVERING AND CHARACTER

Therefore, since we have been justified through faith, we have peace with God through our Lord Jesus Christ, [2] through whom we have gained access by faith into this grace in which we now stand. And we rejoice in the hope of the glory of God. [3] Not only so, but we also rejoice in our sufferings, because we know that suffering

produces perseverance; [4]perseverance, character; and character, hope.
[5]And hope does not disappoint us, because God has poured out
his love into our hearts by the Holy Spirit, whom he has given us.
(Romans 5:1-5)

The role of perseverance in producing Christlike character cannot
be understated. Our lives are being molded and forged by God, and
that takes time. Therefore the journey of pursuing God's abundant life
is a journey of *becoming*. We are always changing in life, either *toward*
or away from God's life for us. Our ability to become can have a dramatic
effect for good or evil in our lives and in the world.

PERSEVERING THROUGH TIMES OF SUFFERING

As the passage from Romans highlights, part of the process of being
conformed into Christlikeness is simply rejoicing in the hope of the
glory of God. When life seems to be working well, this rejoicing in
the hope of God's glory might seem easy. For others it's a challenge to
keep practicing dependence on God in good times. The real test
comes when God allows suffering into our lives. Some lessons in life
can only be learned through suffering, and suffering by its very nature
demands perseverance. While persevering, we can be called into
extended seasons of "waiting on God," which God will use to develop
character strengths in us. Every man and woman must be placed into
the crucible of suffering, and no one else can know another's suffering
entirely, for each of us has different thresholds. The point is, while
we're in that crucible, we make decisions that will shape the trajectory
of our lives: Through suffering we become either *bitter* or *better*. By
looking to God and drawing on His perspective and strength in times
of suffering, we can find that our experience of His love increases in
us, even in the middle of the hardship.

I lift up my eyes to the hills—
Where does my help come from?
My help comes from the Lord,
The Maker of heaven and earth. (Psalm 121:1-2)

As we receive that help from the Lord in our suffering, it is inevitable that we then have more to give. One woman was going through a terrible family crisis while she attended a Community Bible Study in her town. As she ventured to share some of what she was suffering, the other members reached out to her with various expressions of love and help, just as we saw in the case of Mike's family in Chapter Six. This was moving enough, but what really surprised her was the way these other women responded to her at the end of that year. They all *thanked her* for what she had *given them*! In her mind, she'd been sustained through their prayers, helped with meals, childcare, financial contributions and all manner of generosity overflowing with love. Yet these women all thanked *her* because she had been so transparent that year, causing them to open up their hearts to more of God in turn. They thanked her for being an inspiration to them, helping them to be more courageous through her example. Yet it was their prayers that had helped her receive that courage. Do you see the wonderful way God knows how to prime the pump and create an overflow of good even from difficult circumstances? He conformed this brave woman more closely to His likeness as she looked to Him. The women in the Bible study reached out to help their sister stay in God's hope; her continual choosing to look to God for help released greater hope back to them. A godly, win-win cycle was created, whereby they witnessed the wisdom and grace of God in action through this one woman's life. That witness unlocked the hearts and lives of everyone in the group.

Suffering comes into all of our lives, whether we love God or not. *How* we persevere or journey through suffering makes us who we are and sets the trajectory of who we will become. When we put our hope in God, He sustains us and creates yet more hope to spread around. Again, this cannot be *achieved*, but it can be *received*. We receive by abiding in the vine, the vine being a perfect picture of humility and dependence. If you live a life in which you're loving people and engaging in the hard work of seeking God, then you're building into yourself those habits that *will* form your character.

IMITATION OF CHRIST

As we persevere, God will take us to places and through experiences that will make us more like Him. When it came to my discus-throwing experience, there was a point at which I reached my potential; other things then replaced it as worthy life goals. But the coaching break-through taught me one of life's most valuable lessons: I am the wrong person to assess my shortfalls and guide me forward. We need the insights of others on the journey of growth towards Christlikeness, which is truly the journey of realizing His greatness.

Ω

How about you? *Do you find it difficult to set God-discerned goals and invite others into your life to help coach you toward their accomplishment? Are you easily discouraged, or do you put your hand to the plow and pursue what God has guided you to do? How have you and your family responded to difficult seasons in your lives? Can you look back on times when you've had to persevere? What do you think would aid you in pursuing God's growth process?*

CHAPTER 17

Lining Up Your Sights

LAW 17

The Law of Alignment: *Regular evaluation, planning and realignment with God's mission leverages time through increased focus.*

You are now standing at a good vantage point: You've reached the fifth and sixth levels on the Life Focus Process, which are entitled Stay the Course and Revelation and Adjustments.

In rifle marksmanship, the key skill needed is the alignment of sights, from the rear of the rifle barrel to the front and from there to the center of the target. Any shift of the body requires a realignment of these sights. The Apostle Paul understood this alignment process when he spoke of sin as "missing the mark."

In football the role of alignment is equally crucial. When I played football at Brown, our coach would drill us incessantly in proper alignment. After breaking down games for years, the coaching staff had concluded that 75% of the success of each play was attributable to proper alignment before the snap. Our strategy was based on knowing the plays our opposing team used, having studied the film of their previous games. With proper alignment based on our opponents' tendencies, we could actually gain a strategic advantage and set ourselves up for success.

Similarly, an improvement in how we daily align our lives with God's ways dramatically increases the likelihood that we will achieve God's mission for us. Alignment will also give us a strategic advantage over our enemy, the Evil One, in that we will be well positioned to defend against his attack. Knowing the main tactics and weapons of your opponent is a formidable advantage. Our enemy is relentless, of course. Therefore we need to overcome the intensity of the Evil One's desire to destroy us with a greater, proactive intensity in discipleship. This means **preparation, alignment and execution.**

"You will seek me and find me when you seek me with all your heart." (Jeremiah 29:13)

The promise is very simple, but you and I both know that it's not always simple to seek God with all our heart. Our heart, soul, mind and strength are subjected to the daily shocks of our fast-paced life. Like a car with worn-out struts, we are easily bumped off the track of our best intentions to stick close to God. We want to stay aligned with Him, but we do veer off, some days more than others. If you remember nothing else from this book, you're going to remember that no one naturally drifts into righteousness. Our disciplines and regular times of planning and recalibration with God are like a hand on the tiller to realign us with our main objectives. God is faithful as we come to Him; usually we need only a short period of stillness to become realigned with Him. We can come into a stillness of heart, soul, mind, strength, and circumstance in these times with God. Some people call it "quiet time," some call it their "power hour;" others go into their "secret place." Whatever your style, it's a time to connect and refuel. As we enter into this connection time with God, we can review our personal growth plan, order our day in alignment with that plan and ask God for discernment about what needs changing. In addition to structuring our day and receiving our marching orders, it is important to open our lives up prayerfully to God and ask Him to search us, know us and reveal if there be any wicked ways in us. You might consider praying through Psalm 51 and/or Psalm 139 to prime your pump and get yourself in a teachable place of listening and submission before God. It is during this alignment that God will convict us of our sin and give us insights as to how we can properly align our lives.

There is one further requirement, even though some Christians suppose it is necessary only after some gross violation of God's will, and that is repentance. Repentance is more of a daily washing than a special drama episode. If we confess to God and one another frequently, we find our spiritual engine is running with more freedom and power. Even if you can't discern where you are walking in sin, you can always ask God to show you and meanwhile confess the drift pattern of your sinful nature and your need for God every day in every way.

The main point in spiritual planning and tracking is not to take back control over our lives from God but to plan, track and evaluate what's working and what's not. We don't remember to do these things until we realize that they are imperative to training in righteousness. We need all the help we can get to maintain focus in this uphill battle.

THE ROLE OF YOUR PERSONALITY

Of course, people's personalities can make for added variety in this realignment process. At one end of the spectrum are the hyper-structured people who lead very focused and organized lives; at the other end are the spontaneous, decide-on-the-go, structure-averse people. There are pluses and minuses to each of these predispositions. A structured person will welcome the journey of planning, tracking and evaluating but might miss out on when and how the Spirit is trying to make mid-course adjustments. A spontaneous person will be better at being open to the Spirit changing plans in an instant, but not as good at sticking to a regimented time-management and life-training plan. A reasonable middle ground is to have a God-discerned structured plan while holding it loosely and remaining open to God's promptings so you can shift as you are led.

We can also shuttle between different ends of the spectrum depending on what we're trying to do. For instance, if we are striving to complete a detailed project in a compressed timeframe, the more planning and structure we engage in, the better. On the other hand, if we're striving to solve a relational problem, spontaneity and "going with the flow" may be a more helpful approach.

SET YOUR SAILS

Transformation is voluntary abandonment. God commands it ("be transformed") and we choose to allow it. Once we're in the boat, it's an ongoing process. I have always liked this vivid illustration from John Ortberg:

"One of the analogies that's kind of been helpful to me is the difference between a motorboat, a raft, and a sailboat. In a motorboat I'm in charge. I determine how fast we're going to go, and in what direction. Some people approach spiritual life that way. If I'm just aggressive enough, if I have enough quiet times, I can make transformation happen on my own. Usually that results in people becoming legalistic, then pride starts to creep in, and things get all messed up.

Some people have been burned by that kind of approach. So they go to the opposite extreme and will say, "I'm into grace." It's like they're floating on a raft. If you ask them to do anything to further their growth, they'll say, "Hey, no. I'm not into works. I'm into grace. You're getting legalistic with me." So they drift. There are way too many commands in Scripture for anybody to think we're called to be passive.

On a sailboat, however, I don't move if it's not for the wind. My only hope of movement is the wind. I can't control the wind. I don't manufacture the wind. Jesus talks about the Spirit blowing like the wind. But there is a role for me to play, and part of it has to do with what I need to discern. A good sailor will discern, where's the wind at work? How should I set the sails?" [28]

Aligning our lives with God and His transformational path for our life is indeed like sailing. Ortberg captures the concept with that picture, just as a good sailor catches the wind. Once we have discerned where, when, and how God is moving, we align our lives (set our sails) in alignment with the Spirit (wind). In doing this, we stay connected to both the guidance and power of God. This doesn't mean we don't have a plan for how to live each day. As it is with sailing, we can have a plan for setting our sails a certain way in roles and relationships in our lives where we have discerned there is a prevailing wind. But, just like sailing, it also means that as we are moving through the day and we see the wind change directions, we change our plan (adjust our sails) to better align with the wind (Spirit). This is an intimate dependence on God's leadership and power in our lives! Our Father is trying to guide and empower us through this life, but we need to seek Him and align our lives with His.

A counselor friend shared with me what a typical day looks like for her when the wind changes directions:

"It's full of divine appointments! The other day, one of my clients was scheduled to come at 12:30, but they forgot they were double-booked and didn't show. If I'd been dead-set on sticking to my schedule, I would've been frustrated and had a hard time shifting plans. But I checked in with the Holy Spirit instead, and I began to use the extra time to journal. God started revealing certain insights from Scripture, and we were really on a roll. Then in the middle of that, I felt an urgent prompting to go find my husband. I know that sounds really ODD, but that's not usually the way I am. I had no idea why or where he'd gone, but felt a nudge to look down the street. Sure enough, there he was talking to two friends, one whose car wouldn't start and the other who'd come to help. As it turns out, the insights God had just given me fit perfectly with what they were all sharing. The one with the stalled car needed prayer, and we had a joyful ministry time out there on the sidewalk. I never would have been open to that had I not listened to God and stayed flexible when I had that no-show. When God breathes on my daily plans like that, it truly is the breath of life!"

Now then, my sons, listen to me; blessed are those who keep my ways. [33]*Listen to my instruction and be wise; do not ignore it.* [34]*Blessed is the man who listens to me, watching daily at my doors, waiting at my doorway.* [35]*For whoever finds me finds life and receives favor from the LORD.* [36]*But whoever fails to find me harms himself; all who hate me love death. (Proverbs 8:32-36)*

This Scripture defines death as separation from God and His mission for our lives. Jesus daily realigned His life with the will of the Father. We gather from Scripture that it was His habit to draw away early in the morning to pray alone. It was during this time with the Father that He aligned His life with the will of the Father and received His guidance and empowerment for the day. We also know He rested weekly on the Sabbath and recalibrated His entire being with the Father. We need to follow in Jesus' footsteps in this area of aligning our lives with God.

PLANNING AND TRACKING

There are natural planning and recalibration times that we are encouraged to observe in Scripture. These keep us in sync with God and help us to follow the rhythm of life. The Scriptures discuss at least four different **time perspectives** that we should pay attention to and use as a guide: We notice a *daily* perspective in the admonition to live one day at a time. There's a *weekly* perspective in God creating the world in six days, resting on the seventh and commanding us to follow this pattern. We have a *quarterly* or *seasonal* perspective with the changing of the four seasons. And finally, God gives us an annual perspective as the cycle of seasons begins to repeat itself, the earth circles the sun and we begin a new year. In response to this, I recommend a rhythm to your planning: annual and quarterly "big-picture" planning, in addition to weekly and daily "detail planning."

"BIG PICTURE" PLANNING AND TRACKING

Annual: You are encouraged to plan annual retreats to seek God's wisdom for any major readjustments in your life. It is during this kind of retreat that you can embark on some holistic thinking through your long-range plans, establish your annual mega-goals and plan annual events for the year with the key people in your life.

Quarterly: This would be establishing your three-month seasonal goals and discerning the three roles you are going to focus on developing over that period. Your quarterly goal-setting is best done with the help of your mentors. It's a time to review your big-picture roles and goals, evaluate your progress, and synthesize any new revelations, projects, tasks and appointments into your personal growth plan.

> *"Suppose one of you wants to build a tower. Will he not first sit down and estimate the cost to see if he has enough money to complete it?* [29]*For if he lays the foundation and is not able to finish it, everyone who sees it will ridicule him,* [30]*saying, 'This fellow began to build and was not able to finish.'* [31] *Or suppose a king is about to go to war against another king. Will he not first sit down and consider whether he is able with ten thousand men to oppose the one coming against him with twenty thousand?* [32]*If he is not able, he will send a delegation while the other is still a long way off and will ask for terms of peace.* [33]*In the same way, any of you who does not give up everything he has cannot be my disciple.* [34]*Salt is good, but if it loses its saltiness, how can it be made salty again?* [35]*It is fit neither for the soil nor for the manure pile; it is thrown out. He who has ears to hear, let him hear."* (Luke 14:28-35)

Our willingness to constantly seek out God's plan for our lives, align our lives with His plan and remain attentive to His directional changes along the way is the only hope we have of truly thriving as His disciple in this world. Trying to commingle our plans with God's plans for our lives will only end in futility. This is where the rubber meets the road in our faith journey. God's encouragement for us is to spend time with Him and discover the path that will produce abundant living. For wherever God guides, God provides!

In the illustration of the king going off to war in this Scripture, I like to think of it as a simple equation that leads to life or death. The 10,000 men opposing the 20,000 men are like people who think that they are going to be able to find the abundant life in their own guidance and power (10,000 men). In reality, our sinful nature (10,000 men) and the influence of the evil one (10,000 men) co-conspire to lead us away from God's abundant life for us. A wise person would give up on this plan because they understand that it is destined to fail. On the other hand, if we give up everything and become a disciple of Christ, we will be guided and empowered to live as more than conquerors. When we do this, we live into our true destiny and become the salt and the light that we were created to be!

"DETAIL" PLANNING AND TRACKING

Weekly: You may do this already, but inviting God into it makes the difference between a to-do list and a TA-DAH list. Review the previous week, evaluate your progress and synthesize any new revelations, projects, tasks, disciplines and appointments into your calendar and personal growth plan. On a higher level, set aside time weekly to review your current plan, consider adjustments, and readjust your long-term plan. Use your weekly role planning chart and a day timer. Consider the following suggestions for weekly planning:

1. Find a place that is relatively free from distractions.
2. Prayerfully review your Mission, Goals and Disciplines.

3. Think back through the week and evaluate what happened, record any major God-sightings and create plans to respond to any revelations from God.
4. Create a task-and-appointment list, prioritize them and begin to decide when you will accomplish them.
5. Anticipate obstacles.
6. Ask God for His guidance and power to live in Him that week!

Daily: We need to practice daily planning as a form of discipline. This includes conducting a daily overview, prioritization and alignment of our lives before God. We also need to remember to submit to the Holy Spirit to empower us to live out God's mission for our lives. At the beginning of each day, during your planning time, pull out your day-timer, prioritize your tasks and plan the flow of your day. Become familiar with a notation system that works for you and use it to help plan and track your activities and projects. A suggested routine:

1. Find a place that is relatively free from distractions.
2. Prayerfully review your plan for the day and any new adjustments you need to make.
3. Review your daily task-and-appointment list.
4. Anticipate obstacles.
5. Prioritize your daily activities.
6. Ask God for His guidance and power to live in Him that day!

Projects: For areas in our lives where we are tackling projects covering a certain time-span, it will be helpful to use a project worksheet and figure out how we are going to go about completing the various tasks. Use of timelines and other project completion devices can be very useful for planning things that don't fall into our regular rhythm of daily and weekly disciplines.

THE USE OF PLANNERS

Planners can help us stay on track and focus our lives. They are great tools to help us plan our work and work our plan. We also use our planners to track how we are truly investing our time, which can serve as a mirror of our true beliefs. They should be used to plan not just our business time but also our personal lives. I recommend that you experiment with multiple views. The two most common are the day-at-a-glance and week-at-a-glance. Take your time and find one that is effective for you and your work habits. For you right-brained folks out there, I wouldn't rule out a planner that includes sketches and doodles or mind-maps instead of a linear listing. To some extent we need to adjust to the fact that we do live with linear time now. But you can adjust your approach to planning to suit your more creative outlook.

Every planning tool should also have a monthly view, and for many people this view is the most important one. This is the first calendar you might reference when scheduling appointments, because it will have everything written on it. Also, there are sections associated with the monthly calendar that will aid you in setting monthly goals and establishing disciplines. After entries have been made on the monthly calendar, if you use one, enter them on your weekly or daily planning pages. There are many helpful tools on the market that provide a monthly view, a weekly view, and a daily view. You can also use electronic planners that sync with PDAs.

Special planning pages will help too. You may ask yourself, "I'm so engaged in this major project, when am I ever going to sit down and read the book I've been wanting to read for so long, or take up the creative endeavor that I've been postponing for so long?" A season may open up: Implement pronto! One of the things you may need to do is actually schedule your "open space." That is, downtime is important too and you may not have it if you don't make an appointment with yourself and hold the space.

REVELATION AND ADJUSTMENTS

As we have mentioned already, when reviewing plans, we need to keep listening for adjustments and revelations that God may have for us along the way. If God speaks to us in the middle of the planning process, we need to be prepared to do a complete about-face, if that's what's called for.

Regular evaluation of our lives happens all the time. We are always evaluating our satisfaction with life, either consciously or subconsciously. It is helpful to plan times of reflection and evaluation to see if you are spending your time doing activities that meet your God-given needs and to help you accomplish your mission in life. God desires to speak into our lives and reveal truths to us about who we are and whether we are truly following His path toward abundance. It is therefore important to be listening constantly for God's revelation in our lives and making the appropriate adjustments.

There is no project or challenge in life where the Lord cannot be found. His Kingdom is His perfect rule, and that includes His order, His efficiency, His planning details, His everything. God's perfect rule leads to God's favor—even the gratifying glow of anticipating it—and nothing could exceed the benefit of His favor in our lives. Following a mere abstract plan will often bring failure and in any case will not bring about any opportunity to discover God's life in the middle of the situation.

> *See to it, brothers, that none of you has a sinful, unbelieving heart that turns away from the living God. ¹³But encourage one another daily, as long as it is called Today, so that none of you may be hardened by sin's deceitfulness. ¹⁴We have come to share in Christ if we hold firmly till the end the confidence we had at first. ¹⁵As has just been said: "Today, if you hear his voice, do not harden your hearts as you did in the rebellion." (Hebrews 3:12-15)*

Waiting daily at His door and continuing to listen for His guidance with soft hearts that want to obey God will guide us to life. In this process we will become aware of several sin areas in our lives; making adjustments and following through on the cycle of renewal, as we have discussed in previous chapters, is necessary if we are going to mature in our relationship with God. Remember that the Cycle of Renewal is built on this admonition:

> *All Scripture is God-breathed and is useful for teaching, rebuking, correcting and training in righteousness, ¹⁷so that the*

*man of God may be thoroughly equipped for every good work.
(2 Timothy 3:16-17)*

Recalibrating and planning is not merely setting goals and plotting the steps toward those goals and then writing "amen" at the end. God isn't asking us just to check in once in a while; He's asking us to submit all the time. We submit because we have the promise and understanding that love flows out of a well-aligned and growing heart and life.

Did you ever watch a room full of toddlers and their mothers? Imagine the mothers sitting together and talking, while their toddlers play in the center of the room. Every few minutes, one will run and crash into his mother's knee, leaning his head into her lap for a little while. The mother caresses his head and pats his little body with her hand as she continues talking. In a minute or two, he runs back to play. They all do it with almost predictable frequency. Psychologists call it "refueling." Those toddlers don't need specific attention or information; they just get a refill on love and security before running back into the fray.

Our times of alignment with God may be more sophisticated than that picture; we have an understanding of God's plan, use lots of tools and engage in regular evaluation and adjustments along the way. But the love refill is the same. If our purpose in life is to experience and express love, then we never outgrow our need for His perfect, everlasting, unconditional love. Alignment with God might look very business-like, and we do mean business. But the bottom line is, staying aligned has everything to do with love. If He is the Vine and we are the branches, our alignment is a matter of keeping that stem (our connection to Him) strong and clear so we can receive all the life sap we need to become great and fruitful.

Ω

You can start in on your free alignment right here: *Do you have regular time set aside to go over your plans with God? How do you adjust when the wind changes? Does your use of time reflect your priorities in life? Where in your big-picture planning is God prompting you to change directions? What areas of your life are being highlighted for attention right now, and what are some ways you see yourself addressing them in your daily and weekly plans?*

CHAPTER 18

Training for LIFE

LAW 18

The Law of Training: *The life you live trains you for the life you are going to lead!*

START WHERE YOU ARE

Have you ever tried to not be where you are? It's not easy, is it? Sometimes it's like quicksand: The harder we try, the more stuck we get. But here's a liberating thought: What if your current set of circumstances, including anything you can't stand right now, is the perfect training ground for your best possible life? Everything in your daily life, depending on how you react to it, can be a tool for training in godliness. It can become training the minute you go to God with it. **Ask Him: "Lord, what are you wanting to develop in me right now that you've allowed these circumstances in my life?"** If you ask it often, this one question will be the difference between stagnation and dramatic growth in your life. Classes, conferences and programs are fine and can be useful, but one of the fastest ways to grow is through everyday challenges. God's training program of permitted difficulties might sound like the school of hard knocks to you. However, your attention to the Master Teacher puts you in the advanced track! If you react to each difficulty by depending on God all the more, your holy dependence releases an even greater supply of grace and power into your life. That power is then available to meet the next difficulty. You enter a cycle of grace and growth, not a cycle of grief and corruption. Your relationship with God deepens, and your *stumbling stone* becomes a cornerstone upon which you can truly build something solid.

YOU'RE ALREADY ENROLLED IN THE HUMAN RACE

Do you not know that in a race all the runners run, but only one gets the prize? Run in such a way as to get the prize. ²⁵Everyone who competes in the games goes into strict training. They do it to get a crown that will not last; but we do it to get a crown that will last forever. ²⁶Therefore I do not run like a man running aimlessly; I do not fight like a man beating the air. ²⁷No, I beat my body and make it my slave so that after I have preached to others, I myself will not be disqualified for the prize. (1 Corinthians 9:24-27)

Drifting or training—which will it be for you? In every way, it's easier to drift toward the ways of the world. As we said when we started, no one ever drifts toward a life of virtuous living. Even if your goal is to simply remain the same, there is no way to accomplish that; you are either getting better or getting worse all the time. If you don't make the specific decision to embrace God's training and stay in training, then what takes over your life is the phenomenon of drift, and the drift is always downward. And if you are going to train, don't do it half-heartedly; train to win—with all your heart! Remember, our lives affect everyone we meet. The reality is, there is much at stake.

Have nothing to do with godless myths and old wives' tales; rather, train yourself to be godly. For physical training is of some value, but godliness has value for all things, holding promise for both the present life and the life to come. (1 Timothy 4:7-8)

Training isn't an option; it's part of life. The question is, who we'll look to for our training and whether we'll go for the prize. What is the prize? Is it the afterlife with all its heavenly rewards? Yes, but there's more. Note that the verses in 1 Timothy speak of training being valuable for the life to come *and* for the present life. While there's certainly reward in Heaven, we don't have to wait until we die to experience rewards. In fact, we're *not supposed* to wait. Without experiencing rewards now, we'd fall short of our full destinies.

How many times do you find yourself in mildly oppressive circumstances and say, "Oh, I can't wait until we're out of here and then I can..."[Fill in your blank.] But why wait? True, you may not be free to act in certain ways in certain situations, but that doesn't mean you put your life or identity on hold.

GETTING BACK ON TRACK

I know some parents of teenagers who've shared with me what life was like in their household a couple of years ago. The music coming through the floorboards of their kids' rooms was not exactly what these parents were in the mood to hear all day. When they played their own "grownup" music, the kids rolled their eyes and expressed disdain for its lame style. The teens also didn't want to have family dinners and preferred to grab something and run out the door or up to their rooms. Anyone would easily be intimidated or antagonized by living in this atmosphere. The grownups felt like they were being held hostage in their own house.

But these parents were praying one day, and God reminded them who was paying the mortgage on their home. (Big clue: It wasn't the kids.) "Oh, yeah," they said to one another. "Why are we allowing them to rule over us?" God directed them to love their teenagers but not let them infiltrate or cramp their style. There's something to be said for putting others first and adapting to them for the sake of respect and kindness in the family and community. But that needs to be distinguished from "enabling," which is putting another in God's place, forgetting who you are and neglecting to do what you're called to do. Big difference. The latter is nothing short of allowing your life in Christ to be trampled flat.

The shift these parents experienced was more internal than external at first, but it did begin to show up in the form of certain changes. They set a time limit on noise: Quiet in the house after 9 p.m. and during the parents' home gatherings. Mom and Dad played their own music without apology, and even began to sing with it, worshipping and praying out loud, including blessing their children. They ignored the eye-rolling and blessed them even more. Soon the kids began to crack smiles and acknowledge that their parents were "crazy but pretty cool." The daughter found her mother dancing with God in the living room one day, and said to her friend on the cell phone, "My mom is, like, having a party all by herself in the living room right now!" Sometimes Mom put on headphones and went about her business oblivious to the kids' noise, but instead of feeling like she was retreating in frustration or running away from the problem, she saw it as a way to proactively cultivate joy in the Lord in the midst of chaos.

Their home began to feel *more theirs and more God's.* When facing everything that bugged them about their kids, they stepped up the prayer and blessing first, which helped them pick their battles more wisely. These parents began to see their children transform before their eyes as they prayed more and griped less. And it all began with remembering that they were supposed to make God Lord of their lives, not their kids. Then God guided them to create an environment conducive to the kind of training in righteousness that they all needed for growth.

> *"If anyone comes to me and does not hate his father and mother, his wife and children, his brothers and sisters—yes, even his own life— he cannot be my disciple. ²⁷And anyone who does not carry his cross and follow me cannot be my disciple." (Luke 14:26-27)*

JESUS FIRST AND LAST

Jesus is not advocating literal hatred here. His point is that our training is not possible without our putting Him first. We need to let go of all else. If our minds are not *fixed on Him,* who is the one constant, then we are perpetually out of alignment due to our wobbly nature.

Those parents had gotten out of alignment, not realizing they'd allowed their kids to dictate their lifestyle instead of God. Once they realigned and obeyed God's promptings, they were strengthened by that training, and its benefits extended to their children. It wasn't just about getting along with one another or surviving the teen years; it was about lining up with God's will. Our motto must become, *"Thy will be done, Lord!"* Or as Peter exclaimed to Jesus before the miraculous catch of fish, *"because you say so I will"* *(Luke 5:5)*. It doesn't mean we'll understand all the time, or not ever feel exasperated. Simon Peter sounded fit to be tied as he explained to Jesus how they'd already fished all night:

> When he had finished speaking, he said to Simon, "Put out into deep water, and let down the nets for a catch." ⁵Simon answered, "Master, we've worked hard all night and haven't caught anything. **But because you say so, I will** let down the nets." ⁶When they had done so, they caught such a large number of fish that their nets began to break. ⁷So they signaled their partners in the other boat to come and help them, and they came and filled both boats so full that they began to sink. ⁸When Simon Peter saw this, he fell at Jesus' knees and said, "Go away from me, Lord; I am a sinful man!" (Luke 5:4-8)

Notice that Simon Peter's crusty attitude didn't prevent Jesus from performing a miraculous catch. Jesus knew Peter's heart even better than Peter did. That can encourage us to be honest with God; Peter was real and honest with the Lord. Then, of course, his awe and conviction were as strong as his previous complaints. The main thing was, he was *trainable*. We can expect much of our training to resemble this fishing story in Luke's gospel. We receive guidance from God that doesn't make sense to us from our human perspective. Then we are forced to decide whether or not we are going to obey and trust God's training, or disobey and miss out on God's preferred future for us. The decision to trust imparts actual power to obey. Of course, when God moves mightily as He did in this Scripture, we're often blown away as Peter was in verse 8 when he exclaimed, *"Go away from me, Lord; I am a sinful man!"* Being in the presence of His holiness produces awe and reverence, a holy fear of God. Whenever you step out in faith and do something God is prompting you to do even when you don't understand it totally, you'll be cracking open more of Heaven on Earth and you'll find yourself growing in awe of God.

TRAINING AND NURTURING THE FRUIT OF THE SPIRIT

As we live in the Spirit, God begins to produce fruit in our lives. Remember He's training us to become people through whom He can bear *much* fruit, pruning and nurturing us the way a vine dresser watches over the grapevine for maximum yield. Let's look again at the list of the ninefold fruit of the Spirit in Galatians 5:22-23. As I mentioned earlier, these describe not just *what* the Spirit will do in and through us but also *how* it will be done. Think about this: The way in which you do things speaks even louder than what you do. When the fruit of the Spirit are showing up and growing in your life, Christ is being formed in you, which opens the way for the Spirit to bear even more fruit. What might this fruit look like in the everyday life of a disciple? I've jotted down some characteristics below:

• **Love** – This is the fullness of life. No accident this one is listed first, as God is Love and everything else is to flow from love. To experience and express love is to reflect the very likeness of God, His very image. How do we tap into this love? If He lives in us, then that reservoir *is there already*. When we feel like the love we have is running dry, especially if we're facing an encounter with a person we find difficult to love, we can draw on that reservoir by asking the Lord and acting in faith. We typically ask for more; we ask Him to "fill" us. But in actuality we're *tapping into* His life *within* us, something already given, much the way we might pump water from a well. God does not expect us to love with our own human desires, feelings, thoughts and capabilities only. That's but a fraction of the love that He has to pour through us. He's given us the well (Holy Spirit), and our part is to draw on it as we step out in faith, submit to Him and love with the strength He provides. Corrie Ten Boom demonstrated this stepping out in love after surviving a Nazi concentration camp;

she found that she did not feel able to express any friendliness toward a former Nazi being introduced to her. However, out of obedience, she extended her hand. Just then she saw God express His faithfulness by pouring love through her toward this man.

- **Joy** – Joy is not the same as happiness. It is far deeper, not dependent on happy circumstances. Even in the most adverse situations we can know this joy. It's based on an assurance that God is in charge and caring for us, guiding us, working to use the adversity for His purposes. He did it for Paul when he was in the Philippian prison, for Joseph after he was sold into slavery by his jealous older brothers and for Jesus as he approached the cross. He promises to come through for us too as we obey His will. Joy comes from being on mission with God! Just the fact that we have a mission given to us by God gives us a firm basis for joy. We don't have to be like many in this world who go forward wondering whether or not their lives are making a significant impact. The knowledge that there is a reason and purpose to whatever we're going through can usher in a joy that keeps us going. *The joy of the Lord is my strength (Nehemiah 8:10).* This joy is first God's joy over us, which is so encouraging that we are strengthened. If you know that God is delighted with you, does that not give you a boost? Our joy comes from His joy, and once we have tasted it, we are not to let anyone steal that joy!

- **Peace** – We think of peace as being the opposite of war. But peace, like joy, can also prevail in us in the midst of difficulty. The war that needs to cease is *within* us. When we stop pulling against God's ways and line up with His will, the abrasive disconnect between our lives and God's ways disappears and we experience the grace-filled shalom (peace) of God. Why not take five minutes right now to focus on the reality that God is present with you as your Lord, your Helper, your Light, and your Strength? If you want *the peace that passes understanding (Philippians 4:7),* you may need to let go of having to *understand* everything! Interestingly enough, as we let go, as we trust and live in the shalom of God, we grow in understanding without trying so hard. *A word study in the New King James version for SHALOM says: Completeness, wholeness, health, peace, welfare, safety, soundness, tranquility, prosperity,*

perfectness, fullness, rest, harmony, the absence of agitation or discord.
Not only that, but people around us take note of this peace; our groundedness in Christ is such a contrast to their everyday concerns that they will want to know how we can be so peaceful. Peace is a powerful witness in and of itself.

• **Patience** – "Give me patience, Lord, and hurry!" Have you ever prayed that prayer? Sometimes we might be wary of asking God for patience, fearing that He'll give us more opportunities in which we will *need* that patience. But this fruit too is within us for the tapping. We are to depend on the Lord's well within us for patience, especially at moments when we're most tempted to struggle in an effort to work up our own patience. The short prayer, "Over to you, Holy Spirit!" has saved many from a rash decision or a harsh expression. When people see God's patience through you, they will feel His love. *Love is patient...* (*1 Corinthians 13:4*). You can pray for your love to increase, and then patience will come with it as part of the package! When we remember the graciousness of God for *us*, it is much easier to express graciousness toward others. *The Lord is not slow in keeping his promise, as some understand slowness. He is patient with you, not wanting anyone to perish, but everyone to come to repentance (2 Peter 3:9).* Also helpful to remember is the fact that God's timing is not ours, as His ways are higher than our ways (see Isaiah 55:9). An acceptance of that truth will save us much fretting and impatience. The King James Version translates patience as longsuffering. We need the patience of God during times of suffering in order to remain faithful and bear witness to God's grace and providence over all things. Especially over our lives and circumstances. After all, our lives belong to Him.

• **Kindness** – Is it possible to be hospitable and kind, even to our enemies? When the Holy Spirit has been working in us, the answer is yes. As we keep relying on the Lord, we begin to develop two sensitivities that work together: one, a sensitivity to whoever is with us; and two, a sensitivity to what God might want us to say to the other person through us. The result is more kindness than we might have thought possible. I love the phrase, "kill 'em with kindness." Of course, the person we are killing in this process is not a human being but the Evil One and his influence in people's lives. *The kindness of God leads you toward repentance...(Romans 2:4).* God's first choice is kindness. If that is not well received, a different messenger may be needed. But God's kindness expressed through us does have the power to awaken people from their self-centered stupor and sensitize them to God's heart for them. They may be baffled at how you can be so kind to them, especially if they have been mean to you. *Do not repay evil with evil or insult with insult, but with blessing because to this you were called, that you may inherit a blessing (1 Peter 3:9).* To be able to bless someone who has not been kind to you, you'll need to be drawing upon God's kindness indeed.

• **Goodness** – *Taste and see that the LORD is good; blessed is the man who takes refuge in him (Psalm 34:8).* Goodness is something we have to taste in order to know well. We can hear about God's goodness, but we need to submit our lives to God in order to taste and see it for ourselves. We need to know first-hand the overwhelming generosity of God, the abundance of His love and goodness towards us. Then we can more easily discipline ourselves to choose Him more consistently and experience His goodness in increasing measure. Our goodness or generosity towards others is from God; we can't give what we haven't received. When expressing His goodness, we can expect to go against the grain of the surrounding culture with its insistence on "looking out for number one." But the human goodness pales in comparison to the goodness of God. True goodness is the power of God flowing through us. James 1:17 says it this way: *Every good and perfect gift is from above, coming down from the Father of the heavenly lights, who does not change like shifting shadows.* With God's goodness, you will find yourself able to serve far more generously than you thought you could, and others will then taste and see.

• **Faithfulness** – *If we are faithless, He will remain faithful, for He cannot deny who He is (2 Timothy 2:13).* This Scripture should be a big comfort. The other truth hidden in that verse is that your faith grows stronger through those times when you feel faithless. Again, it's all from Him. Certainly it will be amazing to hear from God's lips, *"Well done, good and faithful servant"*...but by that time, there will be no doubt in our minds that He is the Source of that faithfulness. As good stewards empowered by the Holy Spirit we are empowered to remain faithful to the guidance of our Lord. When we open ourselves to hear what He loves and then submit to His power flowing through us to accomplish what He loves, complete faithfulness becomes possible. It is by seeing the many ways God fulfills His promises that we can then be counted on to fulfill *our* promises. Notice, too, how each fruit builds on the last; our experience of God's faithfulness, for example, so often takes the form of His great patience, kindness and goodness toward us. It's the Holy Spirit in us we're experiencing, manifesting Himself in the form of this steady faithfulness. In a world of constantly changing devotions, the faithfulness of God through us will shine brightly and draw many to Him.

> *Therefore, my dear friends, as you have always obeyed—not only in my presence, but now much more in my absence—continue to work out your salvation with fear and trembling, ¹³for it is God who works in you to will and to act according to his good purpose. ¹⁴Do everything without complaining or arguing, ¹⁵so that you may become blameless and pure, children of God without fault in a crooked and depraved generation, in which you shine like stars in the universe ¹⁶as you hold out the word of life—in order that I may boast on the day of Christ that I did not run or labor for nothing. (Philippians 2:12-16)*

- **Gentleness** – When is gentleness needed most? In situations where someone is fragile or breakable, wounded or helpless, requiring special care. When we send a package that has fragile contents, we label it, "handle with care." We need gentleness when correcting others or tending to people's healing. It is Biblical to correct and confront, but it needs to be done with gentleness and respect, without judgment or harshness. Much of our current culture's hypersensitivity to judgment has come from people's experience of excessive criticism received in their younger years. Later, this gets in the way of their ability to receive correction that is actually good for them. The Holy Spirit's gentleness can address that issue and deal with the wounding without harming the person. You might compare it to the skill of a fine surgeon who knows how to remove the tumor without cutting the patient's vital organs. Gentleness includes the Holy Spirit's discernment; it is knowing where to cut. Just as that doctor may expose one part of the body in order to remove the diseased tissue, we are to gently confront one another as we address delicate issues in the Body of Christ.

• **Self-control** – If you recall from my description of meekness in Chapter 14, self-control is about being well harnessed to the Lord; it is about the power of God working through a well-aligned heart and life. This is my favorite fruit of the spirit, and I think the Apostle Paul put it last in his list to emphasize the point. We have no chance of living self-controlled lives apart from the Holy Spirit. Self-control is not like self-help and self-empowerment, which are deceptive paths encouraged by the Evil One. Rather, it is the fruit born of submission, a self that has been submitted to God. When we align our being with God, His guidance and power become operative in a big way. Self-control might sound like someone has got a "handle" on things, not needing any help. But quite the contrary; self-control is the result of "double dependence:" Full dependence on the Holy Spirit within us as well as free and mutual dependence on God working through other believers around us. Perhaps more than any other fruit, self-control arises in a context of covenant community and mentoring relationships.

All of this fruit is made possible through *abiding*: Hanging strong on the stem, connected to Jesus who is the Vine, rooted and grounded in love. The Scriptures are full of organic pictures to show us how to grow in Christ. As we begin to get the hang of it, we'll see a harvest in our lives: *He is like a tree planted by streams of water, which yields its fruit in season (Psalm 1:3).*

Ω

Reflect for a moment: *What fruit do you see God producing in and through your life? Which fruit seem to be absent or less abundant? Are you aware of experiences throughout your life in which you may have been trained to short-circuit God's fruit production?*

Where you've seen your growth stunted, what can you do to begin to engage in new training and invite God to nurture these areas?

TRAINING THAT IMPACTS THE WORLD

...be on your guard so that you may not be carried away by the error of lawless men and fall from our secure position. [18] But **grow in the grace and knowledge of our Lord and Savior Jesus Christ**. *To him be glory both now and forever! Amen.* (2 Peter 3:17-18)

Many who desire to live rightly lament the decline of cultural norms. Some have a hand-wringing sense of helplessness as they express their concern, coupled with an exasperation at other people who need to change before the tide will turn. There's a better way, and that is for each of us to be so transformed that we influence the culture for good.

"You are the salt of the earth. But if that salt loses it saltiness, how can it be made salty again? It is no longer good for anything, except to be thrown out and trampled by men." (Matthew 5:13)

How do we stay salty? How do we retain our flavoring and preserving qualities as Christians? Through transformational training. Through the kind of nurture and growth that I've been describing throughout this book. The main weakness in the Church in our culture is its emphasis on accepting Christ without the *growing up in Christ* that needs to follow. People have learned to call Him "Savior" but have not understood the full implications of calling Him "Lord." A Christian cannot go straight from accepting Christ to the effective practice of following Him any more than a marine can go directly from the recruiter's office to the battlefield, be expected to perform properly for his commanders and come out alive. A Christian who stops growing and transforming once receiving forgiveness of sin is one who will not engage in the future effectively. This is not a subtle nuance; it makes all the difference between impotence and impact.

ACCOUNTABILITY AND AUTHORITY IN ACTION

What then must we do? Or as theologian Francis Schaeffer put it as a book title some years back, *How Should We Then Live?* We need to ask that question, both individually and corporately.

The Christian walk was never intended to be a solo journey. We looked at the identity roles of Mentor/Mentee in an earlier chapter, but I want to dig in a little deeper here. As we undergo training in righteousness, we need the encouragement, advice, and understanding of others. That's called accountability, and it's not about being caught, disrespected and embarrassed. People who cringe at the thought of accountability have never experienced it done well. Accountability done well always includes the mercy and encouragement that come from humble and wise people who understand that we are all sinful human beings. We relate to God as one who is pure and perfect, but we relate to others as sinful human beings. Mentoring is helping others find God and grow deeper in their relationship with Him. It is one sinner in the power of the Holy Spirit showing another sinner how to find the life that is truly life.

When you're in a relationship with Christ at the center, that relationship is full of grace and truth. It encourages your obedience and challenges you when you are going off mission. In our efforts to resist temptation, we know we will remain weak unless we confess to one another where we have failed, a practice that will produce healing. This kind of accountability also has the power of prevention; just thinking of the fact that you'll be speaking with your mentor next week may help you stay on track and resist temptation *this* week.

In the larger church, mentoring addresses the issue of *moral decline* head-on. As the Christian believer is expected to reflect a higher standard than the secular person, any falling short of that standard is met with greater judgment and disappointment by those watching our lives. Even more destructive is the display of spiritual gifts and miracle-working power alongside poor character and moral decadence or helplessness. The very word "demoralizing" captures the discouragement born of that gap between the standard and the actual. However, if you allow the growth and development of the *fruit* of the Spirit in your life, the *gifts* of the Spirit will not seem showy, hypocritical or abusive but loving and helpful. Gifts are given and used; fruit is nurtured and developed. There is no nurturing without a *nurturer*. A mentor nurtures that fruit.

GOD IS THE AUTHOR

When you're in a position of real authority in someone's life as a mentor, your mentee is allowing you to shape his understanding of life. The desires, feelings, thoughts and capabilities you affirm as good, healthy, true and possible will be caught and taught through your life. This is why it is so important to understand that there is always a chain of consequences. Because of our interconnectedness, we become "co-authors" of—or influencers in—one another's lives. The ideal is to let God be the Author of our lives, then let Him influence the lives of people through us. When this happens, we take part in His story all the more fully. His story is the story of the Kingdom of God, and it is the only story that will last.

You may fear that submission to God and His training in righteousness will rob you of your true self, but the opposite is the case. The more you submit your life to God, the more you become your true self and realize your life's true potential. Those fears come from an awareness of the danger of submitting your entire will to another person, which is brainwashing, not mentoring. That kind of submission is very different from putting your life under God's authority. In the Lord, you are set free. In the Lord, you are acting in His name, with His authority. In the Lord, the subordinate's decisions carry the same authority as the leader's. This is not oppression but empowerment. When you speak and act in line with the will of God and in the power of God, using the name of Jesus in the character of Jesus, your words and actions carry His authority.

When done well, mentoring is like spiritual parenting. Because we are all children with respect to God, we have plenty of maturing to do; we need continual parenting until we die. A godly human father holds onto God with one hand and holds onto his child's hand with the other until the child reaches the age of accountability (about the age of 12). At that point he takes the hand of his child and places it into the hand of God, explaining that it is God's job to do the parenting more directly from this point forward and his child's job to seek out God's parenting. It is a gradual process, letting go, but ideally there is also a rite of passage in which the authority is transferred. After that, especially in the teen years, it is still important to remain engaged and available, yet the real parenting and spiritual guidance should be seen and affirmed as in God's hands. Each child needs to develop his or her own relationship to the Father. He or she may continue to respect the human parents but needs to have his or her own testimonies and opportunities to grow in the faith.

CHRIST IS THE PLUMBLINE

What is the standard we use in all this parenting? How do we measure our effectiveness? In Amos 7:7-9 the Lord speaks to Amos about a plumbline that He's setting in the midst of His people. Ultimately, Jesus is the Plumbline. The straightness of the building (His Church) is to be measured against His standards, for He IS the Standard. He is straight and true; He is also above all other standards. *When the enemy comes in like a flood, the Spirit of the Lord lifts up a Standard against him (Isaiah 59:19).* Some read that verse with the emphasis on the Lord being like a flood; either way, He is the Standard that is lifted higher, outlasting the work of the enemy.

Just as you can't build a house by measuring once and then sawing away, you can't grow by making just one decision. Embracing the Standard of God's authority in your life requires many daily decisions. Many moments of choice. On the one hand, you might say that all this "measuring" is tedious. But consider the alternatives: What kind of building do you think you would produce if you had no way to measure? Not only would it not fit together well, which would cause much more tedium in construction, but it would also not last long. Gravity would do its work over time, causing any part of the building not aligned to quickly sag and buckle. No, you are better off with a plumbline and a measuring tape. Furthermore, your Standard happens to be the King of Kings, Lord of Lords. You are going to the top! In the world of large organizations, it is a mark of distinction to be one of the "direct reports" to the chief executive without anyone in between. For the Christian, God is the Chief Executive of the universe and, amazingly, each of us has the opportunity to be one of His direct reports. If He created the universe, it's more than likely He can oversee your training without any problem. I consider it a privilege to report to Him often!

BUILT TO LAST

"...upon this rock I will build my church, and the gates of Hades will not overcome it." (Matthew 16:18)

Fellowship based on common beliefs is powerful, but the secular world can also mount challenges that are powerful. What we see lately is evangelism in reverse; that is, the spirit and values of the world are infecting the church. The world has *its* training program also. In fact it's a better training program than the church if you measure effectiveness based on lifestyles. It looks to many as though the "gates of hell" might be overcoming the church after all. The seven deadly sins are on full display all the time in our secular culture. In order to thrive as Christians and overcome this influence, we need to be trained like Navy Seals for God; this is no ordinary battle and requires no half-hearted focus. It is clear that the forces working against Christianity have redoubled their efforts.

However, if God's church is strengthened through mentoring networks, we'll have the guidance and power that can turn the tide. The infiltration will work the other way around. Evangelistic efforts won't even be viewed as "efforts," because the transformation that will take place in our lives will be a witness in and of itself. Sharing will be inevitable as people see God at work. What we're talking about is a moral and spiritual climate that is far above what prevails in secular surroundings. We're talking about the kind of authority and power that not only turns back the storm but clears the skies for miles around. This spiritual climate will be unmistakable and unshakable.

Ω

Is a lifetime of focused discipleship possible? It is if you enter into mentoring relationships and covenant community as a way of life. To keep you on track and growing, your task is to seek God's mission for your life, engage His transformational work within you, and engage His training in righteousness.

You may remember the stark contrast I pointed out in the Foreword to this book: What a difference between our cushy Western culture and others around the world. Whereas we've been lavished with success and freedom, many other cultures have much less materially but are now more fully submitted to God than we are. Just as it's a challenge for an individual to seek God when not so desperate, it's equally challenging for a whole culture to turn back to God when every need is met and the illusion that we've done it ourselves is allowed to go unchallenged.

What should we do? The answer for us corporately is the same as individually: Embrace the authority of God and seek His mission for our lives. As Paul said in 1 Corinthians 6:12, *Everything is permissible for me—but not everything is beneficial. Everything is permissible for me—but I will not be mastered by anything.* Add to this the thought from Luke 12:48: ***"From everyone who has been given much, much will be demanded; and from the one who has been entrusted with much, much more will be asked."*** **Those (we) who have more freedom will require more accountability and training, not less.** We will have to seek and discern where we are not submitted to God and repent, in order that we might not be mastered by anything other than God. We now have the opportunity and responsibility to choose the limitations that will benefit us. We CAN live counter-culturally, if we do it together.

The task now is to bring the church to full strength for the purpose of reaching the world. This strengthening requires the empowerment of the Holy Spirit. It also requires great coaching.

Just as I needed others to draw out more of my potential, the church at large needs to foster an environment of Spirit-led, positive peer pressure that nurtures the growth of disciples. We need to go beyond information, inspiration and education. We need transformation! Most churches already have the essential infrastructure in place for this transformation. They have preaching, worship services, Sunday school, pastoral care and small groups. All that is missing is transforming the culture of the Church. If the Church begins to tap into the power and love of the Holy Spirit and consider discipleship and mentoring as *normal* for every believer, there will be no stopping her! When we're all coaching each other with fervor and focus, we create an environment where Christlikeness is understood to be healthy and good. In essence, the church becomes a gym or health club where we are building one another up in the faith *(Ephesians 4:11-13)* instead of functioning only like a hospital by binding up the wounded, important as that is. The church becomes proactive, not just reactive.

I am convinced that a major frontier in the evolution of the modern church lies in its becoming a mentoring network. This vision culminates in communities of Christians who are obeying Jesus' great commission to make disciples *(Matthew 28:18-20)*. Can we love God with all our heart, soul, mind and strength and love our neighbors as ourselves? Can we engage in the transformation process and partner with God in His reproductive disciple-making engine that unleashes our full potential? I believe so. On our own, it's impossible. But God calls us to work with Him by the power of His Spirit. If He didn't think it could be done, He wouldn't have commanded us to do it.

So what is keeping us from such an abundant life? I strongly believe it is our desire to self-help our way through life and not submit ourselves to God. I also believe it's our unawareness of who God is in us and who we're called to be in Him that limits our ability to embrace that life.

DEALING WITH DECAY, GOD'S WAY

A pastor friend was sharing with his peers how it felt to be associated with a denomination that was departing from Scripture and growing corrupt. He and his church were in a position where they were not yet permitted to remove themselves from this corrupt organization. It stifled their freedom and the waiting was hard. "It feels like I'm chained to a corpse," he said. He recalled how one of the methods of execution in ancient times was to chain someone to a corpse. The decay of the dead body would spread to the living person, and death was slow and painful.

One of those listening heard his complaint and thought a minute. Then she came back with a challenge to him. "What about the wife whose husband had died? She prayed for his resurrection for four days and even dragged his embalmed body to one of Reinhard Bonnke's crusades. Even though there wasn't enough room for her to bring his body up front, the anointing was so strong in that place that he was raised from the dead! If you're chained to a corpse, why don't you pray for it to come back to life?"

These words brought the pastor up short. He found himself rightly rebuked, reminded of his opportunity to pray. If the same Spirit that raised Christ from the dead dwells in us (see Romans 8:11), who are we to passively allow ourselves to be slowly killed by corruption and decay? All it takes is remembering who we are to start reversing the flow. When we remember that we're bound to Christ who has overcome death; if we realign ourselves with God's mission and impart life to that corpse, we will thrive and not die. The corpse may or may not be resurrected, but at the very least, the life in us will not have been snuffed out. That resurrection life is at the very core of Christianity. Why would we be called to anything less?

CONCLUSION

Christians in the West may feel like that pastor chained to the corpse. Is it because the church is in a state of drift? Many people have received the forgiveness of God through Jesus Christ, but they have not been applying the guidance and power of God to many aspects of their lives. Because of this, their defenses are down in the face of the cultural tide.

They are like a ship that has drifted off course. The natural tendency has been to turn in on ourselves and deal with the challenges in a self-oriented way. The real answer is to consult the charts and adjust our course. Christ is the Way, and He is either Lord of all our lives or he is not our Lord in any sense that makes a difference.

It is impossible to make this transition over to the full acceptance of His Lordship without each other. God has already set up the ideal paradigm for a thriving church, and in that paradigm we need to mentor one another. If we are not advancing together, we are not advancing.

This book is not just an attempt to describe the water we are drifting in. My aim has been to teach you how to sail by harnessing the wisdom of Scripture. However a book like this can only be the beginning. What's needed is a *response*. Even coaching is only as useful as the ensuing actions of the one being exhorted. It is heartening for me to know that communities of faith are now beginning to take their people through the Omega Experience in order to build up the power of a Christ-centered mentoring network in their midst. This is a start.

LAUNCHING INTO THE DEEP

In this book I've laid out disciplines, strategies and principles. I've done this to help you connect with God and work proactively to align yourself with His mission for your life. I'm aware that this doesn't come naturally. I've exhorted you to focus, enter into accountability, stay open to support from the community of faith and empowerment by the Holy Spirit to keep you moving along on the Road of Life. As you continue to grow and be trained by Him, you will experience more and more of the abundant life He has for you. And you will become contagious with life; you will be a more powerful conduit of His Love to a world in desperate need. Remember, **He has *blessed us in the heavenly realms with every spiritual blessing in Christ***

(*Ephesians 1:3*). He has already given you everything you will need for the journey ahead.

The time is short. Evidence abounds that the Christian worldview has been disappearing, even among churchgoers, at a velocity that is stunning. Social dysfunctions have multiplied to where the moral recession is deeper than anything involving the economy. Even atheism is gaining ground once held by Christians. Do we submit to the corruption and decay, or submit to God and impart life? The moment for action is now.

We need to start where we are, but we mustn't stop there! The urgency of our circumstances, like the stifling corruption that pastor was lamenting, is the perfect training ground for strengthening the Church. Even the darkest challenge can be transformed as we submit to God. If we begin with the idea that our lives are not our own but the Lord's, then it's a short and easy step toward serving one another and overcoming together. When our churches are fully networked with mentoring relationships, the joy and impact of a healthy and dynamic community will be self-evident to all its members. The impact on the surrounding culture will be astounding, nothing short of new life for that corpse. I look forward to building His Kingdom together.

Let's give 'em heaven!

ENDNOTES

1 David Myers, 2000, *American Paradox: Spiritual Hunger in an Age of Plenty*, Yale University Press, New Haven, CT

2 Andrew Murray, 1981, *With Christ in the School of Prayer*, Whitaker House, New Kensington, PA

3 Franklin Covey, 1994, *First Things First*, Simon & Schuster, New York Arthur Quiller-Couch, ed., 1922, The Oxford Book of English Verse, Oxford University Press, Oxford, UK

4 Thomas à Kempis, 1941, *The Imitation of Christ*, Catholic Book Publishing Co., New York, NY

5 James Lawrence, 2002, *Developing a Vision*, Arrow Leadership Training Module. Sumas, WA. For more understanding see James Lawrence, 2004, *Developing Leaders*, The Bible Reading Fellowship, Oxford, UK. p. 63-64

6 Dallas Willard, 2002, *Renovation of the Heart: Putting on the Character of Christ*, NavPress, Colorado Springs, CO

7 *The Best of Elton Trueblood*, 1979, an anthology edited by James R. Newby, Impact Books, Nashville, TN

8 *The Book of Common Prayer*, 1990, Oxford University Press, New York, NY

9 Eugene D. Genovese, 1974, *Roll, Jordan, Roll: The World the Slaves Made*, Random House, New York, NY

10 Viktor E. Frankl, 1946 (Germany) 1959 (U.S.), *Man's Search for Meaning: An Introduction to Logo Therapy*, Beacon Press, Boston, MA

11 Ed Silvoso, 1994, *That None Should Perish*, Regal Books, Ventura, CA

12 Liberty Savard, 1992, *Shattering Your Strongholds*, Bridge-Logos, Alachua, FL

13 Jim Glennon, 1978, *Your Healing Is Within You*, Bridge-Logos, Gainesville, FL

14 J. D. Unwin, 1934, Sex and Culture, Oxford University Press, New York, NY

15 Christopher Peterson, and Martin E.P. Seligman, 2004, *Character Strengths and Virtues: a Handbook and Classification*, American Psychological Association, Washington, DC

16 Tom Siciliano and Jeff Caliguire, 2005, *Shifting into Higher Gear: An Owner's Manual for Uniting Your Calling and Career*, Josey-Bass, San Francisco, CA

17 Gary Chapman, 1995, *The Five Love Languages*, Northfield Publishing, Chicago, IL

18 Hyrum W. Smith, 1994, *The Ten Natural Laws of Successful Time and Life Management*, Warner Books, New York, NY

19 Teresa of Avila, 1904, *The Life of St. Teresa of Jesus of the Order of Our Lady of Carmel*, Benziger, New York, NY

20 Thomas Aquinas, 1952, *My Way of Life, The Summa Simplified for Everyone*, Confraternity of the Precious Blood, Brooklyn, NY

21 Thomas Merton, 1968, *Conjectures of a Guilty Bystander*, Image Books, Garden City, NY

22 Hannah Whitall Smith, 1998, *The Christian's Secret of a Happy Life*, Barbour 20 Publishing, Inc. Uhrichsville, OH

23 Meister Eckhart, 1982, *Classics of Western Spirituality*, Paulist Press, Mahwah, NJ

24 François Fenelon, 2008, *The Complete Fenelon*, Paraclete Press, Orleans, MA

25 *The Best of Elton Trueblood*, 1979, an anthology edited by James R. Newby, Impact Books, Nashville, TN

26 John Ortberg, 2002, *The Life You've Always Wanted*, Zondervan, Grand Rapids, MI

27 Richard Foster, 1998, *Celebration of Discipline*, Harper San Francisco, CA

28 John Ortberg, 2002, *The Life You've Always Wanted*, Zondervan, Grand Rapids, MI

OTHER RESOURCES
FROM LIFE SPRING NETWORK

THE OMEGA EXPERIENCE

The Omega Experience encompasses the Omega Course and additional training seminars that can be easily adapted to small groups, entire congregations or even one-on-one mentoring. The Omega Course guides participants through a transformation process culminating in a personal growth plan. The Omega Course has proven effective over a decade of development and refinement. Omega debuted in 2002 at Stanwich Church in CT as a discipleship training course, teaching people how to steward their lives from God's perspective. In 2006, the Life Spring Network was commissioned from Stanwich.

PARTICIPANT RESOURCES

Omega Course Workbook

The Omega Workbook is a great way to follow along and take notes with the Omega sessions. You'll also find all of the graphics and descriptive charts that we use in the power point presentations. Included in this workbook is an extensive appendix filled with additional Scripture references and in-depth descriptions of various content found throughout Omega. Lastly, each session includes a set of reflective questions to help you process the information individually and with your group or mentor.

Omega Personal Development Guide

This guide complements your Course Workbook, takes you deeper into the Scriptures covered in the session and contains your homework. Each session branches out into three daily devotionals using the Scriptures found within each session of the Omega Course. This helps you absorb the content as you spend time reflecting on and applying each Scripture. The homework is designed to guide you towards creating your Personal Development Plan. Used in conjunction with the Omega Course Workbook and mentoring relationships, this guide helps you process and record God's wisdom and guidance for your life.

Omega Course DVDs

Watch or listen to the Omega Course at your convenience: in the kitchen, on the train, or even in the living room in your pajamas (we won't tell). Supplement your live seminar experience and revisit sessions that you would like to see or hear again. You can also use these resources to run an Omega Seminar (one session) or the entire Omega Course (series of 24 sessions/seminars) for your own family, small group, church or organization.

The Six-part Omega Course Workbooks

We have created bite-sized workbooks to help you introduce the Omega Course to your community four sessions at a time. Each workbook combines the content of the Omega Course Workbook and the Personal Development Guide so that the material for each session is all in one place. You can follow along and take notes, find all of the graphics and descriptive charts that we use in the PowerPoint presentations, and reference an extensive appendix filled with additional Scripture references and in-depth descriptions of various content found throughout Omega.

Part 1 - Abundant Living - Sessions 1-4
- Stewarding Life
- Unpacking Mission
- Abundant Living
- The Seven Values of Abundant Living

Part 2 - Biblical Humanity - Sessions 5-8
- Our Core Identity
- Being Fully Human
- Essential Intimacy
- Contagious Community

Part 3 - Calling of Servanthood - Sessions 9-12
- Called to Serve
- Stewarding Resources
- Empowered to Serve
- The Freedom of Servanthood

Part 4 - Commit to Transformation - Sessions 13-16
- The Journey of Transformation
- Choosing to Transform
- Resistance to Transformation
- Blessings and Curses

Part 5 - Know Thyself - Sessions 17-20
- Realizing Life's Potential
- Pressing into God's Purpose
- Power of Believing
- Seven Deadly Sins

Part 6 - Running the Course- Sessions 21-24
- The Joy of Discipline
- Godly Goal Setting
- Aligning with God
- Training for Abundant Living

LEADER TRAINING RESOURCES

Creating a Connection Culture Workbook

In this practical and inspiring four-hour seminar, you will learn the three key elements and two core elements that can empower you to transform even a lethargic, disconnected church, ministry or business into an impassioned, innovative, and thriving environment by unlocking the potential of your corporate Heart, Soul, Mind and Strength. This seminar is based on the best-selling book book *Fired Up or Burned Out* (Thomas Nelson).

Fired Up or Burned Out Book (Paperback)

Co-authored by Jason Pankau, this book reveals how to reignite your teams passion, creativity and productivity.

Creating a Connection Culture Video DVDs

- The Case for Connection
- Inspiring Identity
- Human Value
- Knowledge Flow
- The Enabling Elements

Omega C.O.R.E. Small Group L.E.A.D.E.R.'s Guide

Take your group to a deeper level of reproductive disciple-making with the Omega C.O.R.E. Small Group L.E.A.D.E.R.'s Guide. Built on the four objectives found in every session of Omega, the Small Group Leader's Guide provides evaluation questions for you to gauge how your members are processing the material. Additionally we provide ideas for methods and moments for sharing your own stories, personal mentoring questions, and learning experiences.

Omega Experience Masterplan
Seminar Video DVD

This four-hour training helps people understand what Biblical discipleship looks like and how we have built the Omega Experience to take congregations to a new level of disciple-making. The notes for this training are found in the beginning of the C.O.R.E. Small Group L.E.A.D.E.R.'s Guide.

- A Taste of the Omega Experience
- Why Make Disciples?
- How? Big Picture
- How? Implementation
- What is an Omega Course?

Omega C.O.R.E. Small Group L.E.A.D.E.R.
Training Seminar Video DVD

This two-hour seminar, in conjunction with the four-hour Omega Experience Masterplan Seminar, gives your leaders: an overview of the Omega Experience, shows them how to utilize the C.O.R.E. Small Group L.E.A.D.E.R.'s Guide for maximum effectiveness in facilitating their group and takes small group leadership to the next level with Life Spring Network's C.O.R.E. small group L.E.A.D.E.R. paradigm.

- C.O.R.E.. Small Groups
- The L.E.A.D.E.R. Job Description

Omega Mentoring and Life Coaching Handbook

This manual provides you with concepts, questions and strategies that will make your mentoring and life coaching truly transformational. Included are practical principles and coaching points for all of the major aspects of each session of the Omega Course. This guide is the distillation of our best mentoring paradigms, tools and training to aid you as a mentor and life coach of others.

**Omega Mentoring Training
Seminar Video DVD**

- The Power of Transformational Ministry
- What the C.O.A.C.H. Does - The VIM Model Part 1
- What the C.O.A.C.H. Does - The VIM Model Part 2
- Principles of Mentoring and Life Coaching
- Using Omega to Guide the Mentoring Process Part 1
- Using Omega to Guide the Mentoring Process Part 2

Omega Site Coordinator and Trainer Handbook
Everything you need to know to facilitate the Omega Experience in your own context. Role portraits help you to select just the right people for your Omega team. A full year planning checklist addresses all of the logistical needs. The Trainer Planning Guide comes with complete outlines, time frames, objectives, and follow-up learning experiences that will ensure a rich and full experience for all Omega participants. This handbook includes reproducible resources that you can use to track, personalize and promote your Omega Course.

**Omega Site Coordinator and
Live Trainer Seminar Video DVD**

- Site Coordinator Training
- Live Trainer Training

Omega Live Trainer's Disk
This disk contains all 24 sessions of the Omega Course, the Creating a Connection Culture seminar, the C.O.R.E. Small Group L.E.A.D.E.R. Seminar and Omega Mentor Training Seminar on PowerPoint and Keynote, in addition to the video clips and reproducible resources that you can use to promote all aspects of the Omega Experience.

OTHER LIFE SPRING NETWORK SEMINARS AND WORKBOOKS

Empowered Servanthood

This seminar is designed to help people better understand their unique call to servanthood, including understanding and identifying spiritual gifts and pursuing next-step ministry opportunities! More than just another Spiritual Gifts course, this one-day (eight-hour) seminar helps people understand their divine P.U.R.P.O.S.E. (Passions, Upbringing, Resources, Personality, Original Abilities, Spiritual Gifts and Experience with Love) and how we are created to serve one another. It further develops and expands the P.U.R.P.O.S.E. paradigm introduced in the Omega Course and personalizes the application. This material is perfect for weekend retreats or a multiple-session class format.

Making Cent$

This seminar is designed to help people achieve financial freedom from God's perspective. This seminar examines what the Scriptures say about money and money management in the areas of earning, saving, giving, borrowing, consuming, budgeting and investing. It then translates that knowledge into wisdom and helps people develop a personal financial plan for stewarding the resources entrusted to them. This four-hour seminar can easily be taught on a Saturday morning or Sunday afternoon after regular church services.

U.N.I.T.Y. in Marriage

This seminar is designed to help you build a marriage that experiences and expresses the love of God. This seminar examines what the Scriptures say about marriage and uses the U.N.I.T.Y. in Marriage paradigm to help couples build a Godly foundation for their marriage. This material is perfect for weekend retreats or a multiple-session class format.

For more information visit
www.lifespringnetwork.org

LaVergne, TN USA
17 January 2011
212643LV00004B/2/P